REAL ESTATE LICENSE PREPARATION COURSE FOR THE UNIFORM EXAMINATIONS
for Salespersons and Brokers

Jack C. Estes, REALTOR®

President, Jack C. Estes, Inc.
President, Jack C. Estes Real Estate School
Lecturer, Instructor, Appraiser
Falls Church, Virginia

John Kokus, Jr., Ph.D.

Associate Professor
Real Estate and Urban Development Studies
School of Business Administration
The American University
Washington, D.C.

McGraw-Hill Book Company

New York   St. Louis   San Francisco   Auckland   Bogotá
Düsseldorf   Johannesburg   London   Madrid   Mexico
Montreal   New Delhi   Panama   Paris   São Paulo
Sinapore   Sydney   Tokyo   Toronto

Library of Congress Cataloging in Publication Data

Estes, Jack C, date.
    Real estate license preparation course for the uniform
examinations.

    1. Real estate business.   2. Real estate business—
Licenses—United States.   I. Kokus, John, joint author.
II. Title.
HD1375.E84   333.3'3   75-6790
ISBN 0-07-019670-2

4 5 6 7 8 9 0   HDHD   7 8 5 4 3 2 1 0 9 8 7

The editors for this book were W. Hodson Mogan and
Margaret Lamb, the designer was Elliot Epstein, and the
production supervisor was George Oechsner. It was set in
Journal Roman by Hemisphere Publishing Corporation.

Printed and bound by Halliday Lithograph Corporation.

Contents

Preface

The primary purpose of this book is to prepare a real estate license applicant to successfully complete the Uniform Examination for either a broker's or salesman's license, and, at the same time, to provide a basic understanding of the fundamentals of real estate.

This book blends the theoretical and the practical aspects of real estate, giving the reader the benefits of both. It is co-authored by a practicing real estate broker and a professor of real estate. It is presented in a down-to-earth manner to make it easy for the layman to understand.

This work is actually the end product of two successful editions of an earlier book. The *License Preparation Course for Real Estate Salesmen* was first printed in 1971, in turn followed by a 1973 edition. It was originally written at the request of the Virginia Association of REALTORS® to prepare licensee applicants for the Uniform Real Estate License Examination as prepared by the Educational Testing Service (ETS) of Princeton, New Jersey. The present book is therefore a highly improved, third-generation product which has been finely honed by the hard test of public usage and found to be most helpful. As additional state licensing commissions adopt the Uniform Examination in the future, this book should become the standard preparation text in the real estate licensure field.

The principal reference sources for this book are the manuals published by the various state Real Estate Commissions. In addition, numerous reference sources and materials have been researched and thoroughly reviewed in an effort to make this book as comprehensive as possible for the beginning real estate salesperson, as well as for the broker-aspirant.

The authors have made every effort to thoroughly cover every subject the license applicant will encounter in the Uniform Examinations; yet, at the same time, every effort was made to keep the presentation of that material clear, concise, and practical.

Previous users of the book have included the Virginia Association of REALTORS, through their home study program; community colleges; The American University; adult education programs; distributive educational programs; and real estate corporations preparing their own license applicants in their in-house training programs.

An extensive listing of concepts and definitions of real estate terms has been provided, with pertinent comments added by the authors. An understanding of these terms is of prime importance in understanding the lessons. Much of the comprehension of real estate results from knowing its terminology. (See Chapter 16, Definitions of Words and Phrases.)

The sample questions in the practice examinations following the chapters as well as the sample final examination are comprehensive and designed to be typical of but not identical to questions found on the Uniform Real Estate Examination, which is used in the 22 states which have adopted the Educational Testing Service examinations.

Although this book has been carefully prepared with the assistance of many outstanding authorities, it should be emphasized that the contents should never be used as a basis for giving an opinion on legal matters. It is not a legal opinion, and it is not a substitute for an attorney's advice.

A sincere acknowledgment is extended to the many experienced contributors who have helped make this book, as well as the successful earlier editions, possible. Early contributors to the 1971 and 1973 editions included John R. Urciolo III, M.S., Washington, D.C. and John J. Coyle, M.S., Jackson-Cross, Philadelphia, Pennsylvania, both of the Real Estate and Urban Development Planning Studies Program of The American University; Ms. Wyatt Rider, B.A. MAT(Mathematics), Arlington County Public Schools, Arlington, Virginia; Robert H. Alsover, MAI, ASA, SRA, AFA, retired Chief Appraiser for the Department of Justice, Washington, D.C.; Frederick H. Goldbecker, A.B., M.A., Fairfax, Virginia, the Lawyers Title Insurance Company; Gregory U. Evans, attorney-at-law, Arlington, Virginia; Marilyn E. Bransom, B.A., Special Reading Teacher, Fairfax County School System, Fairfax, Virginia; and Edward A. Doran, Falls Church, Virginia, who worked on the chapters on land description and preparation of listings, offers to purchase, and settlement statements.

Our sincere thanks to the above contributors as well as the many, many others who have made helpful suggestions and given moral support. Special thanks are due to the sales associates of Mr. Estes and the students of Dr. Kokus, who furnished many hours of research, as well as countless hours of reading and rereading of the manuscript. Special thanks also to Ms. Ann M. Thompson for her familiarity with the dictionary and for her typing skills.

Considerable time and effort are required to successfully complete this course and pass the state license examination. However, the rewards of a career in real estate amply justify this effort.

How To Best Use This Book

There are many preferred means of study, based upon individual preference and prior experience with examination results.

The authors feel that the student will obtain the most benefit from this book by first reviewing thoroughly Chapter 1 on the Uniform Real Estate Licensing Examination, used by almost half of the 50 states, and Chapter 2, "How to Take a Test." The applicant will thereby be reassured about the contents and procedure of the examination, and will also begin to develop a frame of mind and attitude geared to test-taking.

Next, the applicant should carefully study each chapter in sequence, and upon completion, thoughtfully complete the practice examination at the end of each chapter. Answers will be found at the end of the book.

The comprehensive practice examinations have been designed to require very careful reading and thought. Many of the answers are partially correct. However, an applicant must always select the answer which is *most* correct.

The authors realize there can be room for disagreement on many of the recommended answers. The purpose of the practice examinations will be fulfilled, however, if they lead an applicant to study the subject matter in order to understand its substance better. The authors hope that each applicant, as well as the general reader, will develop a finely honed, more acute perception of the richly varied, but unfortunately not easily understood, "answers" in real estate.

Each question missed on the examinations should be reviewed to learn if it was misread or misunderstood, or if a review of the textual material would be helpful. Many wrong answers are directly attributable to a lack of understanding of the concepts and definitions used in real estate. A comprehensive listing of definitions and clarifications is provided in Chapter 16. Applicants and readers would do well to understand them completely. Indeed, your examination will require you to do so.

The full-length practice final examinations provide a last test of your skill. Try to complete them within the time limits given without using any reference material—just as you must do on your actual examination. Following the Index are blank forms for use with the corresponding examinations; they are perforated for easy removal.

In summary, then, a thorough study of the subject matter, along with careful review of the practice examinations and reference to the definitions as needed, should enable an applicant to successfully complete the real estate license examination in the various states and embark on a successful real estate career. Similarly, general readers of the book may find their interest sufficiently aroused or their knowledge increasing in degree to either pursue a like route or embark on a personal program of real estate investments.

Chapter 1
The Uniform Examination

ORIGIN

Between 1968 and 1970, the Uniform License Law Committee of the Washington Area Council of REALTORS* began a movement to bring about a more uniform system of reciprocity between the jurisdictions of the metropolitan Washington area—namely, Virginia, Maryland, and the District of Columbia. This movement was soon joined by North Carolina.

Early in 1970, under the chairmanship of Mr. Ralph A. Wells, vice president of the Yeonas Companies, and with the strong support of the various real estate associations as well as the real estate commissioners of the four jurisdictions, meetings were held with the Educational Testing Service (ETS) of Princeton, New Jersey. The goals of these meetings were:

1. To establish uniform qualifications for a real estate license

2. To establish a basic uniform license examination for salesperson and broker applicants

3. To develop a program leading to national certification for real estate licensees

4. To take a great step toward professionalism of the real estate industry

As a result of these meetings, the first Uniform Real Estate License Examination was conducted by ETS in Virginia and North Carolina on January 27, 1971.

During the very short period since that first examination, an increasing number of other states have adopted the Uniform License Examination administered by the Educational Testing Service.

States that have adopted the Uniform Examination include:

Alaska	Nevada
District of Columbia	New Hampshire
Hawaii	New Jersey
Iowa	North Dakota
Kansas	Ohio
Kentucky	Pennsylvania
Maine	South Dakota
Maryland	Vermont
Massachusetts	Virginia
Montana	Wyoming
Nebraska	Virgin Islands

With the tremendous growth of the Uniform Examination concept, it is most probable that other states will join the program as this book is being printed and published.

The authors believe that this is one of the most significant strides forward that has ever been taken by the real estate industry. Every present or future real estate licensee owes a great debt of gratitude to the members of the various REALTOR associations involved, as well as to the commissioners of the various initial states.

Special thanks should be given to Ralph A. Wells, chairman of the committee, as well as to Turner N. Burton, past director, Department of Professional and Occupational Registration for the Commonwealth of Virginia, and A. P. "Red" Carlton, past chairman, North Carolina Real Estate Licensing Board.

Another debt of gratitude should be extended to the men and women of Educational Testing Service (ETS), who labored so long and hard, and who furnished the expertise to make the Uniform Examination so successful.

The authors hope and expect that these giant steps will result in the fulfilling of the goals set by the original committee.

The rest of this chapter is composed of major portions of the *Bulletin of Information for Applicants, 1974-75,* which are reprinted here with the permission of the Educational Testing Service.* This *Bulletin* is sent to each applicant upon acceptance for the license examination

---

*REALTOR® is a registered trademark of the NATIONAL ASSOCIATION OF REALTORS® which identifies a professional in real estate who subscribes to a strict Code of Ethics as a member of that association.

*Copyright © 1973 by Educational Testing Service. All rights reserved. Reprinted by permission.

and answers most applicants' questions. A thorough review of the *Bulletin* should be most helpful to every applicant.

> This bulletin contains information of interest to candidates for the Real Estate Salesmen and Brokers Licensing Examinations. Descriptions of both examinations are included, as well as sample questions of the types found in the tests. (Sample questions for the salesman examination begin on page 5, those for the broker test, on page 8.) Candidates are advised to familiarize themselves with this material before the day of the tests.

INTRODUCTION

The Real Estate Salesmen and Brokers Licensing Examinations program was developed in 1970 to provide examinations to measure competence in those abilities and skills required of real estate salesmen and brokers. Representatives of several state licensing agencies worked with test development specialists from Educational Testing Service (ETS) in developing the examinations, which were first administered in two states in 1971. By 1973 more than 20 states and jurisdictions, in all parts of the country, were using the tests. It is the hope of the states involved that this is the first step toward eventual reciprocity.

NATURE OF THE EXAMINATIONS

Both the broker and the salesman examinations enable applicants for licenses to demonstrate their understanding of the laws, rules, regulations, and other aspects of real estate practice that apply within their own jurisdictions, as well as their ability to perform basic arithmetic computations. In addition, the broker examination measures applicants' knowledge of the basic regulations pertaining to the practice of real estate and the ability to prepare such documents as listings, offer-to-purchase agreements, and contracts for the sale and leasing of real estate. The examination for salesmen contains sections designed to measure applicants' reading comprehension and ability to follow written directions.

ELIGIBILITY, REGISTRATION

Eligibility to sit for either the salesman or the broker examination is determined by the licensing agency for the jurisdiction in which an applicant wishes to be licensed. Applicants who meet eligibility requirements are informed by the agency of the proper procedures for registration, payment of fees, and so forth.

The examinations are given on dates established and announced by the individual agencies. In some jurisdictions the tests are administered every month, in others every other month, and in others two or four times a year. Depending on the jurisdiction, test centers are established by either ETS or the licensing agency. In all cases, applicants are assigned to test dates and centers by the agencies. (See pages 17–19 for agency addresses.)

For detailed information about eligibility requirements and registration procedures for either examination, contact the licensing agency for your jurisdiction.

ADMISSION TO THE EXAMINATION

After an applicant has registered to take the appropriate examination, he will be sent an admission ticket that he must take to the test center on the day of the test. The admission ticket contains the name of the test for which the applicant has registered, the date of the test, the code number and address of the test center, the applicant's unique examination number, and the time at which he should report to the center. An applicant who has not received an admission ticket a week before the test date should contact ETS, as should anyone who loses his ticket. A lost admission ticket will be replaced with either a duplicate ticket or a special authorization wire.

TAKING THE TEST

You should report to the test center on the date and at the time indicated on your admission ticket. In addition to the ticket, take with you at least three No. 2 pencils and an eraser, your driver's license or other positive identification, and a watch to time yourself during the test. At some centers, photo-bearing identification may be required.

Regulations at the Test Center

To ensure that all applicants are tested under equally favorable conditions, the following regulations and procedures are observed at every test center:

- Applicants are not permitted to bring dictionaries, books, or papers of any kind (including scratch paper) into the testing room and are strongly urged not to bring such materials with them at all. Similarly, the use of slide rules, rulers, protractors, compasses, and stencils is not permitted. If an applicant is found to have any of these materials, he will not be allowed to continue the test.

- Under no circumstances will applicants be permitted to work beyond the allotted times for the tests: four hours for the salesman examination, four and a half hours for the broker examination.

- All scratch work must be done on the blank pages included in the test books, *not* in the margins of the answer sheets. Aside from the identifying information applicants enter before they begin the test, answer sheets should contain nothing but responses to the test questions.

- If an applicant wishes to leave the room while the test is in progress, he must have permission from the examiner.

- Applicants discovered engaging in any kind of misconduct—giving or receiving help, using notes, books, or papers, taking part in an act of impersonation, or removing test materials or notes from the testing room—will be reported to the licensing agency. Decisions regarding disciplinary measures are the responsibility of individual licensing agencies.

GENERAL INSTRUCTIONS

Both the salesman and broker examinations consist entirely of multiple-choice questions. When you get your test book, read carefully the directions it contains and be sure you understand them before attempting to answer any questions. If you skip over the directions or read them too fast, you could miss something important and possibly lose credit.

Once you begin the test, use your time economically. Take the questions in order, but do not waste time on those that contain extremely difficult or unfamiliar material. Go on to the other questions and return to the difficult ones later if you have time.

You are to record your answers on a separate answer sheet; no credit will be given for an answer written or indicated in the test book. Answer spaces on the answer sheet are lettered to correspond with the letters of the suggested answers printed in the test book. For each question, you are to decide which one of the four suggested answers is best and blacken the appropriately lettered space on your answer sheet. The example below illustrates how answers are to be marked.

Chicago is a
(A) state   (C) country
(B) city   (D) town

Sample Answer Spaces

Multiple responses to a single question will be scored as incorrect. Therefore, if you change an answer, be sure that any previous marks for that question are erased completely.

Your scores on the test will be the number of questions you answer correctly in each part of the examination. Do as well as you can, but—since very few applicants answer *all* questions correctly—do not be concerned if there are some you cannot answer. If you do have some knowledge of a question, even though you are uncertain about the answer, you may be able to eliminate one or more of the answer choices as wrong. In cases such as this, it is often better to guess at the correct answer rather than leave the answer spaces blank.

Identifying Information

Before you begin the test, the examiner will give you instructions for entering certain identifying information on your answer sheet. All the required information is printed on your admission ticket, and if it is not transferred correctly to your answer sheet your scores could be delayed or reported inaccurately.

A correctly completed identification section of an answer sheet is shown below. If you study this sample before going to the test center, you will have no difficulty following the instructions given by the examiner.

As the sample shows, you will be asked to record the first 12 letters of your last name, the first 8 letters of your first name, your middle initial, and the examination number that appears on your admission ticket. To enter these items properly, print each letter or number in the box at the top of the column and fill in the space below that corresponds to the letter or number. For example, the examination number of the applicant who completed the sample is 340372. He printed a "3" in the first box under COPY EXAMINATION NUMBER HERE and filled in the appropriate space in the column beneath it, printed "4" in the second box and filled in the appropriate space, and so on. Note that zeros are treated in the same way as any other digit.

SCORES AND SCORE REPORTS

Each examination is divided into parts that are scored separately; the score for each part is the number of questions answered correctly. Applicants must obtain passing scores (as established by the licensing agencies) on *each* part of the examination in order to pass the test.

If an applicant passes the examination, the score report he receives after the test will indicate PASS only. For those applicants who fail, separate scores will be reported for all parts of the test. These applicants can thus determine their weak points and plan their preparation for a future examination accordingly.

Score reports are sent to applicants by either ETS or the licensing agency. All inquiries about scores, however, are to be directed to the agency.

THE EXAMINATIONS

Both the salesman examination and the broker examination consist entirely of multiple-choice questions. Each question in a test book is followed by four suggested answers, lettered A, B, C, and D. After you choose the answer you think is the best response to a question, you are to blacken the appropriate space on a separate answer sheet.

Salesman Examination

The examination for salesmen is a four-hour test made up of 100 questions. It is divided into three parts:

A. Arithmetic (30 questions)—measures applicants' basic computational ability

B. Comprehension of Real Estate Subject Matter (40 questions)—measures applicants' comprehension of data presented in various forms—written, coded, and pictorial; ability to read and comprehend information concerning real estate transactions; ability to follow written directions by correctly interpreting coded information; ability to read plats; understanding of terms and phrases common to real estate

C. Laws, Rules, and Regulations (30 questions)—measures applicants' understanding of the real estate laws, rules, regulations, and other aspects of real estate practice appropriate to their own jurisdiction

SAMPLE QUESTIONS

The following questions illustrate the types of questions in the examination for real estate salesmen. They do not, however, represent the full range of content or the levels of difficulty found in the test. An answer key is provided on page 8.

Salesman, Part A: Arithmetic

1. An apartment building sells for $160,000. If the tax rate in the jurisdiction in which the building is located is $3.40 per hundred based on 45 percent of a property's market value, how much is the annual tax on the building?

   (A) $1,836   (C) $2,992
   (B) $2,448   (D) $3,536

2. If a 6 percent brokerage fee is agreed upon for the sale of a house listed at $29,000, what is the loss to the broker if the actual sale price of the house is 10 percent less than the listing price?

   (A) $156.00   (C) $272.60
   (B) $174.00   (D) $290.00

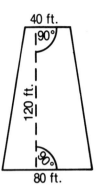

3. The lot diagrammed above is sold for $10,800. What is the price per square foot?

   (A) $1.50   (C) $2.00
   (B) $1.75   (D) $2.25

Salesman, Part B: Comprehension of Real Estate Subject Matter

Questions 1–2 which follow measure your comprehension of information concerning a real estate transaction given on a summary card.

IMPROVED PROPERTY SUMMARY CARD

Description. A one-story redwood ranch—has living room, dining room, den, kitchen, three bedrooms, two baths. Electric furnace and 52-gallon electric hot water heater in a partial basement. Municipal water and sewer connected. Property located at 312 Crestwood Avenue, Outbound City.

Owner/Financial Data. Owned free and clear by John Jones. Tax assessment for the current calendar year is $25,000 with a rate of $5 per $100.

Listing/Transaction History.
June 1—property listed for sale, listing price $29,500, 6 percent brokerage fee, 3-month exclusive authorization to sell.
July 1—property shown to Mr. and Mrs. Frank Leone; made cash offer of $27,500. Received from Leone personal check for $1,000 as earnest money deposit.
July 2—Jones signed the Leones' offer to purchase.
August 1—Closed.

1. Which of the following can be determined from the data on the summary card?

   I. Annual taxes on the property amount to $1,250.
   II. Taxes for the current calendar year have been paid.

   (A) I only   (C) Both I and II
   (B) II only   (D) Neither I nor II

2. Which of the following statements about the Jones property is (are) correct?

    I. It has a full basement.
    II. It has public water and sewer service.

(A) I only   (C) Both I and II
(B) II only   (D) Neither I nor II

Questions 3-6 are based on your ability to interpret correctly information about houses and to transfer specific details from one kind of document to another.

Below, each of four houses is described by a four-digit code (for example, house No. 3 is coded 2 2 2 0). To the right of this code, the meaning of each digit in the code is given. Your task is to recode the data for each house, choosing the appropriate letter (A, B, C, or D) as follows:

(A) if the house is suitable for a couple wanting a ranch style home priced under $30,000

(B) if the house is suitable for a family wanting to be within walking distance of both a public elementary and a public high school

(C) if the house is suitable for an executive wanting central air conditioning and a swimming pool

(D) if the house does not fit any of the categories above

Meaning of Descriptive Code

Type of Dwelling:
0 = Ranch
1 = Split-level
2 = Colonial

Asking Price:
0 = Under $20,000
1 = $20,000 to $30,000
2 = Over $30,000

Luxury Features:
0 = None
1 = Central air conditioning
2 = Central air conditioning and swimming pool

Schools:
0 = Must take bus to all schools
1 = Can walk to public elementary and intermediate schools
2 = Can walk to all public schools

Descriptive Code

Question	House	Type of Dwelling	Asking Price	Luxury Features	Schools
3.____	3	2	2	2	0
4.____	4	0	0	0	1
5.____	5	1	2	1	0
6.____	6	1	1	0	2

Questions 7-8 are to be answered on the basis of the information given on the plat of Far Hills Estates shown on the opposite page.

7. Which of the following lots has the greatest footage on Lambert Drive?

(A) Lot 10, Block E   (C) Lot 5, Block L
(B) Lot 4, Block M   (D) Lot 13, Block D

8. Which of the following statements is (are) true?

    I. In Block L there are four lots with frontage on two streets.
    II. The individual parcels for the land on the easterly side of Lambert Drive should appear on the sheets numbered 3 and 4.

(A) I only   (C) Both I and II
(B) II only   (D) Neither I nor II

9. Chattel is another name for

(A) a wife's equity in her husband's estate
(B) personal property
(C) survivorship rights
(D) an improvement to property

10. In each of the following pairs, the words are synonyms EXCEPT

(A) mortgagee . . . lender
(B) vendee . . . purchaser
(C) grantee . . . seller
(D) lessor . . . landlord

11. Which of the following statements concerning appurtenances is correct?

(A) They are objects attached to a building.
(B) They pass with the land.
(C) They are fixtures.
(D) None of the above is correct.

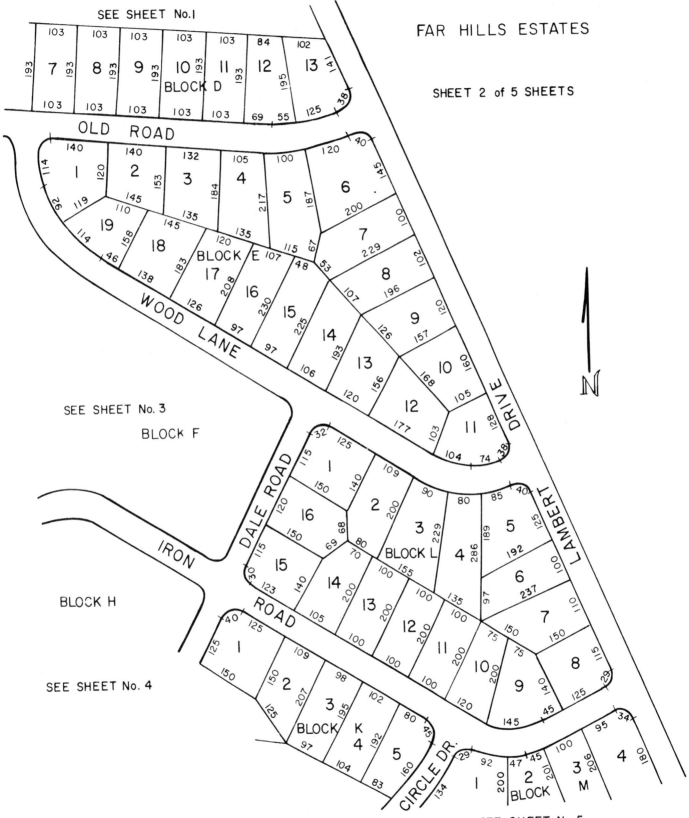

FAR HILLS ESTATES

SHEET 2 of 5 SHEETS

Salesman, Part C: Licensing Laws, Rules, and Regulations

1. Which of the following actions on the part of a real estate broker or salesman could result in revocation of his license?

    I. Failing to submit to an owner, before his acceptance of an offer, all formal, written offers received for property listed for sale

    II. Quoting to prospective buyers of a property a sale price other than the one stipulated by the owner

    (A) I only   (C) Either I or II
    (B) II only   (D) Neither I nor II

2. In order to sell property placed under his control by court order, a receiver in bankruptcy must have which of the following?

    I. A salesman's license
    II. A broker's license

    (A) I only   (C) Either I or II
    (B) II only   (D) Neither I nor II

3. A licensed salesman can legally do which of the following?

    I. Establish his own real estate business
    II. Advertise as a Realtor

    (A) I only   (C) Both I and II
    (B) II only   (D) Neither I nor II

Answer Key—Salesman Examination

Salesman, Part A

1. (B)   2. (B)   3. (A)

Salesman, Part B

1. (A)   2. (B)   3. (C)   4. (A)
5. (D)   6. (B)   7. (B)   8. (A)
9. (B)   10. (C)   11. (B)

Salesman, Part C

1. (C)   2. (D)   3. (D)

Broker Examination

The examination for brokers is four and a half hours long and consists of 130 questions. It is divided into four parts:

A. Instrument Preparation (30 questions)—measures applicants' ability to prepare a listing agreement, an offer-to-purchase contract for the sale of real estate, and a settlement statement for both buyer and seller. The instruments used in the examination appear in the brokers' section.

B. Arithmetic (20 questions)—measures computational ability

C. Real Estate Transactions (50 questions)—measures applicants' knowledge of the basic elements of real estate values, deeds and contracts, leases and property management, financing (including FHA and VA loans), and legal and governmental aspects of real estate (including the Federal Fair Housing and "Truth-in-Lending" acts)

D. Laws, Rules, and Regulations (30 questions)—measures applicants' understanding of the real estate laws, rules, regulations, and other aspects of real estate practice appropriate to their own jurisdiction

SAMPLE QUESTIONS

The following questions illustrate the types of questions in the examination for real estate brokers. They do not, however, represent the full range of content or the levels of difficulty found in the test. An answer key is provided on page 9.

Broker, Part A: Instrument Preparation

The first part of the broker examination measures an applicant's ability to prepare and interpret real estate instruments (including closing statements). The applicant is asked to record in three separate documents the details considered relevant in a data sheet describing a real estate transaction. After he has done this, he will hand in the data sheet to the examiner, who will then give him his test book containing the multiple-choice questions for the test. The applicant is expected to answer the questions in Part A using the information recorded in the three documents.

Because of the nature of the questions in this part of the examination, sample questions are not provided here.

Broker, Part B: Arithmetic

1. A broker has a house listed for $42,000. A prospective purchaser offers $40,000 provided the seller pays 3 points discount on an FHA loan of $37,000. If the brokerage fee is 6 percent, what is the net amount, assuming no other closing costs, that the seller will realize if he accepts the offer?

    (A) $36,490   (C) $38,890
    (B) $37,600   (D) $39,600

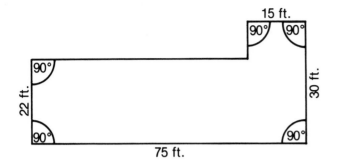

2. The building with the floor plan above was built at a cost of $12 per square foot. If the reproduction cost today is $56,640, the increase in cost per square foot has been

(A) $8   (B) $12   (C) $20   (D) $32

3. An investor bought a 120-acre tract at a price of $1,500 per acre. The taxes he has paid on the property for 5 years have averaged $700 annually. What must be his selling price if he wishes to realize a net profit of 10 percent of his total investment?

(A) $180,000   (C) $201,850
(B) $183,500   (D) $236,500

Broker, Part C: Real Estate Transactions

1. Concerning the valuation of residential property, which of the following is (are) true?

    I. The value of the ordinary single-family residential property should be based on the income it is capable of producing if rented.
    II. In valuing a residence, functional accessories (such as a built-in china closet or breakfast set) are seldom taken into consideration.

(A) I only   (C) Both I and II
(B) II only   (D) Neither I nor II

2. A lease can provide for which of the following on the part of the lessee?

    I. Payment of real estate taxes
    II. Payment of property repairs

(A) I only   (C) Both I and II
(B) II only   (D) Neither I nor II

3. Borrowers of which of the following are subject to a service charge for the preparation of papers?

    I. VA loans
    II. FHA loans

(A) I only   (C) Both I and II
(B) II only   (D) Neither I nor II

4. Of the following, the largest estate or ownership in real property is

(A) estate at sufferance   (C) life estate
(B) estate at will   (D) fee simple

Broker, Part D: Licensing Laws, Rules and Regulations

Questions are the same as for Salesman, Part C. See page 8.

Answer Key—Broker Examination

Broker, Part B

1. (A)   2. (C)   3. (C)

Broker, Part C

1. (D)   2. (C)   3. (C)   4. (D)

Broker, Part D

See answers for Salesman, Part C, page 8.

Chapter 2
How to Take a Test

Reading has been defined by some as the interpretation of written verbal symbols. It is not an easy process, and yet it is the method by which we communicate, test knowledge, and confirm legal agreements, among other things.

This chapter is designed to give some pointers on how to take a test and to suggest ways of improving reading comprehension. Reading involves many skills—locating facts, predicting outcomes, getting impressions, noting details, grasping the main idea, and following directions, to name a few. It requires a working knowledge of both general and technical vocabulary. The technical real estate terms are given in the back of this book. A thorough study of them is recommended.

The following has been included solely for the benefit of the applicant—to emphasize the extreme importance of careful reading of the lessons and examinations.

The Uniform Licensing Examination will usually be a completely objective test composed entirely of multiple-choice questions. For each question you will be given four possible answers, from which you must choose the one you think is *best*. Several answers may contain elements of truth, but you must select the *best* or *most complete answer*. Do not be misled by the seemingly simple format of such a test. Although the correct answer is actually provided for you, finding it may be no easy task.

GENERAL SUGGESTIONS

There is no substitute for a thorough knowledge of the subject matter. This cannot be obtained through a last-minute cram session. Several comprehensive readings and an in-depth study of this book should give you an adequate background for the examination.

Do not spend too much time on any particular question. If necessary, skip a question temporarily and return to it later. *Be sure to indicate the omission in some way so that you do not forget to return to it.*

Since your answers will be marked on a separate answer sheet, be sure to mark your answers in the proper place. Be sure that the number of the question and the number of the answer coincide. Do not mix symbols. If the answer is "deed" (choice B), do not get careless and mark D rather than B. In the event that you should make a mistake, *be very certain that the incorrect answer is completely erased and the correct choice is plainly indicated.*

Be hesitant about changing an answer unless you are absolutely sure of your second choice. In most instances the first impression is correct. This is hard to believe, but several research studies have showed it to be the case. Frequently, the more you think about a question, the less clear your thinking or reasoning becomes. Make an educated selection to begin with, and then leave it.

Read the Entire Question Carefully

Be sure to really see the words; otherwise you may overlook significant details. For example, note this question:

Which one was a pre-Depression President?

(A) Calvin Coolidge   (C) F. D. Roosevelt
(B) Herbert Hoover   (D) John F. Kennedy

A hurried reader might not notice the "pre" and would select Hoover rather than Coolidge, feeling confident of having chosen the one who was the President in office at the time of the Depression.

Likewise, a true-false statement might be carelessly read.

The Parthenon, built in the fifth century B.C., is today among the most beautiful sights in Paris.

This is all true *except* the very last word, but that makes it false. (The Parthenon is in Athens, not Paris.)

Consider All Possible Answers

Do not jump to conclusions too rapidly. An answer may be partly right, but it may not be the correct answer. If several possible answers are listed, do *not* select the first one that seems possible. Examine all answers. Try this.

Which of the following fruits does not grow on a tree?

(A) Lemons   (C) Potatoes
(B) Grapes   (D) Apples

The careless reader might immediately realize that

potatoes do not grow on trees and mark that answer. The more thoughtful reader will recognize that potatoes are a vegetable, not a fruit. The correct choice is therefore grapes, since grapes grow on vines, whereas lemons and apples are both fruits which grow on trees.

Employ Shrewd Inferences

It is sometimes possible to reason out answers you are not completely certain about. You can use what you do know and then continue from that point by clever reasoning. For example:

Which of these is a poisonous snake?

(A) boa constrictor   (C) viper
(B) garden snake   (D) chameleon

You probably recall from playing with garden snakes as a child that they are not poisonous. If you think carefully you will remember that, although deadly, the boa constrictor is not poisonous. It literally squeezes the life out of its victim. The chameleon, though physically similar to a snake, is actually a kind of lizard. Thus, by inference, you choose (C) viper as the correct answer.

Variations often used in multiple-choice questions include "all of these," "none of these," or "both A and B" answers. These stimulate more careful thinking because you can never be sure the correct answer is really there. Sample:

F.H.A.-insured loans incorporate which of the following features?

  I. Low down payment
 II. Mortgages of standard quality

(A) I only   (C) Both I and II
(B) II only   (D) Neither I nor II

This type of question has to be read extremely carefully. To answer questions such as these correctly, the applicant not only must know the material covered, but must be able to reason, in order to select the *best* answer. The correct answer is (C).

To summarize rules to follow for multiple-choice questions: *know what the question asks, eliminate obviously incorrect answers, then choose the best answer from the remaining possibilities.*

SPECIFIC TEST TECHNIQUES

Locating the Main Idea

The good reader quickly learns to find the main idea or central thought in each paragraph. It is important to note immediately the author's style of writing so that you can determine where the main idea is likely to be found in the paragraph. Most authors writing nonfiction material will place the main idea at the beginning of the paragraph. Occasionally the author will place the main

idea at the end of the paragraph as a kind of summary. Be certain to read the first and last sentences especially carefully.

Read the following paragraphs and note the placement of the main idea. (It is italicized for you.)

One of the major areas of concern in the modern high school is the drug traffic. Today's adolescent population has grown up during the turbulent sixties, and their problems are perhaps more complex than those faced by either their parents or their teachers. Although much research has been done and efforts are continually made to alleviate the situation, little seems to have been accomplished. Administrators and teachers both agree that yesterday's headaches over truancies and tardies seem minor when compared with the drug problem of today's schools.

The neatly trimmed yard and stately shade trees were the first things we saw when the real estate agent pulled up in front of the little brick house. The inside tour took us through each of the rooms, including the large den-kitchen combination with its large raised fireplace. We had both previously agreed on the necessity for two baths, which this house had. The back yard was spacious, and the sturdy fence immediately caught my attention. *All in all, it seemed to be the perfect house for our young family.*

In some instances the author may not state the main idea in one particular sentence. It may take more than one sentence to express the central thought, or perhaps it may take the entire paragraph. Note the paragraph which follows:

Like a dog without a boy, what's a home without a family? One of Kingsport's most delightful Ridgefield homes is awaiting an occupant ... and it could be *you*, if you're looking for such features as 2-story privacy ... a full 3,400 square feet of living area ... four bedrooms, with the master suite a hall apart ... three baths, two up and one down ... very large, handsomely paneled family room ... separate utility room ... built-in kitchen with deluxe cabinetry ... living room and dining room in the traditional manner ... two-car attached garage ... partial basement ... patio ... *and* a heated indoor swimming pool that opens to the fresh air in summer by way of sliding glass doors! This house has two Fedders heat pumps, and has qualified as a Gold Medallion home by meeting the highest standards of the electrical industry. Sound great? It is! Call Century 21, Estes Inc. to make an appointment to see it.

In selecting the main idea of a passage, find the statement which best expresses the thought of the entire selection. Be careful to avoid a statement that is too narrow (one that covers only a part of the paragraph) or that is too broad (one which involves more than the paragraph included). Also beware of a statement which misstates information or includes information not given in the paragraph at all. Read the following paragraph and note why the third choice is the best statement of the main idea.

In today's busy, often hectic, world, it is interesting to note how many Americans can find time to devote to their hobbies. There seems to be little correlation between the amount of time spent and the usefulness or value of the particular hobby. Hours may be spent in anything from glass blowing or decoupaging to knot tying or tower climbing. The kinds of hobbies are as varied as the persons who engage in them.

1. Some hobbies are of greater value than others.

2. Stamp collecting is still the most popular American hobby.

3. Many people spend valuable time engaged in hobbies.

4. People throughout the world spend more time involved in hobbies than in any other single pastime.

Statement 1 is too narrow, 2 involves information not included in the paragraph, and 4 is too broad.

Noting Details in Reading

Many people are best described as careless readers. They "read" what they think the words say rather than what the author has actually written. In a test situation it is especially important that you pay close attention to details.

BE SURE TO READ CAREFULLY ALL PRINTED DIRECTIONS

Do not lose valuable time or credit by not following directions.

Do not add, change, or drop words from a question or answer, thereby distorting the intended meaning. The same kind of careful attention given to arithmetical computations should be given to the reading of all questions and answers. Word problems involving arithmetic must be carefully read. Many applicants know how to perform the correct computation, but they cannot decide on the right formula because they get lost in reading the problem itself.

Reading is a thinking process, and your brain must be "in gear" if you are to comprehend fully the material you are reading. *Concentration is essential.* The human brain must be tuned in on only one subject at a time if clear thinking and reasoning is to occur. This is especially true in reading.

SAMPLE SENTENCES

The following sentences are to be read and marked T (true) or F (false). Time yourself, allowing 2 minutes to complete the exercise. Mark your answers in the space to the left of the question.

____ 1. December is always a winter month.

____ 2. Parents are always people.

____ 3. Balanced meals during childhood guarantee good health in adulthood.

____ 4. Ice can be carried in a person's hand for 300 miles.

____ 5. The inauguration of a club president precedes his or her election.

____ 6. Gregarious people prefer the life of a hermit.

____ 7. A situation not without danger is an entirely safe one.

____ 8. Only human beings can make up a society.

____ 9. Snow is not necessarily white in winter.

____ 10. Teenagers who brush their teeth daily never have cavities.

____ 11. A coquette is a mixture of meat and vegetables covered with bread crumbs and then fried.

____ 12. Students often become lethargic with the passing of a school year.

____ 13. A principal who prohibits physical punishment may demand the whipping for an act of insubordination.

____ 14. High school seniors are invariably younger than their true parents.

____ 15. A girl who sells her record collection lock, stock, and barrel reserves no part of it for herself.

____ 16. Reading comprehension is an inherited trait and therefore not susceptible to training.

____ 17. A couple who buy a house without having it appraised by an authority may be buying a pig in a poke.

____ 18. Jewels obtained fraudulently are subject to confiscation.

____ 19. A dollar, a quarter, two dimes and four pennies total one hundred and forty-nine cents.

____ 20. Nonbreakable dishes are not without advantage to the restaurant owner.

Explanation

Some of these questions involved merely common sense and a test of comprehension. Questions 4, 18, and 19 are examples of this. Question 4 does not preclude the possibility of a vessel of some kind, nor does it rule out use of a jet plane. Questions 18 and 19 are likewise simple statements of fact.

Several of the questions use "limiting" words—words which leave no room for any exceptions. *Beware of words such as "all," "none," "always," "invariably," and "never."* Words such as "many," "some," "few," "sometimes," "frequently," "often," "occasionally," and "seldom" allow for exceptions. Note questions 1, 2, 3, 8, 9, 10, 12, and 14. Find the limiting or nonlimiting word in each question. In question 1, although December is a winter month for us, it is a summer month for those countries south of the equator. Question 2 involves the definition of the word "parent." Technically, a parent is one having an offspring and thus may be human or animal. Questions 3, 8, and 10 have limiting words—"guarantees," "only," "never"—and thus do not allow for exception. Question 9 says "not necessarily" and 12 says "often," thus allowing for exceptions. Question 14 has a limiting word, "invariably," and also the word "true," which makes it positively a true statement.

Some questions contain double negatives, which make the statements positive. Questions 7 and 20 are examples. If something is "not without" danger, then it "is with" danger and therefore dangerous; likewise dishes which are "not without" advantage "are advantageous."

Several questions contain phrases or idiomatic expressions which do not have literal meanings. Questions 15 and 17 contain these expressions—"lock, stock, and barrel," meaning "all" or "totally," and "a pig in a poke," meaning "of unknown value."

Other questions may have tricky words or implications. Question 5 illustrates this. Obviously an inauguration cannot possibly come before (precede) a candidate's election. Question 13 has a similar situation. A principal who prohibits physical punishment cannot then demand a whipping (physical punishment) for an offense.

Question 11 defines a word which is very similar to the one given and thus may fool the reader. The definition given is for the word "croquette," but the word used is "coquette," meaning "a female flirt."

Questions 6 and 16 are not particularly tricky. Question 6 demands familiarity with the word "gregarious," meaning the opposite of a hermit, or one who likes people. Question 16 is one of simple logic. Comprehension (unfortunately) is not an inherited trait. Therefore, the entire sentence is false.

Do not let yourself be lulled into a state of false security. Read each statement carefully and be sure it actually says what you think it says.

Following Directions

Allow yourself 1 minute to complete the following exercise. Do not take a sneak preview before beginning the 1-minute timing.

EXERCISE IN FOLLOWING DIRECTIONS

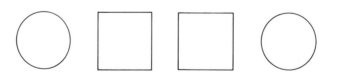

1. Read through the entire quiz before starting to write.

2. Write today's date in the circle at the bottom.

3. Draw three circles at the bottom right.

4. Write the sum of 6, 4, and 2, in the circle at the right.

5. In the left-hand margin, write your birth date.

6. Draw a face in the square at the top left.

7. Cross out all the letter o's in the title of this exercise.

8. Write your age in the circle at the top left.

9. In the square at the bottom, write the first letter of the alphabet.

10. Now that you have read through all the questions, only put your initials in the box at the top right.

Did you follow the directions carefully or did you frantically spend your 60 seconds writing ridiculous data in circles and squares? This is a simplified illustration which may help to point out a careless reading pattern.

Skimming

The following is an exercise in skimming which will help you to concentrate and also to see just how carefully you read. Allow yourself 45 seconds to complete the exercise.

CROSS OUT THE FOLLOWING SENTENCES EACH TIME THEY APPEAR IN THE EXERCISE BELOW: Read faster. Comprehend better. Skim to advantage.

Example: Concentrate when you read. Skim for a purpose. ~~Comprehend better.~~ Skim to save time. ~~Read faster.~~

Skim the article. Comprehend better. Skim the book. Skimming is easy. Read faster. Skim to advantage. Read faster. Concentrate when you read. Skim for a purpose. Skimming is easy. Comprehension can be improved. Read and learn. Skim to advantage. Speed your reading. Comprehend well. Read faster. Comprehend better. Skim to advantage. Comprehend what you read. Reading can be fun. You can learn to skim. Comprehend better. Read more swiftly. Comprehend what you read. Read for an answer. Skim to advantage. Read faster. Read faster. Read for an answer. Improve your reading. Read for experience. Comprehend better. Skim the article. Comprehend better. Skim the book. Skimming is easy. Concentrate when you read. Skim for a purpose. Read and learn. Skim to advantage. Speed your reading. Read faster. Comprehend better. Skim to advantage. Comprehend what you read. Reading can be improved. You can learn to skim. Comprehend better. Read more swiftly. Skim to advantage. Read faster. Read for an answer. Improve your reading. Read for experience. Comprehend better. Skim to save time. Comprehension can be improved. Read more swiftly. Skim for a purpose. Skim the article. Read faster. Read faster.

Were you able to find all the correct sentences in the allotted time? This simplified illustration may show you that you lack concentration and need further work to read with ease.

READING RATE

Few aspects of reading have received as much public attention during the recent past as has reading rate. Much has been said and written, but perhaps little has been done. This may be because each person's reading rate is different; it is hard to change patterns to read faster.

One's reading rate should be determined by one's purpose in reading and general background knowledge of the material. There is no such thing as "the" ideal reading rate. It will vary, depending upon these factors.

In order to get some idea of your reading rate, read two separate selections and have someone time your reading. Allow 1 minute for each timing. At the end of the minute, count the number of words you read. It would be better to choose material which is neither extremely difficult nor overly technical.

Although there is no minimum reading rate per se, most adults should be able to read 200 to 250 words per minute or better. This is the national average (and is actually quite slow). If your reading rate is slower than this, you may find you will have difficulty in completing the examination material in the allotted time.

Many habits prevent people from reading faster. Some of these are unconscious habits practiced so long that the person is completely oblivious to them. Perhaps the most common such habit is regressing or rereading. Because the person is not really concentrating on what is being read, he or she goes back and reads material over again. An easy way to eliminate this habit is to cover each line of print with a white card. Thus, once the line has been read, it is covered by the card and cannot be reread.

Another common habit is subvocalizing. The reader "pronounces" each word in the throat, thereby slowing down the reading process. A more severe and worse form of this is lipreading, or forming every word with the lips in a kind of silent whisper.

Although the market is flooded with devices, courses, and machines designed to increase one's reading rate, you can accomplish a great deal on your own. One simple suggestion is to time yourself while reading. Choose a relatively readable passage, such as an article in *Reader's Digest* or some other popular magazine. Allow yourself 1 minute to read it, then count the number of lines you read. Repeat the process and see if you can increase the number of lines read. Another suggestion is to predetermine the length of time you wish to devote to reading a selection. Then see if you can complete the selection in the desired time limit.

VOCABULARY

There is no substitute for a wide general vocabulary, and there is no quick or easy way to acquire one. A person's vocabulary is probably best increased through extensive reading and listening. The technical vocabulary needed in any field must be mastered by those who wish to achieve success.

You might put unfamiliar terms and words on small index cards to be reviewed during spare moments. The word can be placed on one side of the card, with the definition on the other side. It then becomes a simple matter to look at the word, think of the definition, and then check yourself by looking at the correct definition on the reverse side. (Also, this exercise can be reversed by reading the definition first, then attempting to state the word or the term. This exercise may be especially useful for learning technical real estate terms.)

A FINAL WORD

There is no substitute for an alert mind and a refreshed body. Do your studying and reading practice *well in advance* so that you can get a good night's rest the night before the examination. Even the best reader can become confused and careless if he or she is not properly prepared and adequately rested. Moreover, the combination of being well-prepared and well-rested is conducive to a confident attitude on the part of an applicant, and the attitude that an applicant carries into the examination room is extremely important in determining whether the results will be success or failure.

Prepare early, study diligently, and good luck!

Chapter 3

License Laws, Regulations, and Ethical Conduct

A real estate license law is an act or statute passed by the state legislature which is added to and becomes a permanent feature of the state constitution. The license law contains provisions relating to the licensing and regulating of all real estate licensees, and it also authorizes creation of a regulatory body, usually called a Real Estate Commission, which has broadly defined powers and duties.

License laws generally give the Commissions the authority to interpret, enforce, and administer the laws. In addition, the Commissions are authorized to set forth certain requirements, usually called *rules and regulations,* that clarify the license laws for applicants, licensees, and the general public. These rules and regulations and the license laws govern the conduct of real estate activity in the state.

PURPOSE

The real estate license law is an expression of the police power of the state which protects the public in real estate transactions. Successful license applicants must have exhibited the knowledge necessary to protect the interest of the public. In addition, periodic revisions of the laws serve to upgrade the standards of the real estate industry.

While all 50 states, the District of Columbia, and certain Canadian provinces have license laws, these laws vary. The qualifications, application, and procedures for examination and licensure of applicants in each state also vary.

The Uniform Examination which has been prepared by the Educational Testing Service (ETS) is standard in all those states which have adopted the examination *except* for questions relating to each state's license laws and rules and regulations.

While there is a great deal of similarity between the various states' laws and rules and regulations, each applicant should keep in mind that *one entire part* of the Uniform Examination will be devoted to the particular state's specific real estate laws and rules and regulations. The applicant should read and understand them thoroughly.

It is most important, therefore, for each applicant to request copies of the state's real estate license laws, *rules and regulations of the Commission, application for examination, and other material dealing with licensure.*

LOCATIONS OF REAL ESTATE COMMISSIONS

Write to the proper authority in your state or province for a copy of the state licensing laws, rules and regulations, application forms for examination, and any other materials regarding qualification for licensure.

For your convenience, the addresses of the Real Estate Commission or Department to contact in each state and province for the necessary materials are listed below.

United States

ALABAMA. State of Alabama Real Estate Commission, 562 State Office Building, Montgomery, Alabama 36104.

ALASKA. State of Alaska, Department of Commerce, Division of Occupational Licensing, Pouch D, Juneau, Alaska 99801.

ARIZONA. State Real Estate Department, 1645 W. Jefferson, Phoenix, Arizona 85007.

ARKANSAS. Arkansas Real Estate Commission, 1311 W. 2d Street, P.O. Box 3173, Little Rock, Arkansas 72201.

CALIFORNIA. State of California Department of Real Estate, 714 P Street, Sacramento, California 95814.

COLORADO. State of Colorado, Department of Regulatory Agencies, Real Estate Commission, 110 State Services Building, 1525 Sherman Street, Denver, Colorado 80203.

CONNECTICUT. State of Connecticut, Connecticut Real Estate Commission, 90 Washington Street, Hartford, Connecticut 06115.

DELAWARE. Chairman, Delaware Real Estate Commission, State House Annex, Dover, Delaware 19901.

DISTRICT OF COLUMBIA. Secretary, Real Estate Commission, 614 H Street, N.W., Washington, D.C. 20001.

FLORIDA. Florida Real Estate Commission, State of Florida Office Building, West Morse Boulevard, Winter Park, Florida 32789.

GEORGIA. Georgia Real Estate Commission, 166 Pryor Street, S.W., Atlanta, Georgia 30303.

HAWAII. State of Hawaii Professional & Vocational Licensing Division, Department of Regulatory Agencies, Real Estate Commission, P.O. Box 3469, Honolulu, Hawaii 96801.

IDAHO. Idaho Real Estate Commission, State Capitol Building, Boise, Idaho 83707.

ILLINOIS. Director, Department of Registration and Education, Real Estate Department, 628 E. Adams, Springfield, Illinois 62706.

INDIANA. State of Indiana, Indiana Real Estate Commission, 1022 State Office Building, 100 N. Senate Avenue, Indianapolis, Indiana 46204.

IOWA. Iowa Real Estate Commission, State Capitol, Executive Hills, 1223 E. Court Avenue, Des Moines, Iowa 50319.

KANSAS. Kansas Real Estate Commission, Room 1212, 535 Kansas Avenue, Topeka, Kansas 66603.

KENTUCKY. Kentucky State Real Estate Commission, 100 E. Liberty Street, Louisville, Kentucky 40202.

LOUISIANA. Real Estate Commission, Department of Occupational Standards, P.O. Box 44095, State Capitol, Baton Rouge, Louisiana 70804.

MAINE. State of Maine, Maine Real Estate Commission, State House Annex, Capitol Shopping Center, Western Avenue, Augusta, Maine 04330.

MARYLAND. Real Estate Commission of Maryland, 1 S. Calvert Street, Room 600, Baltimore, Maryland 21202.

MASSACHUSETTS. Executive Secretary, Board of Registration on Real Estate, Brokers and Salesmen, 100 Cambridge Street, Boston, Massachusetts 02202.

MICHIGAN. State of Michigan, Department of Licensing and Regulation, 1033 S. Washington Avenue, Lansing, Michigan 48926.

MINNESOTA. State of Minnesota, Department of Commerce Central Licensing Unit, Real Estate Licensing Section, 2d Floor, 260 State Office Building, St. Paul, Minnesota 55155.

MISSISSIPPI. Mississippi Real Estate Commission, 505 Woodland Hills Building, 3000 Old Canton Road, Jackson, Mississippi 39216.

MISSOURI. Missouri Real Estate Commission, 222 Monroe Street, Jefferson City, Missouri 65101.

MONTANA. Real Estate Commission, State Office Building, Helena, Montana 59601.

NEBRASKA. State of Nebraska, Nebraska Real Estate Commission, State Capitol Building, Lincoln, Nebraska 68509.

NEVADA. State of Nevada, Department of Commerce, Real Estate Division, 111 W. Telegraph Street, Suite 200, Carson City, Nevada 89701.

NEW HAMPSHIRE. State of New Hampshire Real Estate Commission, 3 Capitol Street, Concord, New Hampshire 03301.

NEW JERSEY. State of New Jersey, Division of the New Jersey Real Estate Commission, Department of Insurance, 201 E. State Street, Trenton, New Jersey 08625.

NEW MEXICO. New Mexico Real Estate Commission, Room 1031, 505 Marquette, N.W., Albuquerque, New Mexico 87101.

NEW YORK. State of New York, Department of State, Division of Licensing Services, 162 Washington Avenue, Albany, New York 12225.

NORTH CAROLINA. North Carolina Real Estate Licensing Board, P.O. Box 266, 813 BB & T, Raleigh, North Carolina 27602.

NORTH DAKOTA. North Dakota State Real Estate Commission, 410 E. Thayer Avenue, Box 727, Bismarck, North Dakota 58501.

OHIO. State of Ohio, Department of Commerce, Ohio Real Estate Commission, 33 North Grant Avenue, Columbus, Ohio 43215.

OKLAHOMA. The Oklahoma Real Estate Commission, Executive Office, Suite 100, 4040 Lincoln Boulevard, Oklahoma City, Oklahoma 73105.

OREGON. State of Oregon, Department of Commerce, Oregon Real Estate Division, Commerce Building, 158 12th Street NE, Salem, Oregon 97310.

PENNSYLVANIA. Commonwealth of Pennsylvania, Department of State, Commission of Professional and Occupational Affairs, State Real Estate Commission, Box 2649, Harrisburg, Pennsylvania 17120.

RHODE ISLAND. Rhode Island Real Estate Division, 169 Weybosset Street, Providence, Rhode Island 02903.

SOUTH CAROLINA. South Carolina Real Estate Commission, Office of the Commissioner, P.O. Box 11979, 900 Elmwood Avenue, Columbia, South Carolina 29201.

SOUTH DAKOTA. South Dakota State Real Estate Commission, P.O. Box 638, Pierre, South Dakota 57501.

TENNESSEE. State of Tennessee Real Estate Commission, 556 Capitol Hill Building, Nashville, Tennessee 37219.

TEXAS. Texas Real Estate Commission, 4th Floor Archives Library Building, P.O. Box 12188, Capitol Station, Austin, Texas 78711.

UTAH. State of Utah, Department of Business Regulation, Real Estate Division, 330 East 4th South Street, Salt Lake City, Utah 84111.

VERMONT. Vermont Real Estate Commission, 7 East State Street, Montpelier, Vermont 05602.

VIRGINIA. Commonwealth of Virginia, Virginia Real Estate Commission, Department of Professional and Occupational Registration, P.O. Box 1-X, Richmond, Virginia 23202.

WASHINGTON. State of Washington, Department of Motor Vehicles, Real Estate Division, P.O. Box 247, Highways-Licenses Building, Olympia, Washington 98504.

WEST VIRGINIA. West Virginia Real Estate Commission, 402 State Office Building No. 3, 1800 East Washington Street, State Capitol, Charleston, West Virginia 25305.

WISCONSIN. State of Wisconsin, Department of Regulation and Licensing, Real Estate Examining Board, 819 North Sixth Street, Milwaukee, Wisconsin 53203.

WYOMING. Wyoming Department of Agriculture, Commissioner, Wyoming Real Estate Commission, 2219 Carey Avenue, Cheyenne, Wyoming 82002.

Canada

ALBERTA. Government of the Province of Alberta, Office of the Superintendent of Insurance, The Superintendent of Real Estate, 9919-105 Street, Edmonton, Alberta, T5K-2E8.

BRITISH COLUMBIA. Secretary, Real Estate Council, 502-475 Howe Street, Vancouver 1, British Columbia.

MANITOBA. Registrar, The Real Estate Brokers Act, 1075 Portage Avenue, Winnipeg, Manitoba, R3C-0T9.

NEW BRUNSWICK. Province of New Brunswick, Department of Provincial Secretary, Office of the Deputy Minister, Fredericton, New Brunswick, E3B-5H1.

NEWFOUNDLAND. Government of Newfoundland, Department of Provincial Affairs and Environment, St. John's, Newfoundland.

NOVA SCOTIA. Province of Nova Scotia, Consumer Services Bureau, P.O. Box 998, Superintendent, Real Estate Brokers Licensing Act, Province of Nova Scotia, Halifax, Nova Scotia, B3J-2X3.

ONTARIO. The Ministry of Consumer and Commercial Relations, Commercial Registration Division, Central Registry, The Registrar of Real Estate, 5th Floor, 555 Yonge Street, Toronto, Ontario, M4Y-1Y7.

QUEBEC. Gouvernement du Quebec, Department of Financial Institutions, Companies & Cooperatives, Real Estate Brokerage Branch, Hotel du Gouvernement, Quebec, Quebec.

SASKATCHEWAN, PROVINCE OF. Superintendent of Insurance, 308 Legislative Building, Regina, Saskatchewan, S4S-0B3.

MODEL REAL ESTATE LICENSE LAW

Since 1958 the License Law Committee of the NATIONAL ASSOCIATION OF REALTORS, with the assistance and cooperation of members of the National Association of Real Estate License Law Officials (NARELLO), has published a model real estate license law, entitled *Suggested Pattern: Real Estate License Law and Supplementary Rules and Regulations*. Improvements and revisions were added in 1961, 1969, and 1974, culminating in the fourth revision, January 1975. Individual states are encouraged to pattern their real estate license laws after this model. Many states have done this, thus working toward uniformity and providing more similarity between states.

In addition, the basic purpose of each state's law is the same—the protection of the public—which creates more similarity, even among states which do not use the Model Law.

YOUR STATE'S LICENSE LAW PROVISIONS

The rest of this chapter discusses the *most commonly found* provisions of the various states' license laws and rules and regulations. After each subject, space has been provided for the applicant to note how the subject is treated in his or her jurisdiction. The importance of sending for the previously mentioned materials will become apparent.

Many states' laws start out with definitions of various terms, such as real estate, real estate broker, associate broker, and salesperson. The following definitions are fairly standard in most jurisdictions. (See also Chapter 16, Definitions of Words and Phrases.)

Real Estate

This term includes the land and buildings and any other improvements thereon, including any interest or estate in land, air rights above the land as well as subsurface rights within and beneath the surface.

(YOUR STATE'S DEFINITION:)

_____

_____

_____

_____

_____

_____

Broker—Real Estate

Any person, partnership, association, or corporation who, on behalf of another, and for a compensation or valuable consideration, or with the intent or expectation of receiving the same from another, negotiates or attempts to negotiate the listing, sale, purchase, exchange, lease, or option for any real estate or of the improvements thereon, or collects rents or attempts to collect rents, or who advertises or holds himself or herself out as engaged in any of the foregoing.

(YOUR STATE'S DEFINITION:) _____

_____

_____

_____

_____

Associate Broker—Real Estate

Any person, partnership, association, or corporation who is licensed as a broker, and is either employed by another broker or is associated with another broker as an independent contractor, to perform any of the activities noted above under "Broker." (A broker working for another broker.)

(YOUR STATE'S DEFINITION:) _____

_____

_____

_____

_____

Salesperson—Real Estate

Any person, partnership, association, or corporation who either is employed, directly or indirectly by a real estate broker to perform, under the supervision and responsibility of the broker, or is associated with the broker as an independent contractor to perform, any of the activities noted above under "Broker."

(YOUR STATE'S DEFINITION:) _____

_____

_____

_____

Additional Activities

In addition to the activities covered above, some states also require licensure of anyone who: (1) auctions or attempts to auction real estate; (2) buys or sells, or offers to buy or sell, options on real estate; (3) assists in the procuring of prospects to buy, sell, or lease real estate; (4) appraises, or offers or attempts to appraise, real estate; and (5) subdivides land, other than a public agency, when such subdivision is larger than a minimum number of lots as set by each individual state. (Generally included would be any subdivision which is or should be registered under the Interstate Land Sales Full Disclosure Act.) Anyone who does any of the above acts would be acting as a broker or salesperson.

One recent addition covered in a small but growing number of states includes any person or business entity who charges an advance fee for promoting real estate for sale or lease by listing in a publication or referring information to brokers or others.

In most states a person cannot sue for compensation for services rendered in connection with real estate transactions if the services rendered are prohibited by the laws of the state. Such a provision prevents a nonlicensed person from suing for a sales, listing, or referral fee.

(YOUR STATE:) _____

_____

_____

_____

_____

_____

_____

Note: The key phrases in the Broker, Associate Broker, and Salesperson definitions seem to be "who for a compensation or valuable consideration" and "acting on behalf of another." Keep in mind that all these definitions apply to individual persons, as well as to business entities such as companies, associations or corporations. Note also that anyone who, directly or indirectly for another, with the expectation of receiving a valuable consideration, offers or agrees to perform any of the foregoing acts would be acting as a broker or salesperson. Anyone who "acts" as a broker or salesperson or who receives a portion of a commission should be licensed.

Associate and REALTOR-ASSOCIATE

Sometimes the term "associate" is used in lieu of "salesman." To many persons, the term "salesman" has an unfavorable connotation; "associate" creates a more favorable image in the eyes of the public. It also minimizes a master-servant relationship.

Use of the term "associate broker" in lieu of "salesman," however, is *not* suggested because a number of states now use this designation for a person licensed as a broker, but who is employed by another broker in the capacity of a salesperson.

The term "associate" should not be confused with "REALTOR–ASSOCIATE," a fairly recent (January 1, 1974) category of membership of the NATIONAL ASSOCIATION OF REALTORS. The REALTOR–ASSOCIATE is a licensed salesperson, employed by or affiliated with a REALTOR, as an independent contractor.

Associations of Brokers

There is a growing tendency for individual licensed real estate brokers to form real estate firms in which all active participants are brokers. Advantages include the pooling of talents to enable a higher degree of specialized services, and the impact on regionwide or nationwide advertising of a knowledgeable group of brokers. In addition, some brokers prefer to operate their firms this way rather than employing and supervising a group of salespeople. In a sense, the real estate broker continues to operate his or her own real estate brokerage business, but associates with others of similar "independent" mind.

The present real estate sales agent's license, however, permits no such business options. It requires that its holder be under the supervision of a real estate broker. In any event, whether a person is acting as a real estate broker, associate broker, or salesperson, it shall be unlawful to operate without first obtaining a license.

A New Concept in Real Estate

The small to medium-sized brokerage office finds it more and more difficult to compete with the big chain brokers, which may have several branch offices in nearby cities or areas. The smaller brokerage firm lacks the resources for recruiting, training, and mass media advertising. The largest chains may have over 50 offices and more than 500 brokers and salespeople. Even in the largest metropolitan areas, as few as five or six of these large, multi-office firms may do over 50 percent of the business.

As a result, one of the most revolutionary new developments in the real estate field is franchising. Franchising is the formal licensing by contractual agreement of individual brokers as corporate members of a nationwide real estate organization whose purpose is to compete more effectively with the large metropolitan realty chains. Members' fees vary. There is usually a lump sum payment for initial membership, plus assessments for common advertisements and a percentage of gross sales.

Under the stewardship of national franchising chains like Century 21 and Red Carpet, two of the more successful franchisors, the small or medium-sized broker is able to compete on more equal terms. Familiar to others in rural and recreational areas are the United Farm Agency and Strout Realty, long-standing and reputable concerns. Services are provided over many states in many different areas of the country, rather than concentrated in metropolitan areas. Realizing this, some real estate observers have predicted that the day of the small brokerage office is drawing to a close; many brokers are joining together under one corporate banner in order to project the large corporate image.

Among the services provided, franchisors (1) help member brokers acquire new sales agents (some brokers have doubled their sales forces within 6 to 8 months after becoming franchisees), (2) help them conduct ongoing training programs which will enable their agents to improve their performance and become better professionals, (3) offer brokers management counseling to suggest ways to increase business, and (4) assist and help in problem areas.

Referrals are another important advantage. As more brokers elect to become enfranchised, they will automatically come in contact with a greater number of buyers, as referrals would be made from one member broker to another—e.g., from San Diego to a franchisee in Miami or Washington, D.C. Also, the word "buyers" is emphasized rather than "prospects," as these referrals would more likely include a higher percentage of serious purchasers who were moving from one section of the country to another.

Last but not least, the member brokers working together now project a large corporate image by using the same logo in their classified ads and on their "For Sale" signs and by sharing in radio and television advertising. Smaller brokers who, prior to joining a franchise, found TV advertising prohibitively expensive are now receiving this mass media exposure at a fraction of the cost by sharing the expenses with 50 or 60 other brokers.

Disadvantages of the franchise system would include the loss of some personal freedom to operate a business the way the small broker might desire, or being bound by certain national policies as to radio and TV advertising. The will of the group would be superior to the will of the individual. Also, the malfeasance of one poor performer could injure others by association. Thus, the risks of association must be measured against the benefits of association. In illustration of a basic real estate principle, the potential for higher profits also must carry with it the potential for higher risk. All things considered, for the future it would appear that the franchise concept and method of operation in real estate is here to stay. Certainly, it is a viable alternative for the small to medium-sized broker.

Exemptions from Licensure

State license laws usually exempt certain individuals who deal in real estate from the obligation to obtain a real estate license. They are:

1. Owners of real estate who wish to handle their own property (and in some states, whose principal vocation is *not* real estate) and their employees

2. Those who by court order must handle the property of others, such as a receiver, trustee(s) selling under a deed of trust, trustee(s) in bankruptcy, administrators, executors or guardians, and appraisers for tax purposes

3. Public officials (federal, state and local) who are performing their public duties

4. Officials of regulated utilities and their employees whose real estate activities are related to their principal business

5. Attorneys-in-fact (operating under a duly executed and recorded power of attorney from an owner or lessor where empowered specifically to contract and convey)

6. Attorneys-at-law as part of their professional duties for clients

7. Resident managers of apartments who show vacancies for rental purposes

Some states have recently added auctioneers to the exempt status, as long as they act only as criers at an auction.

Generally anyone not specifically covered above would have to be licensed before acting as a broker or sales agent.

(EXEMPTIONS IN YOUR STATE:)

_____

_____

_____

_____

_____

Penalties for Violation

Most state laws provide for penalties, such as fines or imprisonment, for acting as a broker or sales agent without licensure or otherwise violating the licensure laws. Penalties for an individual who violates the law generally run to a maximum of $500 with imprisonment of up to 1 year. If the violation is by a business entity such as a corporation, fines may be as much as $2,000, and the person within the corporation who is responsible can often be treated as an individual and fined or imprisoned as such. In most jurisdictions, violation of the license law is a misdemeanor.

Note: It should be kept in mind that, in addition to suspension or revocation of a license, any licensee who violates the civil or criminal laws could be further prosecuted under those laws.

(YOUR STATE:)

_____

_____

_____

_____

_____

_____

_____

Real Estate Commissions

As previously stated, the real estate license laws create regulatory bodies called Commissions, whose duties include enforcement of those laws. They are also given the authority to promulgate rules and regulations to clarify the policy of the Commission as well as to complement and clarify the license act itself.

The number of commissioners may vary from 1 to as many as 15, depending on the size and needs of the individual state. Some states have departments instead of Commissions.

Membership on these Commissions is most often by appointment of the Governor. In some states, the appointment must be with the consent of the State Senate.

Qualifications for appointment usually include residency in the state plus real estate experience as a broker or sales agent for a certain period (5 or 10 years). Often there is a requirement that no two commissioners can be from the same county or congressional district.

The average term for commissioners is 4 or 5 years, usually with provision for reappointment for one additional term. The appointments of the commissioners are usually staggered so that only a small number leave office each year.

Funds collected by the Commissions from fees charged to licensees and from other sources are usually put into the state's treasury, but earmarked for use by the Commission for such expenses as office space, an executive director, and clerks and assistants, as needed. *In a small but growing number of states, a certain percentage of these funds are being set aside for educational purposes for the benefit of licensees.** (See also the section on bonding later in this chapter.)

Commissioners usually receive compensation for each day they work, as well as their actual expenses. A few states pay the commissioners an annual salary plus their expenses while working.

*Section 19, *Suggested Pattern: Real Estate License Law* (Model Law), NATIONAL ASSOCIATION OF REALTORS, Fourth Revision, January, 1975, p. 10.

Generally, each year the commissioners select one of their members to serve as chairperson for that year.

(YOUR STATE:)

HOW MANY MEMBERS? 3

HOW ARE MEMBERS SELECTED?

Governor

HOW IS CHAIRPERSON SELECTED?

Elected By Members

WHEN IS CHAIRPERSON SELECTED?

GEOGRAPHICAL REPRESENTATION

COMPENSATION

$25 Per Full Day & Expenses

TERM 3 Years

REAPPOINTMENT Governor

HOW VACANCIES ARE FILLED

Governor

QUALIFICATIONS OF COMMISSION MEMBERS

Citizen At Least 10 Years
10 Years Broker Experience

Qualifications and Procedures for Licensure

Some of the more common requirements and qualifications for real estate licensure are listed here.

AGE

In many states, there is no minimum age for sales agent applicants. However, for broker applicants, the minimum age requirement is usually the same as the age of majority in that state. This varies from age 18 to 21. The reason for this is that a broker must be able to enter into legally binding contracts.

(YOUR STATE:)

SALESPERSON: 18

BROKER: 18

APPLICATION

The applicant must apply on forms provided by his or her state. Included in the application would normally be statements made by a number of citizens of the state attesting to the applicant's character, competence, and reputation for honesty, truthfulness, and fair dealing.

The application usually must be filed at least 30 days prior to the date of the examination desired by the applicant.

(YOUR STATE:)

FEES

Along with the completed application form, the applicant usually must enclose the examination fee and the fee for original license. In some states these are combined into one charge. In addition to these original fees, other charges are made for transfer of license, change of address, etc.

(YOUR STATE:)

EXAMINATION FEE FOR BROKER $

FOR SALESPERSON $

ORIGINAL LICENSE FEE FOR BROKER $ _7.50_

FOR SALESPERSON $ _3.75_

RENEWAL FEE FOR BROKER $ _7.50_

FOR SALESPERSON $ _3.75_

DUPLICATE FEE FOR BROKER'S LICENSE $ _____

FOR SALESPERSON $ _____

TRANSFER OF LICENSE FEE FOR BROKER $ _____

FOR SALESPERSON $ _____

CHANGE OF ADDRESS FEE FOR BROKER $ _____

FOR SALESPERSON $ _____

OTHER FEES _____

_____

_____

EDUCATIONAL REQUIREMENTS

The educational requirements for licensure vary from being able to read and write and understand the English language, to having a high school diploma or the equivalent, to having completed real estate courses at the college or university level. Whatever the requirements, proof of attaining them is usually a part of the original application before licensure.

An increasing number of states are instituting long-range educational requirement programs. These programs provide for progressively more educational qualifications each year, with allowances being made for substitution of experience. Generally, over a long period, such as 10 years, these programs will result in a 2 or 4-year college degree being required for real estate licensure. These programs also include "grandfather clauses," providing for exemption of present licensees.

After licensure, some states require the licensee to complete certain courses within a stipulated time. For instance, a state may require as a condition for renewal of a license that the licensee have completed a stipulated number of classroom or credit hours in real estate subjects in an approved institution. Provision would usually be made for substitution of experience or an approved correspondence course, or an approved Institute program (such as Graduate, Realtor's Institute, with the awardee being entitled to display the initials GRI after his or her name).

(YOUR STATE:)

EDUCATION BEFORE LICENSURE (at time of application)

_____

_____

_____

CAN SUBSTITUTE

_____

_____

EDUCATION AFTER LICENSURE

_____

_____

CAN SUBSTITUTE

_____

_____

SPONSORSHIP

Most application forms for salespersons require a statement from a licensed real estate broker agreeing to sponsor the applicant.

(YOUR STATE:)

_____

_____

_____

FINGERPRINTING

A few states require each applicant to send in a fingerprint card which has been completed by appropriate authorities.

(YOUR STATE:)

_____

_____

MINIMUM EXPERIENCE/APPRENTICESHIP

None is usually required for a sales agent applicant. Some states do provide arrangements for a sales agent applicant to serve an apprentice period under a sponsoring real estate broker before examination and obtaining a license. On the matter of qualification for a broker's license, most states require that applicants have a minimum amount of experience as a salesperson, with a certain percent of their working time prior to application for a broker's license having been devoted to the actual business of real estate. In many states, an applicant can substitute courses in approved educational institutions for all or part of the experience requirement.

(YOUR STATE:) _____

BROKER: _____

SALESPERSON: _____

SUBSTITUTION: _____

BONDING

Many states require an applicant, before licensure, to file a bond or, in lieu of bonding, supply proof of financial responsibility. Certain state laws now are replacing the personal bonding of applicants with a mandatory contributory fund for purposes of consumer restitution. The intent is to make the aggrieved party more nearly "whole" in case of licensee misconduct (fraud, misrepresentation, or deceit) in real estate transactions. At time of licensure or renewal, a restitution fee is collected along with other license fees and placed in a *real estate recovery fund.*

(YOUR STATE:) _____

CONVICTIONS

Most states have some restrictions for licensure if an applicant has been convicted of a felony or other like offenses within a certain period of time prior to application.

(YOUR STATE:) _____

OTHER REQUIREMENTS

These are some of the most common qualifications and requirements for licensure. They should convey to the applicant the scope of the license law and rules and regulations. Above all, an applicant should realize the steps taken to protect the interest of the public.

Other requirements of your state may include specific provisions covering the case where a previous license has been suspended or revoked; previous rejection of an application; previous violations of the license laws, such as acting as a broker or salesperson without a license; numbers of prior attempts to pass the examination; lack of citizenship or residency; and more. Each should be recorded below.

(YOUR STATE:) _____

EXAMINATION

Perhaps the most important tool the various Real Estate Commissions use to test an applicant's competency and knowledge is the examination. As was previously pointed out, the Uniform License Examination is administered by testing experts. It is not a test of the applicant's ability to sell real estate, but rather a test of the knowledge that an applicant should possess *before* dealing with the public.

While some states provide for waiver of the examination under certain conditions, or deferral for a certain period of time, most applicants will be required to complete the examination successfully.

States using the Uniform Examination usually require the applicant to pass successfully each section of the three-part examination for salesperson, or the four-part examination for brokers. Some states will now allow an average grade from all parts of the examination, providing a minimum score has been made on each part.

The Uniform Examination is conducted on dates established according to the need of each state. It may be given as often as once each month or only two or three times a year.

REAL ESTATE LICENSES

Licenses remain in effect for limited and definite terms only and must be renewed, for example, every 1, 2, or 3 years.

Many states have some provision whereby license holders who are not currently active in real estate may place their licenses on an inactive status. Typically, such licensees would continue to pay the regular license fees, as well as a fee to reactivate the license if they wish to do so. A licensee would not be permitted to engage in real estate activities while his or her license is on an inactive status.

In order to make sure that all active licensees are qualified to protect the public, some states have requirements which must be met before they will reactivate a license which has been inactive for more than a stipulated period of time, such as 2 years. Those states with educational requirements before or after licensure will often require that the licensee meet the ever more stringent current educational requirements before reactivating the license. In addition, some states have instituted or are considering a requirement that any licensee whose license has been inactive for more than 2 or 3 years retake the regular state real estate examination prior to reactivation. Other states are considering a time limitation for a license on an inactive status. Such a limitation would mean that the license would lapse after a specified period (e.g., 2 years) on an inactive status. While licenses are in effect, the state Commissions oversee and regulate the licensee's conduct, including disciplinary action for any violations. Such action may include suspension or revocation of the license.

Suspension or Revocation of License

The license laws of most states grant the Commission or regulatory body authority to suspend or revoke the license of any licensee who violates the license laws or the rules and regulations. In reviewing grounds on which a licensee may lose his or her license or have it suspended, one should keep in mind the purpose for which these laws and rules and regulations have been enacted, and that is to protect the interests of the public. Generally, any action on the part of the licensee which could harm a member of the public would be questionable and would constitute possible cause for suspension or revocation.

The applicant should keep in mind, however, that the authority given to the Commissions is authority to enforce the license laws and rules and regulations. They generally have no authority to govern the licensee's ethical or moral conduct, nor can they adjudicate disputes between brokers or other licensees regarding commission splits or any matters other than those relating to enforcement of the license laws or rules and regulations.

The most common reasons for suspending or revoking a real estate license are discussed below.

1. DISCRIMINATION

According to the Federal Fair Housing Law, it is unlawful for a licensee to deny equal opportunity in housing. All prospects, potential clients, and clients are to be treated alike. Refusal to show, sell, or lease real estate to any party because of race, color, national origin, sex, or ethnic group could result in suspension or revocation of license.

2. MAKING ANY SUBSTANTIAL MISREPRESENTATION

Misrepresentation is an unknowing misstatement of fact. Generally a substantial misrepresentation would be interpreted as one in which someone acting on the misrepresentation has been harmed or hurt financially.

3. MAKING ANY FALSE PROMISE OF A CHARACTER LIKELY TO INFLUENCE, PERSUADE, OR INDUCE

Inasmuch as most real estate commissioners or members of regulatory bodies have had considerable real estate experience, they have a good understanding of what constitutes good sales techniques and what constitutes high-pressure tactics. While good sales procedures are admired, high-pressure methods are not.

4. MAKING FALSE PROMISES THROUGH AGENTS OR ADVERTISING

This primarily covers misleading advertising designed to attract calls and solicit business—for example, untruthful statements in ads regarding either the property itself or the financing available.

5. ACTING FOR MORE THAN ONE PARTY IN A TRANSACTION WITHOUT THE KNOWLEDGE OF ALL PARTIES

This would cover collecting a commission from each party to a transaction without the knowledge of the other party. This does not mean that a broker may not collect a commission from each party, if both parties are aware of that fact. A growing trend in commercial and industrial real estate is to have each party to the transaction pay a share of the total commission. When this is done, it is wise to incorporate that agreement into the contract itself.

6. USING THE TRADEMARK OR INSIGNIA OF AN ASSOCIATION OR ORGANIZATION OF WHICH YOU ARE NOT A MEMBER

Licensees must not hold themselves out as members of any association or organization if in fact they are *not* members of that association or organization.

7. ACCEPTING COMMISSIONS OR FEES FOR REAL ESTATE SERVICES RENDERED FROM ANYONE OTHER THAN THE EMPLOYING BROKER

A licensee cannot receive a commission for real estate services from anyone except his or her employing broker. This does not mean that an agent cannot sell property listed by other brokers, as long as it is done with the knowledge and consent of the employing broker. This is standard procedure in multiple-listing services and other cooperative listing groups. Any commissions generated by the licensee in this way must be paid to the employing broker, who then pays the salesperson involved.

8. FAILURE TO PROTECT FUNDS BELONGING TO OTHERS

In most states, it is required that the broker maintain a separate account for monies which belong to others. Generally these funds must be placed in an insured depository and not commingled with the broker's own funds.

9. FAILURE TO REMIT MONIES TO OTHERS WITHIN A REASONABLE TIME

When a person whose money the broker is holding requests it, the broker should always make an immediate accounting to that person and disburse the requested funds. The broker may not arbitrarily delay disbursing these funds to pressure the owner of the funds into some action. Especially covered here, for example, would be the case in which a prospective purchaser had made an earnest money deposit accompanying an offer which was not accepted, and the broker felt that continuing to hold the deposit would give more time to find and sell the prospect another house. Many states also require that the broker maintain accurate records of all monies received, showing the date of receipt, dates deposited and withdrawn, and the disposition of those funds. These records must be kept available for inspection by the Commission for a certain period of time, such as 3 or 5 years.

10. PAYING A COMMISSION OR VALUABLE CONSIDERATION TO ANY PERSON IN VIOLATION OF THE LICENSE LAW OR RULES AND REGULATIONS

This covers payment of a commission to an unlicensed person. The person paying the commission and the person receiving the payment would both be in violation of the license laws.

11. FAILURE TO POST A BOND AND KEEP THE SAME IN FORCE WHEN REQUIRED TO DO SO

In those states with bonding requirements, the licensee must continually keep the required bond in force. Failure to do so could result in suspension or revocation of license.

12. FAILURE TO GIVE COPIES OF ANY AGREEMENT OR CONTRACT AT THE TIME OF EXECUTION

Anyone signing a listing, sales agreement, lease, or other real estate document should immediately be given a copy of that document.

13. FAILURE TO HAVE A SPECIFIC TERMINATION DATE IN ANY LISTING

Generally, in a listing agreement, a specific termination date, including the day, month, and year, must be used. This is intended to prevent the situation in which a broker lists a property with the provision that in order to terminate the agreement, the owner must give the broker 30 days notice. In some states this would only apply to exclusive listings. In other areas it would cover any written listing.

14. PLACING A SIGN ON A PROPERTY WITHOUT THE CONSENT OF THE OWNER

In some jurisdictions, oral consent is permitted, but it is always better to have consent in writing. This provision would tend to eliminate the practice in some areas of having numerous signs on one property.

15. BEING CONVICTED OF FELONIES OR CERTAIN OTHER CRIMES

In most jurisdictions, conviction of a felony or other offense would constitute grounds for automatic revocation of license. Generally, a plea of *nolo contendere* is considered to be the same as a conviction. In most cases, revocation of license for any of the above offenses would be for a minimum period, such as 3 to 5 years, and the individual would then have to requalify for a license.

16. FAILURE TO IDENTIFY YOURSELF AS A LICENSEE IN ANY TRANSACTION

Generally, any person holding a real estate license who is entering into any real estate transaction with a member of the public should clearly state in the contract itself that he or she is licensed. This would tend to serve notice to the other party that they are dealing with someone with superior knowledge regarding real estate, thus putting the other party on guard.

17. ACCEPTING, RECEIVING, OR PAYING ANY UNDISCLOSED COMMISSION, REBATE, COMPENSATION, OR PROFIT ON EXPENDITURES MADE FOR A PRINCIPAL

This provision would prevent a licensee from receiving a "kickback" from a worker who performs repairs on a principal's property. This would not, however, prevent a licensee, such as a property manager, from charging a commission for repairs made for a principal, as long as the principal is aware of the commission charged. For example, a commission may be charged on repairs requiring the obtaining of several estimates and supervision of the work performed.

18. FAILURE TO PRODUCE RECORDS, OR TO PROVIDE INFORMATION TO THE COMMISSION

A broker or other licensee must produce all records in his or her possession for the Commission, or its agents, concerning any real estate transaction in which the licensee was involved. This would include records of financial transactions as previously covered, as well as other documents such as contracts, closing statements, and leases. This would also require any licensee to provide information which he or she possessed, or be in violation of the license laws.

19. GUARANTEEING FUTURE PROFITS

A licensee should not guarantee, or authorize anyone else to guarantee, a prospective purchaser a profit from the future sale of property the prospect is considering purchasing.

20. OFFERING PROPERTY FOR SALE OR LEASE WITHOUT PERMISSION OR ON TERMS OTHER THAN THOSE AUTHORIZED

This provision prevents any licensee from offering any property for sale or lease without the permission of the owner or the owner's authorized representative. A few states require that such permission be in writing. It also prevents the licensee from quoting prices or terms other than those authorized by the owner.

21. INDUCING ANY PARTY TO A CONTRACT TO BREAK THAT CONTRACT

A licensee should not encourage any person who has entered into a contract to purchase or lease real estate to breach the contract in order to purchase or lease through the licensee.

22. FAILURE TO DELIVER SETTLEMENT STATEMENTS TO ALL PARTIES TO A TRANSACTION

It is generally the broker's responsibility to deliver to the buyer and seller detailed settlement statements showing receipt and disbursement of all funds pertaining to that transaction. The broker is also usually required to maintain copies of such statements in his or her files for a certain number of years, usually 3 to 5.

23. FAILURE TO DELIVER FUNDS TO BROKER

An associate broker or sales agent must, as soon as practicable, deliver to the broker any funds obtained which belong to others. The broker is then obligated as in clauses 8 and 9 above.

24. FAILURE TO INFORM PURCHASER OR SELLER OF CLOSING COSTS

It is the responsibility of every licensee to fully inform all purchasers and sellers of all costs required to complete the purchase or sale of real estate. A few states require that the licensee submit a detailed list of such charges and obtain the signatures of the purchasers and sellers, showing they have received such a list.

25. FAILURE TO SUBMIT ALL OFFERS

The licensee should submit all bona fide written offers to the owner for consideration. This would include all such offers received prior to the owner's accepting a previously submitted offer and the licensee's being made aware of such acceptance. The licensee must submit all such written bona fide offers, regardless of the licensee's opinion of the merits of the offer.

26. ACCEPTING OTHER THAN CASH DEPOSITS

If other than cash is accepted as earnest money, the seller must be made aware of the form of the deposit. The form of the deposit should be clearly shown in the offer to purchase agreement and the earnest money receipt.

OTHER REASONS FOR SUSPENSION OR REVOCATION OF LICENSE

In many states, in lieu of specific reasons for which your license may be suspended or revoked, general statements are made which would cover most improper dealings, such as:

1. Being unworthy or incompetent to act as a broker or salesagent in such a manner as to safeguard the interests of the public; or

2. Any conduct which constitutes improper, fraudulent, or dishonest dealings; or

3. Any conduct in a real estate transaction which demonstrates bad faith, dishonesty, or incompetence.

After reviewing these many reasons for suspension or revocation of license, it is suggested that the applicant amend the above list as well as cite additional specific reasons which apply in his or her own state in the spaces below.

(YOUR STATE:) _____

_____

_____

_____

_____

_____

_____

_____

_____

_____

_____

_____

_____

_____

_____

_____

_____

_____

_____

_____

_____

_____

Procedures Prior to Suspension or Revocation of License

Incorporated into the license law or rules and regulations of each state would be the procedures involved in the conduct of an investigation and the hearing afforded a licensee before his or her license is either suspended or revoked by the Commission. In most cases these procedures would incorporate:

1. Formal notification to the licensee of the complaint

2. A request for licensee's answer to the complaint

3. Reasonable notice to the licensee of the date and place for any hearing

4. Notice to the licensee of the procedures to be followed during the hearing, such as licensee's rights to be represented by counsel and to question any parties to the hearing

5. When the decision of the Commission will be rendered and when it will become effective

6. The licensee's right to appeal, and the procedures to be followed, if the licensee feels the decision of the Commission is unfair or unjust.

The applicant is again advised to review procedures in his or her state and note the pertinent ones below.

_____

_____

_____

_____

_____

_____

_____

Reciprocity for Nonresident Licensees

While some states feel that a real estate license issued in one state is good in, and applicable to, all states, certain other states will honor licenses only from those states with similar license requirements, or those which require a similar (written) examination to establish competency to transact business. Inasmuch as each state is sovereign in its own jurisdiction, the right of reciprocity is determined by each state.

(YOUR STATE:)

Summary: License Laws; Rules and Regulations

It is most important to reemphasize that the materials presented here on real estate license law and the Commission's supplementary rules and regulations are not all-inclusive, but rather only indicative of the types of provisions and rules that may be adopted and in force. It would be too complicated, and would make the chapter too long, to recite all the variations and all the regulations applicable in each state. Since each real estate license applicant will be examined on the laws, rules, and regulations of his or her particular state, there can be no substitute for requesting a complete set of licensing, regulatory, and application materials and studying them carefully.

ETHICS AND BUSINESS PRACTICES

It is important to realize that the application and practice of ethics is a voluntary commitment on the part of each real estate licensee. The way each person conducts his or her everyday business will convey to others a certain meaning for the term "ethics." The ethics of the real estate business will be the sum of the individual ethics of each of its members. As each real estate licensee fulfills his or her individual duties and responsibilities to others—whether prospect, client, fellow licensee, or the public—each will individually achieve a measure of dignity and respect in the eyes of others, and the real estate industry will achieve lasting reputation and professional standing.

The role of the state regulatory body (the Real Estate Commission) is usually limited by legal statute to carrying out the provisions of the license law, without authority to take disciplinary action for unethical conduct. In cases of unethical or improper conduct of business by REALTORS, the ethics committee of a local Board of REALTORS or some such duly constituted regulatory body would provide an appropriate forum for hearing, discussing, and resolving controversies and disputes. In this logical approach, local members solve local problems and self-regulate their own profession and business.

Should unethical practices be followed by *non*-Realtors, the only recourse would be to the courts. Most unethical practices, however, do not violate the laws of the state. Thus a practice would have to be sufficiently grievous as to constitute an illegal act, with complainant subsequently pursuing legal action for redress of wrongs committed, in order for the matter to be resolved.

Beyond the threat of enforcement, hopefully, is a broader goal. That goal is a voluntary, self-regulatory one, pursued in the appropriate spirit. It is that all aspirants for a real estate license and all present licensees, both those in practice and those temporarily out, regard their role as one involving the highest standard of personal service to others. Moral, ethical, social, and sound business concepts should govern the individual's conduct, not the possible censure of fellow associates or the threat of legal action for wrongdoing.

The licensed real estate salesperson performs his or her work as a subagent of (or an independent contractor for), and under the supervision of, a licensed real estate broker. Both can be REALTORS, or members of the local Board of REALTORS. All REALTORS subscribe to and uphold the Code of Ethics of the NATIONAL ASSOCIATION OF REALTORS.

The Code of Ethics stipulates, among other things, that REALTORS conduct themselves in a professional and businesslike manner by being thoroughly knowledgeable and informed about the nature of their work. In their relations *with the public*, licensees will thus contribute to the public thinking on matters of real estate. In their relations *with clients*, licensees will protect and promote the interests of their clients. In relations *with their fellow-REALTOR* or fellow-broker or fellow-sales agent, licensees will willingly share personal lessons of knowledge and experience, and will cooperate with them.

It can be seen that the concept of sound and good business practices involves a multisided responsibility to others on the part of the licensee. Regardless of whether an inquiry is about a specific property or about legislation, taxation, mortgage interest rates, economic matters, or other general information, a licensee's obligation is to be of service to others. To practice sound, high-caliber business, therefore, is to practice a high level of personal service to others.

The specific articles in the just-revised NATIONAL ASSOCIATION OF REALTORS Code of Ethics convey a thorough and well-rounded sense of service to others in the practice of real estate. Following is a presentation of those sound and good business practices. Most appropriately, they are produced in their entirety.

CODE OF ETHICS
NATIONAL ASSOCIATION OF REALTORS®

Preamble . . .

Under all is the land. Upon its wise utilization and widely allocated ownership depend the survival and growth of free institutions and of our civilization. The REALTOR® should recognize that the interests of the nation and its citizens require the highest and best use of the land and the widest distribution of land ownership. They require the creation of adequate housing, the building of functioning cities, the development of productive industries and farms, and the preservation of a healthful environment.

Such interests impose obligations beyond those of ordinary commerce. They impose grave social responsibility and a patriotic duty to which the REALTOR® should dedicate himself, and for which he should be diligent in preparing himself. The REALTOR®, therefore, is zealous to maintain and improve the standards of his calling and shares with his fellow-REALTORS® a common responsibility for its integrity and honor. The term REALTOR® has come to connote competency, fairness, and high integrity resulting from adherence to a lofty ideal of moral conduct in business relations. No inducement of profit and no instruction from clients ever can justify departure from this ideal.

In the interpretation of his obligation, a REALTOR® can take no safer guide than that which has been handed down through the centuries, embodied in the Golden Rule, "Whatsoever ye would that men should do to you, do ye even so to them."

Accepting this standard as his own, every REALTOR® pledges himself to observe its spirit in all of his activities and to conduct his business in accordance with the tenets set forth below.

ARTICLE 1

The REALTOR® should keep himself informed on matters affecting real estate in his community, the state, and nation so that he may be able to contribute responsibly to public thinking on such matters.

ARTICLE 2

In justice to those who place their interests in his care, the REALTOR® should endeavor always to be informed regarding laws, proposed legislation, governmental regulations, public policies, and current market conditions in order to be in a position to advise his clients properly.

ARTICLE 3

It is the duty of the REALTOR® to protect the public against fraud, misrepresentation, and unethical practices in real estate transactions. He should endeavor to eliminate in his community any practices which could be damaging to the public or bring discredit to the real estate profession. The REALTOR® should assist the governmental agency charged with regulating the practices of brokers and salesmen in his state.

ARTICLE 4

The REALTOR® should seek no unfair advantage over other REALTORS® and should conduct his business so as to avoid controversies with other REALTORS®.

ARTICLE 5

In the best interests of society, of his associates, and his own business, the REALTOR® should willingly share with other REALTORS® the lessons of his experience and study for the benefit of the public, and should be loyal to the Board of REALTORS® of his community and active in its work.

ARTICLE 6

To prevent dissension and misunderstanding and to assure better service to the owner, the REALTOR® should urge the exclusive listing of property unless contrary to the best interest of the owner.

ARTICLE 7

In accepting employment as an agent, the REALTOR® pledges himself to protect and promote the interests of the client. This obligation of absolute fidelity to the client's interests is primary, but it does not relieve the REALTOR® of the obligation to treat fairly all parties to the transaction.

ARTICLE 8

The REALTOR® shall not accept compensation from more than one party, even if permitted by law, without the full knowledge of all parties to the transaction.

ARTICLE 9

The REALTOR® shall avoid exaggeration, misrepresentation, or concealment of pertinent facts. He has an affirmative obligation to discover adverse factors that a reasonably competent and diligent investigation would disclose.

ARTICLE 10

The REALTOR® shall not deny equal professional services to any person for reasons of race, creed, sex, or country of national origin. The REALTOR® shall not be a party to any plan or agreement to discriminate against a person or persons on the basis of race, creed, sex, or country of national origin.

ARTICLE 11

A REALTOR® is expected to provide a level of competent service in keeping with the Standards of Practice in those fields in which the REALTOR® customarily engages.

The REALTOR® shall not undertake to provide specialized professional services concerning a type of property or service that is outside his field of competence unless he engages the assistance of one who is competent on such types of property or service, or unless the facts are fully disclosed to the client. Any person engaged to provide such assistance shall be so identified to the client and his contribution to the assignment should be set forth.

The REALTOR® shall refer to the Standards of Practice of the National Association as to the degree of competence that a client has a right to expect the REALTOR® to possess, taking into consideration the complexity of the problem, the availability of expert assistance, and the opportunities for experience available to the REALTOR®.

ARTICLE 12

The REALTOR® shall not undertake to provide professional services concerning a property or its value where he has a present or contemplated interest unless such interest is specifically disclosed to all affected parties.

ARTICLE 13

The REALTOR® shall not acquire an interest in or buy for himself, any member of his immediate family, his firm or any member thereof, or any entity in which he has a substantial ownership interest, property listed with him, without making the true position known to the listing owner. In selling property owned by himself, or in which he has any interest, the REALTOR® shall reveal the facts of his ownership or interest to the purchaser.

ARTICLE 14

In the event of a controversy between REALTORS® associated with different firms, arising out of their relationship as REALTORS®, the REALTORS® shall submit the dispute to arbitration in accordance with the regulations of their board or boards rather than litigate the matter.

ARTICLE 15

If a REALTOR® is charged with unethical practice or is asked to present evidence in any disciplinary proceeding or investigation, he shall place all pertinent facts before the proper tribunal of the member board or affiliated institute, society, or council of which he is a member.

ARTICLE 16

When acting as agent, the REALTOR® shall not accept any commission, rebate, or profit on expenditures made for his principal-owner, without the principal's knowledge and consent.

ARTICLE 17

The REALTOR® shall not engage in activities that constitute the unauthorized practice of law and shall recommend that legal counsel be obtained when the interest of any party to the transaction requires it.

ARTICLE 18

The REALTOR® shall keep in a special account in an appropriate financial institution, separated from his own funds, monies coming into his possession in trust for other persons, such as escrows, trust funds, clients' monies, and other like items.

ARTICLE 19

The REALTOR® shall be careful at all times to present a true picture in his advertising and representations to the public. He shall neither advertise without disclosing his name nor permit any person associated with him to use individual names or telephone numbers, unless such person's connection with the REALTOR® is obvious in the advertisement.

ARTICLE 20

The REALTOR®, for the protection of all parties, shall see that financial obligations and commitments regarding real estate transactions are in writing, expressing the exact agreement of the parties. A copy of each agreement shall be furnished to each party upon his signing such agreement.

ARTICLE 21

The REALTOR® shall not engage in any practice or take any action inconsistent with the agency of another REALTOR®.

ARTICLE 22

In the sale of property which is exclusively listed with a REALTOR®, the REALTOR® shall utilize the services of other brokers upon mutually agreed upon terms when it is in the best interests of the client.

Negotiations concerning property which is listed exclusively shall be carried on with the listing broker, not with the owner, except with the consent of the listing broker.

ARTICLE 23

The REALTOR® shall not publicly disparage the business practice of a competitor nor volunteer an opinion of a competitor's transaction. If his opinion is sought and if the REALTOR® deems it appropriate to respond, such opinion shall be rendered with strict professional integrity and courtesy.

ARTICLE 24

The REALTOR® shall not directly or indirectly solicit the services or affiliation of an employee or independent contractor in the organization of another REALTOR® without prior notice to said REALTOR®.

NOTE: Where the word REALTOR® is used in this Code and Preamble, it shall be deemed to include REALTOR®-ASSOCIATE. Pronouns shall be considered to include REALTORS® and REALTOR®-ASSOCIATES of both genders.

The Code of Ethics was adopted in 1913. Amended at the Annual Convention in 1924, 1928, 1950, 1951, 1952, 1955, 1956, 1961, 1962, and 1974.

PRACTICE EXAMINATION:
LICENSE LAWS, REGULATIONS, AND ETHICAL CONDUCT

This practice examination is included solely to show the type of question likely to be found in the Uniform Examination. Keep in mind that your state may have provisions contrary to those presented.

1. Real estate license laws originate with the

   (A) state real estate Commissions
   (B) NATIONAL ASSOCIATION OF REALTORS
   (C) state legislatures
   (D) state regulatory bodies

2. Upon adoption, real estate license laws

   (A) remain in effect for 1 year from date of passage
   (B) become a temporary part of the state constitution until ratified by a majority of the state's local boards of REALTORS
   (C) become a permanent part of the state constitution
   (D) become a permanent part of the state constitution until either amended or voided by the state real estate Commission

3. An associate broker is

   (A) a licensed broker who is self-employed
   (B) a licensed broker who works for a principal broker
   (C) a broker in an association
   (D) a licensed salesperson who associates with a broker

4. Generally a nonlicensed person who collects a real estate commission is guilty of

   (A) duress   (C) negligence
   (B) a felony   (D) a misdemeanor

5. A person appointed by a court to manage and settle the estate of a deceased person who left no will, and for that purpose is exempt from real estate licensure requirements, is a (an)

   (A) executor   (C) intestate
   (B) administrator   (D) trustee

6. Which of the following is usually exempt from real estate licensure?

   (A) Owners of real estate handling their own property, or delegating such right to an attorney-in-fact
   (B) a salesperson showing the new homes of a subdivision
   (C) A public official handling the property of a fellow official
   (D) A self-appointed guardian selling the property of a minor

7. A real estate license law is an expression of

   (A) the police power of the state
   (B) gubernatorial authority
   (C) the right of eminent domain
   (D) none of these

8. Each state has its own license laws. While they vary, their main purpose is generally the same. It is

   (A) to obtain revenues for the state
   (B) to control anyone selling real estate
   (C) to protect the public
   (D) to control ethical conduct of licensees

9. A phrase (phrases) common to the definitions of real estate broker, associate broker, and salesperson is (are)

   I. who for a compensation or valuable consideration
   II. acting on behalf of another

   (A) I only   (C) Neither I nor II
   (B) II only   (D) Both I and II

10. Which of the following statements is (are) correct?

    I. A real estate licensee could usually have his or her license suspended or revoked for making a substantial misrepresentation.
    II. Any real estate licensee who is a REALTOR could have his or her license suspended or revoked for violation of the Code of Ethics of the NATIONAL ASSOCIATION OF REALTORS.

    (A) I only   (C) Neither I nor II
    (B) II only   (D) Both I and II

11. The state real estate license law generally is administered and enforced by

    (A) each individual local Board of REALTORS
    (B) the NATIONAL ASSOCIATION OF REALTORS
    (C) the real estate licensee
    (D) the state real estate Commission

12. In addition to other requirements for licensure, a broker applicant usually must

    I. have reached the age of majority
    II. have had a minimum period of apprenticeship as a salesperson or equivalent educational credits

    (A) I only   (C) Neither I nor II
    (B) II only   (D) Both I and II

13. With regard to real estate Commissions, which of the following statements is (are) true?

    I. They generally have no authority to control the licensee's ethical or moral conduct.
    II. They cannot adjudicate disputes between brokers or other licensees regarding commission splits.

    (A) I only
    (B) II only
    (C) Neither I nor II
    (D) Both I and II

14. In common parlance, when a broker commingles funds, it means that he or she

    (A) mixes personal funds with those of salespeople
    (B) mixes his or her savings account with his or her checking account
    (C) mixes the clients' funds with personal operating funds
    (D) separates clients' down payments from the sales commission

15. A real estate licensee should generally reveal that he or she holds a real estate license

    (A) in any real estate transaction
    (B) when representing a principal to third parties
    (C) in all transactions except personal ones
    (D) as the licensee deems advisable, based on firsthand knowledge of the situation and careful judgment

16. Which of the following would normally be a reason for suspension or revocation of a real estate license?

    I. Charging more than a regular commission.
    II. Offering property for sale on terms or at a price other than that stipulated by the owner.

    (A) I only
    (B) II only
    (C) Neither I nor II
    (D) Both I and II

17. The meaning of reciprocity is that

    (A) one state may substitute its license law for that of another state
    (B) one state may institute legal action against another state
    (C) one state may recognize the licensing requirements of another state
    (D) one state may trade its rules and regulations for those of another state

18. A licensed real estate salesperson can only receive commissions from which of the following?

    I. Clients he or she successfully represents.
    II. Builders whose property he or she sells.

    (A) I only
    (B) II only
    (C) Neither I nor II
    (D) Both I and II

19. As agent for an owner, a broker

    I. may not collect an undisclosed commission on expenditures made for the owner
    II. must account for the principal's funds

    (A) I only
    (B) II only
    (C) Neither I nor II
    (D) Both I and II

20. A licensee collects one-half of the sales commission from both buyer and seller without either of them knowing the other paid half. Which of the following statements is (are) true?

    I. This would generally be grounds for suspension or revocation of the real estate license.
    II. This action would not be grounds for suspension or revocation because each only paid one-half of the commission.

    (A) I only
    (B) II only
    (C) Neither I nor II
    (D) Both I and II

Chapter 4
Equal Opportunity in Housing

FEDERAL FAIR HOUSING LAW, TITLE VIII, CIVIL RIGHTS ACT OF 1968

On April 10, 1968, the United States Congress adopted the Civil Rights Act of 1968 (Public Law 90-284), which included the Federal Fair Housing Law, Title VIII, Sections 801 to 819 inclusive, and Section 901. On April 11, 1968, the very next day, the measure was signed into law by the President.

The law declares that, "It is the policy of the United States to provide, within constitutional limitations, for fair housing throughout the United States" (Section 801).

According to the law, "discriminatory housing practices" are acts that are *unlawful* under Sections 804 to 806. These sections of the law declare that it shall be unlawful to (1) discriminate in the sale or rental of housing (Section 804), (2) discriminate in the financing of housing (Section 805), and (3) discriminate in the provision of brokerage services (Section 806).

No person shall be denied any real estate services whatsoever because of his or her race, color, religion, national origin, or sex.* All persons and families are to enjoy equal opportunity in housing.

The purpose of this chapter is to clarify the Fair Housing Law for the real estate license applicant, the practicing professional, and the general public. The purpose of the Federal Fair Housing Law (Title VIII) is to ensure equal opportunity in housing for everyone. Its goal is free and open access to housing for all people everywhere.

IMPORTANCE OF THE FAIR HOUSING LAW

Housing is a major determinant of the quality of life of an individual and of a family unit. All persons, regardless of race, color, religion, national origin, or sex, need to share in the opportunity to select the housing of their choice, wherever it may be found. The progress and well-being of the nation are dependent on such freedoms as freedom of speech, freedom of the press, freedom of personal travel and mobility, or freedom to seek the housing one wants.

The home and the neighborhood in which it is located constitute the environment in which a family lives and raises children. Unfortunately, as a result of overt (open and flagrant) or covert (hidden and subtle) discrimination, members of minority groups are often denied access to houses and neighborhoods they might otherwise have chosen. The denial of a choice of housing and neighborhood is thus a denial of a family's efforts toward self-improvement, and in that denial America's betterment—its well-being, progress, and character—is undermined. To deny open housing is to deny the American dream as well—the desire to buy your own home.

Of particular importance to real estate license applicants are the following words of the U.S. Commission on Civil Rights:

Housing is a key to improvement in a family's economic condition. Homeownership is one of the important ways in which Americans have traditionally acquired financial capital. Tax advantages, the accumulation of equity, and the increased value of real estate property enable homeowners to build economic assets. These assets can be used to educate one's children, to take advantage of business opportunities, to meet financial emergencies, and to provide for retirement. Nearly two of every three majority group (white) families are homeowners, but less than two of every five nonwhite families (black, Mexican-American, Puerto Rican, Indian, and other minorities) own their homes. Consequently, the majority of nonwhite families are deprived of this advantage.*

The real estate license applicant, as well as the practicing professional and the general public, should also

---

*The Housing and Community Development Act of 1974 amends the Federal Fair Housing Law of the Civil Rights Act of 1968 by adding the word "sex" in those sections which prohibit discrimination on the basis of race, color, religion, or national origin in the sale, rental, or financing of housing.

The 1974 Act also prohibits discrimination on the basis of sex in granting a federally related mortgage loan.

*Understanding Fair Housing, U.S. Commission on Civil Rights, Clearinghouse Publication 42, February 1973, p. 1.

realize that restricting or limiting housing choice also restricts or limits the securing of civil rights in other areas. Segregated residential patterns in metropolitan and rural areas limit opportunity in employment and education. If minority workers cannot follow jobs to the suburbs or elsewhere because housing is denied them, then discrimination in housing—unlawful as it is—leads to other social problems, as well as other violations of our constitutional freedoms.

Similarly, equal opportunity in education is also denied when discriminatory housing practices prevent fair and open housing selection. Travel patterns of school busing show the great distances minority children have had to travel to receive the benefits of equal education. Looking toward the future, when personal and national efforts toward conservation of fuel and other resources should intensify, the real estate license applicant and realty professional cannot help but realize the crucial and helpful role that fair housing can play if it is applied as the law—and human decency—intend.

Background of the Federal Fair Housing Law

It is useful to know that the Fair Housing Law did not represent a dramatic shift in the philosophy of housing the nation. Rather, other laws prohibiting discrimination in housing were enacted earlier over a period of years, and the Federal Fair Housing Law is the culmination of these earlier efforts.

For example, President John F. Kennedy signed an Executive Order on Equal Opportunity in Housing in November 1962, prohibiting any discrimination in housing where public funds were obtained through federally assisted programs. Then, in 1964, Title VI of the Civil Rights Act of that year forbade discrimination in low-rent public housing and urban renewal, as well as other federally assisted programs, thus continuing the nation's attack on discrimination in housing.

On June 17, 1968, the Supreme Court of the United States entered the picture with its decision in *Jones v. Mayer* barring discrimination in all housing, both public and private, without exception. To cite the *REALTORS Guide to Practice Equal Opportunity in Housing* on this subject, comments by counsel noted:

> The short of the matter is that no one may refuse to sell, lease or rent to another because of race or color, and no real estate licensee may do so, regardless of his principal's directions. Should a principal seek to restrict a listing according to race or color, the licensee must refuse to accept the listing.*

To continue, should a property owner (of either real or personal property) seek to restrict a listing or a sale of the property to another on the grounds of race, color, religion, national origin, or sex, the real estate licensee must refuse to accept the listing. After the listing, the

*REALTORS Guide to Practice Equal Opportunity in Housing, prepared by the Equal Opportunity in Housing Committee and the Department of State and Urban Affairs of the NATIONAL ASSOCIATION OF REALTORS, October 1973, pp. 9–10.

property owner may not refuse to sell to minority group members. According to counsel, "Every interpretation will be taken by courts in favor of the fullest application of the law." It is true that Title VIII relates only to "dwellings" and land intended to be used for a "dwelling," but *Jones v. Mayer* applies to *any* real and personal property. To cite the early (1968) HUD slogan, "Unfair housing isn't just unfair, it's illegal."

U.S. Department of Housing and Urban Development (HUD)

In the November 1965 Housing and Urban Development Act, five separate administrations were combined [Public Housing, Federal National Mortgage Association (FNMA or "Fannie Mae"), Federal Housing Authority (FHA), Urban Renewal, and Community Facilities] into one central organization, the Department of Housing and Urban Development (HUD). It is a federal department, and the Secretary is a member of the President's Cabinet. Its main purpose is to solve the complex problems of our American cities by utilizing the vast resources of the federal government, in coordination with state and local governments. This includes fair housing practices and equal opportunity for all.

HUD's Fair Housing Objectives: Conciliation, Contracts, and Cooperation

The Federal Fair Housing Law creates the position of Assistant Secretary for Equal Opportunity at HUD. This firmly establishes the importance of equal opportunity in housing, because only at HUD and the Department of Justice are civil rights responsibilities placed at so high a level.

The office is responsible for investigating and conciliating complaints of discrimination in housing. Its action steps are: to get the complainant the house or apartment denied because of discrimination; to also get the complainant reimbursement for out-of-pocket expenses as well as possible other compensation for the embarrassment and humiliation of discrimination; and lastly, to get the broker, builder, or management agent who discriminated to undertake remedial, corrective, and *affirmative* action to overcome the causes and effects of past discriminatory policies.

EXAMPLE OF AN AFFIRMATIVE HOUSING ACTION

Increasingly, focusing national attention on recent energy shortages has also focused attention on the desirability of close-in city land. In particular, local public urban renewal agencies acquire run-down properties and then get the sites ready for development. To prospective developers, a prospectus is sent for each of the parcels offered as development sites, followed later by a Developer's Kit, containing fuller particulars (i.e., a complete description of the parcel(s) and of the surrounding area, design guidelines and other objectives established for the parcel(s), sample sales contract and lease agreement, appropriate HUD forms, and a sample letter of interest forwarding the developer's statements of qualifications).

Within the statements of qualifications, the developer must provide, in addition to financial responsibility and other documented standards of performance, two documented types of "affirmative" actions:

1. A written affirmative action program in accordance with HUD Form 907 and in support of Affirmative Action under Executive Order 11246

2. An affirmative marketing plan in conformance with HUD Circular 8030 and in support of Title VIII (the Fair Housing Act) of the Civil Rights Act of 1968

The written affirmative action program is a program for providing opportunities for displaced and minority businesses and for community investment participation. The affirmative marketing plan is a plan to attract minority and majority buyers or tenants, providing a complete range of housing choices to every prospective buyer or tenant. Advertising of property listings and vacancies in minority media is one method of affirmative housing action. Another is contacting community organizations. The affirmative plans must include ways of reaching out to those groups not likely to apply for the housing or for employment or other opportunities.

FOR THE FUTURE: AN AFFIRMATIVE MARKETING AGREEMENT

During 1975, the NATIONAL ASSOCIATION OF REALTORS and officials of the Departments of HUD and Justice continued working on a real estate industry-wide affirmative marketing agreement to assure minorities of free and open access in housing. Comprehensive, voluntary programs are sought for the future that will institutionalize fair housing practices. Such actions should help to clarify the responsibilities of local real estate boards and REALTORS in the realm of fair housing, and

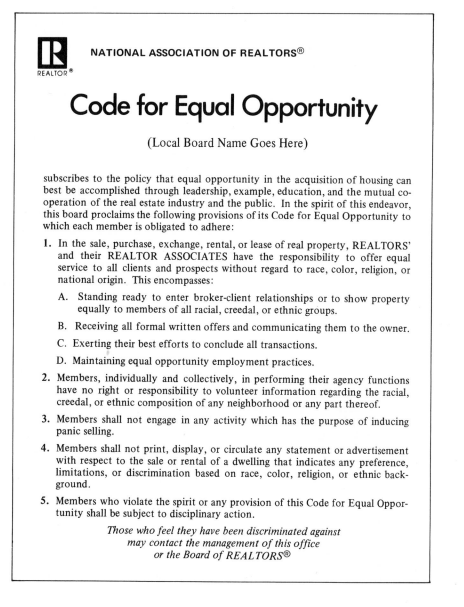

NATIONAL ASSOCIATION OF REALTORS®

Code for Equal Opportunity

(Local Board Name Goes Here)

subscribes to the policy that equal opportunity in the acquisition of housing can best be accomplished through leadership, example, education, and the mutual co-operation of the real estate industry and the public. In the spirit of this endeavor, this board proclaims the following provisions of its Code for Equal Opportunity to which each member is obligated to adhere:

1. In the sale, purchase, exchange, rental, or lease of real property, REALTORS' and their REALTOR ASSOCIATES have the responsibility to offer equal service to all clients and prospects without regard to race, color, religion, or national origin. This encompasses:

   A. Standing ready to enter broker-client relationships or to show property equally to members of all racial, creedal, or ethnic groups.

   B. Receiving all formal written offers and communicating them to the owner.

   C. Exerting their best efforts to conclude all transactions.

   D. Maintaining equal opportunity employment practices.

2. Members, individually and collectively, in performing their agency functions have no right or responsibility to volunteer information regarding the racial, creedal, or ethnic composition of any neighborhood or any part thereof.

3. Members shall not engage in any activity which has the purpose of inducing panic selling.

4. Members shall not print, display, or circulate any statement or advertisement with respect to the sale or rental of a dwelling that indicates any preference, limitations, or discrimination based on race, color, religion, or ethnic background.

5. Members who violate the spirit or any provision of this Code for Equal Opportunity shall be subject to disciplinary action.

*Those who feel they have been discriminated against
may contact the management of this office
or the Board of REALTORS®*

should also reduce the exposure of real estate licensees to federal investigations and litigation which would otherwise harass them and take valuable time away from earning a livelihood.

In the future, every board and every REALTOR will need to be prepared to *prove* his or her compliance with the law of the land and also to *document* such proof of compliance, if necessary. According to NAR's general counsel, William North, of Chicago, "This means that every Realtor and his salesmen must truly be 'racially neutral.' "*

Generally, real estate licensees must not restrict access to listing information to minority buyers or renters; or discriminate in the terms, conditions, or financial arrangements offered; or downgrade integrated schools or neighborhoods; or observe a double standard in the services rendered to clients.

Neither should real estate licensees make, print, or publish any notice, statement, or advertisement with respect to the sale or rental of a dwelling that indicates any preference, limitation, or discrimination based on race, color, religion, national origin, or sex. The "Code for Equal Opportunity" in housing (page 41) is printed by the NATIONAL ASSOCIATION OF REALTORS as a guide for usage and posting by local Boards of REALTORS.

Newspapers advertising housing for sale or rental, and other real estate services such as financing, also must comply with the federal law. For example, the advertisement shown at right appears with every edition of the real estate section of *The Washington Post.* Should there be two or more sections, it appears prominently in each and every one.

Notice that the logotype features the national symbol for equal housing opportunity. This is the outline of a house with an equals sign enclosed.

In addition, HUD has prescribed a fair housing poster which must be displayed in all real estate and rental offices and at model homes in all new subdivisions.

As can be seen, the poster lists the prohibitions of Title VIII and advises individuals who believe they have been discriminated against where to file complaints. Two additional points require amplification: (1) "blockbusting" and (2) complaint procedures.

BLOCKBUSTING IS ALSO ILLEGAL

Blockbusting, or panic-peddling, is the illegal practice of inducing fear among property owners and residents in a neighborhood, large apartment complex, or building so that they will move and cause abnormally high turnover rates in their area. This practice disrupts the stability and tranquility of residential neighborhoods by trading on people's fears of the unknown, such as learning or even suspecting that a minority family or other "alien" person or group is moving into the neighborhood. If such anxieties are fostered either overtly or covertly by sales

*"Realtors Pledge Aid to Open Housing Goal," *The Washington Post,* March 9, 1974, p. E37. (Based on "The Executive Officer," NATIONAL ASSOCIATION OF REALTORS, March 1974.)

EQUAL HOUSING OPPORTUNITY

EQUAL HOUSING OPPORTUNITY

All real estate advertised in this newspaper is subject to the Federal Fair Housing Act of 1968, which makes it illegal to advertise "any preference, limitations, or discrimination based on race, color, religion, or national origin, or an intention to make any such preference, limitations, or discrimination."

This newspaper will not knowingly accept any advertising for real estate which is in violation of the law. Our readers are hereby informed that all dwellings advertised in the newspaper are required to be available on an equal opportunity basis.

and rental agents, or even by the neighbors themselves, it is illegal. It is unlawful for *anyone* to coerce, influence, intimidate, or encourage such property turnover, with its resultant social and human costs.

COMPLAINT PROCEDURES ARE DIRECT

The various posters illustrated indicate that complainants who feel that they have been discriminated against may file complaints with HUD, the management of the brokerage firm or the apartment building, or the local Board of REALTORS. Should complainants still feel dissatisfied after conciliation, they have the option of pursuing their cases in court.

However, the provisions of Title VIII of the law permit complainants to go *directly* to court without ever filing a complaint. Direct access to the courts, combined with HUD's "hot line" telephone system (operated on a toll-free, 24-hour basis) and its clarification, explanation, and promulgation of the law, has markedly increased the effectiveness of the Federal Fair Housing Law. Also, the U.S. Department of Justice, in bringing over 100 cases to court, has yet to lose one case on appeal.

Fair Housing Law and Civil Rights Law Combine to Include All Housing

It is important for the real estate licensee to realize that in essence *all* housing is covered by antidiscrimination law, either by the Fair Housing Law or by the Civil

Rights Law. Initially, in 1968, the Federal Fair Housing Law in its first stage prohibited discrimination on the grounds of race, color, religion, or national origin in federally owned or assisted housing only. In 1969, the second stage of the law covered almost all conventionally financed apartment units and subdivision housing as well. On January 1, 1970, the third stage of the law further covered the sale or rental of all single-family houses where the services of a real estate licensee are engaged and the houses are still occupied by owners when they are marketed. Owners of property who are renting or selling on their own and who advertise, use written or posted notice, or make statements which indicate an intention to discriminate are also covered. HUD has estimated that about 80 to 85 percent of the housing units in America are covered under Title VIII. The remaining 15 to 20 percent are covered with respect to racial and sex discrimination by the various civil rights acts enacted through the years, dating back to the first Civil Rights Act of 1866. Finally, the stated provisions of the Housing

and Community Development Act of 1974 which prohibit discrimination can be seen as a fourth stage.

Clearly, housing discrimination—which occurs when persons seeking, purchasing, selling, renting, occupying, or financing housing are treated differently because of their race, color, religion, national origin, or sex—is illegal and is prohibited.

The Law Includes Appraisal Reports as Well

The statements of real estate appraisers in property valuations are also covered by the letter and the spirit of the Federal Fair Housing Law. An appraisal report must not include racially oriented statements. Great care must be exercised in using terminology such as "changing neighborhood" and "declining property values," or making declarations as to whether a neighborhood is a "desirable" or "undesirable" place to live, lest there be an inference that racial considerations have played a negative role. This would be especially so in an area where blockbusting is being carried on.

Racial fears must not be commercially exploited. Nor may appraisal terminology be a contributing factor to the segregation or desegregation of neighborhoods. Racial doubts and fears should not be aroused by careless language. Should the courts be called upon to render judgment as to discrimination in housing, findings would revolve around four criteria: the accuracy of the appraisal statements, the intent with which they were made, the degree to which they conformed to objective and noninflammatory criteria, and the good faith of the appraiser.

Unfortunately, statements are often used for purposes quite different from those of the person who made them. It is important, therefore, that the disclosure of all pertinent facts in an appraisal report or an opinion of value not be phrased in a way which will make them easy to misconstrue or misuse in order to profit from the misfortunes of minorities and others.

Reporting Service

The U.S. Department of Housing and Urban Development contracted with Prentice-Hall, Inc., in 1971 to develop and maintain an equal housing opportunity reporting service for use by federal, state, and local officials involved in administering and enforcing fair housing laws.

The subscription service is also available to the real estate industry, including REALTORS, lawyers, builders, lenders, appraisers, and others concerned with and affected by fair housing laws.

FAIR HOUSING IN PRACTICE, NOW AND IN THE FUTURE

The following examples may help to convey a sense of what fair housing is now and what it is likely to become in the future. Such examples clarify the concept of equal opportunity in housing.

1. An equal hiring policy in recruiting a sales staff is now in force; for example, minority real estate licensees are hired by suburban sales offices.

2. Use of all white or all black models is seen as a violation of the law; it is viewed as a subtle form of "racist" advertising.

3. Prominent display and use of the HUD equal housing logotype or slogan in advertisements is required for each subdivision project.

4. Real estate sales staffs must be trained to become sensitive to discriminatory practices and the social and human damage they cause.

5. Heavier expenditures and more extensive institutional advertising and support for the affirmative fair housing marketing approach, by REALTORS and other groups, are required.

6. HUD will collect and disseminate racial data on loan applicants, on house and apartment turnover, and on neighborhood composition.

7. Greater publicity is given to terms such as "racial steering" (which describes a variety of unlawful practices designed to influence a minority prospect's choice of housing locations). To limit a minority applicant's housing or neighborhood choice is to "steer" him in certain directions. Instead, applicants must choose for themselves and their families, from the full range of offerings available, those listings and neighborhoods they wish to see and consider. The prospect makes the choice of location, not the agent.

8. Broker-client responsibilities are clarified. By law, sellers may *not* discriminate and limit their listings to "whites only" or "nonblacks," and brokers may *not* accept such illegal listings. Rather, the broker should explain the law and the nature of fair housing, and the legal proceedings and penalties that may arise should the law be violated. Brokers should not wish to place their clients or themselves in jeopardy.

9. The performance of brokers and salespersons will be more closely monitored. Brokers increasingly will be held responsible for the misconduct of licensed agents as well as other staff personnel under their supervision. According to William D. North, "This means that any salesman, no matter how productive, who steers or otherwise violates the law, is too expensive to have around."*

10. "Testers" have the right to represent themselves as home seekers in order to discover racial discrimination in the sale or rental of housing. Recent court decisions have upheld this practice.

REALTORS, REALTOR–Associates, and sales agents are in business to provide the full range of real estate and housing services desired. To the extent that a client's request is lawful, the real estate licensee has the opportunity to enhance his or her professional standing in the community by the caliber of his or her performance. Knowing federal laws, and explaining and clarifying them for clients, prospects, and the general public, are critical aspects of that performance.

---

*"Realtors Trade Group, HUD Negotiating to Devise Industry-wide Marketing Accord," *The Wall Street Journal*, March 4, 1974, p. 8.

PRACTICE EXAMINATION: EQUAL OPPORTUNITY IN HOUSING

1. Should the client ask, the real estate licensee is obligated to provide the following information:

   (A) locations of "white only" neighborhoods
   (B) descriptions of minority neighborhood locations
   (C) identification of neighborhoods changing from majority to minority residents
   (D) none of these

2. Housing discrimination occurs when persons seeking, purchasing, selling, renting, occupying, or financing housing are treated differently because of their

   (A) race, color, religion, national origin, or sex
   (B) race, color, religion, or national origin
   (C) race, color, or religion
   (D) race only

3. Definitive interpretations of the Federal Fair Housing Law are established

   (A) by the minority complainant
   (B) through the U.S. Department of Housing and Urban Development
   (C) through the judicial process
   (D) through compliance and conciliation

4. "Racial steering" means to

   (A) steer brokers to minority prospects
   (B) steer minority prospects toward a limited number of choices
   (C) steer minority prospects toward the center of town
   (D) apply two of the above alternatives

5. Does the 1968 act prohibit racial steering?

   (A) Yes   (C) Usually never
   (B) No   (D) Almost always

6. What are the broker's responsibilities under the 1968 act?

   (A) To show all houses to all prospects
   (B) To show all neighborhoods
   (C) To defer to minority prospects
   (D) To treat all prospects equally

7. May a broker answer requests for racial information from sellers or prospects?

   (A) Yes
   (B) Yes, but only factually and with a disclaimer of any intention to show or offer homes on a racial basis
   (C) Both of the above
   (D) None of the above

8. If a minority prospect does not ask to be shown homes in white neighborhoods, what does the broker do?

   (A) Inquires why the minority prospect is not interested.
   (B) Explains why white neighborhoods contain better buys.
   (C) Never controls the selection of houses.
   (D) Obliges and only shows homes in nonwhite neighborhoods.

9. When a seller wants to sell to whites only, the broker

   (A) honors the listing request
   (B) does not honor the listing request
   (C) adds these words to the listing agreement
   (D) tries to comply as well as possible

10. If a minority prospect asks to be shown homes in white neighborhoods, the broker

    (A) obliges and shows homes in white neighborhoods
    (B) responds and shows homes as requested
    (C) both A and B
    (D) asks the neighbors if it would be all right

11. "No one may refuse to sell, lease, or rent to another because of race or color, and no real estate licensee may do so, regardless of the principal's directions."

    (A) The statement is absolutely correct.
    (B) The statement is only partially accurate.
    (C) The statement does not include discriminatory practices.
    (D) The statement is absolutely false.

12. The 1968 Federal Fair Housing Law

    (A) does not establish a set of required business practices, but all practices must be consistent with nondiscrimination in housing
    (B) does establish a set of required business practices, and all practices must be consistent with housing discrimination
    (C) establishes neither business practices nor intent with regard to nondiscriminatory practices in housing
    (D) none of the above

13. In blockbusting, racially transitional neighborhoods have

    (A) an increasing percentage of minority residents
    (B) a higher rate of turnover
    (C) none of the above
    (D) two of the above

14. Blockbusting is an acceptable practice

    (A) only under the supervision of real estate licensees
    (B) only when approved by either HUD or the Justice Department
    (C) under no circumstances
    (D) only if the seller and buyer mutually agree

15. Complaints about discrimination may be made to

    (A) the courts
    (B) HUD
    (C) either A or B
    (D) neither A nor B

16. The broker's obligation in promulgating equal opportunity in housing

    (A) is to replace white residents with minority homeowners
    (B) is to avoid any acts which would make housing unavailable to someone on account of race
    (C) is to exclude white residents from minority neighborhoods
    (D) is to avoid openness and honesty with minority prospects who are interested in his area

17. In blockbusting, a broker or agent may be held liable for accurate statements such as "a declining neighborhood" or "property values are falling" if there is any reasonable likelihood the listener will take them as racial inferences.

    (A) This statement is not at all true.
    (B) This statement is true.
    (C) None of the above.
    (D) Clearly, no one is liable.

18. The Federal Fair Housing Law (Title VIII of the Civil Rights Act of 1968) states that it is illegal to discriminate against any person because of race, color, religion, or national origin

    (A) in the sale, rental, or financing of housing or residential lots
    (B) in advertising the sale or rental of housing
    (C) in the provision of real estate brokerage services
    (D) in all of these

19. Should a REALTOR violate the Fair Housing Law, the local Board of REALTORS

    (A) may prosecute
    (B) may conduct a hearing to determine guilt or innocence
    (C) may report the alleged violation to the appropriate governmental authority
    (D) none of these

20. An affirmative fair housing marketing plan is one that

    (A) seeks out minority home buyers and renters
    (B) deals fairly with minority prospects
    (C) explains the full range of housing services open
    (D) stresses its nondiscriminatory aspects

Chapter 5

Contracts, Agency, and Listings

It is essential that a person licensed to sell real estate have a fundamental knowledge of the instruments used in the real estate business. *Contracts* establish the legal relationship between parties and set forth various duties between them. Contracts, also known as agreements, are used extensively in real estate. For example, a real estate broker gets the authority to sell or rent real estate through an *agency agreement* from the principal. Also, the sale or lease of real property is accomplished through a *sale* or *lease agreement*, and the closing or transfer of title to real estate is consummated through use of another instrument called a *deed*. All the above become contracts of one type or another between the parties involved.

In addition to knowing about these instruments, one should also have a fundamental understanding of the laws that govern contracts in order to avoid legal problems at a later date.

CONTRACTS

The laws governing real estate activity in the United States are generally based on the English common law. "Common law" refers to that body of unwritten law governing human and business relations which was developed in England by usage and court decisions prior to the American Revolution. This law was carried over into the American system of justice after the revolution.

The common law has been modified or altered to some degree by many states, but while these modifications are important, the basic legal principles governing real estate transactions are much the same throughout the United States.

This chapter sets forth the common-law principles with regard to real estate. It has been prepared with the assistance of authorities in the field to give the prospective licensee a working knowledge of the subject matter, but it should never be used as a basis for legal opinions. These are best left to your attorney.

Types of Contracts

To have a better understanding of contracts, a few specific definitions should be understood.

A *valid* contract contains all the essential elements of a contract and is legally binding on all parties.

A *void* contract is not really a contract, because it has no legal force or effect. An example is a contract made to commit an illegal act.

A *voidable* contract is one that can be made void, but one of the parties must take action to have it declared void. For example, A was induced by fraud to enter into a contract with B. A can have the contract declared void.

An *unenforceable* contract is a good contract which for some reason cannot be enforced, such as an oral contract entered into for the sale of real estate.

A *bilateral* contract occurs when two parties exchange promises, such as when A promises to buy B's house and B promises to sell it to A.

A *unilateral* contract occurs when one party promises to do something upon the completed act of another; for example, A promises to pay B $10 for walking across the Brooklyn Bridge. Here there is no exchange of promises, and no contract is formed until B actually walks across the bridge, which is at the same time B's acceptance of A's offer.

An *express* contract is one expressed in words, either oral or written.

An *implied* contract is one that is implied by the acts and conduct of the parties.

Oral and Written Contracts and the Statute of Frauds

Many contracts, or agreements, between parties may be made orally and will be legally enforceable in a court of law. Some contracts, however, to be enforceable must be in writing. In most states, contracts involving real estate are governed by a law enacted during the reign of Charles II of England in 1677. This law, commonly referred to as the Statute of Frauds, was enacted to prevent fraudulent practices in certain types of contracts—including the transfer and lease of real estate—by requiring that the agreements be in writing in order to be enforceable by the courts.

A statute of frauds is in effect in virtually all states and is applied in transactions involving real estate as follows:

1. No contract for the sale or purchase of real estate shall be enforceable unless it is in writing and signed by the parties made accountable therein.

2. No contract for the lease of real estate for more than 1 year shall be enforceable unless it is in writing and signed by the parties made accountable therein.

It should be noted that the law stating that a real estate contract must be in writing does not make an oral contract illegal or nonbinding. It only means that if any differences arise under an oral contract for the sale of real estate, the courts would not enforce it. The same holds true for oral leases when they are for more than 1 year. Oral agreements are valid, but they cannot be enforced in a court of law should disputes arise.

While it is the general rule that all real estate contracts coming under the Statute of Frauds must have all the terms in writing, there are nevertheless some very limited instances where verbal statements will be allowed. These instances occur when one of the written terms is ambiguous and requires verbal clarification, such as when a term consistent with the purpose of the contract has obviously been left out by oversight or when it appears that the written terms were not actually intended to be a final agreement. A court will also usually allow verbal interpretation of the written terms where one party is attempting to set aside the contract on the basis of fraud or mistake.

Essentials of a Contract

There are five essential elements that contracts must have in order to make them valid. The absence of any element would make the contract void or voidable.

1. There must be an offer and an acceptance.
2. There must be a seal and/or a consideration.
3. The parties must have legal capacity to contract.
4. There must be a reality of consent.
5. The object of the contract must be legal.

1. AN OFFER AND AN ACCEPTANCE

The first element for any contract is that there must be a real offer and a genuine acceptance. The offer may originate with the seller (a contract of sale), in which case all terms and conditions must be met by the buyer, or the offer may originate with the buyer (a contract of purchase), in which case all terms and conditions must be met by the seller. In either case the offeree must *exactly* meet the conditions of the offeror.

For example: A offers property for sale for $30,000 with the offer to include certain chattels, such as a washer or dryer. B makes an offer to purchase the property at a price of $29,500 without those chattels. Is there a contract?

No. No contract exists because there has been no acceptance. Two offers do not equal one acceptance. B in this case made a new offer, or counteroffer, which A could accept or reject. B did not meet all A's terms and conditions.

This is a common form of negotiation. In actual real estate transactions final agreement may sometimes be reached only after several such offers and counteroffers. Both sides must become satisfied and thereby agree to the contract.

2. CONSIDERATION OR SEAL

Consideration may be generally defined as a promise made by a person to do something he or she is not otherwise obligated to do in order to induce another party to make the same contractual type of promise. Thus, in a contract for the sale of real property, the promise to pay the sales price is exchanged for the promise to convey title. The law only requires that the consideration exchanged meet the above definition; the law, on the other hand, is usually not concerned with whether the value of one of the promises is equal in value to the other. This means that the fact that the sales price is perhaps too much or too little will ordinarily not be grounds for setting aside a contract.

In earlier times the placing of a seal—which could be a device or a unique mark—on a contract by one party and delivery of the contract to another party meant that no consideration was required. Although seals are often used on contracts today—sometimes by the traditional metallic device, other times by the mere indication of "Seal" or "L.S." (*locus sigilii,* place for the seal) by the signature line—the effect of the seal has generally been changed by legislation to be at most a presumption that consideration has passed. Such a presumption, of course, is not conclusive and may be shown to be false. Most jurisdictions have legislated away even this small effect of the seal (except in special circumstances, such as where corporations are specifically required by state law to use a seal).

3. LEGAL CAPACITY TO CONTRACT

Not all persons have the legal capacity to enter into a contract. Generally, insane persons, intoxicated persons, and minors cannot enter into a binding contract. Should any of these persons enter into a contract, either they or their guardians could void the contract. Thus such contracts are voidable by these categories of persons, but not by the other party to the contract.

In the case of a minor (one who has not reached majority) he or she can disaffirm or make void any contract entered into during infancy, or for a reasonable time after reaching his or her majority (legal age). Traditionally this has been age 21, but many states have lowered the legal age requirements to age 18 or some other age.

However, in some cases a minor can be held liable for a contract entered into involving real estate, if it can be proven that it was *a necessary*. Necessaries are essentials for existence, such as food, shelter, and clothing. Real estate is classified as shelter, a necessary, and a contract of sale or a lease of property to a minor may be judged both necessary to the minor's actual needs and in keeping with his or her ability to contract.

4. A REALITY OF MUTUAL CONSENT

In order to be recognized as valid, a contract must be free from mistake, misrepresentation, fraud, undue influence, or duress. The consent of the parties to the contract must be real, and the contract's terms must reflect the real or true intention of the parties. Otherwise, the contract is either void or voidable.

Mistakes made in the preparation of a contract have varying effects, depending upon the nature of the mistake. Generally, mistakes are mistakes of fact or mistakes of law.

Mistake of fact. These mistakes include errors which do not state the true conditions of the contract, such as identity of a party to the contract or the identity of the subject matter. If curable, these mistakes of fact generally do not void the contract, but make the contract voidable.

Mistake of law. A mistake of law happens when a party having full knowledge of the facts comes to an erroneous conclusion as to their legal effect. A party to a contract operating under a mistake of law cannot disavow or void the contract based on the erroneous conclusion. If, however, the contract itself is in violation of the law or requires one of the parties to do an illegal act, then it is void.

Misrepresentation. This is an unknowing or innocent misstatement of fact, with no intent to deceive. A misrepresentation of a material fact would make the contract voidable at the option of the party to whom the misrepresentation was made.

Fraud. This is the knowing or deliberate misrepresentation of a material fact, made with the intent that the other party act on the false information and possibly cause himself or herself some harm or injury. Such contracts would usually be voidable at the option of the aggrieved party.

Undue influence. This is the taking of unfair advantage of another because of the particular and peculiar relationship of the parties. Such contracts would be voidable at the option of the person unfairly induced.

Duress. This is the forcing of someone, by threat of personal injury or restraint, to enter into a contract against his or her own free will. Contracts obtained under duress are voidable by the aggrieved party.

5. LEGAL OBJECT

The subject matter of the contract must not violate any laws—local, state, or national. A contract between parties to commit a criminal act would be void.

Contract Provisions

There is no "one absolute correct form" for any real estate contract. Any form used should specify all the terms and conditions of the agreement between the parties. As a beginning, the agreement would necessarily include the above five essentials. In addition, other provisions would include:

1. Date of the agreement
2. Names and signatures of the parties to the contract
3. Legal description of the property
4. Consideration (see above section)
5. Terms of payment
6. Any special agreements or contingencies between the parties
7. Date and place of closing

The Contract Is Merged in the Deed

A contract for the sale of real estate incorporates future actions. It is an executory agreement that calls for the future completion of stipulated terms. When the sale is completed, the seller transfers ownership to the buyer by means of a deed, which is an executed contract and supersedes and replaces the contract of sale.

It should be noted that in most jurisdictions any provisions in the contract of sale which were not included in the deed are no longer enforceable once the buyer has accepted the deed. In order to prevent this merger of contract of sale into the deed, it is advisable to insert in the contract form a provision which states that "the provisions hereof shall survive the execution and delivery of the deed aforesaid and shall not be merged therein." (See also the section of Chapter 7 on execution, delivery, and acceptance.)

Doctrine of Equitable Conversion

This doctrine states that when a purchaser and seller sign a sales contract for a property, the purchaser immediately acquires "equitable title" to the property and the seller acquires a similar "equitable right" to the purchase price.

The doctrine further states that when the purchaser obtains the equitable title to the property, he or she also becomes liable for the loss or destruction of the property. Thus, if the property were a building which was destroyed before conveyance, the purchaser would still have to pay the full price to the seller.

One way to avoid such a result would be for the purchaser to insure the property when the contract is signed. But the easiest and least costly way is to include a clause in the contract providing that liability for loss remains with the seller until closing and transfer of the legal title. In many jurisdictions, state law requires that such a provision be a standard part of every contract for the sale of real estate. (See also the section of Chapter 7 on equitable title and legal title.)

The Contract May Be Assigned

Unless expressly precluded in the contract, a buyer retains the right to assign his or her "equitable title" to a third party, called the *assignee*. The assignee takes over all the rights of the assignor, and also all the responsibilities. However, the assignor remains liable to the seller, as contracted, for performance of the terms of the contract.

Breach of Contract

When one of the parties to a contract fails to perform, it is a breach, and the nonbreaching party has certain legal rights.

Specific performance. The nonbreaching party could initiate court action to force the breaching party to go through with the terms of the contract.

Recission of the contract. Both parties may agree to rescission, in which case the purchaser would be entitled to the return of the deposit and any payments made, and the seller would be entitled to the return of the property, had possession been granted to the buyer.

Damages. The nonbreaching party may offer to perform, then sue for actual damages incurred if the other party fails to fulfill the terms of the contract.

Liquidated or stipulated damages. Occasionally the contracting parties insert a clause in the contract stating an amount of money payable in case of a breach.

Forfeiture of purchaser's consideration. Most contracts contain a clause which states that if the purchaser defaults, the seller may declare a forfeiture of the purchaser's deposit, or without the forfeiture proceed as under "Damages," or "Specific performance" above.

AGENCY

The Principal and the Agent

Agency is a contractual relationship in law whereby one party gives to another party the authority to act for him or her in a particular business transaction. The authority can be specifically expressed either orally or in writing, or can be implied through negotiations and agreement. The principal is the party conferring the authority, and the agent is the party accepting the authority to act for the principal.

A real estate broker is an agent who acts for a principal, usually the seller. A real estate salesperson working for a real estate broker is known as an agent, but is not a party to the agency contract.

Minors and insane persons cannot be principals because they lack the authority and capacity to act and contract for themselves. However, corporations and partnerships are legal entities and do have the capacity to contract and can be principals. Any person who can be a principal can also be an agent, subject to licensure laws imposed by the state.

Creation and Termination of Agency

Although the agent's authority can be either express or implied, it is good business practice to proceed only on an express authority in writing. If a dispute were to arise out of an implied or oral authority, the agent would have to prove in court that an agency relationship actually existed in order to collect a fee. In many states, either statutes or license laws require that all agency agreements to sell real estate be in writing.

In order to end or release an agency agreement, the general rules of contracts apply. Termination of the agency relationship may occur either by acts of the parties or by operation of the law.

ACTS OF THE PARTIES

Mutual consent of the parties. Both agent and principal agree to end their agency contract.

Completion of the agreement. For example, an agency contract ends when the property has been sold.

Expiration of time. The agency contract may stipulate that it will end after a certain period of time. If an expiration date is not included, it would terminate at the end of a reasonable time. (Many states require that all agency agreements have a definite termination date, such as a day, month, and year.)

Revocation by the principal. The principal may revoke the authority of the agent any time. However, an agent may be entitled to damages sustained as a result of the breach of the contract, or a wrongful improper revocation. If the principal shows the agent to have been incompetent, dishonest, or disloyal, the principal would not be liable for damages to the agent.

Renunciation by the agent. An agent may also renounce or end the relationship with the principal at any time. However, the agent also can be held liable for damages to the principal, as for failure to accomplish the object of the agency contract.

OPERATION OF LAW

Insanity of either principal or agent. This would terminate any agency agreement, because the insane person can no longer act for himself or herself, or perform the terms of the contract.

Death of either principal or agent. This would usually terminate the agency agreement. It is possible, though unusual, for an agency to survive death by including a contractual provision that makes the agency agreement binding upon the estate.

Destruction of the object. If the object or subject matter upon which the agency was created is destroyed, this will terminate the agreement.

Bankruptcy of either party. Bankruptcy of either agent or principal would usually terminate an agency contract.

Duties and Liabilities of an Agent

Duty to perform. The agent has a duty to perform the work assigned. While inadequate performance may only lead to a breach of the agency contract, if the agent commits acts which cause the principal loss, the agent may be liable to the principal.

Loyalty. The principal has put faith and trust in the agent because of the knowledge and experience of the agent in that profession. Therefore, an agent acts for the best interests of the principal, subordinating personal interest, and owes complete loyalty to the principal. The agent must realize that his or her actions will reflect on the principal, and that he or she has a duty to act in the most professional and ethical manner. Acts of disloyalty are illegal under the law.

The agent selling property for a principal may not purchase it for himself or herself, even through a third person, without permission of the principal. Should the agent make such a secret purchase, the principal, upon discovery, may cancel the sale, or, where the agent has disposed of the property, possibly recover the value of the property plus any profits. The rationale of this rule is to prevent unjust enrichment of the agent.

An agent also may not work for two principals with conflicting interests, as for example both buyer and seller, unless *both* principals are fully informed and have *consented* to the arrangement. Without such *information*

and consent the transaction may be voided by either principal and the agent may be denied fees from both, regardless of how innocent or honest the agent's motives were.

After termination of the agency employment, the agent may accept employment from a client with interests adverse to the former principal, but the agent may not disclose any confidential information obtained during the previous employment. Though the requirement of loyalty is very broad, it does not require an agent to cover dishonest acts of the principal which the agent may discover. The agent must act in a legal manner at all times.

Notice. The agent is required to report any information about the property that is acquired through his or her agency to the principal within a reasonable time after becoming aware of it. When knowledge is obtained by the agent within the scope or performance of duties, the law imputes knowledge to the principal regardless of actual notice.

Obedience. The agent must act in the manner stated by the principal, even if the agent thinks it unwise, unless the principal's instructions are illegal. The judgment of the agent should never be substituted for the principal's specific instructions. Failure to follow instructions will render the agent liable for damages. Should the principal deliver no instructions, the agent is then to be guided by local established sound business practices in real estate. If the agent knows the principal's action to be unwise, he or she is under an obligation to explain to the principal the illogic of the unwise action. If the principal still insists that the agent carry out the unwise action, the agent must do so.

Fiduciary responsibility. The agent stands legally in a fiduciary relationship to the principal. This relationship imposes upon the agent a higher standard of care or responsibility than is found in most business relationships.

The agent must exercise due care in acting for the principal. Due care is "that degree of care which any average, reasonable, prudent person in real estate locally would exercise under similar circumstances." This includes the duty of notice described above, as well as the obligation not to take secret profits, such as rebates, or to conceal essential facts from the principal. Violations of this fiduciary responsibility may give the principal grounds for a civil suit for damages against the agent.

Accounting for the principal's assets. The agent must account to the principal for all funds and property which come into the agent's possession. In addition, the agent must protect these funds to the best of his or her ability. The responsibility logically rests with the agent, and sound business practice will be to establish an "escrow" account, stating the express purpose of the funds. In most states it is required that the broker not commingle escrow funds with the broker's personal or company funds. A separate business account for the agency as well as other matters, generally, is sound business practice.

ACTORS AND THEIR ACTIONS IN REAL ESTATE TRANSACTIONS

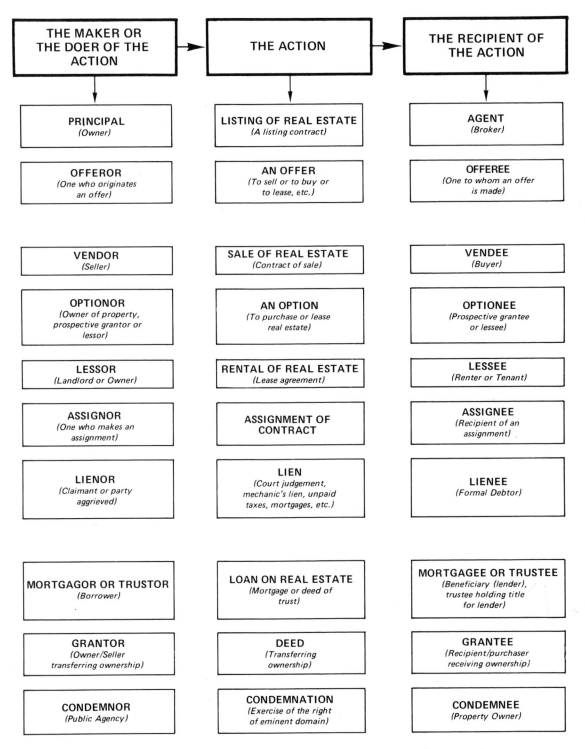

Specially prepared for Jack C. Estes and John Kokus, *Real Estate License Preparation Course for the Uniform Examinations: For Salespersons and Brokers*, New York, McGraw-Hill, 1976.

Compensation of Agent

Many disputes arise as to whether a broker (agent) has earned a fee or not. However, in general an agent earns a fee when he or she can bring to the principal a ready, willing, and able buyer meeting the terms set out by the principal. If the principal fails to complete the sale, through no fault or act of the agent's, the agent is entitled to a fee. If the sale materializes but the principal disputes the agent's claim, then the agent must show that personal efforts procured or brought about the sale. The importance of the written listing contract between the principal and the agent is thereby emphasized.

Today, there have been a great number of court decisions supporting the theory that the true measure of a buyer's ability and willingness to perform is whether or not the contract actually goes to settlement. Many sales agreements incorporate a clause stating that the brokerage fee is payable at settlement. Thus, if settlement does not occur, the fee would not be paid. An exception to this would be if the seller defaulted.

LISTINGS

A listing is a contract between the seller of property (the principal) and the real estate broker (the agent) wherein the seller "lists" property for sale with the broker. Either the seller or the broker may approach the other initially, with the end result being a listing contract.

The usual listing contract is in effect for a certain definite period of time only. The seller promises to list his or her property for sale for a stated period of time, and to pay a fee if it is sold. On the other hand, the broker promises to advertise and undertake other actions to effect a sale. The broker's other obligations to the principal are as noted under duties and liabilities of an agent.

Open or General Listing

An "open" listing is a general listing, in which a seller notifies the broker that he or she is offering a particular piece of property for sale. The broker then lists this property with his or her firm and tries to secure a buyer. The contract consists of an offer by the seller for an act by the broker, which is the finding of a buyer ready, willing, and able to purchase on the seller's terms.

Figure 5-1. The various actors and their actions are shown to help the reader visualize the key transactions in real estate. From top to bottom, the exhibit presents a natural flow of events. Moreover, the wording is expressed in a "grantor-grantee" fashion so that the reader may begin the process of becoming familiar with the difficult "—ee, —or" mode of expression in real estate. The reader may wish to return repeatedly to this exhibit in reading later chapters until the actors, their actions, and these expressions become commonplace.

An open listing, open-ended as the one stated, is hazardous for the broker. The seller has reserved the right to sell the property personally, or to list it with any number of other brokers with varying dates of contract termination, or perhaps no termination dates at all. A fee is earned only by the broker who produces the buyer, and even the amount of the fee may be subject to dispute should it not be specified in the contract. On the other hand, the broker is not bound to exert any efforts, such as advertising, to sell the property.

Open listings are indefinite listings and are likely to result in misunderstandings between the parties involved, in poor relations with the public, and in litigation. It is better business practice in real estate to avoid such ill-defined listings because of the potential harm that may result.

Exclusive Listing

An exclusive listing is a contract wherein a principal agrees to let one broker list the property exclusively. No other broker can obtain or have the right of listing during the period of exclusive listing. Such an advantageous listing for the broker requires consideration on his or her part of promotional expenditures and the performance of other acts such as property showing. In return for the broker's promissory considerations, the seller gives an exclusive listing of the property.

Although the contractual language may vary, there are two categories of exclusive listing.

EXCLUSIVE RIGHT TO SELL

The broker is entitled to a fee regardless of who makes the sale. For example, if the owner sells his own property, the broker is still entitled to a fee.

EXCLUSIVE AGENCY

Under this type of agency the owner retains the right to sell the property personally without being obligated to pay a fee to the broker. However, the particular broker holding the listing contract is the exclusive broker and is entitled to a commission should she, he, or some other broker sell the property.

Multiple Listing

Many types of cooperative listing organizations have been formed over the past several years. The most popular are ones formed by REALTORS who have banded together to share their listings. Their listing services are generally called "REALTORS Multiple Listing Service" (RMLS). In this type of listing an owner generally lists property with a cooperating member on an exclusive right to sell basis. The broker then shares the listing with all other members of the service, cooperating with the other brokers on a negotiated share of the sales fee. Many of these organizations have computerized their operations to expedite selection of properties for the purchaser.

PRACTICE EXAMINATION:
CONTRACTS, AGENCY, AND LISTINGS

1. Contract law, according to the statute of frauds, requires that real estate contracts for the sale of real estate

   (A) be valid for a period of more than 1 year
   (B) be in writing if enforcement is desired
   (C) be consistent with the legal code of the state
   (D) be absolutely clear in their stipulated provisions

2. Reality of consent in a contract means that

   I. the parties' consent to the contract must be real
   II. the terms of the contract must express the real intention of the parties

   (A) I only   (C) Both I and II
   (B) II only   (D) Neither I nor II

3. Principals may sell their own property and not pay the broker any commission

   I. under a general listing
   II. under an exclusive agency

   (A) I only   (C) Either I or II
   (B) II only   (D) Neither I nor II

4. One of the following is not an essential element in the making of a real estate contract:

   (A) an offer and acceptance, and a consideration
   (B) legal capacity of the parties, and a reality of consent
   (C) legal object
   (D) in writing, and signed by the parties to be charged thereby

5. Agent most nearly means

   (A) one who is the source of another's authority
   (B) one who represents and acts for another
   (C) one who has conferred authority to another
   (D) one who settles the affairs of another

6. Consideration in a contract is

   (A) a sum of money
   (B) an exchange of promises
   (C) at least 5 percent of the purchase price
   (D) none of the above

7. The appointment of an agency relationship

   (A) requires no formalities
   (B) requires an express act, such as a contract
   (C) in real estate agreements is better accomplished by implication
   (D) is always derived by express act

8. Agency is a legal relationship

   (A) between broker and agent
   (B) between broker and purchaser
   (C) between principal and agent
   (D) between salesperson and seller

9. Obedience of the agent to the principal's instructions means that

   (A) the agent may disobey those instructions in good faith
   (B) the agent may disobey those instructions in good faith if the agent's good judgment dictates such action
   (C) the agent should disregard those instructions that are contrary to local established procedures and customs of the real estate business
   (D) the agent must follow those instructions regardless of personal feelings about them

10. A contract by which one person with greater or less discretionary power undertakes to represent another in business relations is

    (A) a listing   (C) a power of attorney
    (B) an agency   (D) none of these

11. A contract based on a consideration which consisted of a promise in exchange for another promise is known as a

    (A) multilateral contract
    (B) unilateral contract
    (C) bilateral contract
    (D) binary contract

12. The difference between an exclusive agency and an exclusive right to sell is

    (A) the broker's promise to undertake and bear certain promotional expenses
    (B) the principal's reservation of the right to sell his or her own home
    (C) the principal's reservation of the right to pay broker no commission
    (D) the principal's reservation of the right to pay broker no commission should the principal sell the property

13. When the real estate agent has produced a buyer who is ready, willing, and able, the agent has generally

    (A) accounted to the principal
    (B) earned a commission
    (C) consummated the sale
    (D) established personal competence

14. From the point of view of clarity of intention, a general listing

    (A) is superior to an exclusive listing
    (B) cannot be withdrawn prior to performance
    (C) solves the problems that an exclusive listing poses
    (D) is the most indefinite of all

15. Generally, if a purchaser has signed a contract under duress, the contract is

    (A) void
    (B) voidable by the seller
    (C) voidable by the buyer
    (D) a unilateral contract

16. An agency agreement may be terminated by all the following except

    (A) revocation by the principal
    (B) reciprocity
    (C) renunciation by the agent
    (D) mutual consent

17. In the event of an assignment of a contract, which of the following is (are) correct?

    I. The person to whom the contract is assigned is called the assignee.
    II. The person assigning the contract remains liable to the seller for performance of the terms of the contract.

    (A) I only
    (B) II only
    (C) Both I and II
    (D) Neither I nor II

18. A written contract would best be described as

    (A) an implied contract
    (B) an express contract
    (C) an enforceable contract
    (D) a negotiated contract

19. Generally, unless there are certain provisions to the contrary in the contract, the terms of the contract

    I. are enforceable after settlement
    II. are not binding after settlement, because the terms of the contract merged into the deed

    (A) I only
    (B) II only
    (C) Both I and II
    (D) Neither I nor II

20. A contract would generally be void if it were

    I. based on an illegal act
    II. entered into with a minor

    (A) I only
    (B) II only
    (C) Both I and II
    (D) Neither I nor II

Chapter 6

Real Property Interests

PRIVATE PROPERTY AND PUBLIC PROPERTY

Real property can be defined as "the right or interest which an individual has in lands and fixtures to the exclusion of all others." The definition further suggests the concept of ownership of real property, which includes the owner's rights to possess, enjoy, control, and dispose of his or her property or land at will, subject only to the rights of the state.

Historically, two systems of property ownership have existed, the feudal and allodial systems. In the feudal system the sovereign owned all the land, with subjects possessing only the right to use it. In return they gave the sovereign their services.

Individual ownership characterized the allodial system. In the United States we have operated under the allodial system of ownership, but private ownership rights are subject to certain public limitations by the state.

Limitations on Private Ownership of Real Property

EMINENT DOMAIN

This is the right of the state to take private property for public use upon payment of reasonable compensation to the owner. The right exists at all levels of government: local, state, and federal. The theory behind the power of eminent domain is that the property taken will be used for the greater benefit of the community. The right of eminent domain is exercised by condemnation.

POLICE POWER

This is the right of the state to limit an owner's use of private property if this will mean greater benefit to the community. For example, zoning is the regulatory right of government to enact ordinances that will control and regulate the character and usage of property. Zoning land for residential usage is an example of a public ordinance designed to preserve harmonious family living patterns.

The Standard State Zoning Enabling Act found in state legislation delegates the authority to zone to local governmental units. This act, which has been adopted with varying provisions by 44 states, requires that local jurisdictions zone their land in accordance with a comprehensive or master plan, or a general plan that has been widely and well considered. The act also delegates to the local governmental units the authority to approve amendments to the adopted zoning ordinance, or to approve changes in zoning for individual parcels of land.

TAXATION

The state has the right to tax property and to receive revenues to finance necessary public expenditures, such as schools and government. Should the private property owner fail to pay public taxes, the state could enforce its tax claim and sell the property.

ESCHEAT

This is the right of the state to take private property from deceased owners, should no heirs be found to assert their claim to the property and if there was no will.

Classifications of Property

PUBLIC PROPERTY

This is real property that is owned by the state (or government). Examples include school grounds, public roadways, parks, government wilderness areas, and many others. Besides government's taking private property for public use through eminent domain or because of the failure to pay taxes, lands for public use may be voluntarily dedicated by private owners.

QUASI-PUBLIC PROPERTY

This is real property privately owned by the public in general. Examples include public transportation routes such as rapid transit, rail lines, and bus terminals, as well as utility companies furnishing water, gas, electricity, and telephone service.

PERSONAL PROPERTY

This is not real property. It is not an interest in lands or their fixutres but is an interest in things movable. Personal property is a chattel, and its ownership interests do not constitute an estate in perpetuity lasting beyond the lifetime of the owner, as does real property.

Fixtures were originally items of personal property that had become affixed to the land or its improvements. Then they may or may not have become a part of the real property and passed to the new owner at the time of sale or other transfer of the property. Briefly, one test as to whether an item is real or personal property is whether it is movable or removable without either damaging the real property or making the building or land incomplete. How is an item affixed? Other tests answer these questions: Why was it affixed? What is its purpose? Is it a special item relating to a person's livelihood, such as trade fixtures to conduct business? For example, extra-heavy duty vises and workbenches, though affixed to the property, may be ruled to be personal property and can thus accompany the seller to a new location.

The difference between real and personal property is important to the licensee, as the laws applying to these two forms of property are different.

ESTATES IN LAND

An estate in land can be defined as the degree of interest or the extent of the interest that a person has (or owns) in the land. The estate is of a permanent, substantial nature, a right extending in perpetuity. However, the extent of an estate may range from complete and absolute ownership to mere possession. Generally, estates are classified as freehold estates and estates of less than a freehold.

A freehold estate is an interest in real estate of not less than a life estate. A person holding a freehold estate is said to be seized of it (from the term "seisin," which is the possession of a freehold).

At this point the reader may find it helpful to refer to Figure 6-1 for a visual depiction of the terminology and concepts presented.

Fee, Fee Simple, and Fee Simple Absolute

All these terms have the same basic meaning and may be defined as the largest and strongest estate or interest a person can have in real property. A person holding a fee simple estate enjoys all the rights of absolute ownership, including the right to transmit it by inheritance, so it is sometimes referred to as an *estate of inheritance*. Some of the rights of absolute ownership are: the right to exclusive possession; the right to personal enjoyment and use of all products and assets of the fee; the right to sell

or transfer by deed or will; and the right to use, misuse, or waste. All rights, however, are subject to the limitations imposed by the state.

Fee Tail

This form of ownership has been abolished by statute in most states, and in the others it has been radically altered in its effect. When originally used it ensured, by inclusion in the granting clause of a deed the words "and the heirs of his body," that if the grantee died without heirs of the body the property would revert to the grantor.

Fee Determinable

This form of ownership (also sometimes called *qualified* or *base fee*) and *fee upon condition* are other rarely used fee estates. These fees were used to transfer property to a holder who enjoyed all the rights of fee simple, but from whom these rights could be taken away at a later date if a certain specified event took place. If the specified event occurred, the property reverted to the grantor. For example, property is transferred to A to be used as a school; should it cease to be used as a school, then it would revert to the grantor or grantor's heirs.

Life Estate

This is an estate for the duration of someone's life. The only requirement is that the estate terminate upon the death of a prescribed person. This person can be the owner, the owner's spouse, or any person so designated. Upon the death of this person, the estate reverts back to the property owner or to any other specified person. The person who receives the property upon the death of the life estate holder is called the *remainderman.*

The holder of the life estate is free to sell the interest that he or she holds in the property, which is for the duration of a designated life. The purchaser of the life estate would lose the property upon the death of the designated person. Also, a holder of a life estate would be required to keep the property in good repair and not waste its assets to the detriment of the remainderman. It is possible to acquire the life estate holder's interest plus the remainderman's interest, and thus have a fee simple estate.

OWNERSHIP IN REAL PROPERTY

Real property may be owned by one person alone, called severalty ownership, or with others in some form of concurrent ownership.

When real property is held with other people, they are generally referred to as co-tenants. Types of concurrent ownerships may be joint tenancy, tenancy by the entireties, or tenancy in common.

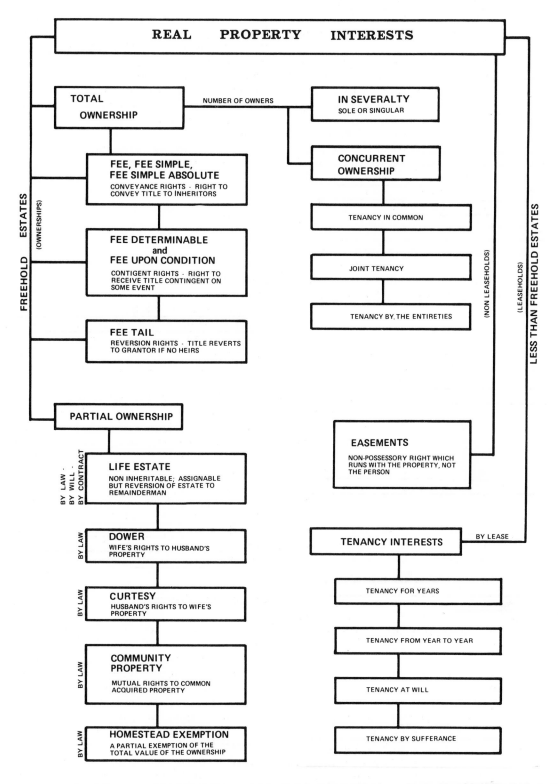

Specially prepared for Jack C. Estes and John Kokus, *Real Estate License Preparation Course for the Uniform Examinations: For Salespersons and Brokers*, New York, McGraw-Hill, 1976.

Figure 6-1.

Joint Tenancy

This is an estate held by two or more persons, but with simultaneously acquired title, with identical interest or shares, acquired from the same source and in the same conveyance.

In some states, upon the death of one of the owners of the joint tenancy, the interest of the deceased passes to the surviving owners or tenants. However, in most states the right of survivorship is not created unless the intention of the parties to have survivorship is expressly written on the face of the instrument by which they acquired title. For example, title is taken by "John Jones and Mary Jones, his wife, as joint tenants, with right of survivorship, as at common law." Otherwise, if the right of survivorship is not expressly written, an estate will pass on to the heirs or devisees of the deceased.

Should it be necessary to separate the joint interests of tenants in common or of joint tenants, court action for partition may be requested. Any tenant with an estate, except husband and wife, may initiate the legal action and thus ascertain the quality of the title. The estate may then be divided physically or a sale may be held and the proceeds divided.

Tenancy by the Entireties

This is a special type of ownership of property intended only for husbands and wives who own property together. As in joint tenancy, tenancy by the entireties requires that property be acquired simultaneously, with identical interest, from the same source in the same conveyance. In addition, there is the requirement that the parties be husband and wife. The theory is that a husband and wife are "one" person and thus hold property as one person. A husband and wife can own property by any of the three means for concurrent ownership—as tenants in common, as joint tenants, or as tenants by the entireties. Survivorship, if intended, usually must be expressly stipulated, as in joint tenancy.

In a tenancy by the entireties a husband and wife can convey property only by mutual consent. Neither can sell his or her interest alone, without the other joining in. Property held in tenancy by the entireties cannot be attached by creditors, unless the creditor is the creditor of both husband and wife.

Tenancy in Common

This exists when two or more persons hold an estate in land, not necessarily acquired simultaneously or from the same source, or with equal interest, with each holding an undivided interest or share in the whole property. An owner may sell his or her share in the whole, or upon death, the share, still undivided, is distributed to the owner's heirs, and they become tenants in common in the same proportion to the whole. Each tenant in common assumes proportional responsibility for taxes, maintenance, and repairs of the property. There is no right of survivorship in a tenancy in common.

OTHER INTERESTS IN REAL PROPERTY

Dower

Under common law, dower is the right of a wife to a life estate in one-third of all real property owned by her husband during the marriage. Until the death of the husband, the wife's dower is contingent or "inchoate." If the husband dies intestate (without a will) and without children, the wife then is entitled to a full life estate in all his property, subject to any rights by the husband's creditors.

Under common law there are cases where the wife's right of dower is not upheld:

Willful desertion or abandonment

Divorce

Murder of the husband to obtain dower interest

Curtesy

This is the right which the husband likewise has in property owned by his wife at her death. Common law declares that all rights of dower also apply to curtesy.

In either case, dower or curtesy, the law is assuring the surviving spouse of a minimal interest in the property of the other. Many states have either abolished or altered dower and curtesy and substituted other statutes to protect the interest of the surviving spouse. In some states, in lieu of dower or curtesy, the surviving spouse is entitled to a statutory share of the estate of the deceased spouse. In other states the one-third share has been modified to some other proportion.

In any event, usually neither spouse can deed this interest away without the other's joining in, nor can either will the other's interest away to heirs or anyone else. Therefore, it is always wise for both signatures to appear in the sale of real property in order to release their joint interest, if any.

Community Property

Some states do not recognize dower or curtesy interests. Instead the interests of the husband and wife are known as *community property.* While individual states treat community property differently, generally property owned prior to marriage by one of the parties, or acquired by gift, will, or inheritance after marriage, is considered separate property and the spouse has no claim upon it. Any property acquired by either spouse after marriage is considered community property owned equally by both, each possessing an undivided one-half interest. There are provisions in most states that have this type of system of real property interest whereby either spouse can purchase property after marriage and have it still considered as separate property.

Even in states using community property, it is still wise to have both husband and wife join in the contract of sale and deed, as their signatures to these instruments will give up any interests they or their heirs may have in the property.

Homestead Exemption

A *homestead* is simply real estate occupied as a home, including the house, the land upon which it is situated, and the accompanying outbuildings. In certain states a homestead law has been passed for the purpose of preserving the family unit, in the interests of public policy. This law protects homes from forced sale by creditors to satisfy certain types of debts. In actual practice, homestead laws specify maximum dollar values and acreage limits for an exemption, which may range, for example, from $2,500 to $12,500, or from a city lot to 180 acres in a rural area. Necessary qualifications for exemption are that the owner or owners (i.e., a marital homestead is husband and wife) must be a family unit of two or more persons living together, under a family head, in actual occupancy of the property, and must have recorded a declaration of homestead.

The homestead declaration does not exempt the property from forced sales: it does not protect it from actions for satisfaction of judgments obtained prior to recorded homestead, mechanic's liens, husband-and-wife debts where they have encumbered the property as security for the debts (such as mortgages or deeds of trust) or where they encumbered the property prior to the recorded declaration of homestead. Other creditors may only seek recourse against that portion of homestead value which is above the specified amount of homestead exemption, if any, by resorting to special legal proceedings to reach the excess value. Should the court-appointed appraiser find such excess value, the property may be sold under execution and the excess applied toward satisfaction of the judgment(s). Also, tax obligations, as a general rule, may not be defeated by a recorded homestead.

In some states a portion of the real estate taxes is waived if the property is owner-occupied and if the owner has filed for the homestead exemption.

Fruits of the Soil

FRUITS BY NATURE

Such things as trees, wild fruits, plants, grass, and other natural growth from the soil of the land in which humans had no part are regarded as "natural fruits" (*fructus naturales*). They are considered to be real property and pass with title to the property. Otherwise, the contract of sale or other instrument of conveyance must expressly state what is considered to be personal property and thus the possession of the seller. Generally, if it is growing, it is real estate, and if it has been severed, it is movable and personalty.

FRUITS BY MAN

Fruits by man (*fructus industriales* or emblements) are things which grow in the soil, but are dependent on human effort for their annual growth; examples are crops which require annual planting or cultivation, such as vegetables, corn, or wheat. Such growing crops are a part of the freehold and go with the land on sale or devise, unless specifically reserved.

Easement

An *easement* is a privilege or right of use or enjoyment which one person has in the lands of another. An example is the right to cross another's land to get to your land, either by car or on foot. This is commonly referred to as a right-of-way. The easement can either "run with the land" (called an easement appurtenant, or simply an appurtenance) or be a personal right that belongs to the individual only and does not run with the land (easement-in-gross).

Some common easements today are:

The right to use a common or party wall

The right to maintain drainage across another's property

The right to receive water which flows through another's land

The right to air and light, without obstruction

All these easements can either run with the land (be expressed in the deed to the property, and thus "follow" ownership) or be bestowed to a person or persons alone (for their use alone). Also, easements may arise or be created by express grant, by reservation to the grantor (seller), by implication of law, by prolonged use under adverse possession, and by prescription of law (when an easement over one property is necessary to the use of another property; and by condemnation proceedings under an eminent domain action).

Note: Easements do not always have to be stated in the affirmative. They may also take the negative form of the "right not to. . . ."

COOPERATIVES AND CONDOMINIUMS

The terms *cooperative* and *condominium* are frequently used interchangeably. This is incorrect. While both concepts denote ownership, the two concepts differ greatly in construction and in the rights of ownership. While co-ownership is a very old form of ownership, its recent popularity in the 1960s was accelerated by Section 234 of the National Housing Act of 1961, which provided FHA mortgage insurance to purchasers of the individual housing units.

Cooperatives

These may be set up in many ways. Among the most popular are: (1) in title form, in which all owners share in a joint tenancy, or as tenants in common; (2) in a trust form, in which the property is held by separate trustees and certificates of interest are issued to the owners; and (3) in a corporate cooperative, in which ownership of shares in the corporation plus an occupancy agreement confers ownership. Of these, the last concept is by far the one most frequently used. Cooperative agreements such as this usually contain certain restraints on alienation, such as giving the corporation a right of first refusal to buy back the "shares." One special advantage of the cooperative is that the liability for injury to third parties in what are called the "common elements" falls upon the corporate entity and not upon the "shareholders."

Condominiums

This form of ownership involves an actual conveyance of title for a given unit with provisions for easements regarding pipes, wires, etc. Also, the "common elements" are held in joint tenancy, which makes each owner jointly and severally liable for injuries to third parties. Unlike cooperatives, condominium titles do not usually restrict or control future sale of the property. Also, unlike the cooperative arrangement where a bylaw violation may cause eviction (mandatory return of shares to the corporation), a condominium owner may only be removed by foreclosure, as in ordinary property. Also, in condominiums, owners do not bear any burden for the default of other owners, whereas in cooperatives, shareholders are responsible if other shareholders default (e.g., do not pay the common mortgage).

Another advantage of condominiums is that lenders are willing to make individual loans on each unit. This is possible because of Horizontal Property Acts, which have been enacted by all states. Under these acts, each unit can be freely and separately sold and mortgaged, and the deeds and mortgages can be recorded in the land records.

The master deed of the condominium development and the condominium's bylaws will be based on the horizontal property and condominium acts of that state. Real estate licensees who wish to provide brokerage and other services in this kind of development will need to be familiar with such legislation.*

The strength of the condominium movement is attested to by various statistics. Late in 1974, the Census Bureau reported that almost one out of every seven housing units started during 1973 was intended for condominium ownership, including single-family houses, townhouses, and units in multifamily buildings. Within metropolitan areas, this figure rises. In a 1974 survey of 292 metropolitan areas in the United States and Puerto Rico conducted by the Economics Department of the National Association of Home Builders, condominiums represented

*Typical of these acts is the Commonwealth of Virginia Condominium Act (Code of Virginia, Title 55, Chapter 4.2, Sections 55 to 79.39, as amended April 5, 1974).

22 percent of the reported housing units completed and for sale. Florida is the leading state in terms of condominium production.

With the popular acceptance of condominium housing units by many younger, as well as older, buyers, professionals in the general real estate brokerage field will come to see an ever-increasing number of them appear as resales in the real estate market. Lenders will also need to become familiar with condominium documentation, or miss a substantial share of the mortgage loan business. For the future, documents will need to be simplified and standardized to facilitate the growing number of condominium property transfers.

In terms of structure, about 80 percent of all condominium units are in 1- to 3-story buildings, while about 15 percent are found in 4- to 8-story structures and about 5 percent are in high-rise structures of 9 stories and over. For older but well-maintained and well-situated rental apartment buildings in metropolitan areas where housing demand is strong, condominium conversion is increasingly being considered as a way to satisfy the popular demand for homeownership in close-in locations.

CONDOMINIUMS ARE SUBDIVISIONS

In the February 28, 1974, issue of the *Federal Register*, the U.S. Department of Housing and Urban Development (HUD) published guidelines which declared that condominiums are covered by the Interstate Land Sales Full Disclosure Act. This act regulates the filing and registration of lots (parcels of land) that are for sale interstate, and a condominium has been judged to be the equivalent of a subdivision, with each unit being a lot. HUD's Office of Interstate Land Sales Registration (OILSR) regulates these filings and protects the consumer. As for intrastate and local dealings, the condominium laws of most states also make the creation of a condominium the subdivision of real property.

CONDOMINIUM HOMEOWNER ASSOCIATIONS ARE TAXABLE

During 1974 also, tax-exempt status for condominium associations was denied in a ruling by the Internal Revenue Service (IRS). Prior to the ruling, a condominium homeowners' association formed under the authority of the condominium's bylaws for the purpose of managing, operating, and maintaining the common elements of a condominium building or community paid no tax on the assessments it received from the individual condominium unit owners.

In its Revenue Ruling (74-17), the IRS noted that the issue revolved around a condominium's qualifications for tax exemption under Section 501(c)(4) of the Internal Revenue Code. This section provides for exemption from federal income tax for civic groups or organizations not organized for profit, but operated exclusively for the promotion of social welfare. Such civic organizations promote "the common good and general welfare of the people of the community." Condominium homeowner associations, on the other hand, are seen as safeguarding the private benefits of their members, the unit owners, and thus they do not qualify for exemption from federal income tax under the Internal Revenue Code.

Under a later ruling (74-99), the IRS expanded its position to remove the income tax exemption for nonprofit homeowners' associations. The new IRS stand creates a presumption that associations are operated for the benefit of their members and therefore do not qualify for tax exemption. The new IRS position is likely to result in few, if any, homeowners' associations being able to qualify for tax-exempt status.

For the future, condominium homeowners' organizations and other homeowners' associations such as those of planned unit development (PUD) communities with common, undivided, shared-ownership areas and facilities (such as green open space, parks, bicycle-riding and walking trails, playground equipment, or swimming pools, for example) can be expected to legally contest the IRS rulings. Assessments levied for common grounds and facilities upkeep are visualized as a reserve fund for maintenance, repairs, and replacement rather than as income, which is taxable.

Summary

The condominium and the cooperative are forms of owned housing. The apartment units in these multifamily housing structures are owned, not rented. While both these forms of co-ownership are very old, their popularity in the 1960s and the 1970s has been nothing short of startling. Such housing developments are proliferating across America, spurred by inflation and the rising costs for land, labor, materials, and both construction and mortgage money, combined with the demographic factor of a youthful adult population joined with an older adult group which needs less housing space.

The condominium movement has also fostered the creation of condominium commercial buildings and office space, warehouse units, and professional doctors' and dentists' offices which are owned instead of rented. The same applies to industrial lots and buildings and offices in industrial parks and developments. Therefore, it is not as much a question for the real estate broker or salesperson whether the condominium will "last" or "stick around" as it is an observation that these units and buildings are already here, with more being constructed or converted every day. Thus the licensee will need increasingly to be prepared to thoroughly serve this significant segment of the market.

PRACTICE EXAMINATION: REAL PROPERTY INTERESTS

1. An example of a freehold estate is

    I. an estate for life
    II. an estate in fee simple

  (A) I only   (C) Neither I nor II
  (B) II only   —(D) Both I and II

2. One of the following is not an example of the exercise of police power by government.

  (A) Zoning ordinance   (C) Health regulation
  (B) Housing code   —(D) Tax bill

3. Another name for items that are not real property is

  (A) chattels   (C) personal property
  (B) personalty   —(D) all the above

4. As the term applies to real estate, partition means

 —(A) the division of real estate between tenants
  (B) a nonbearing wall in a house
  (C) a written request to do or refrain from doing some act
  (D) a bearing wall in a house

5. A life estate

  (A) cannot be sold
  (B) reverts to the heirs upon the holder's death
 —(C) is held by the owner for the period of his or her life only
  (D) can be transferred to the holder's heirs in the grantor's will

6. One of the following is out of place

  (A) The right to go over another's land
  (B) The right to light and air
  (C) The right to use another's land
 —(D) The right to compensation if your property is taken by condemnation

7. One of the following is out of place

  (A) Real estate   (C) Realty
  (B) Land or lands —(D) REALTOR

8. The operation of due process of law governs the "taking" of private property by governmental authorities under the right of

  (A) condemnation —(C) eminent domain
  (B) police power   (D) taxation

9. Any right to, or interest in, land which may subsist in third persons, to the diminution of the value of the principal estate—such as a lien or judgment—is a (an)

 —(A) encumbrance   (C) right-of-way
  (B) fixture   (D) none of these

10. The residue of an estate left in the grantor, to commence in possession after the termination of some particular estate granted out by the holder, is best described as a

  (A) life estate   (C) residuary estate
 —(B) reversion   (D) none of these

11. An easement is created when

    I. a dwelling is placed over your property line onto another's property
    II. you give someone the right or privilege of using your land

  (A) I only   (C) Either I or II
 —(B) II only   (D) Neither I nor II

12. Limitations on private property ownership do not include

  (A) police power   (C) taxation
  (B) eminent domain —(D) homestead exemption

13. A right or privilege that belongs to and passes with property would best be described as

  (A) an easement   (C) a right-of-way
 —(B) an appurtenance (D) none of these

14. The interest or value which an owner has in real estate, over and above the debts against it, is best described as

  (A) value   —(C) equity
  (B) fee simple   (D) estate

15. The act of taking private property for public benefit is called

  (A) eminent domain —(C) condemnation
  (B) police power   (D) none of these

16. An outstanding claim or encumbrance which, if valid, would impair an owner's title to real estate is known as a (an)

  (A) lien   —(C) cloud on the title
  (B) easement   (D) color of title

17. Only husband and wife may hold properties as "one" under the unique tenancy

 —(A) by the entireties (C) in common
  (B) as joint tenants   (D) by law

18. A holder of a life estate

  (A) is not to repair the property
 —(B) is not to waste the property
  (C) owns the property and can do with it what he or she wants
  (D) is under no obligation at all

19. An easement that runs with the property

    (A) cannot be passed to another
    (B) is an appurtenance
    (C) is known as a personal right
    (D) is known as an easement-in-gross

20. Tenancy in common could be created by

    (A) a lease   (C) an oral agreement
    (B) a will or deed   (D) none of these

Chapter 7

Transfer of Title to Real Property

Transfer of title to real property usually occurs by voluntary execution of a deed or by will. Other methods include involuntary alienation such as transfer by a tax sale for nonpayment of taxes, and by adverse possession. The licensee is most concerned with transfer by deed and by adverse possession, and only these will be discussed here.

DEEDS

The definition of a deed is that it is an instrument in writing duly executed and delivered for the purpose of conveying title to real estate. It is another form of contract, and the requirements applicable to contracts apply. State statutes usually stipulate that the instrument of a deed may only be prepared or drawn by a lawyer or by the property owners involved. No broker or salesperson should prepare a client's deed. Nor should a real estate agent advise an inexperienced property owner or owners to prepare their own deed, because of the complications that may later arise. However, real estate agents should become familiar with the form and laws dealing with title transfer by deed, and also by adverse possession, to assist them in their real estate transactions.

Essential Elements

In order for a deed to be valid, certain essential elements must be present.

1. Names of the parties, as grantor and grantee
2. Words of conveyance or transfer and an existing estate being granted
3. Description of the property
4. Consideration
5. Execution, delivery, and acceptance

NAMES OF THE PARTIES, AS GRANTOR AND GRANTEE

The names of the grantors and their marital status should appear on the deed in exactly the form used when they themselves took title (their names would have appeared as the grantees receiving the property in the previous deed). The grantors must be persons legally competent to convey their interests in the property; the grantees need not necessarily be legally competent to accept the deed. However, when it is their turn to convey or transfer their interests, or when they act as grantors, they must have legal capacity to give up their interests in the property. To avoid further confusion, grantees' full names and marital status should be used. Some states require grantors' and grantees' addresses to be included also.

WORDS OF CONVEYANCE OR TRANSFER AND AN EXISTING ESTATE BEING GRANTED

The words of conveyance or transfer of the property actually state that it is the intent or purpose of the grantors to convey the property. Generally a single phrase such as "grantors do hereby grant" would be sufficient. However, customary deed language in use in warranty deeds usually includes a series of words such as "grant, bargain and sell, and convey," or in quitclaim deeds, "release, remise, convey, and quitclaim." All these words of conveyance are sometimes referred to as the "granting clause."

The description of the existing estate being granted could follow the granting clause or come later in the deed under the "habendum clause," which usually begins with, "To have and to hold...." No matter how many times the statement of the estate that is being granted appears, the words "subject to" may sometimes follow. Encumbrances would then be listed and would serve to lessen the quality or quantity of the estate being conveyed.

DESCRIPTION OF THE PROPERTY

The property must be legally described beyond question. No doubt should be left as to the property being conveyed. A legal description is necessary because upon delivery and recordation a deed becomes a permanent record and a new addition to the chain of title. There are four types of legal description used in the United States to describe property: by metes and bounds; by lot and block number of a recorded plat or map, which in turn has been originally described in metes and bounds; by

U.S. public land rectangular system; or by monuments alone. '(See Chapter 8, "Land Descriptions.") The seller or grantor should always use the same description as that in the deed by which he or she took title. To guard against errors in the description, it is advisable to follow the description with a statement that the property being conveyed is the same as that received in the deed preceding it in the chain of title, with recital of date, place, and recording data (book and page of county records, recorder's document number, etc.).

CONSIDERATION

As in a contract, a consideration must also be stated in a deed. However, the consideration expressed can be as little as 1 dollar or 10 dollars, perhaps followed by "and for other good and valuable consideration received." The expression in a deed of some consideration having passed between grantor and grantee is far more important than its amount. It shifts the burden of proving a possible lack of consideration to anyone who would attack and try to invalidate the deed.

EXECUTION, DELIVERY, AND ACCEPTANCE

Execution and signatures by all grantors on the deed both mean the same thing. After signatures, delivery of the deed by the grantors or their designated agent must be intentional and voluntary. However, delivery need not be physical or direct. Any act showing the intent of grantor to make the deed in effect, and to lose control over the property to grantee, would signal a delivery. Delivery of the deed must occur during the grantor's lifetime. Acceptance of the deed is presumed where the grantee benefits, or acceptance may also be by act or words.

Grantee will next want to record the deed. Therefore, acknowledgment of all the grantors' signatures is necessary to prove the validity of those signatures. Acknowledgment is taken by a notary public who either witnesses the signatures of the grantors or accepts attestations of subscribing witnesses to the signatures of the grantors. Failure to record a deed does not invalidate it. The deed is still effective and valid between grantor and grantee and to all others who have knowledge of its existence. However, future purchasers of the property who take the precaution of recording their deeds will establish a prior claim to title to the property through constructive notice to the public. Those grantees who fail to record their deeds stand to lose the property, even though they have recourse to legal action against the fraudulent practices of the grantor.

When a deed is executed, delivered, and accepted, it fulfills and completes the terms of the contract. As stated in Chapter 5, the contract usually merges into the deed and the conditions of the contract of sale or purchase are cancelled. Should it be desired that a provision in the contract live on, a clause in that contract should read that the conditions of the contract are not to be merged into the deed, but are to survive settlement. Many contracts used by REALTORS have this as a standard clause. (See

also the section in Chapter 5, The Contract Is Merged in the Deed.)

Corporate deeds must be executed with the corporate seal in most states. Deeds of persons or partnerships do not usually require a seal.

Nonessential Elements

A deed does not require a date. However, it is advisable to have one. Otherwise, the date of delivery, the date of acknowledgment, or the date of recordation may apply.

Much excess jargon could be eliminated from the wording of deeds without affecting their validity. The essential elements are noted above, with no one particular form of presentation to be preferred over another. Brevity, clarity, and accuracy would perhaps describe the best deed form.

Deeds in General Use

There are three types of deeds in general use to transfer title to real estate.

1. General warranty deed
2. Special warranty deed
3. Quitclaim deed

GENERAL WARRANTY DEED

The general warranty deed is used most extensively. Under a general warranty from the grantor, the grantee receives the highest form of title guaranty and the safest deed that can be received. Besides receiving title to the real property, grantee receives grantor's personal covenant that grantor will defend grantee and grantee's heirs, personal representatives, and assigns against any claim to the title, no matter how far back in the chain of title. Grantor warrants that the title granted is good and sufficient against any possible future claimants.

SPECIAL WARRANTY DEED

In the special warranty deed the grantor warrants good and sufficient title covering only his or her period of tenure in the property, not historically back through the chain of title. Grantor does not warrant or defend grantee's title against all prior defects, but only those attributable to him or her. Thus the special warranty deed conveyed from grantor to grantee covers only that period of time during which grantor had an interest in the property.

QUITCLAIM DEED

In a quitclaim deed the grantor makes no warranty to grantee. Grantor "releases, remises, conveys, and quit-claims" only that interest that he or she held in the property. Without the warranty as to the deed that is being received, grantee cannot be sure of the condition of the title to the real property. Grantee stands the risk against all other potential claimants, rather than grantor.

If "grantor releases to grantee all his claims upon the land," the usual state law provides that such a release deed shall be regarded as a quitclaim. Grantor as well as grantor's personal representatives, all heirs and assigns, forever relinquish all rights upon the land.

Special Deeds and Instruments

DEEDS OF TRUST

A deed of trust is a different type of deed. It too is an instrument in writing duly executed and delivered for the purpose of conveying title to real estate. However, the legal title to the property is delivered to a third person, called a *trustee*, whose function is to hold title to the property in trust until the property is paid for entirely. This debt owed on the property is described in the deed of trust.

The grantee receives a warranty deed and in return executes or grants a deed of trust to secure the indebtedness on the property. The trustor is the borrower on the property and owes the debt. The trustor receives possession, use, and control of the property. The beneficiary is the lender who receives the monthly payments on the property. The trustee retains the power to sell the property on behalf of the beneficiary if the trustor (debtor) fails to fulfill all obligations as recited in the instrument of the deed of trust. The trustor holds equitable title in the property during the period that he or she is paying off the loan. The trustor (debtor) can, in his or her possession, use, and control of the property, do whatever he or she pleases with it as long as this does not place in jeopardy the interest of the beneficiary (lender). Trustor must pay all taxes, maintain the property in an inhabitable condition, and ensure that the asset not waste away.

MORTGAGES

A mortgage is an instrument in writing between two parties, mortgagor (borrower) and mortgagee (lender), to conditionally convey title to land. The condition is usually the payment of the loan advanced to purchase the property, but it may also be the fulfillment of some contract or the performance of some act. Upon full payment, fulfillment of contract, or performance of the act, the mortgage becomes void and the conveyance of title whole. To accomplish this, a release, or a satisfaction of mortgage (called a satisfaction piece), is executed, by the mortgagee, and is then also recorded in the appropriate clerk's office. Recordation of mortgages, deeds of trust, and deeds in the city or county where the property is located serve the purpose of giving effective, constructive notice to future purchasers.

It can be seen that no third party is involved in a mortgage. However, should a default of the mortgage occur, the procedure of foreclosure would become necessary in order for the mortgagee to claim possession, use, and control of the property. A foreclosure of a mortgage can only be accomplished through court action, and this may become a costly, lengthy, contested process. For this reason and others, the mortgage instrument is not commonly used in many states. Lenders do not favor it, and most state laws permit the use of the deed of trust as an instrument to secure indebtedness on real estate.

Difference between a Mortgage and a Deed of Trust

Both a mortgage and a deed of trust are pledges of real estate as collateral securities, usually for the repayment of a loan on real estate. The difference, however, is that the deed of trust *conveys legal title* to a *third-party trustee*, who then holds certain readily usable powers to sell the property upon default of the borrower (trustor) and pay off the loan. Also, a deed of trust *note* evidencing the loan usually accompanies the deed of trust.

The classification of a mortgage is not as simple because different states treat the concept of a mortgage in one of two different ways. The mortgage may be either a *conditional transfer* of real estate (as collateral security) *or* merely a *lien* or *encumbrance* on property. In the event of default, after the property has been foreclosed and sold in payment of the debt, there is still a 1-year period of redemption in which the borrower (mortgagor) may redeem his or her interest in the property by paying off the debts and other related costs against the property.

In the case of the deed of trust, upon default of the debtor (trustor), foreclosure can occur within 120 days as opposed to 1 year or longer in the case of a mortgage).

Table 7-1. Difference between a Deed of Trust and a Mortgage

	Deed of Trust	Mortgage
A pledge of real estate as collateral security	Yes	Yes
Conveys legal title	Yes	Yes or no*
—to third-party trustee	Yes	No
—to mortgagee	No	Yes
Period of foreclosure	120 days	1 year
Period of redemption	None	1 year

*May be merely a lien or encumbrance.

COVENANTS OF TITLE

A covenant of title is a continuing promise by grantor that exists in the deed. A covenant may either cover the past or extend into the future. It may promise or prohibit the performance of certain acts, or may promise that a given state of things either does or does not exist. These convenants or promises by grantor to grantee also may be either implied or expressly stated in the deed. The following covenants by grantor in a warranty deed are in addition to grantor's covenant of warranty that states that grantor will protect grantee's title against any claimant. These covenants, called the English covenants, usually apply whether they are stated or not.

Covenant of the Right to Convey

Grantor covenants or promises that he or she holds good right, full power, and absolute authority to convey title to the real property, as specified in and by the deed.

Covenant of Seisin

Grantor covenants that he or she owns such title and has possession of such property as is being conveyed in the deed.

Covenant against Encumbrances

Grantor covenants that the property being conveyed is presently free of encumbrances and in the future will remain so. Grantor guarantees grantee against grantor's future encumbrances on the property.

Covenant of Quiet Possession

Grantor covenants nondisturbance to the grantee in the possession and enjoyment of the property.

Covenant of Further Assurance

Grantor covenants future voluntary execution of such instruments as are necessary to give grantee the title which grantee believed he or she was receiving and which it was intended grantee should receive. This covenant remedies imperfect execution or otherwise perfects the title. Grantor's later execution of a deed of correction or a quitclaim deed to grantee would be such example of satisfaction of the covenant.

SPECIFIC COVENANTS

In addition to the covenants listed above, other covenants of a specific nature may be placed in a deed. For example, when an oil company purchases a portion of a larger tract of land, it will often insist that the grantor place a covenant on the balance of the land to prevent the sale of petroleum products. Other covenants would be those placed by the developer of a subdivision covering building of fences, keeping of animals, etc. Often these covenants are called "real" covenants and are said to "run with the land" when the covenant directly affects the land and has been included by the seller and buyer with the intention that the covenant will be binding on any future buyers. Covenants which are in violation of the law, however, such as restrictions which violate fair housing laws, are not enforceable.

TRANSFER OF TITLE BY ADVERSE POSSESSION

Adverse possession is a possession of private property which is inconsistent with and detrimental to the rights of the true owner. The title to private property may pass against the owner's will and desire if the adverse claimant takes physical possession of the property for the term specified by the law of the state in which the property is located. The public purpose of adverse possession is to prevent the abandonment of private property.

The following statutory requirements usually must be met for title to pass by adverse possession.

ACTUAL POSSESSION

The adverse claimant must physically occupy and exercise dominion over the property (example, build a house, farm the land, erect fences, etc.).

EXCLUSIVE POSSESSION

The adverse claimant must occupy the property exclusively for personal use alone. The claimant excludes others from a claim to a distinct and definite piece of ground which can be sharply defined.

HOSTILE, OPEN AND NOTORIOUS POSSESSION

The adverse claimant must occupy the property in such a fashion that the true owner, the neighbors, and the general public know about it.

BONA FIDE CLAIM OF TITLE

The adverse claimant must exercise an actual claim of ownership or title against that of all other persons. The claim must accompany the possession; one will not suffice without the other.

CONTINUOUS POSSESSION

The adverse possession must continue uninterruptedly for the statutory period of time, usually 15 to 20 years. Normal residency is required, not a mandatory day-by-day occupancy.

TACKING

A second or follow-up adverse claimant may "tack on" another period of continuous occupancy to that of the first adverse claimant who has sold or otherwise conveyed his or her interest in the property to the second claimant. Together, the successive occupancies may total the necessary period of time.

Title by Adverse Possession

When an adverse claimant has complied with the necessary statutory requirements, he or she obtains valid title to the land so occupied. No deed to the property has been received. Nevertheless, the adverse claimant can execute a deed to another as the grantor, and can compel the grantee to accept the deed. The adverse claimant has become a bona fide owner of the property and can convey his or her interest in the property to another. Such title dates from the date of actual possession of the land.

EQUITABLE TITLE AND LEGAL TITLE

An equitable title (or title in equity) is obtained by the purchaser of a piece of property when the contract of purchase is signed and accepted by the seller. From that time until the time of settlement, the buyer holds an equitable title. The fulfillment of the terms of the contract at settlement date will then result in the purchaser's obtaining legal title to the property, signified by the passage of the deed from seller to buyer.

As has been noted in the section in Chapter 5, Doctrine of Equitable Conversion, during the time the contract of purchase is being fulfilled and the buyer has an equitable interest in the property, the buyer also stands the risk of damage or loss to the property (prior to closing or settlement date). However, most standard contracts of purchase and sale contain a clause or provision that the seller is to stand the risk of property loss until terms of the contract are concluded and legal title is passed by the deed. This is logical for two reasons: (1) the seller is under an obligation to deliver the property to the buyer as they have contracted and subject only to normal wear and tear; and (2) the seller's property insurance would usually remain in effect until passage of legal title by the deed, thereby continuously protecting seller's interest during such time as the terms of the contract of sale were being fulfilled (or even covering the possibility that the contractual terms may never be concluded and the sale not materialize). For example, the purchaser may make the contract to purchase contingent on obtaining favorable financing terms (low interest rates, or a high loan figure with a small down payment) or may stipulate that the property appraisal and/or inspection be reported on favorably by some independent expert.

Again, should there not be a clause in the contract of purchase or sale stating that the risk of loss is to remain with the seller until the time of transfer of deed (at closing or settlement date), the buyer should protect his or her equitable interest in the property by taking out a property insurance policy.

PRACTICE EXAMINATION: TRANSFER OF TITLE TO REAL PROPERTY

1. The essential elements of a deed include

   (A) grantor, grantee, description of the property, and words of conveyance
   (B) estate or interest being granted, consideration, execution, delivery, acceptance, and recordation
   (C) names of the parties, offer and acceptance, signatures of grantor and grantee, and attestation
   (D) trustor, trustee, beneficiary, consideration, description of the property, execution, and acknowledgment

2. From the point of view of the grantee, the safest kind of deed that can be received is a

   (A) general warranty deed
   (B) special warranty deed
   (C) quitclaim or release deed
   (D) trustee's deed

3. In order to transfer title to real estate, a deed

   (A) must be accepted
   (B) must be conveyed
   (C) must be recorded
   (D) must be signed by the grantee

4. Unless specifically prohibited by the terms of the contract,

       I. the vendee may transfer his or her interest to another, called the assignor
       II. the assignee is liable to the seller for performance of the terms of the contract

   (A) I only   (C) Both I and II
   (B) II only   (D) Neither I nor II

5. A deed may legally convey property to

   (A) a minor and an insane person
   (B) a drunkard and a debtor
   (C) both of the above
   (D) neither of the above

6. A foreclosure of a mortgage can be accomplished

   (A) by the trustee
   (B) more quickly than under a deed of trust
   (C) through court action
   (D) without legal recourse

7. Any action showing the grantor's intention to make the deed operative and to relinquish control of the property effects a (an)

   (A) acceptance   (C) delivery
   (B) acknowledgment   (D) closing

8. To hypothecate means to

   (A) fabricate a story
   (B) pledge something as security without giving up possession of it
   (C) dispense medicine or drugs
   (D) render a judicial opinion

9. Under a deed of trust the grantor is

   (A) the buyer   (C) the lender
   (B) the seller   (D) the trustee

10. The history of the title to real estate would best be described as a (an)

   (A) affidavit   (C) title
   (B) abstract   (D) fee simple

11. A deed which contains a guarantee that the grantor will protect the grantee against defects in the title would be

   (A) a quitclaim deed   (C) a covenant of title
   (B) a warranty deed   (D) none of these

12. When a person dies without a will and without heirs, the deceased person's property reverts to the state under

   (A) an executor   (C) escheat
   (B) escrow   (D) eminent domain

13. The clause in a deed which conveys title to the property is the

   (A) habendum clause   (C) granting clause
   (B) covenant of seisin   (D) none of these

14. A privilege, acquired for a consideration, of demanding within a specified time the carrying out of a transaction upon stipulated terms is a (an)

   (A) right-of-way   (C) devise
   (B) covenant   (D) option

15. To die without a will is to die

   (A) will-less   (C) intestate
   (B) testate   (D) escheat

16. An agreement between two or more persons, entered into by deed, whereby one of the parties promises the performance of certain acts, or that a given state does or shall, or does not or shall not, exist, is called a (an)

   (A) grant   (C) covenant
   (B) release   (D) easement

17. A grantor can limit liability to the grantee to anyone claiming by, from, through, or under the grantor with a

    —(A) special warranty deed
    (B) general warranty deed
    (C) quitclaim deed
    (D) release deed

18. The covenant in a deed under which the covenantor assures his or her possession of the exact interest being conveyed is the covenant

    (A) of further assurance
    (B) of quiet possession
    (C) of conveyance
    —(D) of seisin

19. Grantor's responsibilities under a deed of trust include

    (A) payment of all taxes, and property upkeep
    (B) committing no waste
    —(C) both A and B
    (D) none of these actually, because these are the responsibilities of the grantee

20. Which of the following statements is (are) true?

    I. A quitclaim deed transfers whatever interest a grantee has in property.
    II. A quitclaim deed carries a warranty of good title.

    (A) I only   (C) Both I and II
    (B) II only   —(D) Neither I nor II

Chapter 8

Land Descriptions

An integral part of any contract or other instrument transferring a parcel of land from one person to another is a description of that parcel, usually known as the "legal description" or the "deed description." Quite often descriptions are, at best, vague. Some older ones in their entirety might read, "Just ask. Everybody down there knows where it is." Fortunately, most modern descriptions are accurate, in that they clearly define a unique parcel of land on the surface of the earth. No two parcels of land can ever be alike. Each requires its own legal description.

There are four methods of describing land in general use throughout the United States:

1. By metes and bounds

2. By lot and block, referring to a recorded plat

3. By monuments alone

4. By U.S. Government Rectangular Survey

Generally, measurements and dimensions calculated by these four methods of land description are determined by licensed surveyors, civil engineers, and their staffs of draftspersons.

METES AND BOUNDS

This is the oldest method of land description in this country. Its use is generally confined to the 13 original states (although it is now used by a few others). With this method, a parcel of land is described by giving the exact locations of all boundaries that enclose the property, with each boundary stated in terms of its length and direction.

The term "metes and bounds" means "measures and boundaries." It is always used in its entirety.

Let us consider some elements that make up a good metes and bounds description. They are, in order,

1. An accurately and uniquely described beginning point.

2. An accurate description of each boundary line in succession, with the final boundary line returning to the beginning point. This will completely enclose the tract. There is no such thing as a tract of ground not completely enclosed by its boundaries; therefore, a description which does not return to the point of beginning is worthless.

3. The area of the tract described. This is usually given in acres for larger tracts and in square feet for ordinary building lots.

Boundary Lines and Corners

A boundary line has both length and direction. The intersection of two boundary lines is called a *corner*. The physical location of boundary lines and corners may or may not be marked on the ground by some evidence. Such physical evidence (if present) is called a *monument*.

MONUMENTS AS MARKERS

Monuments marking boundary lines may be natural or artificial and may include, but are not limited to, ridge lines, streams, fences, lines of trees, hedgerows, and roads.

Monuments marking boundary corners may include trees, wooden stakes, iron pipes, cut stones, cast concrete cylinders or posts, and road intersections.

The description of a given boundary line should clearly give the length of the line, the direction of the line, and the monuments (if any) one might expect to find on the ground marking the line or its corners.

LENGTH

The length of a line is usually given in feet and decimals of feet, to either the nearest 0.1 foot or 0.01 foot (0.1 foot equals approximately $1\frac{1}{5}$ inches; 0.01 foot equals approximately $\frac{1}{8}$ inch). Some older descriptions might include rods, chains, poles, or perches. Occasionally in records of land transfers in areas of the country that were once under foreign ownership, lengths may be stated in terms of old foreign units, such as the *arpent* (French) or the *vara* (Spanish).

DIRECTION

The direction of a line is given by its *bearing*. A good way to remember this is to think of a bearing as the

Table of Land Measurements

Linear Measure		Square Measure	
1 in	= .0833 ft	144 sq in	= 1 sq ft
7.92 in	= 1 link	9 sq ft	= 1 sq yd
12 in	= 1 ft	$30\frac{1}{2}$ sq yd	= 1 sq rod
1 vara	= 33 in	16 sq rods	= 1 sq chain
$2\frac{3}{4}$ ft	= 1 vara	1 sq rod	= $272\frac{1}{4}$ sq ft
3 ft	= 1 yd	1 sq chain	= 4,356 sq ft
25 links	= $16\frac{1}{2}$ ft	10 sq chains	= 1 acre
25 links	= 1 rod	160 sq rods	= 1 acre
100 links	= 1 chain	4,840 sq yd	= 1 acre
$16\frac{1}{2}$ feet	= 1 rod	43,560 sq ft	= 1 acre
$5\frac{1}{2}$ yards	= 1 rod	640 acres	= 1 sq mi
4 rods	= 100 links	1 sq mi	= 1 section
66 ft	= 1 chain	36 sq mi	= 1 Twp
80 chains	= 1 mi	6 mi square	= 1 Twp
320 rods	= 1 mi	1 sq mi	= 2.59 sq km
8,000 links	= 1 mi		
5,280 ft	= 1 mi		
1,760 yd	= 1 mi		

AN ACRE IS:

43,560 sq ft	660 ft X 66 ft
165 ft X 264 ft	160 sq rods
198 ft X 220 ft	208′8″ square

or any other tract, the product of the length and width of which totals 43,560 sq ft.

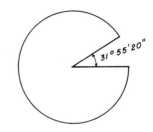

Figure 8-1.

measured in units of degrees, minutes, and seconds. The angle in Fig. 8-1 has an opening of 31 degrees, 55 minutes, and 20 seconds. This is written $31°55'20''$.

Quadrants

A full circle, containing all directions, is made up of four *quadrants* of exactly 90° each (4 X 90° = 360°). These quadrants are the Northeast (NE), Southeast (SE), Southwest (SW), and Northwest (NW). (See Fig. 8-2.)

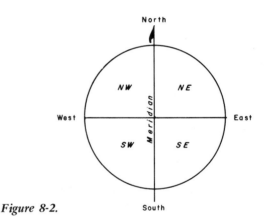

Figure 8-2.

direction you are looking at or traveling toward. To better understand what is meant by the bearing of a boundary line, it would be appropriate to review the definitions of meridians, circles, quadrants, angles, and bearings.

Meridians

A *meridian* is an imaginary line running north and south, extending from the North Pole to the South Pole. Meridians are represented, for example, by lines of longitude on a map. A meridian can be passed through any point on the earth's surface.

Circles

A *circle* contains 360 degrees. Each degree contains 60 minutes, and each minute contains 60 seconds. *Angles are*

Angles

An angle of exactly 90° is called a *right angle*. An angle of less than 90° is called an *acute angle*.

Bearings

The *bearing* of a boundary line is the acute angle the line makes with a meridian. Bearings are written with an angular value and a quadrant. The conventional method of writing a bearing is as follows:

1. The first letter (either N or S) of the quadrant

2. The value of the acute angle

3. The second letter (either E or W) of the quadrant

Description Exercises and Explanations

Now, try to read the bearings in Fig. 8-3.

Figure 8-3.

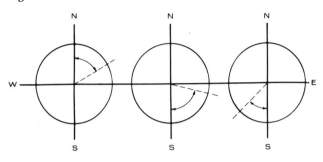

The answers are:

N 60° E   S 79° E   S 45° W

To make these boundary line descriptions complete, the length of the lines and monuments to be found, if any, would be added.

Now try to read the bearings of each side of the four-sided tract shown in Fig. 8-4. Note the location of the North arrow.

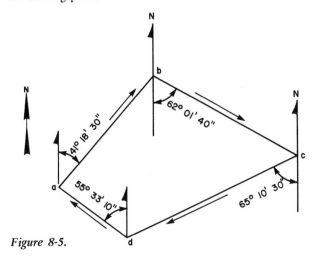

Figure 8-4.

In Fig. 8-5 we have drawn meridians through each corner of the tract shown in Fig. 8-4. These will help to identify the quadrant of the measured angle.

Next we can choose a starting point and a direction in which we will "walk" around the perimeter. Assume that we start at corner *a* and proceed in a clockwise direction toward corner *b*, then to *c*, to *d*, and finally back to *a*, the starting point.

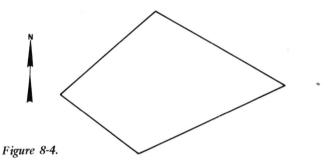

Figure 8-5.

We can now measure the acute angles formed by the meridians and the boundary lines intersecting them, and write the bearings as follows:

Line *a* to *b* = N 41°18'30" E

Line *b* to *c* = S 62°01'40" E

Line *c* to *d* = S 65°10'30" W

Line *d* to *a* = N 55°33'10" W

Note that we traveled around this tract in a clockwise direction. We may proceed in either a clockwise or a counterclockwise direction, but we may never mix the two. If you reverse the direction in which you "walk" a boundary line, the quadrants will be opposite. When reading a plat of land description, remember that you may or may not be "walking" the same direction as the surveyor who drew the plat. Note also that the final course returned to the point of beginning.

A survey plat will not show the meridians and angles at the corners as Fig. 8-5 did. Such a plat will have the bearings written along the boundary lines, as in Fig. 8-6.

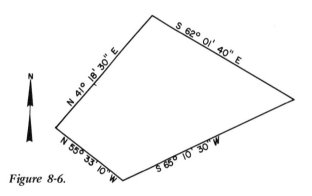

Figure 8-6.

Fig. 8-7 shows the same tract as Fig. 8-6, but the bearings are as they would appear on a survey plat proceeding in a counterclockwise direction.

Note that the angle of the bearing remains the same in each case, but the quadrants are just opposite those of Fig. 8-6.

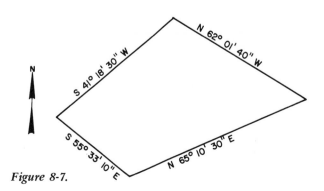

Figure 8-7.

Figure 8-8.

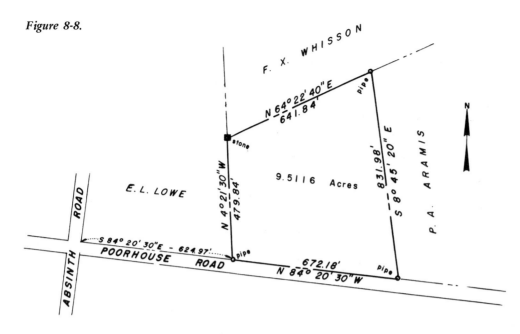

Study Fig. 8-8 for a few moments.

An accurate metes and bounds description of this parcel might read thus:

Beginning at an iron pipe on the north side of Poorhouse Road, and at a fence corner, which pipe is S 84°20'30" E 624.97 feet from the intersection of said north boundary of Poorhouse Road and the easterly boundary of Absinth Road and running with a wire fence on Lowe's line N 4°21'30" W 479.84 feet to a stone; thence with the line of Whisson N 64°22'40" E 641.84 feet to a pipe at the base of a stone wall; thence with the line of Aramis and with the stone wall S 8°45'20" E 831.98 feet to a pipe on the north boundary of Poorhouse Road; thence with said north boundary N 84°20'30" W 672.18 feet to the point of beginning, and containing 9.5116 acres.

Note that in this description:

1. We started at a definite point, i.e., "an iron pipe on the north side of Poorhouse Road, and at a fence corner." The location of the pipe and fence was further clarified by saying that it was 624.97 feet from the intersection of two roads.

2. From this point we traveled along the fence line (a monument marking a boundary line) 479.84 feet to a stone (a monument marking a boundary corner). The fence was also the boundary line of the property belonging to Lowe.

3. From the stone we traveled the common boundary shared by this property and that owned by Whisson 641.84 feet to a pipe at the base of a stone wall.

4. We started in a clockwise direction, and so we must continue clockwise, along the common boundary with Aramis, which is a stone wall, 831.98 feet to the north side of Poorhouse Road.

5. Then we returned along Poorhouse Road 672.18 feet to the point of beginning.

6. The area contained within the boundaries is calculated as 9.5116 acres.

LOT AND BLOCK

Inasmuch as all parcels of land were at one time cut from larger parcels, all descriptions of real estate reflect, in some manner, a previous subdivision of land.

Modern practice when acreage is subdivided into building lots (whether the acreage was originally described by metes and bounds, or by U.S. public land rectangular system) is to record a plat of the subdivision in the land records of the political jurisdiction in which the subdivision is situated. The plats are recorded and filed on a given page of a specific deed book.

These subdivision plats will show, among other things, the building lots in relation to each other, the lot numbers, the length and bearing of each lot boundary, the area of each lot, blocks, sections, streets and other public rights-of-way, areas reserved or dedicated for public use (for example, a school site), easements, any monuments marking lot or subdivision corners, the name of the subdivision, North arrow, date, and scale.

It should be noted that plats of subdivisions recorded this way are not necessarily limited to smaller building lots. For example, a 1,000-acre farm could be subdivided into a number of 80-acre tracts and a plat of the entire subdivision duly recorded.

Once such a subdivision plat is recorded, a lot or parcel may be described by lot and block with reference to the recorded plat. Such a description may read in its entirety:

Lot 14, Block 4, Section 2 of the Early Times Subdivision as recorded in Deed Book 2234 at page 381 of the Land Records of Bourbon County, Virginia.

In order to better understand this description, let us clarify some of the terms that we have used. An exhibit of the Mountararat Subdivision, Section One, is presented in Figure 8-9. Readers should refer to the plat of this subdivision when necessary.

LOT

A lot is an individual parcel of land intended to be conveyed in its entirety to an individual purchaser.

BLOCK

A block is usually a group of contiguous lots bounded by streets or roads. A good way to think of a "block" in a given subdivision is to recall a city block, or all its lots together, side-to-side and back-to-back, without any streets separating them. Another way to think of a block is "all the lots I can walk over, going from one to the other, without crossing a street." (In subdivisions where lots are numbered continuously, the block designation is not used.) A block is usually indicated on a plat by a circle with the block number inside, or the number may be written across the plat in stippled letters and numbers.

SECTION

Frequently it is inconvenient for a subdivider to record all the lots of a given subdivision at one time. In these cases, the subdivider will record different sections at different times. Each section contains a number of lots. Each suceeding section is identified in some way. The subdivider may use cardinal numbers (Section 2), written numbers (Section Two), Roman numerals (Section II), or letters (Section B) to identify sections.

STREETS

A street is an access way to the various lots in a subdivision. The developer so designs and lays out the streets in a subdivision that the use of buildable land is enhanced and its use maximized. The design may include cul-de-sacs, frontage roads, feeder and main roads, and preservation of green space.

A street (or road) on a survey or subdivision plat usually includes all the land contained between the front boundaries of the lots abutting the street. The name of the street is usually written within its boundaries.

EASEMENTS

An easement is the right of the public (or an individual) to a specific portion of land owned by another for a specific use. Easements may be granted for (but are not limited to) the following: roads and streets (often for widening purposes), power lines, sanitary and/or storm sewers, driveways and walkways, and parkland. Easements are usually represented on a plat by dashed lines. Frequently, a lot boundary (shown solid) is also the boundary of an easement.

The specific usage of each easement should be indicated on the plat. This designation may be written within the easement itself, adjacent to it, or in some other appropriate place on the plat.

NORTH ARROW

The reader should note the direction of the North arrow each time he or she studies a survey or subdivision plat. Quite frequently the North arrow does not point toward the top of the page. Just remember that the North arrow, whatever its position, is the meridian to which all bearings on the plat are referred.

SCALE

The reader should also note the scale of a plat. A typical scale might be written $1'' = 50'$. This reads "1 inch equals 50 feet" and means that each inch on the plat is equal to 50 feet on the ground. Knowing the scale of a given plat can be of great help in estimating distances. The scale shown on the plat in Figure 8-9 reads $1'' = 200'$, or 1

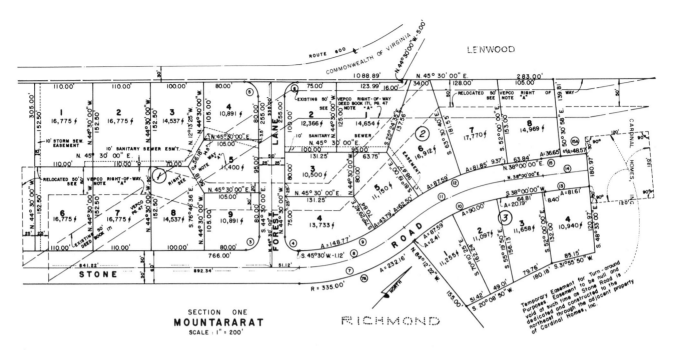

Figure 8-9.

inch equals 200 feet. However, this plat has been reduced in size in order to present all of Section One. Therefore the scale is not correct.

To better understand metes and bounds and descriptions by lot and block, review a typical subdivision plat showing some of the features covered so far (see Fig. 8-9).

1. Notice the location of the North arrow. Especially notice that it does not point directly to the top of the page.

2. At the bottom of the plat you will see the label "Section One, Mountararat." This indicates that this drawing shows only a part (or one page) of a larger subdivision.

3. The scale is usually included just under the subdivision name.

4. You can readily see that Section One contains 3 blocks (heavy numbers in a circle). Note that the blocks are separated by roads.

5. Also note the square at the end of Stone Road with the printed information pertaining to it.

6. Each lot in each block is numbered, and just below the number is the square footage of that lot. (Note the surveyor's symbol for square feet, ⌂.) Note also that most lot lines show their lengths and bearings. Some do not. Lengths and bearings are often omitted if the opposite side of the lot is equal and parallel and contains the length and bearing. This helps to keep the plat from becoming unduly cluttered.

7. The front measurement on lots that front on the curve of Stone Road is prefixed by the letter A.

This is the surveyor's shorthand notation for the length of the arc formed by the curved line. Some plats also indicate the angle subtending the arc, as well as its radius. When this is indicated, the symbol Δ ("delta") indicates the angle and the letter R indicates the radius of the curvature in feet. Sometimes this information is not indicated directly at the lot, but is keyed to a small table located elsewhere on the plat by some suitable notation. Along Stone Road the arc lengths are given on the lots, but the central angles subtending the curves and their radii are keyed to a chart by the small letters within circles. The chart has been deleted here because for our purposes it is not needed.

8. The name "Lenwood" at the top of the plat in stippled (dotted) letters indicates that the property joining the rear of lots 6, 7, and 8, Block 2, is owned by Lenwood. The line extending northward from the rear of Lot 1, Block 2, represents the boundary between Lenwood's land and land owned by the state (Road #600).

9. In addition to showing the ownership of adjoining property, stippled letters are used to indicate the overlap where one plat joins another. This is not used on this plat.

10. Note the easements shown and the purposes for which they were created.

When you have become familiar with the plat of Section One, you may wish to complete Practice Examination A at the end of the chapter.

DESCRIPTION OF LAND BY MONUMENTS

Land parcels, particularly in rural areas, are sometimes described by momuments which mark the boundaries or corners of the property. Monuments, as previously mentioned, can be natural or artificial (created by people). For example, a boundary may be defined by a section of roadway, a fence line, or a streambed. A corner may be defined by a large rock, a pile of rocks, a tree, or a surveyor's pipe. A typical description by monuments might read as follows (refer to Fig. 8-10):

Beginning at a point marked by a concrete-filled pipe on the northeast abutment of the bridge on State Road 619 where it crosses Panther Skin Creek, and located approximately 12 miles east of Partlow and 6 miles west of Oskaloosa, thence along the stream bed of Panther Skin Creek in a northerly direction 425 feet to a cedar post in the fence line marking the land of John Smith, thence easterly along said fence line 600 feet to a post in the fence line marking the land of George Brown; thence southerly along the property line of Brown 415 feet to the right-of-way line of State Road 619; thence westerly 655 feet along the right-of-way line of State Road 619 to the point of beginning, containing 6.05 acres more or less.

Although this description included the lengths of the boundaries, sometimes a description will make no mention of them. The absence of such specifics does not by itself render a land description invalid, but it can

contribute to a great deal of difficulty in the event of a legal challenge. The following is an example of a description made by monuments alone.

The property of Orson Wagon, near Corn Centre City, bounded and described as follows: beginning at the northeast abutment of Waterloo Bridge, thence easterly along the north edge of Waterloo Road to its intersection with Quatrebras Highway; thence northerly along the west side of Quatrebras Highway to its point of intersection with the fence line marking the south boundary of Henry Jones's property; thence westerly along the fence line to the low-water line of the Kwai River; thence southerly along the low-water line of said river to the point of beginning, and containing 450 acres more or less.

Descriptions such as this were often made by the landowner personally in times gone by when people were few, the supply of land was relatively plentiful, and the need for accuracy was not pressing. Because the locations of monuments often change over a period of time, descriptions such as these can become subject to legal contest, and then a professional land surveyor will have to determine the original boundaries.

Remember the explanation given after the metes and bounds description of Fig. 8-8? This explanation deleted any reference to the bearings and referred to monuments alone.

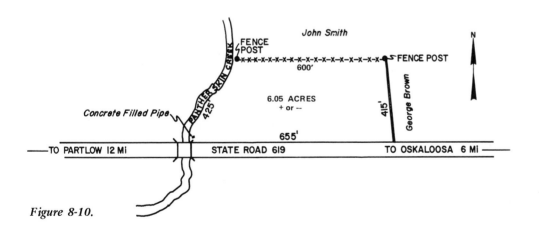

Figure 8-10.

SUMMARY OF METES AND BOUNDS, LOT AND BLOCK, AND MONUMENTS

1. Metes and bounds means measures and boundaries.

2. A meridian is an imaginary line running north and south.

3. A bearing is the acute angle a lot line makes with a meridian.

4. Always note the location of the North arrow.

5. A good description contains:

   a. a definite starting point.

   b. a description of each course in succession, with its length, direction, and monuments, if any.

   c. the area of the parcel described.

6. Directions of the boundaries can proceed either clockwise or counterclockwise.

7. The description must return to the starting point.

8. A parcel of land can be subdivided into lots, blocks, and sections, and the approved plat filed in the land records of the jurisdiction. Once this has been done, a good description need only refer to the particular lot as a part of the recorded subdivision plat, along with reference to the deed book and page number.

9. Some older descriptions, usually prepared by non-professionals, especially in rural areas, described a parcel of land by referring to monuments alone.

U.S. GOVERNMENT RECTANGULAR SURVEY

The rectangular survey is a method of land description that is peculiarly American. Its development was directly related to the problems facing the United States during its first years of independence.

When the government of the United States was formed after the Revolutionary War, the country found itself heavily in debt. The union had acquired vast territories as a result of the war. Therefore, Congress decided to sell the newly acquired land. However, before it could be sold, it had to be surveyed. Because of the vastness of this area and its wilderness nature, the use of the metes and bounds system was not practical.

In 1784, a committee of the Continental Congress worked out a plan, largely attributed to Thomas Jefferson, for locating and selling lands in the Western territory. The plan was adopted in 1785, and the first survey was made in 1786.

The basic concept of the plan was unique; no pattern for it existed anywhere else in the world. Three new theories of land administration were introduced: first, the principle of "survey before settlement"; second, a mathematically designed plan to be followed throughout the entire area of public domain; and third, the creation of a standard land unit, the section, which would be of a uniform shape and have its boundary points physically marked on the ground.

These surveys were referred to as "The United States Public Land Surveys," "Government Rectangular Survey," or just "Rectangular Survey." They are used in the entire continental United States, except for the areas occupied by the 13 original states, certain parts of Ohio, all of Texas, and Hawaii.

Principal Meridians and Base Lines

The general plan of this system is based upon lines running true north and south, called *principal meridians*, and east-west lines, called *base lines*. In any particular survey, a reference point (usually a substantial landmark) is selected. Then a true north-south line, the principal meridian, is run through this initial point. Next, a standard parallel of latitude is run from east to west through the initial point. This is called the base line.

There are at present 36 principal meridians located in different parts of the United States. Some are designated by numbers (e.g., 1st Principal Meridian) and some are given names (e.g., Indian Meridian, San Bernardino Meridian). The Bureau of Land Management of the U.S. Department of the Interior publishes a map, entitled "Principal Meridians of the Federal System of Rectangular Surveys," which shows the area covered by each principal meridian and its base line. It is reproduced in Fig. 8-11.

Each principal meridian is associated with the survey of a particular area. For example, the area associated with the survey of the 5th principal meridian includes Arkansas, Missouri, Iowa, North Dakota, and parts of Minnesota and South Dakota. All subdivisions within that area are based on the 5th principal meridian and its corresponding base line.

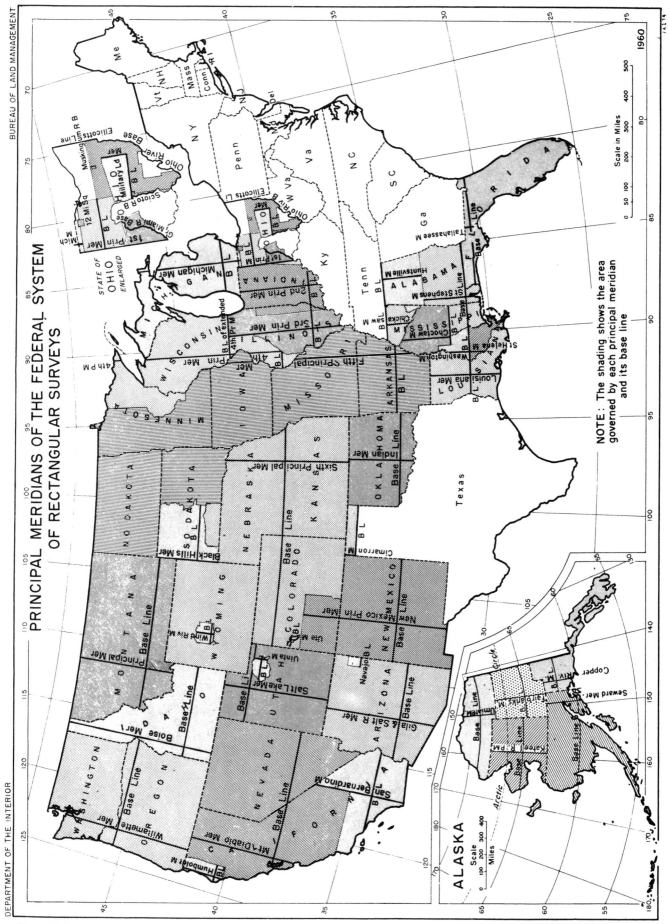

Figure 8-11.

The basic plan of subdivision used in the U.S. Government Rectangular Survey System is presented in Figs. 8-12 to 8-15.

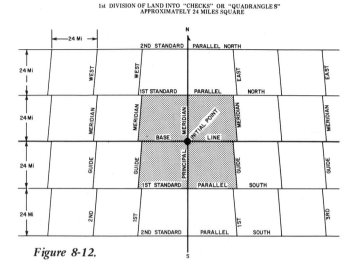

Figure 8-12.

The area shaded in Fig. 8-12 is the entire area shown in Fig. 8-13, in which each of 4 checks is divided into 16 townships.

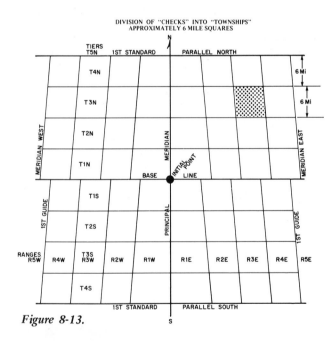

Figure 8-13.

The area shaded in Fig. 8-13 is the entire area shown in Fig. 8-14, in which 1 township is divided into 36 sections.

Figure 8-14.

The shaded area of Fig. 8-14 is shown in Fig. 8-15. One section of 1 square mile, which is 640 acres, is further divided.

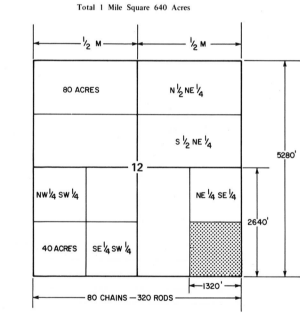

Figure 8-15.

Standard Parallels

You will note from Fig. 8-12 that the land description plan is centered around the initial point, through which pass the principal meridian and the base line. You will also note that north and south of the base line there are other lines parallel to the base line. These are called *standard parallels.*

Guide Meridians

Similarly, east and west of the principal meridian there are north-south lines that run virtually parallel to the principal meridian. They are not continuous, but extend only from parallel to parallel. These lines are called *guide meridians.* In Fig. 8-12 you will note that the guide meridians appear to be segmented and offset slightly at each standard parallel (this is exaggerated here to demonstrate the nonalignment more clearly). This non-alignment partially compensates for the curvature of the earth and the convergence of all meridians at the North and South Poles. The check, township, and section are thus not true squares. The variations in each particular case, although accurately accounted for, compensate for earth curvature and therefore result in some relatively minor differences in length and area from the standard check, township, and section. For our purposes, however, these are of little concern. A more detailed explanation may be found in any standard text on surveying.

The principal meridian, the base line, standard parallels, and the guide meridians are all called *standard lines.* The distance between any two successive guide meridians, as well as between any two successive standard parallels of latitude, is 24 miles. The area bounded by two successive standard parallels and by two successive guide meridians is the basic quadrangle called a *check*, which contains 16 townships.

Checks, Townships, and Sections

CHECKS

Starting at the initial point (the intersection of the principal meridian and the base line), as shown in Figure 8-12, land is laid out in a gridlike fashion on either side of the principal meridian and the base line. The grid divides the land into squares or quadrangles called checks that measure 24 miles to the side. Each check is in turn divided into 16 squares called *townships*, each of which contain 36 square miles and measures 6 miles on each side. A township is further divided into 36 squares of 1 square mile each called *sections*, containing 640 acres each. The section is the smallest whole unit of land division dealt with in the government survey system.

TOWNSHIPS

Referring to Figs. 8-12 and 8-13, you will see that each standard parallel is designated either north or south, according to its relationship to the base line. The guide meridians are designated according to their position east or west of the principal meridian.

Now study the check that is bounded by the base line, the 1st standard parallel south, the principal meridian, and the 1st guide meridian west. The 16 townships contained within the check are identified in each case according to the standard plan of designation that applies throughout the public lands survey. The letters "T" and "R" stand for "tier" and "range," respectively.

Tier

A *tier* is best thought of as a column of townships, one on top of the other, running north and south. Townships are numbered consecutively from the base line, and are designated as T1N, T2N, etc. (or T1S, T2S, etc., if the township lies south of the base line).

Range

A *range* can be thought of as a row of townships running east and west. Ranges are numbered consecutively eastward from the principal meridian as R1E, R2E, etc. (or R1W, R2W, etc., if the range is west of the meridian).

The designation of a township is always given with the tier number stated first, for north or south direction, followed by the range number for east or west direction. A township whose tier number is T3N and whose range number is R2E would be identified as "Township three North, Range two East." The word "tier" is understood but not expressed.

SECTIONS

Sections within a township are also numbered according to a standard system. Fig. 8-14 illustrates the method used. The numbering starts from the northeast corner and proceeds to the west boundary; then down to the next south range, then back from west to east; down once more, then from east to west on the next south range; and so on. Consider Fig. 8-14 as a magnification of Township 3 North, Range 3 East (the shaded area of Fig. 8-13).

The full description of the shaded portion of Fig. 8-14 would be "Section 12, Township 3 North, Range 3 East, of the _____ Principal Meridian (or Section 12, T3N, R3E, _____ PM)."

We have already learned that a section is a square, 1 mile by 1 mile, which is 1 square mile, or 640 acres, in area. Public land laws also provide for subdividing sections into quarter sections, although this is rarely done by United States surveyors.

Sections are normally marked on the ground, however, by eight permanent monuments—one at each corner, and one midway between each two corners.

Aliquot Parts

The basic subdivision of a section is accomplished primarily by successive quartering. The divisions of a section obtained by quartering are known as *aliquot parts*, which are described as fractions of a section located with reference to the four points of the compass. These can be expressed in terms of a fraction of a section, a fraction of a fraction, etc.; e.g., "the northwest quarter of the northwest quarter of Section 3," written "NW$\frac{1}{4}$, NW$\frac{1}{4}$, Sec. 3." Thus the shaded portion of Fig. 8-15 would be described as the "southeast quarter of the southeast quarter of Section 12." In abbreviated form, the description would be "SE$\frac{1}{4}$, SE$\frac{1}{4}$, Sec. 12."

One can most easily locate a property described by the public lands survey system by *reading the description in reverse*; i.e., read the principal meridian, then the range, township (tier), section, part of section, part of part of section, and part of part of part of section.

To calculate the area contained in a fractional part of a section, multiply the fraction or the fraction of a

fractional part of the section by the area contained in a complete section (640 acres).

Examples: The NE$\frac{1}{4}$ of Section ____ contains 160 acres.

$$\frac{1}{4} \times 640 = \frac{640}{4} = 160 \text{ acres}$$

The N$\frac{1}{2}$ of the NW$\frac{1}{4}$ of Section ____ contains 80 acres.

$$\frac{1}{2} \times \frac{1}{4} \times 640 = \frac{640}{8} = 80 \text{ acres}$$

The NE$\frac{1}{2}$ of the NE$\frac{1}{4}$ of the NE$\frac{1}{4}$ of the NE$\frac{1}{4}$ of Section ____ contains 5 acres.

$$\frac{1}{2} \times \frac{1}{4} \times \frac{1}{4} \times \frac{1}{4} \times 640 = \frac{640}{128} = 5 \text{ acres}$$

SUMMARY OF U.S. GOVERNMENT RECTANGULAR SURVEY SYSTEM

1. The basis of the U.S. Government Rectangular Survey method is a series of north-south lines called principal meridians and east-west lines called base lines. The intersection of these is called an initial point.

2. North and south of the base lines at 24-mile intervals are parallel lines called standard parallels.

3. East and west of the principal meridians at 24-mile intervals are parallel lines called guide meridians which are staggered (or slightly adjusted) at each standard parallel to partially compensate and correct for the curvature of the earth.

4. These 24-mile grids formed by the standard parallels and guide meridians are called checks, and they are further divided into townships, which are 6 miles square (16 townships in one check).

5. Each township is further divided into sections, which are 1 mile square (36 sections in one township).

6. Tiers are columns of townships running north and south. They are numbered according to their position north or south of the base line and their distance from it.

7. Ranges are rows of townships running east and west. They are numbered according to their distance and direction from the principal meridian.

8. Each section can be further divided into fractional portions which are identified with reference to the quadrants of the compass.

9. The easiest way to read a description using the Government Rectangular Survey system is to read it backward, from the largest fractional part down to the smallest.

10. To calculate the area contained in a fractional part of a section, multiply the fraction or fractions by 640 acres.

PRACTICE EXAMINATION A:
METES AND BOUNDS, LOT AND BLOCK, AND MONUMENTS
(*Refer to Fig. 8-16*)

1. Locate the following: "A point on the northwesterly boundary of Section 1, Mountararat, which point is N 45°30'00" E 178.00 feet from the corner of Lenwood and the State." This describes:

   (A) the rear corner common to Lots 7 and 8, Block 2, Section 1, Mountararat
   (B) the front corner common to Lots 6 and 7, Block 2, Section 1, Mountararat
   (C) the rear corner common to Lots 3 and 4, Block 3, Section 1, Mountararat
   (D) none of the above

2. Read the following metes and bounds description:

   "Beginning at a point on the southeasterly boundary of Route 600, which point is N 45°30'00" E 110.00 feet from the westerly corner of Block 1, and running with Route 600 N 45°30'00" E 110.00 feet to a corner; thence S 44°30'00" E 152.50 feet to a corner; thence S 45°30'00" W 110.00 feet to a corner; thence N 44°30'00" W 152.50 feet to the point of beginning and containing ____ square feet."

This description might be more briefly written as follows:

(A) Lot 1, Block 1, Section 1, Mountararat
(B) Lot 2, Block 1, Section 1, Mountararat
(C) Lot 7, Block 1, Section 1, Mountararat
(C) Lot 6, Block 1, Section 1, Mountararat

3. Stone Road to the northeast was completed and dedicated last year. The easement through Cardinal Homes property:

(A) still exists   (C) no longer exists
(B) never did exist (D) will always exist

4. If Lot 8, Block 2, Section 1, Mountararat, were described by metes and bounds, its northwest boundary would be described as running with:

(A) Smith   (C) State Road 600
(B) Lenwood   (D) Cardinal Homes, Inc.

5. The easement at the rear of Lot 3, Block 1, Section 1, and Lot 8, Block 1, Section 1, Mountararat, is for:

(A) a sanitary sewer   (C) electric service lines
(B) a storm sewer   (D) none of these

6. The lot having the greatest frontage along Stone Road is:

(A) Lot 3, Block 3, Section 1, Mountararat
(B) Lot 4, Block 2, Section 1, Mountararat
(C) Lot 5, Block 2, Section 1, Mountararat
(D) Lot 8, Block 2, Section 1, Mountararat

7. A house built on Lot 5, Block 2, Section 1, Mountararat, would probably face:

(A) North   (C) East
(B) South   (D) West

8. The bearing of the front boundary line of Lot 2, Block 1, Section 1, Mountararat, is most likely

(A) S 38°00'00" W   (C) N 44°30'00" W
(B) S 45°30'00" W   (D) N 45°30'00" E

9. Block 2, Section 1, Mountararat, contains

(A) 9 lots   (C) 17 lots
(B) 8 lots   (D) 4 lots

10. Lot 7, Block 2, Section 1, Mountararat, contains

(A) 16,775 square feet
(B) 17,770 square feet
(C) 16,912 square feet
(D) none of these

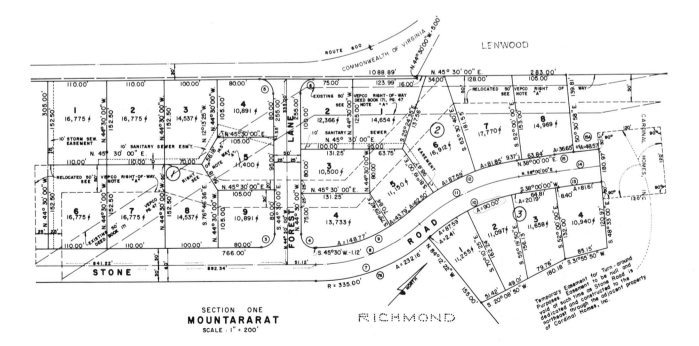

Figure 8-16.

PRACTICE EXAMINATION B: GOVERNMENT RECTANGULAR SURVEY

1. The parcel of ground marked 7 in Figure 8-17 would best be described as

    (A) NW$\frac{1}{4}$ of NW$\frac{1}{4}$ of SE$\frac{1}{4}$ of Section ____
    (B) W$\frac{1}{2}$ of NE$\frac{1}{4}$ of SE$\frac{1}{4}$ of Section ____
    (C) N$\frac{1}{2}$ of NW$\frac{1}{4}$ of SE$\frac{1}{4}$ of Section ____
    (D) NW$\frac{1}{4}$ of SW$\frac{1}{4}$ of Section ____

2. The parcel of ground marked 10 in Figure 8-17 would contain

    $\frac{1}{2} \times \frac{1}{4} \times \frac{1}{4}$

    (A) 10 acres   (C) 40 acres
    (B) 20 acres   (D) none of the above $\frac{1}{32}$. 640

3. Referring to Figure 8-17, the NE$\frac{1}{4}$ of the SW$\frac{1}{4}$ of the SE$\frac{1}{4}$ of the SE$\frac{1}{4}$ is parcel number

    (A) 16   (C) 19
    (B) 22   (D) 24

4. The parcel of ground in Figure 8-17 marked 20 contains

    (A) 2.5 acres   (C) 10 acres
    (B) 5.0 acres   (D) none of the above

5. The line 1–4 in Figure 8-18 is properly called

    (A) a guide meridian   (C) the principal meridian
    (B) the base line   (D) none of these

6. The distance between lines 2–6 and 3–5 in Figure 8-18 would be

    (A) 6 miles   (C) 48 miles
    (B) 24 miles   (D) 2 miles

7. Thirty-six sections of land would be

    (A) a check   (C) 24 square miles
    (B) a township   (D) none of these

8. A check would contain

    $\begin{array}{c} 36 \\ \underline{16} \\ 216 \\ 36 \\ \hline 576 \end{array}$

    (A) 376 sections
    (B) 1,156 square miles
    (C) 16 townships
    (D) all these

9. The shaded area in the lower left portion of Figure 8-19 would best be described as

    (A) a check
    (B) T3S, R3W
    (C) Section 8 of the township
    (D) none of these

10. Refer to the shaded portion of a square in the northeast quadrant of Figure 8-19. This area would best be described as

    (A) Section 36   (C) Section 31
    (B) Section 6   (D) Section 1

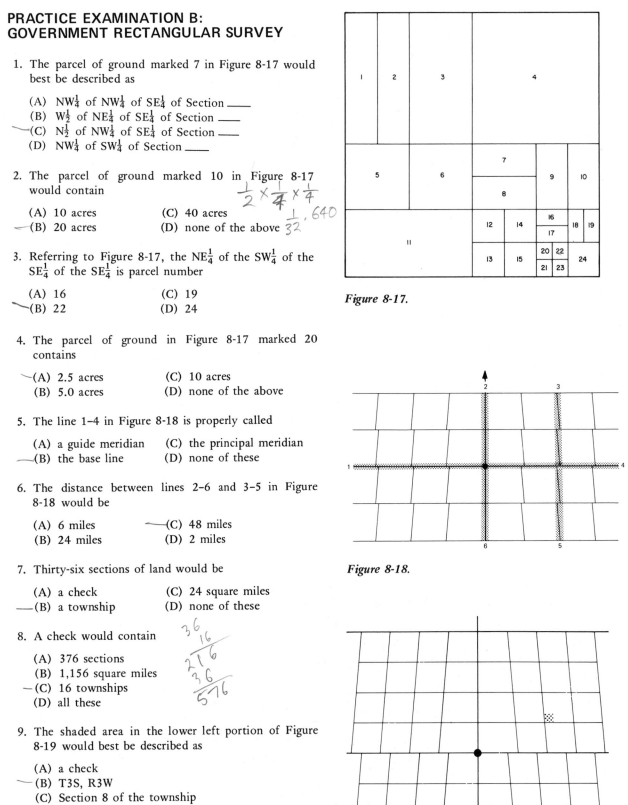

Figure 8-17.

Figure 8-18.

Figure 8-19.

Chapter 9

Title Insurance

NATURE OF TITLE AND PROTECTION OF REAL PROPERTY INTERESTS

To own real estate is to own rights or interests in land or realty. When real estate is sold, these rights or interests are transferred, not the land or realty itself. The word "title" applies to the legal ownership of any rights that an owner of real estate possesses. When sellers sell their rights, they transfer only those rights to which they actually have a valid claim.

The sale of a right that is not owned, however, does not defeat the rights of the true owner. For example, the sale of one's own rights cannot defeat outstanding dower, homestead, or curtesy rights that other persons may possess in the same property. Most importantly, even though a title appears clear at the time of sale, it may be subject to challenge at any future time.

Title Insurance Defined

Title insurance is a policy of insurance which indemnifies the holder for loss sustained by reason of defects in the title. An owner of a home could suffer financial loss or the loss of the home itself should a defect in the title to the property later arise. This is the reason why a purchaser should seek adequate title protection when buying a home. However, to understand the need for title insurance, it is helpful to consider the process of obtaining good title and the variety of risks in the transfer of title to real estate.

The Process of Obtaining Good Title

The buyer wants to know that the seller has a good and clear title to the property which is being purchased. The buyer also wants to know that the property is free of all liens, encumbrances, or other claims. To do this, the buyer requests that a search of title be made for the property.

A lawyer or title examiner then searches the title by examining all public records where claims against the title might be presented or recorded. The history of the property is presented in a report that is known as an *abstract of title*. The abstract shows title passing from owner to owner, or a *chain of title*. The buyer may receive a copy of this title *report*, usually referred to as a preliminary title report, which also shows any outstanding liens and encumbrances against the property.

The next step is a *legal examination* of the abstract and an issuance of a *certificate* or *opinion of title* by a lawyer. This is the lawyer's opinion or judgment as to the current status of the title to the property. It is, the buyer (and seller) hopes, an opinion that the title is clear and good, and insurable.

Where the opinion of title sets out defects or otherwise indicates that the title is clouded, the buyer is placed on guard. The buyer may accept or reject the property, or require that the clouds be removed, depending on the terms of his or her contract of purchase of the property.

Risks or Defects Not Discovered by Title Search

A title insurance company makes a very careful analysis of every title it insures. Its concern as insurer of the title to the property merges with that of the property owner into a mutual concern that no title defect exists that will later affect the title held by the insured owner. Reasonable premium rates, paid one time only for title insurance on real property, indicate that in practice title claims against property are few in number.

However, even though the opinion of title may indicate the title is clear, the buyer cannot be absolutely certain that it is good. Many types of defects in the title may exist and fail to be disclosed through title search:

1. Technical errors by humans, such as the clerk's errors in recording or indexing, or erroneous city and county tax department notations, or omissions by title examiners (called undiscovered defects)

2. Defects hidden from title examiners (called undiscoverable defects), including

   • fraud or forgery in the signing of various papers affecting the property

- execution (signature) of papers by a minor, an insane person, or an incompetent person

- name similarity in the execution of papers

- deeds executed under an invalid power of attorney (for example, one that has expired)

- unrecorded outstanding mortgages

- undisclosed judgments outstanding against the seller

- unpaid real estate taxes and other tax liens not yet recorded

- fraud, misrepresentation, or undue influence in the transfer of title

- easements through adverse possession

- creditor claims on former owners in bankruptcy

- undiscovered marriages and divorces with resultant dower rights of widow or curtesy rights of the widower

- the presence of undiscovered wills naming additional or different devisees

Security for the Purchaser

From the above, it is easy to imagine that there can be a great deal of legal risk associated with title to property. As a result, most title searching is performed by attorneys. Based on their certificates (opinions) of title, title insurance policies are issued. Title insurance companies use their own staffs or outside (fee) attorneys whom they have previously investigated and approved. Many attorneys specialize in the title aspects of real estate law.

An attorney is only personally liable for errors and oversights that would not have been made by some other attorney acting diligently, and then only if loss has actually occurred. An attorney is not liable for loss caused by hidden, undiscoverable defects. Under the statute of limitations in some states, individual liability runs out after a certain number of years. There is no statute of limitations for title insurance companies. They remain liable in accordance with the terms of their contract (policy) with the insured and sustain liability through the insured's heirs.

Since most property is transferred under General Warranty Deeds, a purchaser could have a claim against the grantor (seller) for defective title. It might be surmised that grantor's guarantee of title would eliminate the need for title insurance. However, the purchaser would first have to lose a court action asserting the purchaser's claim to title to the property. Next, another lengthy and expensive court action against grantor would be necessary to acquire a judgment which then could be placed as a general lien against all property of the grantor. Finally, chances of recovery would depend on grantor's financial solvency.

A title insurance policy issued to the purchaser (an owner's policy) protects his or her title to the property against loss resulting from both undiscovered and undiscoverable defects. Thus, human errors and oversights are covered, such as defects in the public record, as well as matters outside the record which also might make the title defective and cause the purchaser a loss (e.g., fraud or forgery). The security of the title insurance policy would be as good as the reputation and financial solvency of the company issuing the policy.

TYPES OF POLICIES

There are three broad types of title insurance policies.

The Mortgagee Policy

The *mortgagee policy* is a policy that protects only the lender against financial loss. The lender, not the home buyer, is the beneficiary. One of the mandatory conditions imposed by a lender before granting a loan is that the home buyer pay for a mortgagee's policy of title insurance. Otherwise, a defect or encumbrance on the property may affect the priority of the lender's lien (the mortgage or the deed of trust).

The mortgagee policy issued to the lender by the title insurance company also insures the lender against loss should the property be unmarketable. A marketable title means a salable title.

The title insurance company, through issuance of its policy, also makes a covenant to defend mortgagee's lien by defending the property's title in any court action. The company promises to defend the insured in any legal action based on a claim of title or encumbrance prior to the effective policy date. There is no limit on the amount of legal services which will be provided.

As the amount owed is reduced, the coverage of the mortgagee's policy is periodically decreased until such time as the loan is paid off. Because a mortgagee policy terminates more quickly and because the risk decreases as the debt is paid, it will carry a lower premium rate than an owner's policy.

The Owner's Policy

An owner's policy insures the property owner (purchaser) against financial loss up to the face amount of the policy, which is usually the purchase price of the property. The owner's policy does not protect the holder from loss as a result of unrecorded mechanics liens or other such items *specifically exempted* in the policy, but undiscovered defects (of record and of person) as well as undiscoverable defects (hidden) not specifically exempted are covered by the insurance policy. The policy also covenants to defend the purchaser in court against any attack on the title as it is stated and insured.

This basic benefit of the owner's policy—protection against loss or damage resulting from defects in (or failure of) ownership title to a particular parcel of realty—usually includes insurance coverage on the marketability of the title. Marketability of title may mean that the title search has failed to disclose severe material defects that would stop the sale of the property, and that a prudent and reasonable buyer would buy the property. In this case title insurance protects the insured purchaser. In the case where a prudent buyer would refuse to purchase the property because of a title disclosure, under insurance coverage the title company could either purchase the property itself (from the insured at the sales price or policy amount) or could go to court to test the validity of the objection to the title (and perhaps enforce the pending contract of purchase).

In contrast to the diminishing liability of the mortgagee policy, under the owner's policy the title insurance company remains fully liable for the original amount insured throughout the ownership tenure of the named insured, as well as that of his heirs and assigns. Three points are important here:

1. Title insurance protects the named insured against possible losses because of events which have happened in the *past*, up to the date of policy issuance. Therefore, title insurance is different from other types of insurance policies, which provide coverage for *future* events, dating from policy issuance forward, such as coverage for life, casualty, or fire insurance. Title insurance has covered the acts of others in the past, and has not provided for the acts of the policyholder in the future.

   On the basis of this reasoning also, a title insurance policy cannot be transferred at a later, future date from the present owner to a new buyer. Title insurance is personal to the insured and to the property, insuring title as of a specified date.

2. Instead of annual premiums, there is only one premium, which is paid when the policy is issued. However, as the market value of the property appreciates over time, a widening gulf could arise between the face amount of the owner's policy and the subsequent market value of the property. Therefore, should another party later assert a successful claim on the title, even with title insurance in effect it is conceivable that the title company's payment to the successful claimant would be lower than the award, and the named insured would stand the additional loss.

3. Should the buyer fail to insure his title with an owner's policy, substantial loss could be suffered. A mortgagee policy alone would satisfy the lender's requirements but would not look after the interests of the property owner. In fact, expenses or losses borne by the title company in defending the owner's title (on behalf of the mortgagee) could be made a lien against the property.

The Leasehold Policy

A leasehold policy is a special title policy which is purchased by a long-term tenant to insure that the landlord (lessor) owns a good, clear title to the leased premises. It would be apparent that a tenant would seek such an assurance prior to signing a long-term lease and being committed to substantial expenditures for customizing the property to the tenant's special needs. A regular-form owner's policy is used, with the face of the policy amended to show that the insured interest is a leasehold. Where the lessee has a loan, the face of the mortgagee policy is also amended to show that the borrower's title is a leasehold interest or estate.

COSTS, COVERAGES, AND BENEFITS

Costs of Title Insurance Policies

While the cost of title insurance varies from state to state, as well as from one area to another within states, the insurance rates quoted here are comparable with the pure basic rates paid to the insurance company. They do not include other charges which are sometimes lumped together with the title insurance charges.

The title premium is a one-time, nonrecurring expense. The mortgagee policy premium covers the mortgagee until the mortgagor's mortgage payments have stopped. The owner's policy premium covers the property owner as long as the owner or the owner's heirs possess any interest in the property. The leasehold policy premium insures the lessee as long as the lessee has an interest in the property.

Where the purchaser takes out two concurrent policies of title insurance for one transaction—an owner's policy for himself and a mortgagee policy for the mortgage lender—the purchaser pays the full premium on the owner's policy ($3.50 base rate per $1,000 of insurance coverage; scaled downward after the levels of $50,000; $100,000; and $500,000 have been reached), on an amount equal to the purchase price of the property, plus a flat fee of only $7.50 for a duplicate policy for the mortgagee.

Example: Assume that a property was purchased for $40,000, with a $36,000 loan.
   Owner's policy premium:

$40,000 ÷ $1,000 = 40 (X) $3.50 base rate =	$140.00
plus mortgagee policy: flat rate	7.50
Total policy insurance cost	$147.50

Added to these charges would be the attorney's fees for binder and application. The legal title examination fee is a separate, additional charge.

The owner's policy rate is $3.50 per $1,000 of insurance coverage whether it is combined with the mortgagee policy or not. However, if the mortgagee policy is taken out by itself, the base rate is $2.50 per $1,000 of insurance coverage (which would be the amount of the loan). This base rate is similarly scaled downward at the same levels of coverage as the owner's policy.

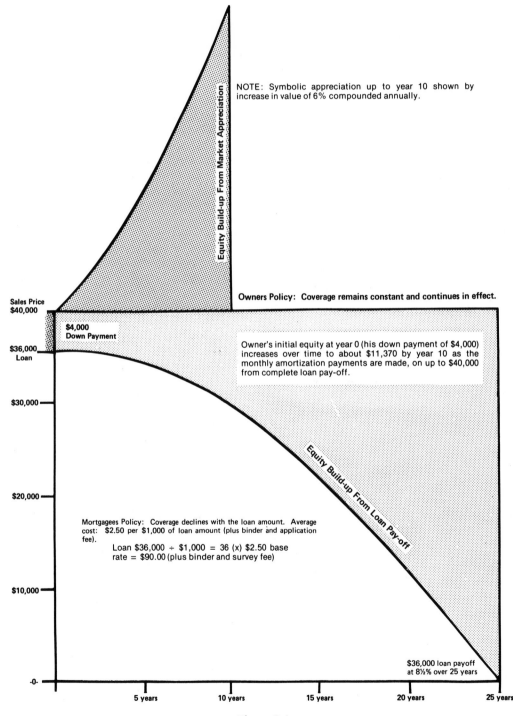

COVERAGE OF AN OWNER'S AND MORTGAGEE'S TITLE INSURANCE

POLICY AND EQUITY BUILD-UP.

(Example of the total equity build-up from market appreciation and loan pay-off on a property that sold for $40,000 with $4,000 down payment and a $36,000 loan at 8½%.)

NOTE: Symbolic appreciation up to year 10 shown by increase in value of 6% compounded annually.

Equity Build-up From Market Appreciation

Owners Policy: Coverage remains constant and continues in effect.

Sales Price $40,000

$4,000 Down Payment

$36,000 Loan

Owner's initial equity at year 0 (his down payment of $4,000) increases over time to about $11,370 by year 10 as the monthly amortization payments are made, on up to $40,000 from complete loan pay-off.

$30,000

Equity Build-up From Loan Pay-off

$20,000

Mortgagees Policy: Coverage declines with the loan amount. Average cost: $2.50 per $1,000 of loan amount (plus binder and application fee).
     Loan $36,000 ÷ $1,000 = 36 (x) $2.50 base rate = $90.00 (plus binder and survey fee)

$10,000

$36,000 loan payoff at 8½% over 25 years

-0-

5 years   10 years   15 years   20 years   25 years

Figure 9-1.

In the previous example, mortgagee policy premium:

$36,000 ÷ $1,000 = 36 (X) $2.50 base rate = $90.00 plus charges for binder and application

It is sometimes customary in settlement statements for title insurance premiums to be included as a total "package of legal fees" of premium, legal title searching fees, and/or other legal fees. In these cases, the title insurance company would receive its due share for issuing its insurance policies.

Refer to Figure 9-1 for an illustration of the salient features of the owner's and mortgagee's policies, including equity build-up as the result of both loan payoff and market appreciation of the property.

Coverage of a Policy of Title Insurance

A policy of title insurance contains a description of the property, the exact nature of the buyer's interest in the described property, and the deed or lease by which the buyer of the policy obtained that interest. The policy also lists any known title defects, liens, or encumbrances. These are shown as exceptions to the coverage. The policy will not pay for any claims arising from these itemized exceptions.

The liability the insurance company assumes, and the coverage the purchaser receives, depends on the type of policy purchased. Two types are common: In one type—a *record title policy*—the title insurance company guarantees only that the purchaser's ownership as shown by the policy conforms to the record. The purchaser is only insured against a poorly done or incompetent title examination. Only the work performed is guaranteed, and only that which the public record discloses.

The second type of policy—a *full-coverage policy*—protects the insured against both undiscovered and undiscoverable, unknown defects in the title or public record. Both poor quality of the work and any hidden defects are covered.

Benefits to the Real Estate Broker and Salesperson

A title insurance policy affords the comfort of property protection that a purchaser usually needs when acquiring title to property. For example, a purchaser can rest easier over a long period of years as a homeowner knowing that the residence is safer from outside claims to the title. In particular, a full-coverage policy protects ownership rights in a home as securely as possible against the unforeseen. Also, a policy of title insurance is stronger evidence of a property's marketability for later resale. In addition, the title policy places the legal resources of a substantial and knowledgeable organization behind the title claim of the homeowner. The policyholder can return to the title insurer with future questions on title and real estate. Also, should legal action later become necessary to defend the title, the title company would undertake it, not the homeowner. Finally, the existence of a policy of title

insurance conveys to all outsiders a strong presumption that that title is valid. It asserts and guarantees the homeowner's estate.

THE TORRENS SYSTEM OF TITLE REGISTRATION

In 1857 Sir Robert Torrens, an English businessman, developed a system of title registration in Australia which has subsequently been legally adopted in various states and localities, but is not widely practiced as yet in the United States. Under the Torrens system the *title* to land is *registered*. Where the Torrens Law has been adopted and is in effect, the law presumes that title to property rests in the registered owner, as a result of that owner's producing evidence to show that he or she does hold title, confirmed by a follow-up examination of that title. However, even after the title is registered, claimants who believe they hold a valid interest in the property are not precluded from later court action.

In the majority or usual system of title registration, recording acts apply by which the *deed* is *recorded*, usually in the office of the registrar by the clerk of the county in which the property is located, as evidence of property ownership. However, as earlier sections in this chapter have explained, title as indicated in the deed may be invalid or otherwise contestable as a result of hidden or undiscoverable (as well as undiscovered) defects. The possible existence of such defects then brings about the next step, which is the obtaining of some form of title protection; the purchasing of an owner's full-coverage policy of title insurance most commonly satisfies that requirement. Under the Torrens system, however, the necessity for title insurance is eliminated.

In the event that a human error or fraud is committed in registering title under the Torrens system, an indemnity or insurance fund is available to provide restitution. Such a fund is maintained by the Registrar of Title (or County Clerk), who, along with any examiner(s) of title, may also be required by state law to execute an indemnity bond. Fees to support the indemnity fund are derived from title registrations. A Torrens Certificate of Registration of Title is legal evidence of presumed ownership.

Allowing for individual variance, the basic procedure is as follows: The owner of the property initiates the action by making application or petition under oath to the appropriate court to have the title registered. The particulars submitted include personal identification (name, age, residence, marital status), property description, title or real property interest held (for example, fee simple absolute), liens (and lienor identification), other claims and claimants against the property, and tenant occupants, if any.

The application is then referred to an examiner of title possessing full authority to conduct an inquiry into the title and the veracity of the facts presented. Depending upon the findings of the examination, the court may then (1) deny the application, (2) defer decision (and request more information), or (3) enter an order that the Registrar issue a Certificate of Registration of Title.

In order for a Torrens system to be effective, in essence it must become a master list of title registrations, and all instruments affecting title must pass through the Registrar's office. It becomes a compulsory system.

While the Torrens system may register title, under the system the property owner still must use the deed to convey title. Therefore, the Registrar will receive two documents, the deed and the Certificate of Title, for registration purposes. Upon filing, a new Certificate of Title will pass along with the deed to the new owner.

The purpose of the Torrens system of title registration is to eliminate the repetitive title search and examination each time a property transfer takes place. Researching the chain of ownership and encumbrances on title impedes the transferability of property. The advantage of eliminating title examination expense is also noted, with "official" (or Torrens) certification of title made conclusive and irrevocable (except for error or fraud) for all to see.

After the first search and registration is performed, no more searches into the past are necessary. Loans and other investment dealings with property are speeded up and facilitated as well. From the property owner's point of view, he or she does not have to worry that the old policy of title insurance may not cover the present value of the appreciated or improved property.

Opponents of the Torrens system point out that the saving of time is merely an illusion because an official title examiner has merely replaced a private title examiner. The public records have to be searched, and the claimant's facts need to be verified each time, regardless, even though subsequent transfers are presumably simpler. The saving of expense may be a similar illusion, since the cost of title registration would supplant the cost of title insurance. Also, heirs and devisees, as well as the original insured, are protected by title insurance, whereas the Torrens system requires a new procedure for registration, plus some additional expense. Moreover, the title registration procedure would create another layer of government bureaucracy, and one which would perhaps respond very slowly during periods of heavy property transfer. Court action and legal proceedings may also be careful and deliberate, rather than easy and speedy.

However, perhaps the greatest difficulty facing the adoption of the Torrens system is the possibility that an individual (or a mortgagee) with a claim against or interest in the property might not receive notice of the Torrens procedure and thus be unconstitutionally deprived of due process of law. Even though restitution would be made from the indemnity or insurance fund, an individual (or mortgagee) could be deprived of rights to the property itself. The property may later be unrecoverable, as in a subsequent transfer where an innocent purchaser obtains an indefeasible title and the right to retain the property.

Serious objections such as these keep the Torrens system of title registration from becoming common practice in the United States.

SETTLEMENT COSTS AND REGULATION

On December 22, 1974, the Real Estate Settlement Procedures Act of 1974 was signed into law by the President. The intent of Public Law 93-533 (12 USC 2601) is to provide advance disclosure to home buyers and sellers of all costs and charges associated with the transfer of title to residential property, wherein federally related mortgage loans are involved. Other reforms include the elimination of referral fees and kickbacks or rebates of any portion of a charge for services not rendered. Payment must be related to services actually and legitimately performed.

With this legislation becoming effective on June 20, 1975, the Secretary of the Department of Housing and Urban Development is to develop a uniform settlement statement, for use as the standard real estate settlement form in all transactions where federal loans, insurance, guarantees, or programs are involved. Also, *any* loan is to be regulated where the lender's volume of business in residential loans totals $1 million or more per year. Accordingly, the Secretary of HUD is to prepare and distribute special information booklets to lenders, who in turn will help borrowers understand the nature and costs of real estate settlement services. The purpose of each cost is to be explained, with examples and descriptions, including choices available to buyers, as well as citings of unfair practices and unreasonable or unnecessary charges.

PRACTICE EXAMINATION: TITLE INSURANCE

1. With regard to title insurance protection,

   (A) a record title policy covers a homeowner's interests best
   (B) a full-coverage policy covers a homeowner's interests best
   (C) a full-coverage policy combined with a mortgagee's policy covers a homeowner's interests best
   (D) none of the above is correct

2. A mortagee policy of title insurance is purchased by

   (A) the lender   (C) the buyer
   (B) the seller   (D) the mortgagee

3. A mortgagee policy is usually required by

   (A) the lender   (C) the seller
   (B) the borrower   (D) the mortgagor

4. Title insurance

   (A) protects against loss in the event there is a legal flaw in previous ownership
   (B) protects future owners as the property is transferred
   (C) only protects future heirs
   (D) protects the previous owner against loss

5. A Torrens system

   (A) regulates deed registrations
   (B) regulates liens and encumbrances
   (C) regulates title insurance
   (D) regulates title registrations

6. A Torrens system eliminates the necessity for

   I. title insurance
   II. title registration
   III. deed recordation

   (A) Both I and II   (C) Both I and III
   (B) Both II and III   (D) III only

7. Which of the following statements are generally true?

   I. Torrens systems are sweeping the country.
   II. The Torrens system is a relatively new development.
   III. Torrens systems of deed registration are very useful for mortgagees.

   (A) Both I and II   (C) Both I and II
   (B) Both II and III   (D) None of these

8. Regarding an owner's policy of title insurance, which of the following statements is (are) correct?

   I. The owner's equity created by an increase in value is not covered.
   II. The owner's equity created by amortization of the loan is not covered.

   (A) I only   (C) Both I and II
   (B) II only   (D) Neither I nor II

9. If the certificate of title sets out defects or otherwise indicates that the title is clouded,

   (A) the seller must remove defects and clear up the title
   (B) principals are referred back to the contract for clarification
   (C) the title company may intercede and remedy defects
   (D) the seller may remove defects and clear up the title

10. An owner's policy of title insurance is only good

    (A) as long as the mortgagee's policy stays in effect
    (B) as long as the owner continues to pay the premiums
    (C) as long as the owner or the owner's heirs have an interest in the property
    (D) as long as the owner lives

11. When the title search indicates a clear title

    (A) the seller owns the property free and clear of debt
    (B) a policy of title insurance becomes unnecessary
    (C) the seller is assured of the marketability of the property
    (D) the buyer cannot be absolutely certain that the title is good

12. If legal action becomes necessary under a title insurance policy,

    (A) the property owner is liable
    (B) the lender is liable
    (C) the title examiner is liable
    (D) the title company is liable

13. A mortgagee policy of title insurance affords protection

    (A) to the lender or the lender's representative
    (B) to the owner of the property
    (C) to the seller who has given a general warranty deed
    (D) to the one who searched the title

14. A policy of title insurance does not protect against

    (A) hidden easements (C) forged signatures
    (B) eminent domain   (D) real estate taxes

15. Title insurance premiums are paid

    (A) at the time of contract of sale
    (B) as long as the policy remains in force
    (C) at the time of loss
    (D) once, when the policy is issued

16. Title insurance, in terms of coverage from its date of policy issuance, is similar to

    (A) fire insurance   (C) either of these
    (B) trustee's insurance (D) neither of these

17. A policy of title insurance will protect against

    I. forgery, minor's signature, undisclosed marriages and divorces, and dower and curtesy rights
    II. undisclosed heirs and wills, technical errors, tax liens, and outstanding mortgages

    (A) I only   (C) Both I and II
    (B) II only   (D) Neither I nor II

18. The process of ascertaining good title includes

    (A) delivery, search, and certificate of title
    (B) search, abstract, and certificate of title
    (C) search, certificate, and opinion of title
    (D) search, opinion, and delivery of title

19. Generally, the title insurance coverage extends to hidden and unknown matters

    (A) whether or not they are of record
    (B) when they are of record
    (C) when they are not of record
    (D) in none of the cases listed

20. The essence of title insurance is that it

    (A) comforts the seller in his or her time of need
    (B) gives the grantor the protection he or she needs
    (C) guards against risks in real estate transfer
    (D) insures the holder against financial loss

Chapter 10
Real Estate Appraisal

The purpose of this chapter is to introduce the reader to the real estate appraisal field. The definitions, principles, and techniques which will be set forth refer only to real property and are not necessarily applicable to the broader appraisal field which encompasses personal and/or intangible properties.

The value of real estate is a focal point of nearly every real estate activity. Every real estate broker or salesperson needs to be aware of the principles and techniques which structure the appraisal function.

NEED FOR APPRAISALS

An appraisal of real estate is made to establish and support an opinion of value. The appraiser becomes familiar with the different kinds of value and the technical methods of estimating them. The broker and salesperson find the need for appraisals arising in many situations. Typically, appraisals are required

- when property is sold
- when property is purchased
- in connection with mortgage financing
- in condemnation and urban redevelopment proceedings
- to establish a basis for taxes
- in connection with real estate insurance work
- to settle estates and partition real property interests
- in establishing rentals

There are different kinds of value other than those recorded here, each of which is of less concern to the license applicant.

DEFINITIONS

Because real estate is such a dynamic part of the world's various economic and governmental structures, the real estate appraiser must rely on specific definitions in order to clearly define and establish the value which must be estimated.

Here are some interesting definitions pertinent to the real estate broker's and salesperson's business.

AN APPRAISAL

An appraisal is an *estimate* or *opinion* of the value of property, based on an appraiser's analysis—(The appraiser is an informed observer of the forces which affect real estate values.) Based on experience, education, and market attunement, the appraiser estimates (but does not determine) property value, and by applying one or more value analysis methods and other techniques adequately supports the finished estimate, called an appraisal.

The general public engages in the appraisal activity to satisfy individual needs. The general real estate vocational group, comprising brokers, salespersons, managers, etc., deals with value problems in its daily work. While members are usually not professional appraisers, their vocation requires a general knowledge of evaluation economics. The professional appraiser is one who has been recognized as competent, knowledgeable, and skillful in real estate economics. This recognition has come about through education, years of real estate exposure, and professional designations.

VALUE

Value has many meanings, but for the real estate appraiser, three basic elements must be present in order to create value. Real estate has value when it has *utility* (usefulness, or the ability to arouse desire to own) and *scarcity*. Both utility and scarcity must be present to some degree. However, another factor must also be present, *purchasing power* (the ability of the public to satisfy its desire to own property).

Market Value

The market value is usually the appraiser's concern. Both the appraisers and the courts have accepted the following definitions of it.

The highest price estimated in terms of money which a property will bring if exposed for sale in the open market, allowing a reasonable time to find a purchaser who buys with knowledge of all the uses to which it is adapted and for which it is capable of being used.

or

The price at which a willing seller would sell and a willing buyer would buy, both being informed and knowledgeable of the property's utility and neither acting under duress.

Probable Selling Price

Brokers use this term interchangeably with "sales value." The probable selling price is important to the real estate licensee, since neither broker nor salesperson can afford to handle a property on which the owner has set a price too far out of line with its "market value."

Simply stated, the informed professional appraiser recognizes the difference between probable selling price and market value as represented by:

1. The value definition, establishing the well-informed, willing, and able parties

2. The background requirements for the market value estimate; for example, the purpose and limiting conditions which the client, the appraiser, or the law might impose

HIGHEST AND BEST USE

The highest and best use is the most profitable likely use to which a property can be put as of the date of the appraisal. It is the legal and economic use which will yield to land the highest present value.

DEPRECIATION

Depreciation is a loss from an initial upper limit of value from all causes.

CAPITALIZATION

The process of computing current value from expected future income is called capitalization.

CAPITALIZATION RATE

The capitalization rate is a percentage. It is made up of the interest rate (return on the land and improvement) and recapture rate (return of the improvement investment, which is a wasting asset).

GROSS RENT MULTIPLIER

The gross rent multiplier (GRM) is a figure which multiplied by the annual or monthly gross income of a property produces an estimate of the value of that property. It is obtained by dividing the value by either the annual or the monthly gross income.

ECONOMIC LIFE

A property's economic life is the period during which it will yield a return on the investment, over and above the economic or ground rent due to land. (It is the life-span during which the improvement on the land can reasonably be expected to pay a return *on* and *of* the improvement investment.)

FORCES AFFECTING MARKET VALUE

In order to arrive at an estimated value, the appraiser must have a firm understanding of the forces which influence prices and costs in the market place, and which consequently affect market value. Four general groups of forces are:

1. Social forces
2. Economic forces
3. Governmental forces
4. Physical forces

Changes in population growth and composition, personal attitudes and preferences, living styles and habits, and environmental movements are typical of social forces. Economic forces include the quality and quantity of natural resources, the availability of money and credit, price levels, wages in effect, and the level of interest rates. Governmental forces include zoning and building ordinances; sewer moratoria and capital improvements budgeting; local, state and federal housing and subsidy programs; and the monetary and fiscal policy of the federal government. Some of the more important physical forces are climate, topography, weather, and ecological considerations. All these forces in varying degrees continually change the value of any parcel of property.

THE APPRAISAL PROCESS

The phrase "appraisal process" denotes the orderly procedure of analysis which an appraiser performs in arriving at a value estimate. Whether the property to be appraised is a residence, vacant land, a warehouse, an apartment building, or a shopping center, essentially the same process is applicable.

First, the appraiser must define the problem to be solved. The problem will center on the nature of the interest in real property to be appraised. The appraiser must establish whether the property being evaluated is a fee simple estate, a leasehold estate, an easement, a reversion, or one of the other types of estate. The appraiser must then identify the property, state the purpose of the appraisal and the value to be estimated, and ascertain the date at which the value estimate applies.

The value indicators, or increments, which the property possesses are to be established. Based on the market's reaction to these indicators, the highest and best use is resolved. These value indicators or increments include the characteristics of the subject property, such as number of bedrooms and bathrooms, as well as neighborhood location, upkeep, and amenity features such as schools, among other things.

Second, the appraiser must determine how much work will be involved in solving the problem. By knowing what must be done, the appraiser can plan and schedule his or her time to complete the work required in the time available.

Third, the appraiser must collect the data to be analyzed and, after collecting it, classify it. Three approaches to analyzing data to arrive at a value estimate have been developed: the sales comparison or market data approach, the cost approach, and the income approach. More will be said about these three approaches later.

Fourth, the results of the different approaches must be correlated so that a defensible value range indicated by the separate approach analyses can be arrived at. A medium or average result is not correct. The appraiser should determine the most reliable estimate supportable by the data collected and the purpose of the appraisal.

Fifth, the appraiser presents the conclusions in a written report.

THE SITE

ANALYSIS

Land and its improvements (buildings, etc.) constitute real estate. The improvements require the land base—the land stands alone. The site analysis covers title and record data, physical data, and relationship of the location to competitive economic forces. Such an analysis enables the appraiser to determine the highest and best use. The appraiser must study other sites and uses of similar land in the area to decide whether the site under evaluation is being utilized to its highest and best use.

UTILIZATION—ACTUAL VS. POTENTIAL

Site valuation compares similar land sales, adjusted for location, time, physical characteristics, and economic utility. Adjusting such sales data to the site under evaluation results in a reasoned and rational value estimate. Most sites have various possible uses, and often the actual use hinders an orderly progression to a potential use. If the land is underimproved, the appraiser must check land sales in areas with several different uses.

This expands the area of research, which leads to a reasoned highest and best use estimate.

There is an appraisal axiom which maintains that land does not depreciate. This axiom is based on the recognition that improvements to land represent wasting assets, while the land itself persists indefinitely.

CONSISTENT USE THEORY

This theory states that a property in transition to another use cannot be valued on the basis of one use for land and another for improvements; this would be inconsistent with the economics of valuation. Therefore, while land is not depreciable, it can be encumbered by an interim use which is an underimprovement (for example, a downtown parking lot). For the licensee's purpose, appraisals of transitional land areas must be based on the value of the present improvements as they relate to the interim period needed to consummate a transition to an ultimate highest and best use. Simply stated, economics will not justify a demolition cost for improvements when such improvements can provide a desirable return to the property for an interim period. In transitional areas, the consistent use theory is a most important tool to the licensee.

PRINCIPLE OF SUBSTITUTION

Simply stated, this principle recognizes that when two or more properties with substantially the same utility are available, the lowest price prevails. This is an appraisal principle applicable in all three value approaches.

1. The value of an equally desirable substitute property tends to establish an upper value limit.

2. A property value tends to coincide with the values informed buyers place on comparable properties.

3. The cost of producing, through new construction, a replica or equally desirable substitute property usually sets the upper value limit.

THREE APPROACHES TO VALUE ESTIMATION

Cost Approach

This approach is based on the axiom that the value of a structure, or improvement, should not exceed the current cost of reproducing or replacing the structure or improvement, less an allowance for depreciation. The informed market will not willingly purchase a property at a price too much in excess of the current reproduction or replacement cost of the improvements, plus the land's contributory value, less the current improvement depreciation estimate. Thus, the following equation has been recognized as representing an upper limit to value:

Land value
+ reproduction or replacement cost estimate
− depreciation estimate for improvements

The basic procedure for estimating land value has been described in the preceding section. In the cost approach, the land is presumed to be vacant. Land does not depreciate but can be affected by the prevailing current use.

REPLACEMENT AND REPRODUCTION COSTS

Replacement cost and reproduction cost are distinguished by the words "equally desirable substitute" and "new replica property."

Replacement cost is the present cost of an equally desirable substitute in which some of the functional obsolescence would be cured; for example, excessive ceiling height or poor or outdated design features.

Reproduction cost is the present cost of producing a new replica property using the same materials and design.

There are several recognized procedures for estimating reproduction or replacement cost new. For the purpose here, the identification of these procedures suffices. The quantity survey, the unit-in-place, and the comparative (square foot or cubic foot) methods are used interchangeably by appraisers. The interested licensee is referred to appraisal textbooks for more information about these methods. There are two important facts to remember. Reproduction means a replica structure; replacement, a substitute improvement having comparable utility. Depreciation estimates must be properly premised on the cost-new estimate employed.

DEPRECIATION

From the cost-new estimate, the appraiser should deduct an amount which will represent accrued depreciation for the improvements. Such depreciation estimates represent a loss in value from the cost-new estimate. The recognized methods of estimating accrued depreciation are:

The breakdown method (observed)

The engineering method (observed)

The straight line method (age-life)

The capitalization method

The market methods

The interested licensee is again referred to the general category of appraisal textbooks.

There are several types of depreciation.

Physical Deterioration

This is the loss of value caused by wear and tear or action of the elements, such as cracks, peeling paint, or structural defects.

Functional Obsolescence

This is the loss from the cost-new value caused by inadequacies within the property, such as poor or outdated design features, high ceilings, or poor room arrangement.

Economic Obsolescence

This is a loss of value caused by factors outside the property. Inharmonious uses, both private and governmental, will result in a loss of value. Examples are conflicting residential and commercial uses, high-use roads, and airport flight patterns.

The various types of depreciation are considered to be either curable or incurable.

Curable

Curable depreciation includes items of physical deterioration and functional obsolescence which are usually repaired or replaced. If the cost to repair or replace an item is greater than the added value resulting from the repairs or replacement, that item would be considered incurable.

Incurable

Incurable depreciation includes those items that are not yet ready to be cured or that it is not economically feasible to cure. Capitalizing the rental loss will measure the value loss.

The cost to cure is usually the best method of measuring curable items.

It is noted that cost data is difficult to gather and analyze. Unless substantial building cost records are handy, older buildings are not easy to estimate. For these and other reasons, the cost approach to value estimation is considered to be less accurate than the other two approaches. The appraiser does recognize that the relative worth of the three approaches depends on the factual worth of the supporting market data used for each approach. The better the input, the better the output!

There are circumstances which require the use of the cost approach. When there are no comparable sales and the subject property is one which is not income-producing, such as a public library, the cost approach must be used. In such cases, the appraiser's supporting data (land, construction, depreciation) become the only value support. However, there are bracketing processes whereby the various data can be reanalyzed and given additional support (for example, one or more depreciation methods can be used).

Sales Comparison or Market Data Approach

This approach is based on the axiom that a subject property will have a value approximating the value of properties similar in location, type, use, and physical characteristics. Through the discovery and verification of similar property sales, a close approximation of the *probable selling price* for a subject property can be made. By researching and analyzing those sales, the indicative value increments (property and neighborhood characteristics) can be compared with the subject property. For example, the appraiser can compare the personal property involved in a sale; difference in lot size, frontage, area, etc.; and improvements' physical condition and functional obsolescence. A value estimate can then be made.

In performing the market data approach, the appraiser searches for similar properties which have sold in that and neighboring areas, as well as available listings and offerings. The next task is to analyze the offering prices and the actual sales prices, and then compare the pertinent characteristics of the subject property and the comparable properties. Based upon such an analysis, the appraiser makes adjustments in price, either upward or downward, from the prices of comparable properties to formulate an opinion of the value of the property being appraised.

The market approach is most commonly used in the real estate brokerage business. The broker finds the supporting data more readily available, and the broker is more attuned to the analysis process. When listing a property, the real estate broker is actually called upon to make an appraisal, for he or she is asked to ascertain the price at which a willing buyer will buy the property from the owner who is engaging the broker.

Income Approach

This approach is premised on the axiom that the informed market will pay the present worth of the net income a property will produce during its remaining economic life. The technique of transforming income into value is called *capitalization*. It is not a difficult process to understand and can be simply illustrated by the following essential steps.

A. Estimate gross income

    1. Deduct estimate of vacancy

B. Effective gross income is the result

C. Estimate fixed and operating expenses

    1. Deduct expense estimate from effective gross income

D. Net income results

E. Select a capitalization rate

F. Divide net income by capitalization rate

G. Value estimate results

Gross income is equal to the total amount of receipts attributable to the real property. Since this approach requires an analysis of both income and expenses, it is obvious that it is used only when the subject property actually generates some income and expense figures. There could be exceptions which are not pertinent to this

text. The appraiser must obtain all the available information concerning rent schedules and percentage of occupancy for the subject property and similar properties. This information is used to estimate gross and effective gross income for the subject property, assuming economic and sound management.

Next, the appraiser estimates the total fixed and operating expenses, again assuming economic and sound management. The detail expense items include taxes, operating and maintenance items, and reserves for replacements, but exclude mortgage expenses. Total expenses subtracted from the effective gross income is the net income.

CAPITALIZATION RATE

The appraiser then selects a capitalization rate. It is sufficient to say that the choice of a capitalization rate is one of the more difficult concepts to grasp for one unfamiliar with appraisal techniques.

When searching for a capitalization rate, the appraiser analyzes the quality, quantity, and durability of income; the expected remaining life of the property; and the earnings expectations of investors in the market. When an appraiser assigns a capitalization rate, it indicates that the appraiser feels that an investor who would be interested in that property would require that capitalization rate. Actually, the capitalization rate incorporates three aspects:

1. Return on the land

2. Return on the building

3. Return of capital invested in the building

Return on the land and return on the building means that the investor who has invested money in the land and building is entitled to receive an investment return on the money. For example, if the investor had deposited money in a Savings and Loan Association, the S & L would credit the account with interest each year. If the investor purchased stock in a corporation, it would pay quarterly dividends on the stock. In the same manner, an owner of investment real estate expects a return on funds invested. If United States Government Bonds pay 6 percent interest per year, and the Savings and Loan Associations pay $6\frac{1}{2}$ percent interest per year, it is reasonable to assume that a real estate investor would expect a rate higher than either of these rates because there are more risks in the ownership of real estate. An investment property that is more risky will require a higher rate of return that an investment property whose income is fairly safe.

Because a building depreciates as it ages, value is lost. To compensate the owner for this loss in value, the capitalization rate includes a provision called return "of" investment, or *recapture*. The recapture rate is derived by dividing 100 by the remaining economic life of the building. For example, a building with a remaining economic life of 25 years has a yearly recapture rate of 4 percent (100 ÷ 25). A building with a remaining economic life of 40 years has a yearly recapture rate of 2.5 percent (100 ÷ 40).

The appraiser then combines the rate of return on the land and building with the recapture rate of the building to arrive at the capitalization rate, using one of several techniques (not discussed here).

Basic arithmetic formulae:

$$\text{Income} = \text{capitalization rate} \times \text{value}$$

$$\text{Capitalization rate} = \text{income} \div \text{value}$$

$$\text{Value} = \text{income} \div \text{capitalization rate}$$

Several examples will illustrate the capitalization process. If an office building has an annual net income of $24,000 and a capitalization rate of 8 percent is applicable, the correct procedure is:

$$\text{Value} = \text{income} \div \text{capitalization rate}$$

$$\text{Value} = \$24{,}000 \div .08$$

$$\text{Value} = \$300{,}000$$

If an apartment house has an annual net income of $80,000 and a capitalization rate of 12.5 percent is applicable, the steps to follow are:

$$\text{Value} = \text{income} \div \text{capitalization rate}$$

$$\text{Value} = \$80{,}000 \div .125$$

$$\text{Value} = \$640{,}000$$

Another example illustrates another formula. If an apartment house has an apparent or indicated value of $500,000 and a capitalization rate of 10 percent, its annual net income should be:

$$\text{Income} = \text{capitalization rate} \times \text{value}$$

$$\text{Income} = .10 \times \$500{,}000$$

$$\text{Income} = \$50{,}000$$

GROSS RENT MULTIPLIER (GRM) FOR SINGLE-FAMILY HOUSES

Single-family residential properties are not usually considered income-producing properties, and the income approach to estimating their value, discussed above, cannot be used. Instead the appraiser relies on the capitalization of the monthly gross rent through the use of a factor called a *gross rent multiplier* (GRM).

Because there is a relationship between the value of a property and the amount of rent that property can command in the market, a factor can be obtained by dividing a property's value by the monthly rent it can command. Example: Property that has a value of $30,000 and can be rented for $150 per month would have a gross rent multiplier of 200 ($30,000 ÷ 150).

This factor can now be used to give an indication of value or to measure certain types of depreciation.

Example: A house is actually rented for $185.00 monthly, and from other similar properties in the area you have developed a GRM of 200. You can then obtain an indication of value of $37,000 ($185 × 200).

Example: A property being appraised lacks a master bedroom bath, which other properties in the neighborhood have. From the market you estimate the rental loss to be $5 per month because of the lack of a master bath. Therefore, the depreciation would be $1,000 ($5 × 200). This would be considered functional obsolescence, incurable if it would cost more than $1,000 to install a master bath.

Note: *The gross rent multiplier can be a very useful tool to help the knowledgeable appraiser get a feel for the market. However, extreme care should be used to arrive at the GRM for each particular area where it is used.*

CORRELATION

In appraisal work, *correlation* refers to the technique of arriving at a final estimate of value by bringing into perspective the value estimates arrived at through the use of two or all three of the separate approaches to value: the cost approach, the sales comparison or market data approach, and the income approach. The appraiser examines the values indicated by each approach. He or she then places emphasis upon the value indicated by the one approach or more which is felt to be most reliable in the circumstances surrounding the appraisal at hand. He or she then adjusts the estimate to arrive at the final value conclusion. The axiom is that the approach which demonstrates the use of the best factual data and the soundest analysis thereof produces the best value estimate.

THE APPRAISAL REPORT

Appraisals are typically presented in one of three ways: a certificate or letter, a standardized form report, or a narrative report. Whether the final report is a one-page letter or a voluminous narrative, certain elements should always be present in any appraisal report. They are:

1. A value estimate

2. The date to which the value estimate applies

3. The certification and signature of the appraiser

4. The purpose for which the appraisal is made

5. Any qualifying conditions

6. Description of the property

7. Analysis of factual data and presentation of any descriptive material required

APPRAISAL ORGANIZATIONS

There are many appraisal organizations, some local in scope and some statewide; some representing specialist groups, such as real estate assessors, and others that present an international position and deal with general areas of real estate activities. Four organizations are noted below.

The American Institute of Real Estate Appraisers

This group covers the total real estate field. It is affiliated with the NATIONAL ASSOCIATION OF REALTORS. Its membership categories are MAI (Member, Appraisal Institute) and RM (Residential Member). A candidate affiliation is part of the membership. The MAI and RM designations are awards based on completion of required courses, examinations, approval of demonstration appraisals, and satisfying experience requirements. The accrediting initials (MAI or RM) may then be placed after a member's name to signal his or her standing as a professional appraiser.

The Institute publishes textbooks, journals, and newsletters and sponsors real estate appraisal courses and seminars.

The Society of Real Estate Appraisers

This group also covers the total real estate field. Its membership categories are SRA (Senior Residential Appraiser), SRPA (Senior Real Property Appraiser), and SREA (Senior Real Estate Analyst). An associate affiliation is part of the membership. The total membership is the largest of any appraisal organization. The membership designations are awards based on requirements similar to those set forth for the MAI's.

The Society also publishes textbooks, journals, and newsletters and sponsors real estate appraisal courses and seminars.

A 1974 survey indicated that the members of both appraisal organizations (The American Institute of Real Estate Appraisers and the Society of Real Estate Appraisers) would like to consolidate into one.

The American Society of Appraisers

This group covers the total real estate field plus the appraisal of personal property, fine arts, and equipment. Its membership categories are Associate, Member, and ASA (Senior Member) and FASA (Fellow, American Society of Appraisers). The designations are broken down to the specialty fields, such as fine arts or machinery and equipment. An associate affiliation is part of the membership. The designations are awarded based on requirements similar to those mentioned before. It also publishes material and sponsors courses.

The American Society of Farm Managers and Rural Appraisers

This is a specialty group, as indicated by its name. The designation of AFA (Accredited Farm Appraiser) is awarded based on the requirements previously mentioned. The group sponsors courses and seminars and publishes material pertinent to the specialty and technical field it represents.

STANDARDS OF PRACTICE

Each organization discussed in this text has a Code of Ethics, all quite similar in scope and purpose. Generally, the appraiser considers it unethical to:

1. Collect a fee contingent upon appraisal findings

2. Have an interest in a property being appraised and not state that interest

3. Make any misrepresentations

4. Reveal the opinion of value or other elements in the report to anyone other than the client without the client's authorization

5. Advertise for appraisal business in a manner not consistent with accepted professional practice

PRACTICE EXAMINATION: REAL ESTATE APPRAISAL

1. In appraising a single-purpose building such as a church, the most reliable approach to an indication of its value would generally be the

   (A) cost approach
   (B) market data approach
   (C) income approach
   (D) both A and C

2. In the application of the capitalization approach to appraising, which of the following statements is (are) true?

   I. The higher the capitalization rate, the lower the appraised value.
   II. The higher the capitalization rate, the higher the appraised value.

   (A) I only   (C) Both I and II
   (B) II only   (D) Neither I nor II

3. The real estate appraiser

   I. Determines the value of property through an orderly procedure called the appraisal process
   II. Estimates the value of property

   (A) I only   (C) Both I and II
   (B) II only   (D) Neither I nor II

4. Which of the following must be present in order for real estate to have value?

   (A) Utility and scarcity
   (B) Purchasing power
   (C) Both A and B
   (D) Neither A nor B

5. Obsolescence in real property has two forms, functional and economic. With regard to these forms, which of the following is (are) true?

   I. Functional obsolescence is the result of factors within the property itself.
   II. Economic obsolescence is caused by factors outside the property.

   (A) I only   (C) Both I and II
   (B) II only   (D) Neither I nor II

6. Depreciation can be caused by which of the following factors?

   (A) Physical deterioration
   (B) Functional obsolescence
   (C) Economic obsolescence
   (D) All the above

7. A capitalization rate incorporates

   (A) return on land and building and recapture of building
   (B) return on land and recapture of land and building
   (C) return on building and recapture of land and building
   (D) return on land and building and recapture of land

8. The return on investment that a real estate investor expects is generally higher than the interest the investor would earn from a savings account because

   (A) banks are more risky
   (B) the real estate investment involves a lower degree of risk
   (C) the real estate investment involves a higher degree of risk
   (D) none of these

9. You are appraising a 20-year-old apartment house. When this building was constructed, the neighborhood was exclusively residential. Today, scattered industrial uses are found in the area. This is an example of

   (A) functional obsolescence
   (B) economic obsolescence
   (C) physical deterioration
   (D) none of these

10. A building 10 years old is being appraised today. It has a useful remaining life of 25 years. The applicable recapture rate is

    (A) 20 percent   (C) 25 percent
    (B) 4 percent   (D) 2.50 percent

11. Reproduction cost is

    (A) the cost of reproducing a building with the same material and design
    (B) the cost of replacing a building with one of the same utility
    (C) the price similar properties have sold for
    (D) none of the above

12. A capitalization rate of 10 percent applied to a net income of $15,000 will indicate a value that is _____ the value indicated when an 8 percent capitalization rate is applied to an income of $15,000.

    (A) less than   (C) equal to
    (B) greater than   (D) none of these

13. The appraisal method most commonly used by real estate licensees in the course of their business is the

    (A) cost approach   (C) income approach
    (B) market approach   (D) none of these

14. The appraisal process refers to an orderly procedure of analysis which is applicable to

    (A) residential property
    (B) industrial property
    (C) commercial property
    (D) all the above

15. The four general groups of forces that affect the value of a given property are

    (A) population, natural resources, prices, and social forces
    (B) money and credit, zoning, building ordinances, and social forces
    (C) economic, social, physical, and governmental forces
    (D) natural, economic, social, and physical forces

16. The first thing an appraiser should know in undertaking an appraisal is

    (A) how he or she is getting paid
    (B) the selling price of the property
    (C) the purpose of the appraisal
    (D) what property has sold for recently in the area

17. It is unethical for a real estate appraiser to

    (A) have a hidden interest in the property being appraised
    (B) collect a fee contingent upon the findings
    (C) both A and B
    (D) neither A nor B

18. Governmental forces affect the value of real property. Which of the following would be a part of the governmental forces?

    (A) Environmental movements
    (B) Ecological considerations
    (C) Housing and subsidy programs
    (D) None of these

19. One type of depreciation is generally not curable. It is

    (A) physical deterioration
    (B) functional obsolescence
    (C) negligence
    (D) economic obsolescence

20. Methods of estimating accrued depreciation include

    (A) the breakdown method
    (B) the engineering method
    (C) the market method
    (D) all of these

Chapter 11
Basics of Real Estate Mathematics

SCOPE

Table of Land Measurements

Linear Measure		Square Measure	
1 in	= .0833 ft	144 sq in	= 1 sq ft
7.92 in	= 1 link	9 sq ft	= 1 sq yd
12 in	= 1 ft	$30\frac{1}{2}$ sq yd	= 1 sq rod
1 vara	= 33 in	16 sq rods	= 1 sq chain
$2\frac{3}{4}$ ft	= 1 vara	1 sq rod	= $272\frac{1}{4}$ sq ft
3 ft	= 1 yd	1 sq chain	= 4,356 sq ft
25 links	= $16\frac{1}{2}$ ft	10 sq chains	= 1 acre
25 links	= 1 rod	160 sq rods	= 1 acre
100 links	= 1 chain	4,840 sq yd	= 1 acre
$16\frac{1}{2}$ feet	= 1 rod	43,560 sq ft	= 1 acre
$5\frac{1}{2}$ yards	= 1 rod	640 acres	= 1 sq mi
4 rods	= 100 links	1 sq mi	= 1 section
66 ft	= 1 chain	36 sq mi	= 1 Twp
80 chains	= 1 mi	6 mi square	= 1 Twp
320 rods	= 1 mi	1 sq mi	= 2.59 sq km
8,000 links	= 1 mi		
5,280 ft	= 1 mi		
1,760 yd	= 1 mi		

AN ACRE IS:

43,560 sq ft   660 ft X 66 ft

165 ft X 264 ft   160 sq rods

198 ft X 220 ft   208'8" square

or any rectangular tract, the product of the length and width of which totals 43,560 sq ft.

INTRODUCTION

The purpose of this chapter is to help you renew your familiarity with the basics of general arithmetic and to present to you the types of mathematical problems which you will face in the various examination questions on real estate technology, sales, and brokerage. There are only a limited number of basic types of problems on which you are likely to be examined. You will be tested on your ability to compute fractions, decimals, percentages, perimeter, prorations, ratio and proportion, and area and volume. Some questions may involve two or more of the above.

The true test of understanding is whether you can *read the problem, interpret what information is given and what must be computed,* actually complete the arithmetic process (generally the easiest step of all), and most important, check that your answer is reasonable and/or correct. Since most problems are written in narrative form or described verbally by a client, the first task is to convert a "word problem" to arithmetic shorthand. The most important thing to remember is to *read the problem*

carefully and not assume anything that is not specifically stated or implied. Probably the next most important thing is to check the final answer. When you are taking an exam, the thoroughness of your checking is naturally going to depend on how much time you have. Most mistakes will generally occur in the simple processes of adding, subtracting, multiplying, dividing, and placing the decimal in the correct place. The most complete way to check for these errors is to review all the arithmetical steps in the "opposite direction"—adding up, reversing the two numbers being multiplied, multiplying the quotient by the divisor, etc. When time is short, a good fast check is to round off the numbers to those you can do in your head to see if the answer is in the "right ball park."

Example: If $\frac{7}{16}$ of the living room floor area (263 sq ft) is carpeted, how much carpet is needed?

(A) 180 sq ft (C) 63 sq ft
(B) 94 sq ft (D) 115 sq ft

After you have computed your answer, check it by the following "thinking process:" Consider that $\frac{7}{16}$ is almost $\frac{1}{2}$ ($\frac{8}{16}$) and 263 is slightly larger than 260. As an approximation, $\frac{1}{2}$ of 260 would be 130. Checking the choices given shows that choice (D) is the most likely. If your computations do not agree, recheck them.

Example: An agent's commission on a $49,000 house is 6%. What is the amount of the commission?

(A) $2,400 (C) $3,200
(B) $2,940 (D) $2,200

Your thinking process would be: $49,000 is approximately $50,000, and 6% of $50,000 would be $3,000, and so the correct answer should be just a little less. In checking you see that choice (B) is the most logical answer.

It is often possible to select the correct answer just by the "thinking process" without doing any computations. Think the problem through, then look at the choices given. If one answer stands out, it is more than likely correct.

Caution should be exercised when using this process. Often an answer will be given that appears correct if you carelessly take the wrong approach to the problem.

Example: What would be the refund due a seller who had purchased a 3-year insurance policy July 10 of last year for $360? The property has now been sold and settlement is scheduled for July 10 of this year.

(A) $120 (C) $140
(B) $160 (D) $240

If you think this through, 1 year or $\frac{1}{3}$ of the total has been used, the total cost was $360, and $\frac{1}{3}$ of $360 is $120. Looking at the choices shows $120 as the first choice, so you might choose it. However, the policy was used 1 year, and a 3-year policy was purchased, so the refund would be for 2 years or $240, choice (D).

Another helpful hint is that "of" can almost always be replaced by "times" and indicates multiplication.

Example: One-fifth of the $100 sales price was profit.

$$\text{Profit} = \frac{1}{5} \times \$100 = \frac{\$100}{5} = \$20$$

In summary, general steps to complete problems are:

1. Read and determine what you are seeking.

2. Rewrite it in arithmetic language.

3. Complete the arithmetic processes.

4. Check your answer to see if it is reasonable.

FRACTIONS

A fraction is the quotient of two whole numbers. It may or may not be a whole number. It is written with the dividend, called the *numerator*, over the divisor, called the *denominator*. Thus, $2 \div 3 = \frac{2}{3}$, where 2 is the numerator and 3 is the denominator. Also, $4 \div 1 = \frac{4}{1} = 4$, so any whole number can be considered as a fraction with 1 as the denominator. When the numerator is smaller than the denominator, the fraction is a *simple fraction* and has a value less than 1. Examples: $\frac{3}{4}, \frac{1}{7}, \frac{19}{20}$. An *improper fraction* has a value greater than 1 and the numerator larger than the denominator. Examples: $\frac{3}{2}, \frac{7}{4}, \frac{11}{6}$. An improper fraction can be reduced to a *mixed number* by completing the division process.

Example:

$$\frac{7}{4} = 7 \div 4 = 1\frac{3}{4} \text{ , which means } 1 + \frac{3}{4}$$

Notice that the remainder of the division, 3, was placed over the divisor, 4, to form the fractional part of the mixed number.

Example:

$$\frac{32}{9} = 32 \div 9 = 3\frac{5}{9} \quad \text{or} \quad 3 + \frac{5}{9}$$

Fundamental Rule of Fractions

When the numerator and denominator of a fraction are both multiplied or divided by the same number, the value of the fraction is unchanged.

Examples:

$$\frac{2}{3} = \frac{2 \times (4)}{3 \times (4)} = \frac{8 \times (3)}{12 \times (3)} = \frac{24}{36}, \text{ etc.}$$

$$\frac{24}{36} = \frac{24 \div (2)}{36 \div (2)} = \frac{12}{18} = \frac{12 \div (6)}{18 \div (6)} = \frac{2}{3}, \text{ etc.}$$

Reducing Fractions

To change a fraction to its lowest terms, divide its numerator and denominator by the largest whole number which will divide both exactly.

Example: Reduce $\frac{56}{84}$ to its lowest terms.

$$\frac{56}{84} = \frac{56 \div 7}{84 \div 7} = \frac{8}{12} = \frac{8 \div 4}{12 \div 4} = \frac{2}{3}$$

Note that it is often easier to reduce a fraction in several steps using numbers you can recognize more easily. If in doubt, try dividing by 2, 3, 5, or 7.

Example:

$$\frac{112}{168} = \frac{112 \div 2}{168 \div 2} = \frac{56}{84} = \frac{56 \div 2}{84 \div 2} = \frac{28}{42} = \frac{28 \div 2}{42 \div 2} = \frac{14}{21}$$

$$\frac{14}{21} = \frac{14 \div 7}{21 \div 7} = \frac{2}{3}$$

or the same problem

$$\frac{112}{168} = \frac{112 \div 8}{168 \div 8} = \frac{14}{21} = \frac{14 \div 7}{21 \div 7} = \frac{2}{3}$$

Changing Mixed Numbers to Improper Fractions

To change a mixed number to an improper fraction, multiply the whole number by the denominator of the fraction, add the numerator to the product, and place the sum over the denominator.

Examples:

$$4\frac{6}{7} = \frac{4 \times 7}{7} + \frac{6}{7} = \frac{28 + 6}{7} = \frac{34}{7}$$

$$\text{or} \quad 5\frac{7}{10} = \frac{5 \times 10}{10} + \frac{7}{10} = \frac{50}{10} + \frac{7}{10} = \frac{57}{10}$$

Adding and Subtracting Fractions

Just as you can't add or subtract apples and oranges or feet and yards until they have been changed to a common unit, you can't add and subtract fractions until they have the same denominator, called a *common denominator*. To get a common denominator, use the fundamental rule of fractions and multiply the numerator and denominator of one fraction by the denominator of the other fraction.

It is necessary to rewrite each fraction as an equivalent one with the common denominator. Then you add or subtract the numerators and place the answer over the common denominator.

Example:

$$\frac{2}{3} + \frac{4}{7} = ?$$

$$\frac{2}{3} = \frac{2 \times (7)}{3 \times (7)} = \frac{14}{21}$$

$$\frac{4}{7} = \frac{4 \times (3)}{7 \times (3)} = \frac{12}{21}$$

Now add these by *adding only the numerators.*

$$\frac{14}{21} + \frac{12}{21} = \frac{26}{21} = 1\frac{5}{21}$$

Example:

$$\frac{1}{3} + \frac{4}{5} = ?$$

$$\frac{1}{3} = \frac{1 \times 5}{3 \times 5} = \frac{5}{15}$$

$$\frac{4}{5} = \frac{4 \times 3}{5 \times 3} = \frac{12}{15}$$

$$\frac{5}{15} + \frac{12}{15} = \frac{17}{15} = 1\frac{2}{15}$$

When adding more than two fractions, you rely on the fundamental rule of fractions, multiplying by all the denominators of the remaining fractions.

Example:

$$\frac{1}{3} + \frac{4}{5} + \frac{6}{7} = ?$$

$$\frac{1}{3} = \frac{1 \times 5 \times 7}{3 \times 5 \times 7} = \frac{35}{105}$$

$$\frac{4}{5} = \frac{4 \times 3 \times 7}{5 \times 3 \times 7} = \frac{84}{105}$$

$$\frac{6}{7} = \frac{6 \times 3 \times 5}{7 \times 3 \times 5} = \frac{90}{105}$$

$$\frac{35}{105} + \frac{84}{105} + \frac{90}{105} = \frac{209}{105} = 1\frac{104}{105}$$

Example:

$$\frac{3}{8} + \frac{1}{2} + \frac{4}{6} = ?$$

$$\frac{3}{8} = \frac{3 \times 2 \times 6}{8 \times 2 \times 6} = \frac{36}{96}$$

$$\frac{1}{2} = \frac{1 \times 8 \times 6}{2 \times 8 \times 6} = \frac{48}{96}$$

$$\frac{4}{6} = \frac{4 \times 8 \times 2}{6 \times 8 \times 2} = \frac{64}{96}$$

$$\frac{36}{96} + \frac{48}{96} + \frac{64}{96} = \frac{148}{96} = 1\frac{52}{96} = 1\frac{13}{24}$$

In some instances a common denominator can be found that is lower in value than the one arrived at by multiplying all the denominators together. The common denominator is chosen by finding some number divisible evenly by all the given denominators.

Example:

$$\frac{1}{8} + \frac{3}{4} + \frac{5}{6} = ?$$

Using the original process the common denominator would be 192 (8 × 4 × 6). However, notice that 24 is also divisible by 8, 4, and 6. Using 24 as a common denominator

$$\frac{1}{8} = \frac{1 \times 3}{8 \times 3} = \frac{3}{24}$$

(8 divides into 24 three times. This was used in the fundamental rule.)

$$\frac{3}{4} = \frac{3 \times 6}{4 \times 6} = \frac{18}{24}$$

$$\frac{5}{6} = \frac{5 \times 4}{6 \times 4} = \frac{20}{24}$$

$$\frac{3}{24} + \frac{18}{24} + \frac{20}{24} = \frac{41}{24} = 1\frac{17}{24}$$

Multiplying Fractions

To multiply a fraction by a fraction, place the product of the numerators over the product of the denominators. (Remember that a whole number is also a fraction with a denominator of 1.) Then reduce it to its lowest terms.

Examples:

$$\frac{7}{12} \times \frac{2}{3} = \frac{7 \times 2}{12 \times 3} = \frac{14}{36} = \frac{7}{18}$$

$$\text{or} \quad 5 \times \frac{11}{14} = \frac{5 \times 11}{1 \times 14} = \frac{55}{14} = 3\frac{13}{14}$$

Dividing Fractions

To divide fractions, invert the divisor (turn it upside down) and multiply.

Examples:

$$\frac{9}{16} \div \frac{2}{3} = \frac{9}{16} \times \frac{3}{2} = \frac{27}{32}$$

$$\text{or} \quad \frac{5}{7} \div 3 = \frac{5}{7} \times \frac{1}{3} = \frac{5}{21}$$

Cancellation

Cancellation is a great time saver and helps to eliminate careless mistakes when multiplying fractions. It consists of taking out factors common to both numerator and denominator before multiplying or dividing.

Example:

$$\frac{\overset{1}{\cancel{16}}}{\underset{3}{\cancel{27}}} \times \frac{\overset{1}{\cancel{18}}}{\underset{1}{\cancel{32}}} = \frac{1}{3}$$

$\dfrac{16}{27} \times \dfrac{18}{32}$ — The numerator 16 and the denominator 32 can each be divided by 16, making the problem now read

$\dfrac{1}{27} \times \dfrac{18}{2}$ — Now by dividing the denominator 27 and the numerator 18 by 9, the problem reads

$\dfrac{1}{3} \times \dfrac{2}{2}$ — The problem has now been reduced by cancellation to read

$\dfrac{2 \div 2}{6 \div 2} = \dfrac{1}{3}$ — Which is 2/6. Now by dividing both the numerator and the denominator by the common factor 2, the problem has been reduced to its lowest possible term 1/3, which is the final answer.

Example:

$$\frac{\overset{1}{\cancel{25}}}{\underset{16}{\cancel{32}}} \times \frac{\overset{\cancel{6}}{\cancel{6}}}{\underset{3}{\cancel{45}}} = \frac{5}{48}$$

$\dfrac{25}{32} \times \dfrac{6}{45}$ — The numerator 25 and the denominator 45 are both divisible by 5, changing the problem to

$\dfrac{5}{32} \times \dfrac{6}{9}$ — The numerator 6 and the denominator 32 are both divisible by 2, changing the problem to

$\dfrac{5}{16} \times \dfrac{3}{9}$ — The numerator 3 and the denominator 9 are both divisible by 3, changing the problem to

$\dfrac{5}{16} \times \dfrac{1}{3} = \dfrac{5}{48}$

Cancellation can never be applied to addition or subtraction of fractions.

Skill Drill

Remember to reduce or change to a mixed number where possible.

1. Fill in the blanks with the appropriate word

   a. A fraction with a value greater than one is a (an) _____ fraction.

   b. The bottom number of a fraction is the _____.

   c. A fraction is a (an) _____ of whole numbers.

   d. Mixed numbers are derived by _____ the denominator of an improper fraction into the numerator.

2. Using the fundamental rule, fill in the missing numbers or signs.

   a. $\dfrac{5 \times ?}{6 \times ?} = \dfrac{20}{24}$ c. $\dfrac{12\ ?\ 3}{48\ ?\ 3} = \dfrac{4}{16}$ e. $\dfrac{15}{63} = \dfrac{5}{?}$

   b. $\dfrac{11 \times ?}{12 \times ?} = \dfrac{?}{108}$ d. $\dfrac{3}{7} = \dfrac{?}{42}$

3. Reduce the following.

   a. $\dfrac{12}{16}$ d. $\dfrac{21}{36}$ g. $\dfrac{16}{32}$ j. $\dfrac{10}{12}$

   b. $\dfrac{9}{33}$ e. $\dfrac{20}{45}$ h. $\dfrac{45}{135}$ k. $\dfrac{36}{54}$

   c. $\dfrac{16}{64}$ f. $\dfrac{14}{42}$ i. $\dfrac{63}{108}$ l. $\dfrac{13}{39}$

4. Change each of the following to mixed numbers. Be sure to reduce all fractional parts when possible.

   a. $\dfrac{17}{3}$ c. $\dfrac{73}{6}$ e. $\dfrac{173}{10}$

   b. $\dfrac{29}{4}$ d. $\dfrac{49}{3}$ f. $\dfrac{73}{8}$

5. Add or subtract the following.

   a. $\dfrac{7}{8} - \dfrac{1}{4} =$ c. $\dfrac{3}{4} + \dfrac{1}{8} + \dfrac{1}{12} =$ e. $\dfrac{2}{3} - \dfrac{1}{4} =$

   b. $\dfrac{1}{8} + \dfrac{5}{12} =$ d. $\dfrac{2}{3} + \dfrac{4}{5} + \dfrac{7}{10} =$

6. Multiply or divide the following. Use cancellation where possible.

   a. $\dfrac{1}{2} \times \dfrac{6}{7} =$ c. $\dfrac{2}{3}$ of 66 =   e. $\dfrac{7}{9} \div \dfrac{2}{3} =$

   b. $\dfrac{3}{5} \div \dfrac{3}{4} =$ d. $\dfrac{3}{4} \times \dfrac{12}{15} \times \dfrac{2}{9} =$

DECIMALS

A decimal is essentially a fraction. The numerator is the numbers following the decimal point, and the denominator is 1 followed by a zero for each number in the numerator. If there is only one numeral to the right of the decimal, the denominator is 10; two numerals to the right of the decimal are put over 100; three are put over 1,000; etc.

Thus .1   .02   .003   .0004   etc.

Are $\dfrac{1}{10}$ $\dfrac{2}{100}$ $\dfrac{3}{1,000}$ $\dfrac{4}{10,000}$ etc.

.1 is one-tenth
.01 is one-hundredth
.001 is one-thousandth
.0001 is one-ten-thousandth

Changing Fractions to Decimals

Divide the numerator by the denominator and write the answer in decimal form. Recall that the decimal point is placed at the *end* of a whole number.

Example:

$\dfrac{3}{4} = 3.00 \div 4 = .75$

Example:

$\dfrac{7}{16} = 7.000 \div 16 = .4375$

If, when dividing, you get a *continuing pattern* of numbers, after the second repetition, round off the third digit. If the third digit is less than 5, leave the second digit as is; if the third digit is 5 or greater, round the second up 1.

Example:

$\dfrac{2}{9} = 9\overline{)2.000}^{.222} = .22$

or

$\dfrac{2}{3} = 3\overline{)2.000}^{.666} = .67$

Changing Decimals to Fractions

Write the decimal as a fraction with a denominator of 1 plus the correct number of zeros, then reduce the fraction.

Example:

$.375 = \dfrac{375}{1,000} = \dfrac{375 \div 25}{1,000 \div 25} = \dfrac{15}{40} = \dfrac{15 \div 5}{40 \div 5} = \dfrac{3}{8}$

or

$.65 = \dfrac{65}{100} = \dfrac{65 \div 5}{100 \div 5} = \dfrac{13}{20}$

Adding and Subtracting Decimals

Decimals are added and subtracted after the numbers are placed in a column with the decimal points in a column. The decimal point of the answer will be in the same column.

Examples:

```
 3.014              16.36
  .021     5.270      .005     1.369
  .007   − 3.104      3.1     −.25
 ─────    ──────    ───────   ──────
 3.042     2.166    19.465    1.119
```

Multiplying Decimals

Decimals are multiplied like whole numbers. In the product, begin at the right and point off (count) the total number of digits to the right of the decimal point in both the multiplier and the multiplicand (both numbers being multiplied).

Example:

```
  43.6     1 digit to the right of the decimal
× .04      2 digits to the right of the decimal
──────
 1.744     3 digits to the right of the decimal
```

Example:

```
  3.42
× .021
──────
   342
  684
──────
.07182
```

Note: It was necessary to place a 0 at the front of the product to get the required 5 decimal places. Remember that an end 0 after the decimal doesn't mean anything.

Example: .160 = .16

Dividing Decimals

Move the decimal point of the divisor to the right until the divisor becomes a whole number. Next, move the decimal point of the dividend the same number of places to the right, adding zeros as necessary. Divide as with whole numbers, placing the decimal point of the quotient directly above the decimal point of the dividend.

Example:

$4.2\overline{)131.88}$ becomes $42\overline{)1,318.8}^{\ 31.4}$

and

$54 \div 1.6 = 16\overline{)540.00}^{\ 33.75}$

Note: Make certain that all the places between the first digit and the decimal contain a numeral. If necessary, use a zero as a place holder.

Example:

$$416 \div .32 = 32\overline{)41,600.}^{\,1,300.}$$

Skill Drill

1. Change fractions to decimals.

   a. $\dfrac{1}{2}$ d. $\dfrac{11}{15}$ g. $\dfrac{4}{25}$

   b. $\dfrac{5}{6}$ e. $\dfrac{3}{10}$ h. $\dfrac{2}{5}$

   c. $\dfrac{3}{8}$ f. $\dfrac{4}{9}$ i. $\dfrac{22}{7}$

2. Change decimals to fractions.

   a. .36   c. .9372   e. .165

   b. .475   d. .43   f. .4375

3. Add and subtract the following.

   a. $3.65 + .12 + .03$ d. $1.631 - .521$

   b. $5.6 + .372 + 16.14$ e. $365.42 - 26.4$

   c. $.03 + .0016 + 1.032$ f. $232.61 - .003$

4. Multiply

   a. $16.3 \times .031$ b. 4.16×2.1 c. $.36 \times .571$

5. Divide

   a. $500 \div 2.2$ c. $1.02 \div 5.4$ e. $.776 \div .69$

   b. $15 \div 6.3$ d. $6.6 \div .37$

PERCENT

Percent is used to indicate that a whole quantity has been divided into 100 equal parts and refers to the number of those parts.

Therefore, 30% means 30 one-hundredths,

or $\dfrac{30}{100}$ or .30

Similarly, $\dfrac{1}{2}$% is one half of a hundredth,

or $\dfrac{.5}{100}$ or .005

Changing Percent to Decimal

Remove the percent sign and move the decimal point two places to the left.

Example:

25% = .25

Example:

2.4% = .024

Note: Remember to put a zero in front of the number if necessary to have enough digits to the right of the decimal point.

Changing Decimal to Percent

Move the decimal point two places to the right and add a percent sign.

Example:

.63 = 63%

.567 = 56.7%

Changing Percent to a Fraction

Divide the percent quantity by 100 and reduce to lowest terms.

Example:

$$25\% = \frac{25}{100} = \frac{1}{4}$$

Arithmetic Processes with Percent

To be on the safe side, it is advisable to convert the percent to a decimal and then do the arithmetic

Example:

$33\% \times 15\% = .33 \times .15 = .0495$ or 4.95%

Example:

$16\% + 12\% = .16 + .12 = .28 = 28\%$

Example:

$4.5 \div 15\% = 4.5 \div .15 = 30 = 30.0 = 3000\%$

Rate Problems

Percent is commonly used in problems as the *rate* or fractional part of some quantity or value which is to be found. These problems are usually associated with the income received from a rate of return (%) on an investment (value). They may be solved with the following formula:

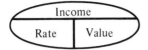

$$\text{Income} = \text{rate} \times \text{value}$$
$$\text{Rate} = \text{income} \div \text{value}$$
$$\text{Value} = \text{income} \div \text{rate}$$

To use this type of formula, you cover the item you want to find and multiply or divide depending on whether the items remaining are side by side or one over the other.

The income used is the *annual net income,* which is that amount remaining after expenses are paid. If monthly income or gross income is given, it must be converted to annual net income. The rate used is expressed as a percentage and should be converted to decimal form. The value used is the amount invested or the worth of the investment.

Before beginning a problem, always decide which formula fits the needs of the problem.

Example: A man owns a building valued at $55,000. He rents it for $450 per month, and he must pay $840 for utilities per annum. What is his annual rate of return?

Formula to use: Rate = income ÷ value

Annual gross income = $450 × 12 = $5,400 (monthly rent × 12)

Annual net income = $5,400 − $840 (expenses) = $4,560

Rate = $4,560 ÷ $55,000 = .0829 = approximately 8.3% rate of return

Example: An apartment house had a gross income of $1,250 per month with annual expenses of $5,900. What price would a buyer who wanted a net return of $6\frac{3}{4}$% per annum on the investment pay for the property to the nearest cent?

Formula to use: Value = Income ÷ rate

Annual gross income = $15,000 (12 months × $1,250)

Annual net income = $9,100 ($15,000 − $5,900)

Value = $9,100 ÷ .0675 = $134,814.81

Example: A woman owns an office building with a value of $235,000. If she has an annual net return of 7%, what is her net annual income?

Formula to use: Income = rate × value

Income = .07 × $235,000 = $16,450

Skill Drill

1. Change to decimals.

   a. 16%   b. 345%   c. $\frac{1}{3}$%   d. .4%

2. Change to percent.

   a. .375   b. 5.25   c. .0625   d. .003

3. Change to a fraction.

   a. .45%   b. 425%   c. .25%

4. Rate problems.

   a. A husband and wife own a store valued at $35,000. When they rent their net return is $6\frac{1}{2}$%. What is their annual net income from the store?

   b. An office building has a value of $150,000. Each of the 10 offices rents for $250 per month. The annual expenses are $13,500. What is the rate of return per year?

   c. What would be the value of an apartment house which has an $8\frac{1}{2}$% annual rate of return? The monthly income is $1,200, and $5,000 is the amount of annual expense.

PERIMETER

The perimeter is the total distance around the boundary of an object or piece of property. The surest way to compute it is to draw a sketch and add up the dimensions of the sides.

Example: Given a rectangular lot with front footage of 325 ft and depth of 270 ft, what is the perimeter of the lot?

$$\text{Perimeter} = 325' + 325' + 270' + 270' = 1,190'$$

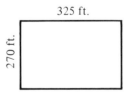

325 ft.

270 ft.

Example: What is the perimeter in yards of a lot with sides of 500 ft, front footage of 420 ft, and a rear lot line of 300 ft? (Remember to convert from ft to yd at 3 ft per yard.)

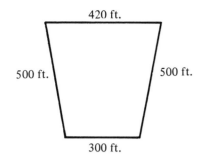

Perimeter $= 420' + 500' + 500' + 300' = 1,720'$

$1,720 \div 3 = 573\frac{1}{3}$ yd

You will occasionally be given a problem involving fence posts.

Example: You are constructing a fence on a lot 120 ft square. Starting at one corner, you put a post every 10 ft. How many posts do you need?

Problems such as this are easily solved by computing the total perimeter and dividing the perimeter by the spacing of the posts.

$120' + 120' + 120' + 120' = 480$ linear ft $\div 10$ ft

$= 48$ posts required

If you are trying to find the number of posts used in a straight line (or anything other than the perimeter of an enclosed area), compute the total length, divide by the spacing of the posts, then add 1. In the above example, if you had 480 linear feet in other than an enclosed figure and the spacing of posts was 10 ft, the number of posts needed would be $48 + 1 = 49$.

AREA

An area is the total surface included within the boundaries of a figure. Remember that all dimensions must be in the same unit (inches, feet, etc.). The answer will be written in square inches, square feet, etc.

Following are some of the most common figures, with the formulas used to calculate the area they contain.

A *rectangle* has two pairs of opposite sides which are parallel and equal, and four angles which are right angles.

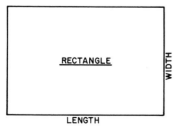

Area = length $\times$ width

A *triangle* has three sides; the angles can vary.

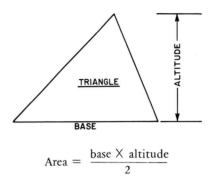

$$\text{Area} = \frac{\text{base} \times \text{altitude}}{2}$$

A *parallelogram* has two pairs of opposite sides which are parallel and equal.

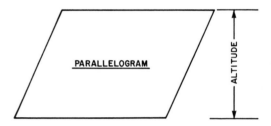

Area = either horizontal parallel side $\times$ altitude

A *trapezoid* has only one pair of opposite sides that are parallel.

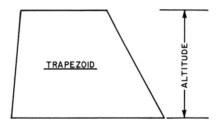

Area = ½ sum of parallel sides $\times$ altitude

Converting Areas

Often it is necessary to get from square inches to square feet or from square feet to square yards. The best way is to make a sketch and multiply it out.

Example: How many square inches in a square foot?

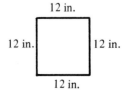

The area in square inches must be

$12'' \times 12'' = 144$ sq in

Note that a 9-foot square is not the same as 9 square feet. A 9-foot square means a square 9 feet on a side; 9 square feet means a total area (length × width) of 9 sq ft.

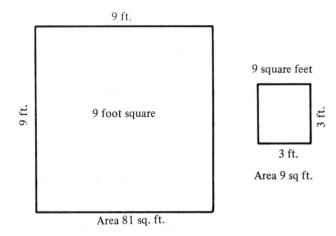

Area 81 sq. ft.

9 square feet

3 ft.

3 ft.

Area 9 sq ft.

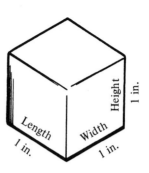

Volume = length × width × height

Remember that all three dimensions must be in the same units—inches, feet, or yards—and the answer will be in cubic inches, cubic feet, or cubic yards.

Acre

A number to *memorize* in real estate is that an acre is 43,560 square feet. To convert area in square feet to acres, divide by 43,560. To convert acres to square feet, multiply by 43,560.

Example: Given a lot whose dimensions are 1,331′ × 180′, what is its total acreage?

Area in feet = 1,331′ × 180′ = 239,580 sq ft

Area in acres = 239,580 ÷ 43,560 = 5.5 acres

Example: What is the area in sq ft of a $3\frac{1}{2}$-acre lot?

3.5 × 43,560 = 152,460 sq ft

Frontage

Land is frequently priced in terms of *front footage* or *frontage*, which is the measurement along the street. The first number indicated in a set of property dimensions is always the frontage. Thus, a lot which is 60′ × 100′ would have a frontage of 60′ on the road or street, and be 100′ deep.

VOLUME

Volume refers to the amount of space any three-dimensional shape contains. It is found by multiplying length times width times height.

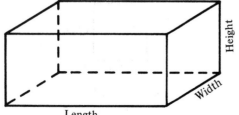

Conversion

You can remember factors to convert from cubic inches to cubic feet, etc., but a simpler method is to draw a sketch and quickly work it out.

Example: How many cubic feet in a cubic yard?

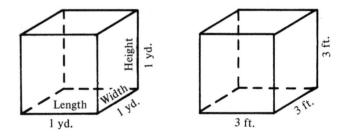

Volume of 1 cu yd = 3′ × 3′ × 3′ = 27 cu ft

Example: What is the volume in cubic yards of a storage shed that is 6′ by 4′ by 6′?

Volume = 6′ × 4′ × 6′ = 144 cu ft

1 cu yd = 27 cu ft (see previous diagram)

144 cu ft ÷ 27 cu ft = $5\frac{9}{27}$ cu yd = $5\frac{1}{3}$ cu yd

Sidewalk or Footing Problems

A typical real estate exam problem treats the construction of a sidewalk "*around the outside of* a corner lot" (and therefore not on the lot) or "*on a corner lot*" (using land from the lot). In every case the first step is to make a sketch of the problem. Keep in mind that the sidewalk would only be installed on two sides of the corner lot.

Example: Construct a 6-ft-wide sidewalk *on* a corner lot 100′ × 60′.

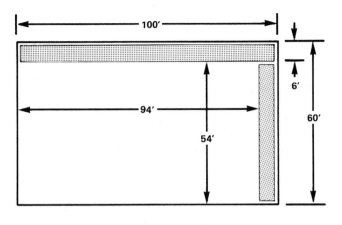

$$A = (100 \times 6) + (54 \times 6) = 600 + 324 = 924 \text{ sq ft}$$

Example: Construct a 6-ft-wide sidewalk *around* a corner lot 100′ × 60′.

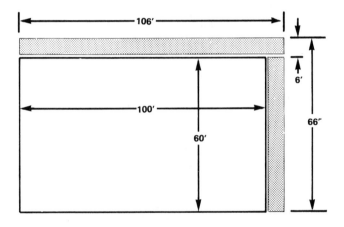

$$A = (106 \times 6) + (60 \times 6) = 636 + 360 = 996 \text{ sq ft}$$

Example: Carrying the previous problem one step further, suppose the sidewalk was to be 6 in deep. How many cubic yards of concrete would be needed to pour the sidewalk?

We have already computed the surface area to be 996 sq ft. If the sidewalk is to be 6 in deep, we can multiply the 996 by $\frac{1}{2}$ (6 in is $\frac{1}{2}$ of 1 ft) and obtain 498 cu ft. Then by dividing 498 cu ft by 27 (there are 27 cu ft in 1 cu yd) we obtain 18.44 cu yd of concrete required to pour the sidewalk.

Skill Drill

1. You are going to fence a lot which has front and rear lot lines of 85′ each. The right side is 167′, and the left side is 3′ longer. How many feet of fencing do you need?

2. You own a rectangular lot which contains 12,420 sq ft. If the front and rear lot lines are 92 ft each, what is the combined length of the side lines?

3. A lot measuring 116 by 143 ft would be what percentage of an acre?

4. A parcel of real estate contains 333,974 sq ft. If it were sold for $2,400 per acre, what would the sales price be?

5. You have dug a basement for a house 42 ft long, 28 ft wide, and 8 ft deep. How many cubic yards of dirt did you remove?

6. You are installing a footing for a building. Its outside dimensions will be 154 ft by 172 ft. The footing will be 18″ wide and 18″ deep. How many cubic yards of concrete will you need?

7. You are going to construct a sidewalk 4 ft wide and 3 in deep around a corner lot 75 ft by 125 ft. How many cubic yards of concrete do you need?

8. A warehouse has outside dimensions of 65 ft by 85 ft; walls 1 ft wide; and 6 interior posts, each 18 in square. How much usable floor space is available?

9. At a price of $15.00 per cubic yard, what would it cost to excavate a basement 30 ft by 26 ft by 6 ft?

10. You own a lot containing 1.56 acres. You sell 12.5% of it, and the state takes 15% of the remainder. You wish to give each of your two children half of the remainder. How many square feet would each child receive?

RATIO AND PROPORTION

A *ratio* is the relationship between two numbers or values. It may be written as a fraction, such as $\frac{3}{4}$, or expressed by the word "per," as in miles per hour. Both terms of a ratio may be multiplied by the same number without changing its value.

A *proportion* is a statement of equality between two ratios. In every proportion both ratios must be written in the same order of value, such as $\frac{2}{3} = \frac{4}{6}$.

Example: If 20 workers assemble 8 machines in a day, how many workers are needed to assemble 12 machines in a day?

One way of thinking of this is 20 is to 8 as x is to 12

The ratios can be set up as follows:

$$\frac{\text{Smaller \# of workers}}{\text{Smaller \# of machines}} = \frac{\text{larger \# of workers}}{\text{larger \# of machines}} = \frac{20}{8} = 2.5$$

Setting up the original equivalence, $2.5 = \dfrac{\text{larger \# of workers}}{12}$

Using the fundamental rule of fractions, remember that

$$2.5 = \frac{2.5}{1}$$

$$\frac{2.5}{1} \times \frac{12}{12} = \frac{\text{\# workers}}{12} = \frac{30}{12}$$

Therefore, larger # of workers = 30

If you are not already familiar with the use of algebra in solving for unknowns, then perhaps your best approach to problems of this sort would be to use logic.

Generally, problems of this type can be solved by reducing the production to what *one* person can produce in *one* unit of time, then using that information to determine the unknown you are seeking.

The procedure in the previous problem would be:

20 workers produce 8 machines in one day, so 1 worker builds .4 of a machine in one day,

$$8.0 \div 20 = .4$$

Then, by dividing .4 into 12 machines,

$$12 \div .4 = 30$$

30 workers are required to assemble 12 machines in one day.

This same logic can also be used to solve the following type of problem.

Example: 14 air conditioners use 4,200 gallons of water in 6 hours. How many air conditioners will use 6,000 gallons in 3 hours?

4,200 gal ÷ 6 hr = 700 gal used by 14 air conditioners in 1 hr

700 gal ÷ 14 = 50 gal used by 1 air conditioner in 1 hr

50 gal × 3 hr = 150 gal used by 1 air conditioner in 3 hr

6,000 gal ÷ 150 gal = 40 air conditioners

REAL ESTATE APPLICATIONS
Scale

You may be required to compute room sizes, given the measurements on a blueprint plus the scale of the blueprint, or you may be required to compute the size of a room on the blueprint, given the room size and the scale.

Example: What is the size of a room if the blueprint is 8″ × 6″ and the scale is $\frac{1}{8}$″ = 1 foot?

If $\frac{1}{8}$″ = 1 foot, then 1″ = 8 ft.

Therefore, 8 × 8′ = 64′ and

6 × 8′ = 48′

Room size is therefore 64′ × 48′

What is the size of a room on a blueprint if the room is 64′ × 48′ and the scale is $\frac{1}{8}$″ = 1 foot?

If $\frac{1}{8}$″ = 1 foot, then for each foot of the actual room the blueprint would measure $\frac{1}{8}$″.

Therefore 64′ ÷ 8 = 8 and 48′ ÷ 8 = 6.

Blueprint size = 8″ × 6″

Profit and Loss

Real estate profit and loss problems are based on the difference between the original cost (purchase price) and the selling price. If the selling price is larger than the purchase price, there is a profit. If it is smaller than the purchase price, then there is a loss.

Example: A person bought a lot for $4,000 and sold it for $5,000. How much profit was made?

Profit = selling price − cost

Profit = $5,000 − $4,000

Profit = $1,000

Example: A person buys a lot for $6,500. After a zoning dispute it is sold for $4,025. What was the profit or loss?

Loss = purchase price − selling price

$6,500 − $4,025 = $2,475

Loss = $2,475

Profit or loss can also be expressed as a percentage by dividing the amount gained or lost by the cost.

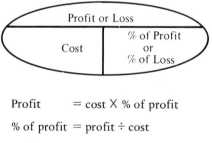

Profit = cost × % of profit

% of profit = profit ÷ cost

% of loss = loss ÷ cost

Example: A person buys a lot for $6,500 and later sells for a loss of $1,475. What is the percentage of loss?

% of loss = loss ÷ cost

$1,475 ÷ $6,500 = .2269, or 23% loss

Example: A person buys a lot for $4,000 and sells it, making $1,000 profit. What is the percentage of profit?

$1,000 ÷ $4,000 = .25 = 25% profit

Example: A book was bought for $10 and sold at a 20% loss. What was the loss?

Loss = cost × % of loss = $10 × 20% = 10 × .20 = $2.00

What was the selling price?

Purchase price − loss = selling price

$10 − $2 = $8

To find the original cost when the selling price and percentage of profit or loss are given, or the selling price when the cost is given, use whichever one of the following applies.

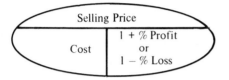

Cost   = selling price ÷ (1 + % profit)

Cost   = selling price ÷ (1 − % loss)

Selling price = cost × (1 + % profit)

Selling price = cost × (1 − % loss)

Note: Used in formulas 1 means 100% (1.0 = 100%).

Example: A table sold for $80. This figure included a profit of 25%. Find the cost.

Selling price = $80.00

Profit = 25%

Cost = selling price ÷ (1 + % profit)

1 + % Profit = 1.25

$80.00 ÷ 1.25 = 64.00 cost

Example: A house was sold for $34,000 at a loss of 5%. What was the original cost?

Cost = selling price ÷ (1 − % loss)

Cost = $34,000 ÷ (1 − 5%) = $34,000 ÷ (1 − .05)

Cost = $34,000 ÷ .95 = $35,789.47

Depreciation

As used in real estate, depreciation is the decrease in value from any and all causes. It can also be shown by:

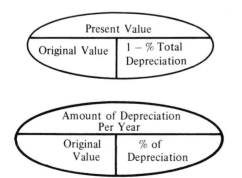

Example: A house cost $30,000 to construct. It is expected to have an economic life of 40 years. What is the percentage of depreciation a year?

Depreciation per year = $\frac{1}{40}$ cost

$1 ÷ 40 = .025 = 2\frac{1}{2}\%$

How much does it depreciate a year?

Amount of depreciation per year = original value × % of depreciation

Amount of depreciation per year = $30,000 × .025 = $750

Example: The value of a house at the end of 8 years was appraised at $7,480. What did construction of the house originally cost if it had depreciated at an annual rate of $1\frac{1}{2}\%$?

Total depreciation = 8 years × $1\frac{1}{2}\%$ = 12%

Original value = $\dfrac{\text{present value (\$7,480)}}{1 - \%\ \text{total depreciation}}$ = $8,500
(100% − 12% = 88% = .88)

Example: A house was bought for $35,000 and depreciates $1,050 in 1 year. What is the percentage of depreciation?

% depreciation = amount depreciation ÷ original value

% depreciation = $1,050 ÷ $35,000 =.03 = 3%

Appreciation

Appreciation is the increase in value brought about by any and all causes. It is represented by the following:

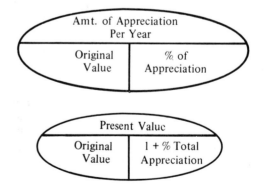

Example: A house is bought for $25,000 and appreciates 2% a year. What is the value of the house after 5 years?

2% × 5 = 10% total appreciation

Present value = original value × (1 + % total appreciation)

Present value = $25,000 × (1 + 10%)

Present value = $25,000 × (1 + .10) = $25,000 × 1.1
                  = $27,500

Example: A house was bought for $35,000 and appreciates $1,050 in 1 year. What is the percentage of appreciation?

% of appreciation = amount of appreciation ÷ original value

% of appreciation = $1,050 ÷ $35,000 = .03 = 3%

Example: What was the original value of a house which has a present value of $17,500 and has appreciated 5% per year for 5 years?

5 X 5% = 25% total appreciation

Original value = present value ÷ (1 + % total appreciation)

Original value = $17,500 ÷ (1 + 25%)
= $17,500 ÷ (1 + .25)

Original value = $17,500 ÷ 1.25 = $14,000

Note: Unless specifically instructed, do not compound depreciation or appreciation.

Commission

Commission is the amount of money paid to an agent for selling goods. When the commission is some percentage of the value of the services performed, that percentage is called the *rate of commission.*

To find the commission, multiply the selling price by the rate of commission.

Example: A real estate salesperson sold a lot for $5,000. The commission rate is $2\frac{1}{2}$%. How much is the commission on the sale?

$5,000 X $2\frac{1}{2}$% = $5,000 X .025 = $125

Example: A real estate agent sold a house for $78,000. The commission rate was 4%. How much was the commission?

4% X $78,000 = .04 X $78,000 = $3,120

Selling Price

A more practical problem for the REALTOR is to determine the selling price which must be asked to net the owner the desired amount (net price) as well as cover the commission and other expenses as stated in the problem. The solution technique is similar to the profit and loss problems.

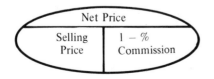

Selling price = net price ÷ (1 − % commission)

Net price = selling price X (1 − % commission)

Example: You are selling a home for which the owner wants to net $15,000 after paying your 5% commission. What would be the selling price?

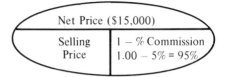

Selling price = net price ÷ (1 − % commission)

Selling price = $15,000 ÷ (1 − 5%) = $15,000 ÷ (1 − .05)

Selling price = $15,000 ÷ .95 = $15,789.47

Taxes

Most of the tax money raised by local governments is obtained through taxes on real estate or personal property. The value of real estate is appraised by tax officers called *assessors,* and the value thus set is called the *assessed value,* or assessment. The assessed value may also be set by local law as a certain percentage of the estimated market value of the property. The total amount of tax to be paid is determined by multiplying the assessed value by the *tax rate.* Tax rates are expressed differently in different areas, but they are normally expressed as a certain number of dollars per $100 of assessed value. Therefore, a tax rate of 3% can be expressed as $3 on $100 of assessed value, or $30 on $1,000.

Problems dealing with taxes, assessments, and rates can be solved with the following formulas:

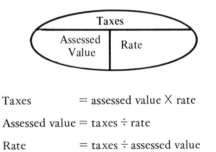

Taxes = assessed value X rate

Assessed value = taxes ÷ rate

Rate = taxes ÷ assessed value

Example: The market value of a piece of property is $18,000. It is assessed at one-third of its market value, and the taxes are $6.30 per $100. What are the taxes?

$\frac{1}{3}$ X $18,000 = $6,000 assessed value

$6,000 ÷ $100 = 60 hundreds

$6.30 X 60 = $378.00 taxes

An easy method of multiplying tax rates when they are expressed in dollars per hundred is to move the decimal point of the assessed value 2 digits to the left.

Example: The market value of a house is $40,000. It is assessed at 60% of its market value, and its taxes are $3.10 per $100. What are the taxes?

60% × $40,000 = $24,000 assessed value

Moving the decimal 2 digits to the left in $24,000 gives 240 hundreds.

$3.10 × 240 = $744

Example: A house is assessed at 50% of its value. The taxes are $2.05 per hundred and are $369 annually. What is the value of the house?

Taxes ÷ rate = assessed value (in hundreds)

$369 ÷ $2.05 = 180 (hundreds); assessed value is $18,000

$18,000 = 50% of market value

$18,000 ÷ .50 = $36,000 market value of house

Example: The taxes on a $65,000 house assessed at 40% are $845. What is the tax rate per hundred?

40% × $65,000 = .40 × $65,000
= $26,000 assessed value

Rate = taxes ÷ assessed value (in hundreds)

Rate = $845 ÷ 260 = $3.25 per hundred

Proration of Taxes and Insurance

This is a necessary step in determining distribution of payments for buyer and seller at time of closing. Taxes are normally computed on an annual calendar year from January 1 to December 31, and fire insurance normally has a 3-year term from date of issuance.

For simplicity on the examination and all problems in this workbook, consider each month as having 30 days and 1 year as having 360 days. Do not worry about who pays for the proration as of the day of settlement; just subtract the dates given from 30 and use the answer for proration.

The first step in solving proration problems is to determine whether you are seeking the amount *that has been used* or the *unused portion*. Pay particular attention to the problem to determine if the item has been paid for or remains unpaid. Then compute the time you are seeking.

Example: An owner paid for a 3-year insurance policy February 10, 1979. What would the refund be if the owner cancelled the policy as of April 20, 1980?

The owner has paid for the entire 3-year policy, and has used only a part of it, and so the owner would be entitled to a refund of the unused portion. The problem is to find the *unused* portion of the policy. This is easily accomplished by adding 2 years 11 months and 30 days (3 years) to the origination date to find the termination date, then subtracting the date of settle-

ment (cancellation date). Write the problem with the year first, month second, and day third.

Origination date	1979	2 months	10 days
Term of policy	+ 2	11	30
Termination date	1981	13 months	40 days
Cancellation date	− 1980	4	20
Unused portion	= 1 year	9 months	20 days

$= 21\frac{2}{3}$ months

The second step is to divide the total premium by the number of months covered to obtain the monthly rate. If the insurance policy had cost $360 for the 3 years, then

$360 ÷ 36 months = $10.00 per month

The third step is to multiply the time determined from step 1 by the monthly rate.

$21\frac{2}{3}$ × $10.00 = $216.60 refund due seller

Or, if you prefer, you may divide the monthly rate by 30 days to obtain the daily rate, then

21 months × $10 = $210.00
+ 20 days × $.33 per day = 6.60
Refund due $216.60

If the problem had been to find the used portion of the policy, it could be solved by subtracting the origination date from the cancellation date.

Cancellation date	1980	4 months	20 days
Origination date	− 1979	2	10
Used portion	= 1 year	2 months	10 days

In some cases the subtraction is not possible because the number to subtract from is less than the number being subtracted. If this is the case, you can borrow from the months (30 days) or the year (12 months).

Example: What is the time lapse from June 20, 1981, to February 10, 1982?

Termination date	1982	2 months (13)	10 days (40)
Starting date	− 1981	6 months	20 days
Time elapsed	= 0 years	7 months	20 days

You cannot subtract 20 days from 10 days, so you borrow 1 month (30 days) and add it to the 10 days. Now you have 40 days, so you can subtract, leaving 20 days. Now, to subtract the months, you try to subtract 6 from 1 and cannot, so you borrow 1 year (12 months). You now have 13 months, and subtracting gives 7 months. You have borrowed 1 year, so you now have 1981 from 1981, or 0. Time lapse is 7 months 20 days.

Example: Prorate the annual taxes as of the settlement date (August 20) if property is valued at $29,000, assessed at 40%, and taxed at the rate of $4.04 per hundred. Seller has prepaid the annual taxes.

$29,000 \times .40 = $11,600 assessed value

$4.04 \times 116 = $468.64 annual taxes

11 months	30 days	(1 year)
− 7	20	(August 20)
4 months	10 days	$= 4\frac{1}{3}$ months time the buyer will be in the house and for which the buyer must reimburse the seller for taxes.

$468.64 \div 12 =$ approximately $39.05 monthly taxes

$39.05 \times 4\frac{1}{3} =$ approximately $169.09

Debit buyer $169.09, credit seller $169.09.

Note: Remember that even though July is the 7th month, the time lapse from January 1 to July 1, is only 6 months.

Skill Drill

1. A family buys a house for $27,500 and sells it for $36,750. What is their profit?

2. A lot is bought for $1,600 and sold for $1,400. What is the percentage of loss?

3. A house is sold for $25,000 at a 4% profit. What was the original cost?

4. A home sold for $75,000 at a profit of 20%. What did it cost?

5. A home sold for $75,000 at a loss of 20%. What did it cost?

6. You bought a house for $32,500. What price would you need to sell it for in order to make a 15% profit?

7. A house cost $32,000 6 years ago. If it depreciates at the rate of 1.5% per year, what is its value today?

8. A house cost $32,000 6 years ago. If it appreciates at the rate of 1.5% per year, what is its value today?

9. You receive a salary of $8,000 per year payable monthly, plus 3% commission on your property sales. If you made $2,664.67 this month, how much property did you sell?

10. You wish to net $30,000 from the sale of your house after paying the present first trust of $22,000, a repair bill of $1,016, and a 6% brokerage fee. What would be the sales price?

11. Your commission arrangement with your broker is that you get 55% of the sales commission. If you sell a $67,500 property at 5% commission, what is the broker's share?

12. If you sell your home on July 10 and the taxes of $840 for the year have not been paid, how much should you pay the purchaser at settlement?

13. Your property is assessed at 50%. Its value is $55,750. The taxes are $1,198 per year. What is the tax rate?

14. You bought a 3-year insurance policy for $316.80 on May 15, 1979, and you sell your house August 10 1980. How much refund would you receive?

15. A property purchased for $15,000 was sold for $21,000. What percentage profit was made?

16. A property purchased for $21,000 was sold for $15,000. What was the percentage loss?

17. What is the value of a house if it is assessed at 45%, the taxes are $495.00 per year, and the rate is $5.00 per hundred?

18. 5 shrubs in 6 ft of hedge is in proportion to how many shrubs in 48 ft of hedge?

19. If you use 2 gal of paint to cover 900 sq ft of wall area, how many gallons would be needed to cover 2,250 sq ft?

20. Four painters can paint 8 rooms in one day. How many painters would be needed to paint 32 rooms in 2 days?

ANSWERS TO SKILL DRILL PROBLEMS

Fractions

1.   a. improper   c. quotient
     b. denominator   d. dividing

2.   a. $\dfrac{5 \times 4}{6 \times 4} = \dfrac{20}{24}$ d. $\dfrac{3}{7} = \dfrac{18}{42}$

     b. $\dfrac{11 \times 9}{12 \times 9} = \dfrac{99}{108}$ e. $\dfrac{15}{63} = \dfrac{5}{21}$

     c. $\dfrac{12 \div 3}{48 \div 3} = \dfrac{4}{16}$

3.   a. $\dfrac{3}{4}$ d. $\dfrac{7}{12}$ g. $\dfrac{1}{2}$ j. $\dfrac{5}{6}$

     b. $\dfrac{3}{11}$ e. $\dfrac{4}{9}$ h. $\dfrac{1}{3}$ k. $\dfrac{2}{3}$

     c. $\dfrac{1}{4}$ f. $\dfrac{1}{3}$ i. $\dfrac{7}{12}$ l. $\dfrac{1}{3}$

4.   a. $5\frac{2}{3}$ c. $12\frac{1}{6}$ e. $17\frac{3}{10}$

     b. $7\frac{1}{4}$ d. $16\frac{1}{3}$ f. $9\frac{1}{8}$

5.   a. $\dfrac{5}{8}$ c. $\dfrac{23}{24}$ e. $\dfrac{5}{12}$

     b. $\dfrac{13}{24}$ d. $2\frac{1}{6}$

6.   a. $\dfrac{3}{7}$ c. 44   e. $1\frac{1}{6}$

     b. $\dfrac{4}{5}$ d. $\dfrac{2}{15}$

Decimals

1.   a. .5   d. .73   g. .16
     b. .83   e. .3   h. .4
     c. .375   f. .44   i. 3.14

2.   a. $\dfrac{9}{25}$ c. $\dfrac{2,343}{2,500}$ e. $\dfrac{33}{200}$

     b. $\dfrac{19}{40}$ d. $\dfrac{43}{100}$ f. $\dfrac{7}{16}$

3.   a. 3.80   c. 1.0636   e. 339.02
     b. 22.112   d. 1.11   f. 232.607

4.   a. .5053   b. 8.736   c. .20556

5.   a. 227.27   c. .19   e. 1.125
     b. 2.38   d. 17.84

Percent

1.   a. .16   b. 3.45   c. .0033   d. .004

2.   a. 37.5%   b. 525%   c. 6.25%   d. .3%

3.   a. $\dfrac{9}{2,000}$ b. $4\frac{1}{4}$ c. $\dfrac{1}{400}$

4.   a. Income = rate × value
      Income = $6\frac{1}{2}$% × \$35,000 = .065 × \$35,000
             = \$2,275

     b. \$250 × 10 = \$2,500 monthly rent
       \$2,500 × 12 months = \$30,000 annual income
       \$30,000 − \$13,500 (expenses) = \$16,500 annual
         net income
       Rate = Income ÷ value
       Rate = \$16,500 ÷ \$150,000 = .11 = 11%

     c. \$1,200 × 12 months = \$14,400 annual income
       \$14,400 − \$5,000 (expenses) = \$9,400 annual net
         income
       Value = income ÷ rate
       Value = \$9,400 ÷ $8\frac{1}{2}$% = \$9,400 ÷ .085
            = \$110,588.24

Perimeter, Area, and Volume

1. $85' + 85' + 167' + 170' = 507$ ft

2.   Area = 12,420 sq ft
    Area = (92′) × (width)
    Area ÷ length = width
    12,420 ÷ 92 = 135 × 2 sides = 270 ft

3.   Area = $116' \times 143' = 16,588$ sq ft
    1 acre = 43,560 sq ft
    16,588 sq ft ÷ 43,560 = .38 = 38%

4.   333,974 sq ft ÷ 43,560 = 7.67 acres
    \$2,400 × 7.67 = \$18,408

5.   Volume = $L \times W \times H$
    Volume = $42' \times 28' \times 8' = 9,408$ cu ft
    9,408 cu ft ÷ 27 = 348.44 cu yd

6.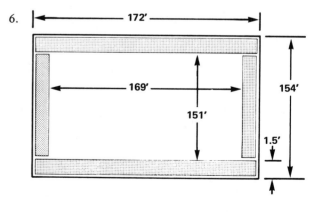

Area = 2 × (172′ × 1.5′) + 2 × (151′ × 1.5′)
    = 516 sq ft + 453 sq ft = 969 sq ft
Volume = area × height
Volume = 969 cu ft × 1.5 = 1,453.5 cu ft
1,453.5 cu ft ÷ 27 = 53.83 cu yd

7.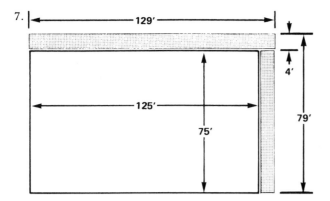

Area = $(129' \times 4') + (75' \times 4')$
  = 516 sq ft + 300 sq ft = 816 sq ft
Volume = area × height
Volume = $816 \times \frac{1}{4}'$ = 204 cu ft
204 cu ft ÷ 27 = 7.56 cu yd

8.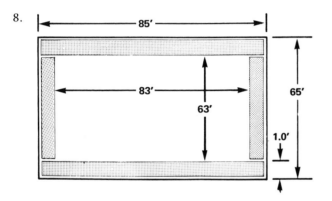

Inside area = $83' \times 63'$ = 5,229 sq ft
Area of one post = 1.5×1.5 = 2.25 sq ft
Area of six posts = 6×2.25 = 13.5 sq ft
5,229 sq ft − 13.5 sq ft = 5,215.5 sq ft

9. Volume = $30' \times 26' \times 6'$ = 4,680 cu ft
  4,680 cu ft ÷ 27 cu ft = 173.33 cu yd
  173.33 cu yd × \$15 = \$2,599.95

10. 1.56 acres × 43,560 sq ft = 67,953.6 sq ft
  100% − 12.5% = 87.5% remaining after sale
  67,953.6 sq ft × 87.5% = 59,459.4 sq ft
  100% − 15% = 85% remaining after taking by state
  59,459.4 sq ft × 85% = 50,540.49 sq ft
  50,540.49 sq ft ÷ 2 = 25,270.25 sq ft to each child

Ratio and Proportion and Real Estate Application

1. Profit = selling price − cost
   Profit = \$36,750 − \$27,500 = \$9,250 profit

2.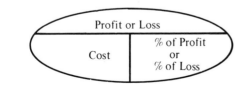

   Loss = cost − selling price

Loss = \$1,600 − \$1,400 = \$200
% loss = loss ÷ cost = \$200 ÷ \$1,600 = .125 = 12.5%

3.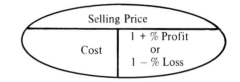

Cost = selling price ÷ (1 + % profit)
Cost = \$25,000 ÷ (1 + 4%) = \$25,000 ÷ 1.04
  = \$24,038.46

4.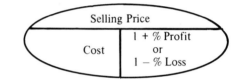

Cost = selling price ÷ (1 + % profit)
Cost = \$75,000 ÷ (1 + 20%) = \$75,000 ÷ 1.20
  = \$62,500

5.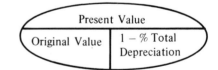

Cost = selling price ÷ (1 − % loss)
Cost = \$75,000 ÷ (1 − 20%) = \$75,000 ÷ .80
  = \$93,750

6.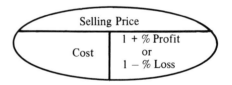

Selling price = cost × (1 + % profit)
Selling price = \$32,500 × (1 + 15%)
  = \$32,500 × 1.15 = \$37,375

7.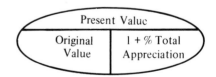

Present value = original value × (1 − % depreciation)
6 years × 1.5% = 9% total depreciation
Present value = \$32,000 × (1 − 9%)
  = \$32,000 × .91 = \$29,120

8. [image]

Present value = original value × (1 + % appreciation)
6 years × 1.5% = 9% total appreciation
Present value = \$32,000 × (1 + 9%)
  = \$32,000 × 1.09 = \$34,880

9. $8,000 ÷ 12 = $666.67 monthly salary
$2,664.67 − $666.67 = $1,998.00 amount made in
  commissions
Amount sold = commissions ÷ 3%
$1,998 ÷ 3% = $66,600 amount sold

10.

Selling price = net price ÷ (1 − % commission)
$30,000 + $22,000 + $1,016 = $53,016 total net
  price
Selling price = $53,016 ÷ .94 = $56,400

11. $67,500 × 5% = $3,375 total commissions
$3,375 × 55% = $1,856.25 your share
$3,375 − $1,856.25 = $1,518.75 broker's share

12. January 1 to July 10 = 6 months 10 days
                = $6\frac{1}{3}$ months
$840.00 ÷ 12 months = $70.00 per month
$70.00 × $6\frac{1}{3}$ months = $443.33 due purchaser

13.
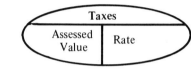

Rate = taxes ÷ assessed value (in hundreds)
$55,750 × 50% = $27,875 assessed value
Assessed value = 278.75 hundreds
Rate = $1,198 ÷ 278.75 = $4.2978 per hundred

14. If the date of origination was May 15, 1979, then the
date of expiration is May 15, 1982.

Expiration date—   1   17
  May 15, 1982 = 1982 year 5 months 15 days
Termination date—
  August 10, 1980 = 1980   8   10

   Unused portion 1 year 9 months 5 days

$316.80 ÷ 36 months = $8.80 per month
1 year 9 months 5 days = $21\frac{1}{6}$ months
$8.80 × $21\frac{1}{6}$ = 186.26

15.
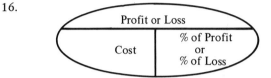

% profit = profit ÷ cost
Profit = selling price − cost
Profit = $21,000 − $15,000 = $6,000 profit
% profit = $6,000 ÷ $15,000 = .40 = 40%

16.
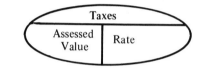

% loss = loss ÷ cost
Loss = cost − selling price
Loss = $21,000 − $15,000 = $6,000
% loss = $6,000 ÷ $21,000 = 28.57%

17.
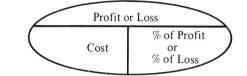

Assessed value = taxes ÷ rate
Assessed value = $495.00 ÷ .05 = $9,900
Value = $9,900 ÷ .45 = $22,000

18. 5 shrubs in 6′ = 1.2′ per shrub (6 ÷ 5)
48′ ÷ 1.2′ = 40 shrubs

19. 2 gal of paint in 900 sq ft = 450 sq ft per gallon (900
  ÷ 2)
2,250 sq ft ÷ 450 sq ft = 5 gal

20. Four painters paint 8 rooms in 1 day, so each painter
covers 2 rooms per day (8 ÷ 4), or 4 rooms in 2 days,
therefore, 32 ÷ 4 = 8 painters required.

PRACTICE EXAMINATION:
BASICS OF REAL ESTATE MATHEMATICS

Instructions: During most real estate license examinations, you are not allowed extra scratch paper for your calculations, and so you must use the margins of the examination book for this purpose. Do not use the answer sheet! To get used to this, use the space between the questions of this examination as your only scratch paper. Your method of computation will not be considered—only the answer checked. *In some cases, the exact answer may not be given, in which case choose the best answer.*

1. You receive $800 per month salary from your broker and 3% commission on your real estate sales. If you were paid $3,091 this month, how much real estate did you sell?

   a. $103,000   c. $76,400
   b. $129,700   d. $93,500

2. A person owns an apartment house from which $460 per month is received. Annual expenses are $1,730. If the annual return is 6%, what is the value of the investment?

   a. $21,200   c. $49,500
   b. $212,000   d. $63,100

3. A lot sold for $6,500, which included a 4% loss. What was the original cost?

   a. $8,125   c. $6,770
   b. $4,875   d. $6,875

4. Four persons decide to purchase a property for $96,000. The first person invests $35,000; the second, 13% of the cost; the third, $33,520. How much of the ownership is left for the fourth owner?

   a. $\frac{1}{6}$ c. $\frac{7}{32}$
   b. 15%   d. 16%

5. What is the difference between a 6-ft-wide sidewalk on a $100' \times 60'$ corner lot and a 6-ft-wide sidewalk around the same lot?

   a. 6 sq ft   c. 36 sq ft
   b. 432 sq ft   d. 72 sq ft

6. A person decides to fence a $155' \times 90'$ lot. Frontage fencing costs $2.75 per linear foot; other fencing costs $1.85 per linear foot. What is the total cost of the fence?

   a. $1,046.00   c. $673.75
   b. $426.25   d. $619.75

7. Four people buy a piece of property. One pays $15,000, another pays $\frac{3}{8}$ of the cost, another pays

$12\frac{1}{2}$%, and the last pays .25 of cost. What was the total investment?

   a. $26,250   c. $120,000
   b. $45,750   d. $60,000

8. An investor buys an office building for $295,000. Each of 20 offices pays $375 per month. Annual expenses are $15,000. What is the rate of return?

   a. 30.5%   c. 2.5%
   b. 3.3%   d. 25.5%

9. A house costs $25,000. If the owner wants to make a profit of 15% after paying the agent's commission of 5%, what should the house be sold for?

   a. $30,000   c. $30,260
   b. $30,250   d. $31,000

10. You decide to pour a footing for a building with outside measurements of $55' \times 40'$. The footing is to be 1 ft wide and 1 ft deep. If concrete is 75¢ per cubic foot, what is the cost of the footing?

   a. $139.50   c. $157.50
   b. $142.50   d. $163.50

11. The original cost of a piece of property was $16,200, and it was sold for $14,500. What is the percentage of profit or loss?

   a. .105 profit   c. 10.5% loss
   b. 10.5% profit   d. 1.05% loss

12. A family owns a lot $95' \times 125'$. The house and landscaped patio occupy 45% of the lot. The family sells 15% of the frontage extending the full depth of the lot to a neighbor. Excluding the area of the house and patio, how much property does the family have left?

   a. 4,750 sq ft   c. 60% of the original lot
   b. 7,125 sq ft   d. 10,094 sq ft

13. You bought a lot 5 years ago for $1,200, and it has tripled in value. The house you bought with the lot cost $13,000 and has increased $4,000 in value. If you sell at the current market value, how much profit will you realize?

   a. $4,000   c. $7,600
   b. $6,400   d. $4,600

14. What was the original value of a house which has a present value of $25,000 and which has appreciated 3% per annum for 7 years?

   a. $19,560   c. $20,660
   b. $24,400   d. $31,645

15. Commission on sales is graduated according to the selling price of the house. An agent receives 4% on a house with value up to $25,000, 5% on a house valued from $25,000 to $50,000, and 6% on every sale over $50,000. What is the agent's total commission on sales of $65,000, $35,000, and $27,500?

    a. $2,300   c. $7,025
    b. $6,750   d. $7,650

16. What is the annual rate of interest on a loan of $45,750 if the monthly interest payment is $266.88?

    a. 7%   c. 6%
    b. $6\frac{1}{2}$%   d. 5%

17. An agent was to receive a 6% commission on a piece of property listed for $43,750. How much will the agent make if the owner reduces the selling price by 12%?

    a. $1,850   c. $2,625
    b. $2,310   d. $7,875

18. The scale of a blueprint is $\frac{1}{2}'' = 1$ foot. If a room on a blueprint measures $6'' \times 8\frac{1}{4}''$, what is the area of the room?

    a. 99 sq ft   c. 1,236 sq ft
    b. 1,230 sq ft   d. 198 sq ft

19. You are going to construct a sidewalk 5 ft wide and 6 in deep around a corner lot $120' \times 75'$. What is the total volume of the sidewalk?

    a. 500 cu ft   c. 475 sq ft
    b. 4,500 cu ft   d. 500 sq ft

20. What is the difference between 10 ft square and 10 sq ft?

    a. 90 ft   c. 20 ft
    b. 90 sq ft   d. 20 sq ft

21. Seven air conditioners use 3,150 gal of water in 6 hr. How many air conditioners will use 3,600 gal of water in 4 hr?

    a. 20   c. 12
    b. 15   d. 10

22. If you receive $6,250 annual income from an investment that is paying 12% interest, what is your investment?

    a. $52,083   c. $75,000
    b. $520,830   d. $7,500

23. If you pay monthly interest of $216.50 on a loan of $35,750, what interest rate are you paying?

    a. 7.1%   c. 7.3%
    b. .61   d. 7.5%

24. Statistics show that an average of 4.2 showings are required to make one sale. If 2,400 sales are made in 6 months, how many showings were there?

    a. 1,008   c. 10,080
    b. 5,714   d. 16,800

25. If property is assessed at 65% of its value, what would the monthly taxes be on a house valued at $70,000 if the rate is $3.90 per hundred?

    a. $147.88   c. $177.45
    b. $1,774.50   d. $1,478.75

26. What is the rate of assessment for a house with a fair market value of $67,000, taxes of $900.79, and a tax rate of $3.82 per hundred?

    a. 35%   c. 28.4%
    b. 23.5%   d. 31.5%

27. You erect a fence around your property, which is $70' \times 90'$. The fencing costs $1.84 per linear foot. How much did the entire fence cost?

    a. $288.42   c. $294.40
    b. $588.80   d. $576.84

28. An owner receives $150 per month for each of 12 apartments. The annual expenses are $3,560, and the total investment was $112,000. What rate of return is being earned on the investment?

    a. 62%   c. 22%
    b. 45%   d. 16%

29. A house was bought for $26,000 and sold for a 16% profit. What was the selling price?

    a. $22,280   c. $27,625
    b. $30,160   d. $29,720

30. Which of the following would net the owner $24,000 after paying your 5% commission and the expenses noted?

	Selling prices	Expenses
a.	26,021	720
b.	26,421	1,100
c.	26,842	1,500
d.	All the above	

Chapter 12

Landlord and Tenant

INTRODUCTION

The terms *landlord* and *tenant* stem from the English system, in which a tenant would, in exchange for services to the king (including military service), receive use of land to farm. In addition, the sovereign would receive some of the crops from the land that the tenant had farmed.

This same concept, using another's land in exchange for something of value, is still valid today. However, military service to and crops bestowed on the landlord have been replaced by rents in the form of money or other considerations.

The landlord-tenant relationship is usually created by an instrument called a *rental agreement*, otherwise known as a *lease*, which is another form of contract. A verbal lease or oral contract is enforceable provided that it is not in excess of 1 year, as prescribed by the Statute of Frauds.

Under a lease or tenancy an owner of the premises, called a *lessor*, leases or lets to the tenant, called the *lessee*. The terms landlord and tenant are being used less in this day and age of consumerism, and are being replaced by owner (or management) and resident.

Under a lease an individual, a family, a group of people, or any business entity such as a corporation may hold, use, and enjoy real property without actually owning it. The tenant's interest created by virtue of the lease is known as a *leasehold*. The tenant's leasehold interest or estate is considered personal property.

CONDITIONS OF A VALID TENANCY

In order to create a valid tenancy, certain minimum conditions must exist.

Occupancy

The tenant must occupy the property with the landlord's consent, which can be either expressed or implied. Without the landlord's consent, the tenant's occupancy might be considered trespass.

Control and Possession

The tenant must exercise or have the right to exercise control of the premises. Provisions of the lease will dictate the terms of control and possession.

Occupancy Subordinate to Landlord

The tenant, in his or her occupancy of the premises, must realize that this possession and control is always subordinate to the landlord's in that the landlord is still the owner of the premises. The tenant does not take on the color of or claim to title even though he or she does have an estate in the premises, and tenant cannot claim title because of that possession.

Reversionary Interest

To be valid the lease must give the landlord the right to recover the premises at some time in the future.

Consideration

Although the rent paid by the tenant is usually in the form of money, it can be another form of consideration. At common law, destruction of leased property did not release the tenant from the obligation to pay the rent. Today statutes often require such releases, and clauses to this effect will be found in most leases.

TYPES OF TENANCY (LEASEHOLD ESTATES—LESS THAN FREEHOLD)

Tenancy for Years

This type of tenancy is the most frequently used one. Use of the word "years" does not mean the tenancy must be for a time measured by years. It need only be for a *definite* period of time (which could be 1 month, 6 months, 1 year, or 5 years) and terminate at the end of that definite period. If a date for termination of the tenancy cannot be determined, the tenancy will usually not be considered as one "for years" but as one "at will" (discussed below). A new lease for a definite period would create another tenancy for years.

The tenancy created is considered personal property and passes to the tenant's heirs at death.

Tenancy from Year to Year

The tenant in a year-to-year tenancy holds an interest in the land for an *indefinite* time, yet makes periodic rent payments. This tenancy may be created by contractual agreement, or in some jurisdictions it may automatically come about if a tenant stays on after the expiration of a tenancy for years, thereby becoming binding for the same term as the original. For example, if a 2-year lease (a tenancy for years, with a definite termination date) is extended by action of the tenant, he or she has created a tenancy from year to year and may be liable for continuing and periodic rent payments for another 2 years. This tenancy is also considered personal property.

Tenancy at Will

Either the landlord or tenant, at their will, can terminate this type of tenancy; it has no definite termination date. Either party gives the other proper notice (usually 30 days) that the tenancy will end.

If the tenant alone holds the right to quit, some courts have ruled this equal to a life estate rather than a tenancy at will.

Tenancy by Sufferance

This tenancy is created when a tenant who originally held possession with the landlord's consent now will not release the premises to the landlord. Tenant is said to hold the premises *by sufferance*, or without the consent of the landlord. The tenant does not have an interest or estate because the premises are held without the landlord's consent, and the owner can treat the tenant as a trespasser. This tenancy can be terminated by either party without notice.

At common law the landlord can choose to either dispossess the tenant who holds the property by sufferance or hold him or her liable for another term the length of the original.

RIGHTS, DUTIES, AND LIABILITIES

Much of the law pertaining to tenancy for residential property has in recent years been greatly liberalized in favor of the tenant. Housing codes specify certain duties which are imposed upon the landlord. Regardless of contrary and earlier contractual agreement with a tenant, new laws and public ordinances may require compliance

by the landlord, and many jurisdictions impose fines or other enforcement measures for violations of housing regulations by the owner of the property.

Traditionally, certain rights, duties, and liabilities belong to the landlord and to the tenant in the absence of any contractual agreement to the contrary. These rights arise as a matter of common law. However, a contract of lease can and often does remove some of the rights, duties, and liabilities of both landlord and tenant, and when this is done, the lease contract takes legal precedence over the unwritten laws. Note, however, that public policy considerations may disallow even a properly concluded written agreement and perhaps restore certain rights which lease provisions attempt to disallow.

Landlord Rights

RIGHT TO RENT

The landlord may lease what he or she owns, and receive payment for it.

RIGHT TO SELL OR TRANSFER

The landlord has the right to sell or transfer his or her interest in the premises without consent of the tenant. The new owner takes title subject to the lease agreement and the tenancy.

RIGHT TO BRING LEGAL ACTION

The landlord retains the right to bring legal action against a tenant or third party for injury to the property.

RIGHT TO REPAIR

The landlord has the right to repair only as is deemed necessary, without the duty to do so unless agreed to by the terms of the lease.

RIGHT OF REENTRY

In many leases (tenancies) for years, the landlord retains a right of reentry which may be exercised should a certain agreed-upon or property-injurious condition occur.

Landlord Duties and Liabilities

DELIVERY OF POSSESSION

The landlord, upon acceptance of the tenant, must comply with the lease terms and surrender the premises to the tenant when agreed and for the specified time of the lease. If the landlord should become wary of the tenant's ability to fulfill the obligations of the lease, the landlord still could not refuse possession if the tenant has fulfilled the obligations, such as advance payment of rent. Most rent payments today are required in advance. This gives the landlord a better opportunity or more time to seek possession for failure to pay before too much unpaid rent accrues. Another device of the landlord to ensure performance of the agreement by the tenant is to require "security deposits." In some areas interest is being paid on these security deposits, and it can be expected that more and more areas will require this.

INJURY TO THE TENANT

The landlord has no duty to perform repairs. However, if the tenant is injured as a result of repairs improperly made by the landlord, or if the landlord leased the premises to a tenant knowing that dangerous conditions existed and did not specify these to the tenant, then the landlord may be held liable.

Contributory negligence on the part of the tenant may be available as a defense to the landlord. For example, if a tenant knows that porch steps were improperly installed, continued use of them despite this knowledge would give rise to a conclusion that tenant contributed to his or her own injury.

In areas of common use by all tenants, such as hallways in apartment buildings, the landlord is responsible for maintenance, upkeep, and safety. Safety usually refers to preventing unsafe conditions in the physical makeup of the property. Nevertheless, some recent court cases have held that the landlord's responsibility for safety extends to providing apartment tenants with security from prowlers. In these cases where the tenant has been physically harmed by a prowler as a result of provable lax security in the building, the courts have given the tenant-victim a right of action personally against the landlord.

IMPLIED COVENANT OF HABITABILITY

A fairly recent doctrine, that of the "implied covenant of habitability," has in certain areas required that the landlord be responsible for the property's measuring up to reasonable living standards.

The inclusion of "as is" clauses in the lease modifies this slightly. An "as is" clause means that the tenant waives any defects when he or she takes the property. But, as already noted, public policy may not allow the waiver of some conditions deemed to be for the good of the community. Waiver of benefits by either landlord or tenant, even if permitted by statute, is usually allowed only as long as no third party or public interests are affected.

INJURY TO THIRD PARTIES

Generally the landlord has liability only for those parts of the leased premises which exist for use by all the tenants or by others in the ordinary course of business.

Tenant Rights

THE RIGHT OF POSSESSION

The tenant has the right of possession of the premises.

USE AND ENJOYMENT

The tenant is entitled to quiet enjoyment and use of the premises for the purpose leased, as if it were the tenant's own property. To use the premises for a purpose other than that covered in the lease could constitute a lease violation. For example, if the premises were leased for residential use and then used for conducting a business, such usage would be in violation of the lease.

EMBLEMENTS

Emblements are things which grow on the land. The tenant has the right to harvest his or her crops after termination of the lease if the crops were planted before the termination and the lease was terminated for some unforeseen reason. However, this is usually not true if the lease has a definite termination date fixed in advance, because the tenant would know well in advance that the lease would end prior to harvest time.

Tenant Duties and Liabilities

RENT

The tenant's first duty is to pay the rent on time. The type and amount, and where and when it is payable, are specified in the lease. Rent may be in the form of money, services, labor, goods, crops, etc.

Amount of Rent

This is usually stipulated in the lease. If not, the tenant owes a reasonable rental value while under a lease. Appreciation or depreciation of the property does not affect the amount of rent due during the time the written lease is in effect. However, a new lease could reflect a rent change.

To Whom and When Rent Is Payable

This is usually stated in the lease. If the time of payment is not stated, the rent is not due until the end of the lease term. Rent must be paid to the landlord or landlord's duly authorized agent, as required.

Assignments of Rents

Unless prohibited in the lease, a tenant may sublease the property to a subtenant. Payment of the rent or a portion thereof is assigned to the subtenant, who must abide by the same terms as the original tenant. However, the original tenant remains responsible for paying the rent if the subtenant does not pay it. Both are liable for payment of the rent to the landlord, and rent is recoverable from either.

REPAIRS

It is the tenant's duty to keep the leased premises in good working order. This means tenant is responsible for maintaining the premises in everyday operating condition, including replacing broken windows, repairing broken doors, stopping simple leaks, and protecting the property from freezing. Tenant is not liable, however, for major repairs unless they are needed because of his or her negligence. Depreciation of the roof, rebuilding sections of the house, major painting work, and furnace or major plumbing repairs are not considered tenant's responsibility. Ordinary wear and tear and ordinary depreciation are expected to occur in rental property, and the tenant cannot be held responsible for this.

INJURIES TO THIRD PERSON

The tenant is normally responsible for injury to persons on the premises leased if the injury occurred as a result of a known defective condition or one which should have been known to the tenant by exercise of reasonable care. The tenant should maintain the property in a safe condition.

TAXES

The tenant might be obligated to pay additional taxes added to the landlord's property tax if the additional taxes are a result of improvements added to the property by the tenant without the landlord's knowledge or consent.

In other cases, a tenant who must pay the property taxes in order to protect his or her lease may deduct them from the rent payment rather than let the property be sold for nonpayment of taxes as a result of landlord's negligence.

WASTE

There is no one overall definition of what constitutes waste, as its meaning will frequently depend upon the situation. In farm property, for example, the tenant's removal and sale of timber from noncultivatable land may be regarded as waste. However, if the land was cultivatable and the removal of the timber was thorough enough to make it usable, such removal would usually not be deemed waste.

Generally there are three categories of waste:

1. Willful injury by the tenant

2. Nonaction by the tenant, such as failing to make certain basic repairs, which leads to deterioration of the property

3. Equitable waste—an act which, while not willful injury, nevertheless decreases the value of the landlord's interest; for example, changing the nature of a commercial property to residential use

The tenant may be held liable for those damages committed over and above ordinary wear and tear. If a jury finds that waste was committed wantonly, judgment may be for double the amount of damages assessed.

A tenant is also responsible for damages committed by third persons while the property is under lease.

FIXTURES

Fixtures are personal property affixed to the real estate so as to make it a part of the real property.

Whether the tenant may remove or must leave fixtures that have been affixed should be decided at the beginning of the lease and stated therein. However, if no agreement was made, a general ruling might be made along these lines:

1. Does removal seriously damage the property?

2. Was the fixture permanently or temporarily attached?

3. What was the original purpose of attaching the fixture to the property?

4. What is the nature of the attachment in regard to the premises?

If, after answering these four questions, it can be determined that the fixture has not become a permanent part of the realty, the tenant may remove it. Trade fixtures left beyond the time a lease expires become the property of the landlord, provided the lease had a definite termination date. If there is not a definite termination date, a reasonable time would be allowed for removal.

TENANCY TERMINATION

A written or oral lease may be terminated at any time by mutual agreement of the parties thereto. Leases also may be terminated by the occurrence of a contingency such as (1) arrival of a definite date, (2) passage of a period of months or years, (3) serious damage by fire or the elements, or (4) other agreed-upon contingencies.

NOTICE TO QUIT

If a tenant holds a year-to-year tenancy, either landlord or tenant may terminate the tenancy by giving 3 months written notice prior to the end of any year. If the tenancy is a month-to-month tenancy, 30 days notice in writing by either party will terminate the monthly tenancy. These conditions can, however, be altered by stipulation of an agreed-upon termination date.

DEATH

Unless there is a contractual agreement to the contrary, death does not terminate a year-to-year lease or a lease for years. The estate is bound to the tenancy. At will or sufferance tenancy is terminated by death.

EVICTION

The landlord or someone of paramount title may recover possession of his or her land and tenements through eviction. Eviction proceedings usually take place because a tenant has not paid the rent when due and is delinquent at the time of the eviction proceedings. Upon eviction, the tenant may treat the tenancy as terminated. Many jurisdictions follow the "forfeiture rule," which holds that tenants may not be evicted until they have had the opportunity to cure the forfeiture, i.e., the nonpayment of rent.

Complications may arise where tenants pay their rent into an escrow fund, but withhold these payments from the landlord or landlord's agent in protest over rental policies. Landlord-tenant law is by no means clear on this subject, nor is the case of eviction. Legal opinion is necessary and presumably will vary, case by case, depending on the facts presented in each situation and the housing codes and laws of the locality.

SALE OF THE LEASED PREMISES

Unless otherwise stipulated in the lease, sale does not terminate a lease. The new owner would assume landlord responsibilities and would be entitled to receive the rent. A properly prepared sales contract should state that the property being sold is "subject to existing tenancies," to provide for buyer-seller information on leases which may be in effect on the property being sold.

Normally the tenant does not have to be notified that a sale is pending. Obviously, in this day of enlightened landlord-tenant relations, keeping the lines of communication open is a good idea.

LANDLORD'S REMEDIES

In many of the states, the landlord holds an automatic lien on the tenant's personal property for payment of rent. To enforce this lien, landlord may use the "distress warrant" or "attachment" proceedings.

The landlord may use the "unlawful detainer" action to secure possession of landlord's property held by a tenant who owes delinquent rent.

TENANT'S REMEDIES

The tenant may refuse to accept the premises leased if the landlord does not deliver possession at the time provided in the lease, or tenant may accept the premises and sue for damages for failure to deliver possession.

VOID LEASES

Leases are generally subject to contract principles governing voidance or invalidity. (See Chapter 5, Contracts.)

TENANT ASSOCIATIONS AND UNIONS

Many younger, well-located rental apartment buildings near shopping and other amenities and close to employment centers, have been converted to condominiums in most of the country's major metropolitan areas. Besides the financial return to property owners who do so, another reason commonly advanced is the desire of owners to get out of the business of rental housing because of rising tenant militancy and pending rent control legislation. In recent years, tenants have increasingly formed associations and unions to assert their tenancy rights and interests in these rental properties. In the face of landlord-tenant (or owner-resident) differences of opinion, as well as rising operating and fixed expenses, it becomes ever more difficult to maintain good will while collecting rental payments and achieving financial goals.

While good and open lines of communication among residents, management agents, and owners are very helpful to everyone involved, the development and maintenance of such lines requires an increasing amount of time. The importance of public relations, the art of explanation and implementation of property management policy, and the solution of newer problems in dealing with increasingly assertive tenant associations and unions take their toll in time, patience, and good will. Combined with the public exercise of a greater degree of rent and other control (for example, the New Jersey legislature in 1972 enacted the first Landlord Security Deposit Ordinance, and the District of Columbia in 1974 enacted a temporary freeze or moratorium on apartment condominium conversions), there apparently is much to be decided in future years on the landlord-tenant issue. The license applicant, as well as the thoughtful reader, is cautioned to make the effort necessary to keep abreast of rapidly changing social needs and legislation in his or her community.

PRACTICE EXAMINATION: LANDLORD AND TENANT

1. When a lease is for years or from year to year, death of either landlord or tenant

   (A) terminates the lease
   (B) terminates the tenancy at sufferance
   (C) terminates delivery of possession
   (D) does not terminate the lease

2. Generally, a tenant is

   (A) liable for ordinary wear and tear, but not liable for waste
   (B) liable for waste, but not liable for ordinary wear and tear
   (C) liable for emblements, but not liable for repairs
   (D) none of these

3. Rent payments are in the form

   (A) of personal service
   (B) of money
   (C) of labor
   (D) specified in the lease

4. Sale of the leased premises by the landlord generally

   (A) terminates the lease
   (B) terminates a tenancy at will
   (C) terminates a rental obligation by the tenant
   (D) does not terminate the lease

5. General rules with regard to tenant installed fixtures are that

   I. a tenant may remove any fixture that has not become a permanent part of the realty
   II. a tenant may not remove fixtures that have become a permanent part of the realty

   (A) I only   (C) Both I and II
   (B) II only   (D) Neither I nor II

6. Liability to third persons who sustain injuries on the leased premises normally belongs to the

   I. landlord
   II. tenant

   (A) I only   (C) Both I and II
   (B) II only   (D) Neither I nor II

7. A tenancy for years

   I. is for a definite period of time
   II. is for an indefinite period of time

   (A) I only   (C) Both I and II
   (B) II only   (D) Neither I nor II

8. Generally speaking, the validity of leases is determined by

   (A) principles of contract law
   (B) recording
   (C) special rules
   (D) none of these

9. The term that specifies a tenant's interest in the property is

   (A) a reversionary interest
   (B) a leasehold estate
   (C) a life estate
   (D) landlord's sufferance

10. The most common form of lease is

    (A) a tenancy for years
    (B) a tenancy from year to year
    (C) a tenancy at will
    (D) a tenancy by sufferance

11. On leased premises, a tenant has the right to

    (A) possession and control
    (B) possession and enjoyment
    (C) possession, control, and enjoyment
    (D) none of these, unless expressly granted in the lease

12. A tenancy at will is a tenancy of

    (A) indefinite duration that the landlord can terminate at will
    (B) definite duration that the tenant can terminate at will
    (C) definite duration that either landlord or tenant can terminate at will
    (D) indefinite duration that either landlord or tenant can terminate at will

13. The interest or estate which a lessee has in real property by virtue of a lease is

    I. less than a freehold
    II. a leasehold

    (A) I only   (C) Both I and II
    (B) II only   (D) Neither I nor II

14. To convey property by lease is to

    (A) demise   (C) sublet
    (B) devise   (D) none of these

15. In order to come under the provisions of the Statute of Frauds, a lease must be for

    (A) 12 months or longer
    (B) more than 12 months
    (C) at least 2 years
    (D) none of these

16. The landlord may recover possession of the property by going into court and obtaining

    (A) an "unlawful detainer"
    (B) a "dejection certificate"
    (C) a "repossession notice"
    (D) none of these

17. In order to create a valid tenancy,

    (A) the tenant must not commit waste
    (B) the tenant must make minor repairs
    (C) the tenant must occupy the property with the landlord's consent
    (D) none of these

18. If a lease is terminated for some unforeseen reason, the lessee may recover

    (A) the encumbrances   (C) the leasehold
    (B) the emblements   (D) none of these

19. General guidelines in determining whether or not an item is a fixture are (is)

    (A) whether removal will seriously damage the property
    (B) what the intent of the party installing it was
    (C) how it was installed
    (D) all of these

20. If a date for termination of a lease cannot be determined, this usually is considered

    (A) a tenancy at will
    (B) a tenancy from year to year
    (C) a tenancy by the entireties
    (D) a tenancy in common

Chapter 13

Real Estate Financing

INTRODUCTION

Most real estate sales require some sort of financing of a portion of the purchase price. The most popular method is with a mortgage loan.

Obtaining financing through the various lending institutions is one of the more difficult steps for the home buyer to understand. Most home buyers are not familiar with the range of loan services available to them from various institutions or their procedural requirements. This is an area where the broker or salesperson can play a vital role in dealing with the potential homeowner. In his or her professional capacity, the salesperson should become familiar with the various lending institutions, including not only their history but also their current operations, requirements, and procedures necessary to qualify potential homeowners for mortgage loans.

The relationship of the real estate agent with lending institutions has been significantly changing over the last few years. Previously, home buyers were required to find their own mortgage financing. Today, however, the real estate agent has become increasingly aware that offering favorable financing has added to sales over the years. In times of "tight" money in 1966, 1969, and 1973-1974, the agent that found and offered favorable financing made the sale, not the one that did little or nothing to help the home buyer.

The agent should keep in contact with several lenders to see if they are in the market for new or existing home mortgages. If they are, the agent should learn their requirements and determine their lending patterns. Then, upon obtaining a contract of purchase, the agent should direct the purchaser to a lender who has indicated interest in that type of loan. After the purchaser's application is approved, the lender will then issue a loan commitment based on an appraisal of the property and the purchaser's ability to repay the loan. The mortgage commitment is a promise by the lender that the firm will make the loan at the time of settlement.

Rates and terms of mortgages vary according to many factors. These include the supply and demand factor, or the supply of mortgage money available versus the demand for loans by borrowers; the degree of risk involved; and what return (called yield) an investor can get from other types of investments, such as government bonds, certificates of deposit, and other similar investments.

MORTGAGES

The term *mortgage* is widely and commonly used, even though in most cases a deed of trust and deed of trust note may have actually been used to obtain and secure a loan on real property. Essentially, a mortgage is a loan.

Purchasers have several types of repayment plans on "mortgages" from which to choose. The ones most commonly used in residential real estate are:

1. Straight mortgage

2. Amortized mortgage

3. Flexible-payment mortgage

Straight Mortgage

The *straight mortgage* is a mortgage that requires no repayment of principal until the end of the mortgage term. The only payments made are those for the interest due, usually on some periodic basis (i.e., quarterly, semiannually, or annually). The major problem with this is that the entire amount of the original principal falls due at the end of the mortgage term. This type of mortgage, with a "balloon-type" payment at the end, was widely used in the early part of this century by home purchasers, but it is seldom used today in single-family financing. It is still used for construction and interim financing for builders, contractors, and developers, and for some commercial loans.

Amortized Mortgage

The *amortized mortgage* is a mortgage that requires a periodic or systematic repayment of both principal and interest due over the entire life of the mortgage loan. Most borrowers as well as lenders prefer this type of repayment inasmuch as the systematic payment reduces the debt regularly and results in a home that is free and clear of debt at the end of the mortgage term. The popularization of the amortized mortgage has been one of the most important steps in widening the opportunity of home ownership in the United States.

Under the amortized mortgage, monthly payments are most common. In addition to the monthly payment covering principal and interest, most lenders will also set up *escrow accounts* in which each month borrowers deposit one-twelfth of the annual taxes and insurance premiums. This total payment for principal, interest, taxes, and insurance is referred to as PITI.

The use of the escrow fund has great advantages for the homeowner. For instance, the homeowner can plan to pay the amount of money needed for taxes and insurance in twelve equal installments to the lender, so that when the lump sum payments become due sufficient money is available in escrow to pay them. Most lenders prefer the use of an escrow fund to ensure that the taxes are paid promptly, and that the house is continuously insured. Otherwise tax liens could be filed against the property, or it could suffer uninsured damage, causing the lender as well as the owner financial loss.

Currently, some lenders provide that nominal rates of interest be credited to the deposits of these escrow accounts. As consumer actions spread across the country, interest-bearing escrow accounts can be expected to grow along with them.

Monthly payments on amortized mortgages usually take the form of "direct reduction." First, interest is paid against the total balance of the principal remaining, then the balance of the principal and interest payment is applied toward the reduction of the principal. Interest is always calculated on the current balance of the loan and not on the original mortgage amount.

The following Monthly Payment Chart shows the *principal* and *interest* payments necessary to amortize various loans over a given number of years.

Monthly Payment Necessary per $1,000 Loan

Years	8%	9%	10%	12%
1	$86.99	87.45	87.92	88.85
5	20.28	20.76	21.25	22.25
10	12.14	12.67	13.22	14.35
15	9.56	10.14	10.75	12.01
20	8.37	9.00	9.66	11.02
25	7.72	8.39	9.09	10.54
30	7.34	8.05	8.78	10.29

Example: A $35,000 loan at 10 percent for 30 years would have monthly principal and interest payments of $307.30.

Solution: $35,000 ÷ $1,000 equals a multiple of 35, or 35 thousands. Multiply 35 × $8.78 (per $1,000 loan), or $307.30.

A $35,000 loan at 12 percent for 30 years would have monthly principal and interest payments of $360.15 (35 × $10.29).

To compute payments required for rates between those given above, use the following procedure:

Example: What would be the monthly principal and interest payments for a $40,000 loan for 30 years at 9.5 percent?

Solution:

Payment required at 9 percent = $8.05

Payment required at 10 percent = $8.78

$16.83 ÷ 2 = $8.42 per month per thousand ($1,000)

The following Loan Progress Charts show the remaining balance of amortized loans during the lifetime of the loan.

Loan Progress Chart
Dollar Balance Remaining on a $1,000 Loan

	8% Original Term in Years				
Age of Loan	10	15	20	25	30
1	932	964	979	987	992
2	858	925	956	973	983
3	778	883	931	957	973
4	692	837	904	941	962
5	598	788	875	923	951
10	—	471	689	808	877
15	—	—	413	636	768
20	—	—	—	381	605
25	—	—	—	—	362
30	—	—	—	—	—

Loan Progress Chart
Dollar Balance Remaining on a $1,000 Loan

	9% Original Term in Years				
Age of Loan	10	15	20	25	30
1	935	967	981	989	993
2	865	931	961	977	986
3	787	891	938	963	978
4	703	848	914	949	969
5	610	801	887	933	959
10	—	489	710	827	894
15	—	—	433	662	793
20	—	—	—	404	635
25	—	—	—	—	388
30	—	—	—	—	—

Loan Progress Chart
Dollar Balance Remaining on a $1,000 Loan

	12% Original Term in Years				
Age of Loan	10	15	20	25	30
1	945	975	987	993	996
2	883	946	973	986	992
3	813	914	956	977	988
4	734	877	938	967	982
5	645	837	917	957	977
10	—	540	767	878	934
15	—	—	495	734	857
20	—	—	—	473	717
25	—	—	—	—	462
30	—	—	—	—	—

Example: An original 30-year loan of $35,000 at 9 percent would have a remaining balance at the end of 5 years of $959 for each $1,000 borrowed, or $33,565 (35 × $959); and a remaining balance of $31,290 after 10 years (35 × $894).

Loan Progress Chart
Dollar Balance Remaining on a $1,000 Loan

	10% Original Term in Years				
Age of Loan	10	15	20	25	30
1	939	970	983	991	994
2	871	936	965	980	988
3	796	899	945	969	982
4	713	858	923	956	974
5	622	813	898	942	966
10	—	506	730	846	909
15	—	—	454	688	817
20	—	—	—	428	664
25	—	—	—	—	413
30	—	—	—	—	—

Flexible-Payment Mortgage

On February 26, 1974, the Federal Home Loan Bank Board, the regulatory agency supervising federal savings and loan associations, announced that it had adopted regulation changes allowing flexible-payment mortgage loans by federal savings and loan associations. A home borrower and a savings-and-loan lender can now negotiate a payment schedule based on the borrower's financial position. This type of mortgage was created because of the rising prices of housing. A purchaser, especially a younger couple with an optimistic expectation of rising income, may wish to make lower payments during the early years of their loan and "catch up" later. For example:

On an 8%, $30,000 mortgage, the normal monthly payment to principal and interest would be $220. Using the flexible payment mortgage, the borrower could, instead, pay as little as $200 per month (or payment as low as the interest only) for the first 5 years and then $230 per month for the remaining term. This would enable a family with rising income expectations to purchase a home sooner than they otherwise could afford to.*

News release, Federal Home Loan Bank Board, Washington, D.C., Feb. 26, 1974.

The Federal Home Loan Bank Board placed two restrictions on flexible-payment mortgages:

1. Each monthly payment must at least cover the interest due on the loan for that payment.

2. The loan must be on a fully amortizing basis by the end of the fifth year.

A flexible-payment mortgage could cover a loan of up to 95 percent of the value of the property, provided other private mortgage insurance covers the top part of the loan. (See Savings and Loan Associations and Magic Financing in later sections for further details.)

Also provisions in the Housing and Community Development Act of 1974 authorize the Secretary of HUD to make a limited experimental demonstration of uneven-amortization mortgage financing, ending June 30, 1976.

Difference between Flexible-Payment Mortgage and Variable-Rate Mortgage

In an effort to combat the effects of credit stringency and resulting "tight" money (or nonavailability of money for mortgage loans) in both the new home and the resale housing market, the concept of a *variable-rate* mortgage has been advanced. Technically, this means that the interest rate of a mortgage loan can be either raised or lowered by the lender to account for either the undersupply or oversupply of mortgage (or depositor) funds available for home loans. The purpose of the variable-rate mortgage is to make the return to the lender on a long-term housing loan competitive with the long-term interest rates the lender might receive from alternative investments.

Popular sentiment on the subject of variable-rate mortgages argues instead, however, that the term of the loan be either extended or reduced in response to tight money, rather than changing the interest rate of the loan. As the term of the loan is varied (to make the lender's loanable funds more competitive with long-term interest rates elsewhere in the private marketplace), the monthly payment of the homeowner is allowed to remain constant, simplifying debtor (and creditor) records.

During 1975 the Federal Home Loan Bank Board has authorized a select few savings and loan associations to experiment with the variable-rate mortgage. If feasible, and accepted by the consumer, the practice may spread. However, the concept of the variable-rate mortgage is far from resolved at the moment.

TERMS OF LOANS AND BORROWER QUALIFICATIONS

Most mortgages are long-term, ranging from 20 to 30 years. The term is determined by the type and characteristics of the property itself, the borrower's age and ability to pay, federal or state restrictions imposed on the lender, and the lender's own policies.

Basically two considerations determine acceptability of the property and the applicant: (1) physical security (the property itself), and (2) borrower security (ability to pay).

Physical Security

The lender will look at the property in terms of its location, condition, future marketability, neighborhood, and material used in construction to determine whether or not to make the loan.

Borrower Security

The lender will not only look at the ability of the borrower to make the monthly payments, but will also consider age, marital status, job stability, other expenses, and other family income in an effort to determine the loan applicant's financial and personal stability.

The borrower's income may be broken down into several categories.

PRIMARY INCOME

This type of income usually includes monthly salary from a primary job, less monthly expenses for food, clothing, medical bills, auto and insurance, house maintenance, etc. Each lender will have its own "rule of thumb" guidelines. Most lenders will approve a loan if no more than 20 to 25 percent of gross monthly income is spent on housing. Consumers increasingly have been finding it necessary to spend a higher proportion of their income on housing.

SECONDARY INCOME

This includes any source of income which adds to the primary income (items such as income from stocks, investment property, and part-time jobs). In most cases, all such income is considered, although rarely is 100 percent of it counted as additional income. The major emphasis is placed on the stability of the secondary income rather than its total amount.

As a result of the increased national attention to the matters of women's liberation and civil rights equality, the secondary income brought into a family household by working wives and mothers is seen to be increasingly important. Officials of the U.S. Department of Labor call to the attention of lenders the emerging financial power of working women, either single or married, and the stability of their work patterns. Therefore, lenders have now adopted more liberal attitudes and policies favoring the "net" result of such figures.

Lenders are advised also to be nondiscriminatory as to sex in their loan policies and to advance home ownership loans to women on terms—down payments, interest rates, length of loan, appraisal valuation on the property—equal to those offered to single male adults or family men. Loan policies must not favor either sex, but rather be impartial to all.*

Points (Loan Discounts)

Loan discounts are measured in points. One *point* is 1 percent of the mortgage loan amount. Points are charged by lenders to adjust the effective interest rate so that the yield on the loan is equal to the yield the lender can obtain from other types of more lucrative, sound investments. For example, if a $30,000 mortgage is advanced at a 4 point discount, the lender will make a cash outlay of only $28,800. The borrower, however, is obligated to pay back the full $30,000 mortgage, at the regular mortgage interest rate specified. Lenders consider that 2 loan discount points are equal to an increase in the mortgage interest rate of $\frac{1}{4}$ of 1 percent over the life of a loan. Another variation on the practice of charging points occurs when the lender requests 4 points from the borrower at the time of the mortgage loan commitment as a cost of obtaining the mortgage. Then, at settlement, the $30,000 mortgage is granted to the borrower.

Loan discounts or points are used by lenders in states where usury laws set upper limits on mortgage interest rates. Points are an "adjustment factor" employed by lenders to make the return on a long-term mortgage loan competitive with the interest rates received on other types of loans where usury laws are not in effect. Loan discounts are also used in situations where interest rates set by governmental authorities are lower than competitive rates in the open market. Therefore, the lender is not able to make the loan unless a competitive return can be received.

With a few exceptions allowed by the Veterans Housing Act of 1974, government-backed loans (FHA and VA) do not allow the purchaser to pay more than 1 percent of the loan amount as a loan origination fee; therefore, the seller must pay any loan discounts required to secure the loan. In conventional financing, payment of any loan discounts is usually resolved by negotiation between purchaser and seller.

Prepayment Penalties

Most lending institutions impose a penalty for prepaying a conventional loan before its maturity. While these penalties vary widely from lender to lender, a fairly typical penalty would be the charge of a certain

*The 1974 Housing and Community Development Act requires that lenders consider the combined incomes of husband and wife in extending mortgage credit. Also, 1975 Regulations of the Federal Home Loan Bank Board require that lenders treat female applicants for home loans (i.e., single or divorced women who are fully employed) on a parity with their male counterparts. In addition, the new regulations require every lender making federally related loans to consider "without prejudice" the combined income of both husband and wife in extending mortgage credit to a married couple.

percentage if the loan is prepaid in the first 5 years, and a lesser percentage if the loan is prepaid after 5 years but before maturity. These percentages are computed on either the original balance or the remaining balance at the time of prepayment. Another widely used prepayment penalty is one in which the borrower is charged 30 to 90 days interest on the remaining balance at the time of payoff. These penalties are imposed to reimburse the lender for all the expenses incurred in originating a loan.

Government-backed loans (VA and FHA) do not allow a prepayment penalty to be charged to the borrower on loans for single-family housing.

With the prospects relatively dim for a return to mortgage interest rates at the low 6 to 7 percent levels, many lenders have modified or completely eliminated their prepayment penalty policies. Today's mortgage rates are usually higher than yesteryear's, since the costs to the lender have risen also. For example, lenders must now pay depositors 6 to 7 percent to attract their passbook accounts and even higher rates to attract the larger amount, longer-term certificates of deposit.

As a result, lenders are not averse to having borrowers pay off their old loan balances at the lower rates of interest, with no, or smaller, prepayment fees, since this returns to the lenders new funds to lend to new borrowers at the higher and more competitive rates of interest. High prepayment penalties discourage more rapid loan payoff, keeping mortgage balances outstanding at the lower rates of interest.

Appraisals

All loans are based on the sales price or the appraisal amount, whichever is lower. Purchasers can pay more than the appraisal amount, and often must do so. With government-backed loans, the amount above the loan allowed by the appraisal must be paid in cash.

LENDING INSTITUTIONS

The range of institutions that serve as sources of funds and supply mortgage money to the housing markets includes:

Savings and loan associations

Commercial banks

Mutual savings banks

Life insurance companies

Loan correspondents

Individuals and organizations

Real estate investment trusts (REITs)

Pension funds

The first five are the major sources of mortgage loans for home buyers. They are discussed below. Government-backed loans (FHA and VA) are essential ingredients in the home mortgage loan picture as well, and their roles will also be discussed.

Savings and Loan Associations

Savings and loan associations (S & L's) are local privately managed and privately owned financing institutions which serve as depositories for the personal savings of numerous families and individuals across the United States. These institutions invest the major portion of these savings accounts in home mortgages, including loans for home repair and modernization and for new construction. S & L's are the largest of all residential mortgage lenders.

Competition determines the interest rates that are charged for mortgage loans, as do federal requirements, availability of money, and risk of loans. The interest earned is in turn used by the S & L to pay operating expenses and maintain reserves, and also to pay interest on savings accounts to its depositors.

Federal savings and loans are incorporated under the authority of the Federal Home Loan Bank Board, subject to statutory codes for associations in the state in which they do business. State-chartered S & L's are usually regulated by the State Commissioner of Banking.

All federally chartered S & L's and most state-chartered S & L's are mutually owned. Mutual ownership means that the individual association has no partners and no stockholders—only depositors. While S & L's have been very successful and their record of service to home owners is enviable, a move was started in mid-1974 by the regulatory Federal Home Loan Bank Board to adopt regulations which will permit federally insured mutual associations, both federally chartered and state chartered, to convert to the state-chartered *stock* form of ownership organization if this is permitted by state law. The purpose of converting to stock ownership is to raise equity capital in order to support growth and expanded services to the public. A mutual S & L can look only to retained earnings for its capital. When money is tight and the business climate unfavorable, relying on the inflows of depositors' savings and an excessive portfolio of low-interest-bearing mortgages may not permit the institution to continue to make new mortgage loans.

S & L's principally lend on single-family homes, multifamily apartment buildings (including condominiums), and combination residential-commercial buildings with small amounts of commercial space. Very little S & L money is loaned on large office or commercial buildings.

Usually S & L's require the borrower to make a down payment of at least 10 percent of the amount of the sales price. However, the down payment may range from 5 to 40 percent, depending on risk and market conditions. S & L's have the authority in certain cases to lend 95 percent of the purchase price, but they seldom do this. Their normal down payment ranges from 15 to 25 percent.

S & L's make loans on three major types of real estate:

1. Home construction loans
2. Home purchase loans
3. Loans for other purposes

HOME CONSTRUCTION LOANS

About one-sixth of all S & L funds are placed in new home construction loans. These loans are made to a builder so that the builder can construct primarily single-family houses. Construction loans usually take the form of installment payout, which means that money is released to the builder as certain phases of construction are completed. For example, a certain percentage of the total construction loan may be released after the footings have been set, an equal amount after the roof and framing are in place, and so on until the house is complete and the total loan has been paid to the builder. The S & L's are very careful to see that no mechanic's liens are placed against the property, so that clear title can be given to the new owner. Mechanic's liens arise when the builder fails to pay the subcontractors or the material suppliers for work done on the structures.

During the 1950s, loans made by S & L's for the construction of one- to four-family homes (commonly called single-family homes) amounted to 30 percent of their lending activity. By 1973, however, that share had declined to 17 percent of their mortgage lending. However, S & L's are still important lenders in the production of new homes.

HOME PURCHASE LOANS

The majority of S & L money is placed directly into home purchase mortgages, a critical component of the housing market. Without home purchase mortgages, new construction would not take place at its present volume. These mortgages enable people to "move up" from their present home to one which is larger or more adaptable to their mode or standard of living. The total housing market economy is based on new home mortgages and construction as well as a very substantial existing home mortgage market.

S & L's put over 50 percent of their available mortgage money into existing home mortgages, which represent their major financing activity. This involved $28.2 billion in 1973 alone, for a new record, or 57.1 percent of all the loans made by all S & L's in 1973.* Mortgage loans were placed on 1,240,000 existing homes and 307,000 new homes. This clearly illustrates the "filtering concept" wherein 4 existing homes are sold for each new one built and sold.

MORTGAGE LOANS FOR OTHER PURPOSES

A variety of loans for other purposes account for about one-fourth to one-third of all S & L lending. This includes

*All 1973 figures are obtained from the *'74 Savings & Loan Fact Book,* United States League of Savings Associations, Chicago, Ill.

modernization, repairs, refinancing of existing loans, land development loans, and loans generally on small non-residential income properties. Loans for other purposes amounted to $12.8 billion in 1973, or 25.8 percent of total mortgage lending.

A major shift in the desire for home improvement loans has arisen within the last few years, with S & L's recognizing their value to the security of the underlying home mortgage. Home improvement makes the first mortgage less risky, and also helps to upgrade and stabilize the neighborhood. S & L's try to level out interest rate fluctuations by making more short-term (5-year) mortgage loans. Home improvement loans for insulation, storm windows, and other improvements also help the nation's energy conservation effort. In 1973, home improvement loans totaled nearly $1.5 billion. Since a declared intention of the 1974 Housing Act is to encourage the preservation of the nation's housing stock, more growth in consumer loans of this type can be anticipated. Federal S & L's can now raise their limit on single-family property improvement loans from $5,000 to $10,000 and on loans on multiunit structures from $15,000 to $25,000.

Home improvement loans can range from 3 to 20 years, unless they are incorporated into the first mortgage. The consolidated loan for home purchase and home improvement then broadens into one which can run for as long as 30 years.

In recent years mobile home loans have expanded significantly. These are another form of consumer loan which S & L's are authorized to make; they can be used to purchase either new or used units. Mobile home loans totaled over $1.8 billion in 1973. Since the 1974 Housing Act has broadened the term "rural housing" to include mobile homes and mobile home sites, and has also raised the term of a single-module mobile home loan from 12 to 15 years and the amount which can be loaned from $15,000 to $25,000, more growth can also be expected in the mobile home loan business.

Commercial Banks

Commercial banks play a significant role in the financing of real estate. However, their major role is in areas other than long-term mortgage loan financing. Requirements are placed on them by federal and/or state governing agencies, depending on whether they are national or state banks. These requirements include a smaller loan-to-value ratio, shorter mortgage terms, and an interest rate ceiling. Operating under these limitations, they are less able to compete with other lending institutions.

Commercial banks, nonetheless, play a most vital role in real estate financing. They are the most prominent source of construction or short-term financing, in which the permanent mortgage follows and is placed with another lending institution after completion of construction. Banks also play a vital role in short-term financing of home improvements and repairs, and in making short-term loans to other mortgage institutions. They also hold and service mortgages on real estate in their trust departments.

Between 1960 and 1971, commercial banks improved their national ranking from third place to second place in holdings of conventional first mortgages on single-family homes. In 1971, commercial banks held 2,185,000 mortgages (or 18 percent of the total number of 12,319,000 single-family-home conventional first mortgages) as contrasted to 6,030,000 mortgages held by savings and loan associations (or 49 percent of the total number). By the end of 1974, mortgage holdings on residential properties by commercial banks totaled $81 billion, versus $226 billion for savings and loan associations. In third place, with $62 billion, were mutual savings banks.

Mutual Savings Banks

Mutual savings banks are similar to savings and loan associations in that they are also depositor-type thrift institutions. Mutual savings banks, like savings and loan associations, have a long history in the United States. They were first organized in the industrialized areas of the East, beginning in 1816 with the Philadelphia Savings Fund Society, to encourage savings by factory workers. Unquestionably one of the basic strengths of the home ownership phenomenon in the United States has been the strength and growth of these savings intermediaries which have fostered and pooled together the small accounts of many individual savers to provide mortgage loans and thus the advantages of property ownership to millions.

While mutual savings banks are mutual organizations owned and operated solely for the benefit of their depositors, like savings and loan associations, depositors do not manage or operate them. Management is vested in a board of trustees. More limited in location than savings and loan associations, mutual savings banks are located in 18 states and Puerto Rico, with three-fourths of their total assets concentrated in savings banks located in New York and Massachusetts. Mutual savings banks are state-chartered and regulated.

Even though mutual savings banks may invest in loans other than mortgages, from the beginning they have regarded mortgage loans as prime investments. During World War II, however, mutual savings bank assets were invested substantially in United States Government securities and bonds. Later, the postwar housing boom, with the widespread use of FHA-insured and VA-guaranteed loans, encouraged them to return to single-family-home mortgage financing. In addition to ranking third in single-family mortgage loans outstanding, mutual savings banks also carry $16.8 billion in multifamily residential property mortgage loans (out of a total of $90.4 billion in multifamily mortgages) as of year-end 1973.

Life Insurance Companies

Life insurance companies over the years have typically been conservative investors, because they act as trustees for their policy holders, the major source of their investing funds. Also, state charters limit the amount insurance companies can invest in mortgages to a certain percentage of their assets. The reason for the limitation rests in the fact that real estate mortgages are considered more risky and less liquid (easy to convert to cash) than such alternative investments as government bonds, municipal bonds, or major corporate preferred stock.

Even with this percentage limitation, life insurance companies will not always lend up to their legal limit. They base their investment decisions on market characteristics and alternative yields. During the tight money market of the latter part of the 1960s, insurance companies sought short-term investments rather than long-term mortgage loans. During that time, life insurance companies could find higher yields in investments other than real property. When this situation occurs, demands for money and loans increase and short-term interest rates also tend to increase, with long-term loan requirements becoming more difficult (higher down payments, higher interest rates, and shorter terms). Money markets tend to tighten since money sources compete for available funds.

Life insurance companies have the luxury of regular deposits of funds paid by their policy holders. This is quite different from the erratic nature of the deposits from S & L and mutual savings bank depositors. The predictability of mortality figures, combined with the relative stability of insurance premium payments, enable both long-term and large-scale real property investments. Increasingly, the life insurance company (like every other lender) is seeking to participate in equity investments more fully, in addition to mortgage or debt holdings. An equity position is desired, but this may be combined with the mortgage and construction loans as well. As a result, with large funds to lend, life insurance companies have diversified into large residential and commercial holdings, with an ever-greater say in management policy. Their funds and interest have made possible the construction of large-scale new town developments, such as Columbia, Maryland. The life insurance company is usually not interested in the individual and smaller single-family-home loan unless it is joined in a large-scale undertaking.

Even so, life insurance companies held $21.8 billion in residential mortgage loans outstanding on one- to four-family residential properties as of year-end 1973, to rank number six nationally. However, life insurance companies ranked second to savings and loan associations in multifamily mortgage loans outstanding, or $18.3 billion versus $24.2 billion, as of year-end 1973, and also held second place to commercial banks, with $34.5 billion (vs. $38.4 billion) in commercial property mortgage loans outstanding, versus $21.1 billion for savings and loan associations and $12.1 billion for mutual savings banks.

Loan Correspondents

Often, large institutional lenders such as insurance companies, real estate investment trusts, and pension funds do not have their own mortgage loan departments. Or, they may make mortgage loans many miles from home. In these cases they usually use a local agent or loan correspondent. The local agents are more familiar with the local real estate market, neighborhood characteristics, quality of properties, and local economic conditions. These large and substantial investors select a local agent to act as a loan correspondent to carefully screen and handle mortgage loans.

Loan correspondents generally fall into two major classifications:

1. Mortgage brokers
2. Mortgage bankers

MORTGAGE BROKERS

Mortgage brokers act as agents for large and small lenders. Their job consists of securing applicants for mortgage loans, screening property and applicants, and placing loans. In effect, they match borrowers and lenders, helping one party to find loans and the other party to place loans. For their services they usually receive a percentage of the mortgage amount as a commission or brokerage fee. Loans originated by mortgage brokers are closed in the name of the lender, who will then service the loan (make the monthly collections).

MORTGAGE BANKERS

Mortgage bankers provide the same range of services as mortgage brokers. However, they close loans in their own name. Once they have originated a number of mortgages, these closed mortgages are packaged and sold to an institutional investor in large blocks. (See the section on federally supported agencies later in this chapter.)

To protect themselves against price changes in the market while they are originating loans, mortgage bankers usually enter into a firm agreement with the investor which states that the investor will purchase a given dollar amount of closed mortgages at a certain price. With this agreement the mortgage banker is able to make firm mortgage commitments to builders and real estate brokers to place loans at set prices.

In addition to the origination fee, mortgage bankers will usually retain servicing (collecting monthly payments, maintaining escrow accounts, paying taxes, etc.) of the loans they have originated. For the servicing, they usually receive a fee of $\frac{1}{4}$ to $\frac{1}{2}$ percent of the monthly mortgage payments for the life of the loan.

According to a research report of the Mortgage Bankers Association of America, the cost of originating and servicing single-family mortgage loans rose much more sharply from 1969 to 1972 than gross income received; thus net income fell. The report states that inflation hit mortgage banking, and raises a serious question whether mortgage bankers can continue to profitably service the volume and smaller denomination of the single-family mortgage loan.*

*Mortgage Banking Survey of Single-Family Loan Operations, 1972. Research Committee Operations Report No. 3, Mortgage Bankers Association of America, Washington, D.C., January 1974.

TYPES OF FINANCING

A purchaser of real estate has several types of financing available. The principal types are:

1. Government-backed loans

2. Conventional loans

3. Assumption (taking over an existing loan)

Government-backed Loans

Government-backed loans are either insured by the Federal Housing Administration (FHA) or guaranteed by the Veterans Administration (VA). They have been an important factor in increasing home ownership since World War II.

FHA LOANS

The Federal Housing Administration (FHA) has many programs, including property improvement loans, low- and moderate-income housing assistance loans, programs for persons on active military duty, and many others. Only the regular FHA program [Section 203 (b) of the National Housing Act] will be discussed here.

The FHA does not lend money; it insures the loan. Being insured against loss if the purchaser defaults has encouraged lenders to make loans with small down payments. The FHA operates this insurance program by adding a $\frac{1}{2}$ of 1 percent Mortgage Insurance Premium (MIP) to the regular interest rate on FHA loans. This MIP is used like a mutual insurance fund from which the FHA sets up a reserve to pay for expenses and losses. The MIP is adjusted annually on the outstanding balance of the loan. The historical experience with the *regular* FHA insurance program is that such funds have enabled the FHA to become a self-supporting federal agency. (However, see the following section, FHA's Problems.)

The normal term of a regular FHA-insured loan can be any multiple of 5 years up to a maximum of 30 years. FHA-insured loan amounts can be any multiple of $50, with a maximum of $45,000 for a single-family home. FHA mortgages are amortized by direct reduction, and escrows are collected for taxes and insurance.

Properties to be financed under the FHA insurance program must meet FHA minimum property standards, often referred to as M.P.S.'s. In addition to M.P.S.'s, design and location are additional factors in the qualification of properties.

To obtain an FHA loan, the purchaser usually must certify that he or she intends to occupy the property.

The ratio of loan to value on FHA mortgages varies, depending on when the structure was built and whether an application was applied for before or after construction, as well as the program being used. The insured loan allowed under the regular FHA program for properties over 1 year old or those approved prior to construction is:

97 percent of the first $25,000

90 percent of the next $10,000

80 percent of the amount above $35,000 (up to the maximum insured loan of $45,000)*

The percentages are computed on sales price or appraisal amount, whichever is lower, and loan amounts are always adjusted downward to a multiple of $50 if necessary.

Example 1: Sales price and appraisal of $34,600.

97% of the first $25,000 = loan of $24,250

90% of the next $9,600 = loan of $\underline{\quad 8,640\quad}$

$32,890

The $32,890 is not a multiple of $50, so $40 must be deducted, giving a maximum loan of $32,850, which subtracted from the sales price of $34,600, leaves a required down payment of $1,750.

Example 2: Sales price and appraisal of $40,000.

97 % of the first $25,000 = loan of	$24,250
90% of the next $10,000 = loan of	9,000
80% of the amount above $35,000 ($40,000 − $35,000 = $5,000 × 80%) = loan of	$ 4,000
	$37,250

Subtracting the FHA-insured loan of $37,250 from the sales price of $40,000 results in a required down payment of $2,750.

Example 3: Sales price and appraisal of $48,700.

97% of the first $25,000 = loan of	$24,250
90% of the next $10,000 = loan of	9,000
80% of the amount above $35,000 ($48,700 − $35,000 = $13,700 × 80% = loan of	10,960
	$44,210

The indicated loan of $44,210 has to be lowered to a multiple of $50, which results in a loan of $44,200. The down payment required is the difference between the sales price (or appraisal figure) and the maximum loan, or $48,700 − $44,200 = $4,500 down payment.

Note: In example 3, if the sales price had been higher than the appraisal figure, say $49,500, the buyer would have had to put up an extra $800 down payment ($49,500 sales price − $48,700 appraisal figure), making a total down payment of $5,300. The loan would have remained the same, at $44,200, since this is the maximum FHA-insured loan amount with an appraisal of $48,700 under *any* circumstances.

*Effective with the Housing and Community Development Act of 1974, the maximum mortgage amount for one- to four-family houses insured by the FHA was raised from $33,000 to $45,000 per dwelling unit.

If calculations result in an indicated loan of more than $45,000, the amount between $45,000 (the maximum loan amount under the regular program) and the sales price becomes the down payment required.

Down payments on FHA-insured loans must be paid from the purchaser's assets, as the FHA does not allow second trusts upon origination of the loan. This does not prevent a purchaser who is selling the property at some later date from taking back a second trust, should he or she decide to do so.

FHA's Problems

In 1934, the original concept of FHA was that it would be an actuarially sound, self-supporting, mutual mortgage insurance program. In this respect, Section 203 (b) of the National Housing Act has been a success since its inception, having underwritten or insured the mortgage loans of over 10 million families in more than 40 years.

However, late in the 1960s, it was felt necessary to expand the federal government's commitment to and involvement in insuring low-income, subsidized housing. Accordingly, Section 235, as well as Sections 236 and others, of the Housing and Urban Development Act of 1968 were enacted, enabling home ownership and/or rental subsidies for the low-income family. Unfortunately, in a relatively short time, the FHA acquired, and the U.S. government now owns, an excessively large number of subsidized properties—single-family as well as multi-family—as a result of loan defaults and foreclosures. In popular parlance, Uncle Sam has become a slum landlord.

In addition, the FHA has come under intense scrutiny for improper supervision of subsidized housing operations in certain areas of the country, resulting in Justice Department prosecutions for fradulent practices. Thus the traditional role of the FHA was transformed and expanded, and apparently abuses have resulted. However, the 1974 Housing and Community Development Act gave the FHA a vote of confidence by extending its authority for its "regular," or nonsubsidized, single-family and multifamily operations at the same time it decreed the demise of the various subsidized home mortgage programs by either cutting back or ending their funding.

VA OR GI LOANS

Several groups of people are eligible for a VA-guaranteed loan.

1. World War II veterans who served on active duty for 90 days or more, any part of which was served between September 16, 1940, and July 25, 1947

2. Korean Conflict veterans who served on active duty for 90 days or more, any part of which was served between June 27, 1950, and January 31, 1955

3. Veterans who served on active duty 181 days or more after January 31, 1955 (the end of the Korean Conflict)

4. Servicemen who have been on active military duty for two or more years

5. Unremarried widows and wives of veterans missing in action, or captured, under certain conditions

6. Those who qualify for restoration of previously used eligibility

The time limitations under 1, 2, and 3 above are waived if the veteran was discharged sooner for a service-connected disability. In all cases, the discharge must be other than dishonorable.

The Veterans Housing Act of 1974 amended the law governing VA-guaranteed loans in numerous respects. Significant changes were made in the restoration of previously used eligibility. The new law:

1. Permits the VA Administrator to restore a veteran's entitlement to loan-guarantee benefits after the property has been disposed of and the prior loan has been paid in full or after the Administrator is released from liability under the guaranty or any loss the Administrator has suffered has been repaid in full. It is no longer required that the property be disposed of for a compelling reason.

2. Authorizes the Administrator to restore a veteran's entitlement and to release the veteran from liability to the VA when another veteran has agreed to assume the outstanding balance of the existing VA loan and has consented to use his or her entitlement to the same extent that the entitlement of the original veteran's had been used. The veteran-purchaser assuming the loan and the property must otherwise meet the requirements of the law.

3. Increases the maximum home loan guarantee from $12,500 to $17,500 but makes no change in the maximum permissible percentage of guarantee (60 percent). Thus the new law provides for a guarantee not to exceed 60 percent of the amount of the loan, or $17,500, whichever is less.

   Note: For those veterans who have used their eligibility, but are not eligible for restoration under 1 or 2 above, this provision may provide sufficient partial eligibility to enable the purchase of a home.

4. Authorizes the VA to guarantee loans for the purchase of one-family residential units in a new condominium housing development or project, or in a structure built and sold as a condominium, provided such development, project, or structure is approved by the Administrator under such criteria as he shall prescribe. Projects converted or proposed to be converted to condominium ownership will not be eligible for GI loan financing.

5. Permits the VA to guarantee a loan for the purchase of a lot upon which to place a mobile home already owned by the veteran. Such loans may be guaranteed up to $7,500 (subject to VA's

appraisal) with a term of up to 12 years, 32 days. Prior to this authority, a loan for the purchase of a mobile home site could only be guaranteed if the loan included the purchase of a mobile home unit.

6. Amends the Federal Credit Union Act (12 U.S.C. 1757) to permit such credit unions to make mobile home loans for maturities of 12 years, 32 days for single-wide units and 20 years, 32 days for double-wide units.

7. Amends the existing laws to increase the maximum amount on mobile home loans as follows:
   (A) From $10,000 to $12,500 for the purchase of a single-wide mobile home.
   (B) From $15,000 to $20,000 for the purchase of a single-wide mobile home and an undeveloped lot which includes costs of necessary site preparations.
   (C) From $17,500 to $20,000 for the purchase of a single-wide mobile home and a developed lot.

8. Creates a new category of loans for double-wide mobile homes. For the unit, the loan may be up to $20,000 with a term up to 20 years, 32 days. Loans for the purchase of a double-wide mobile home plus a developed lot (or an undeveloped lot with necessary site preparation) may be guaranteed for up to $27,500.

9. Extends indefinitely the life of the mobile home program.

10. Authorizes the VA to guarantee loans for used mobile homes.

11. Repeals the VA Farm and Business Loan Authority.

12. Extends the insured loan program to post-Korean veterans. This applies only to home loans made pursuant to 38 U.S.C. 1810 (the single-family program).

13. Increases the Specially Adapted Housing Grant to $25,000.

14. Amends 38 U.S.C. 1810 to allow veterans to pay discount points in certain defined circumstances (in addition to refinancing loans) where there will be no seller, or a seller who is legally incapable of paying discounts.

15. Extends the maximum term of home loans to 30 years, 32 days. This will permit the first loan payment to be set at a date not in excess of 60 days from the date of loan closing and permit an even 360 payments, without any risk of violating the statutory maximum term.

Eligibility for VA entitlement does not expire; it is good until used. To use the eligibility, the veteran must obtain a "certificate of eligibility" (VA form 26-1870).

The VA does not lend money on mortgage loans except in certain circumstances, where the Administrator of the VA determines that private financing is not available. These are called "direct loans."

Normally the VA only guarantees the loan up to 60 percent of the appraisal amount or $17,500, whichever is lower. While the VA does not set a maximum loan amount, the limited guarantee tends to cause lenders to limit the amount of their own money they are willing to have "exposed" to loss, and so in effect VA action has controlled the maximum loans usually made.

The VA does not have minimum down payment requirements such as the FHA does. Instead, it leaves the down payment requirements to the lender's own judgment. The normal VA term is 30 years.

Like FHA loans, VA loans are amortized direct-reduction loans with escrow funds being used. Also, like FHA loans, VA loans are based on the appraisal or sales price, whichever is lower, and the purchaser must certify that he intends to occupy the property.

The VA does allow a second trust at time of origination of a VA loan. However, restrictions attached to the use of the second trust make it undesirable, so second trusts are not normally used.

Conventional Loans

The term *conventional loan* refers to a loan which is not government-backed. Conventional loan terms and rates usually respond more rapidly to changing patterns of the economy than do government-backed loans. Interest rates must fluctuate to meet the day-to-day changes in the economy and competition. Because the conventional loan is not insured or guaranteed by a government agency, this type of loan has fewer regulations imposed and lenders are free to make changes as market conditions warrant, subject to their charters and the laws of the state.

For many years conventional loans were made for 75 percent of value, and only occasionally for 80 percent, with a term of 25 years. Increasingly, 80 percent loans seem to be the rule when mortgage money is readily available, and many lenders allow the purchaser to have a second trust for 10 percent of the purchase price, thus requiring only a 10 percent down payment. Terms are mostly 25 years; however, 30-year terms are often permitted.

Conventional loans play a very important role in home financing at all times. In times of tight money and high loan discounts, many owners refuse to sell to a purchaser with a new government-backed loan because of the loan discounts which the seller must pay, leaving conventional loans as the only major source of financing available.

"Magic" Financing (MGIC)

A new type of financing which is being used in many parts of the country instead of government-backed loans is called *Magic*. This financing is insured by a private mortgage insurance company (PMI) on terms similar to those of the FHA's insurance program. The name "magic" came from the initials of one of the first of these private insurers—the Mortgage Guarantee Insurance Corp. (MGIC).

With this type of financing, a regular lender, such as a savings and loan association, will make a loan of perhaps 75 percent, and the PMI will then insure or guarantee the next 15 to 20 percent, making a total loan of 90 to 95 percent and requiring only a 5 to 10 percent cash down payment.

Thus PMIs make mortgages with high loan-to-value ratios available to consumers, many of whom are young and buying their first townhouse or condominium, who otherwise would have been denied home ownership.

For this insurance or guarantee which covers the upper portion of the loan, the PMI will collect additional fees, sometimes in the form of discount points at settlement or sometimes in the form of additional interest over a stipulated number of years.

A new trade association, the Mortgage Insurance Companies of America (MICA), was formed in 1974 by 11 private mortgage insurance companies. The association serves as a forum for discussion of industry-wide standards and represents the members interests before Congress and federal and state regulatory agencies dealing with housing and related legislation.

Assumption, or Taking Over an Existing Loan

In this type of financing the purchaser *assumes*, or takes over, the existing mortgage on the property and either pays the owner the difference between the sales price and the existing loan in cash or pays part of the difference in cash and the balance as a deferred purchase money note.

Assuming an existing loan usually has many advantages for both purchaser and seller. It saves the loan discount fees and the time required to process a new loan, and often the interest rate is lower than that currently available. Another benefit to some is that the purchaser does not have to qualify for the loan.

While the purchaser assumes the responsibility for making the payments, the seller is *not* relieved of responsibility should the purchaser default. In effect the new purchaser becomes a co-guarantor of the note, and the lender has two parties to look to for payment should it become necessary.

In the last few years many conventional lenders have inserted clauses in their mortgages which prohibit assumptions without the lender's approval. Government-backed loans may be assumed without restriction in most cases. If the mortgage or deed of trust is "silent" regarding assumption, the loan may be assumed.

Second Trusts

Occasionally a purchaser will not have enough money to pay the difference between the sales price and the existing or new loan being placed. If the seller is willing, a portion of that difference may be deferred by taking back a deferred purchase money note secured by a trust on the property. This is usually called a *second trust* because it is always recorded after the first trust and is junior to it. Should a default occur, the first trust holder would be

paid first and then, if there are sufficient funds, the second trust holder is paid.

Payments on a second trust are usually not high enough to amortize it over the period of the loan. Therefore, there is a balloon payment to be made when the loan matures.

The reason that payments on a second trust are "lighter," or smaller, is because the borrower usually must make two payments—the first trust and the second trust—concurrently.

Federally Supported Agencies

During the latter half of the 1960s, certain federal credit agencies came to perform increasingly important secondary mortgage market activities. Primary mortgage loans that have been originated by savings and loan associations, commercial banks, mutual savings banks, and mortgage bankers, as well as other lenders, are traded or bought and sold by these federal credit agencies, namely the Federal National Mortgage Association (popularly known as "Fannie Mae"), the Government National Mortgage Association ("Ginnie Mae") and the Federal Home Loan Mortgage Corporation ("Freddie Mac"). These secondary buyers provide support to the primary institutional home mortgage lenders by committing themselves to purchase packages of home mortgage loans from these primary lenders, thereby releasing additional funds back to the primary lenders, which can be used (especially during periods of tight money) to make additional or new primary mortgage loans.

TRUTH IN LENDING (TIL)

Most mortgage refinancing, as well as assumptions of existing loans, comes under provisions of the Truth in Lending (TIL) Act. This act is a part of the Consumer Credit Protection Act (Public Law 90-321) which became law July 1, 1969. Congress selected the Board of Governors of the Federal Reserve System to prescribe regulations and to implement the Act. This it did through Regulation Z.

Provisions of Regulation Z apply to anyone "who in the ordinary course of business arranges or offers to arrange" *for consumer credit of any form to individuals.* Thus plumbers, doctors, consumer finance companies, automobile dealers, banks, savings and loan associations, and mortgage bankers and brokers, as well as many others, are covered.

However, with the exception of those real estate licensees who operate mortgage or other lending services, or those who deal in land contracts, most licensees are not considered as "arrangers of credit," and therefore are *not* covered by provisions of TIL. Even though they are not generally covered, all licensees and applicants should be familiar with the features of TIL. Only its basic provisions as they relate to real estate activity are covered here.

Purpose

The purpose of the Act is to make sure that borrowers know the true cost of credit. This affords them the opportunity to shop for loans in much the same manner as the purchaser of any other goods. Neither the Act nor Regulation Z attempts to regulate maximum or minimum charges for credit. Rather, the emphasis is to make sure *full disclosure* is made to the borrower.

Disclosure Statement

Disclosure is accomplished by requiring that the borrower receive a statement disclosing the finance charges and the annual percentage rate prior to entering a permanent contractual relationship with the creditor. Items covered in such disclosure statements vary with the type of loan, but items listed would generally include:

1. The total dollar amount of the finance charge (except in the case of a credit transaction to finance purchase of a dwelling).
2. The date on which the finance charge begins to apply, if this differs from the date of the transaction.
3. The annual percentage rate (some small loans are exempt).
4. The number, amount, and due date of payments.
5. The total payments—except in the case of first mortgages on dwelling purchases.
6. The amount charged for any default, delinquency, etc., or the method used for calculating that amount.
7. A description of the security for the loan.
8. A description of any penalty charge for prepayment of the principal.
9. The method used for calculating the unearned part of the finance charge in the case of prepayment. Charges deducted from any rebate or refund must be stated.
10. The cash price, down payment, including trade-in, if any, and the difference between the two.

Exemptions

Exempted from the provisions of the Act and Regulation Z are business and commercial loans, and those loans made to business entities such as corporations, partnerships, and governmental agencies, except when made for agricultural purposes. Also exempted are loans to be repaid in four or less installments, and loans on which no finance charges are made.

Enforcement and Penalties

Responsibility for enforcement is divided among nine federal agencies. The Federal Trade Commission (FTC) is charged with enforcement of the Act and Regulation Z as it pertains to real estate.

Penalties provided for violations include:

1. The borrower may sue the creditor for twice the amount of the finance charge, for a minimum of $100, and up to a maximum of $1000, plus court costs and attorney's fees.
2. For conviction of willfully and knowingly violating the Act or Regulation, the creditor may be fined up to $5,000, be imprisoned for one year, or both.

Should the creditor make an error in the disclosure statement, such error may be corrected within 15 days of its discovery.

Rescission

The borrower has the right to rescind any credit transaction in which a security interest is or will be retained or acquired in any real property which is used or is expected to be used as a principal residence of the borrower. Such right to rescind extends until midnight of the third business day following the date of consummation of the transaction, or the date of delivery of the disclosures required and all other material disclosures were made, whichever is later. If the notice of the right to cancel has not been given the borrower, then the time of the right to rescind extends indefinitely as there is no statute of limitations on this right.

Rescission of a transaction must be in writing, either by signing and dating the notice to cancel which every creditor must furnish the borrower, and mailing or delivering the notice to cancel to the creditor at the address shown on the notice. The borrower may also cancel by telegram or letter describing the transaction which the borrower wishes to cancel.

A borrower may waive his or her right to cancel a credit agreement for certain personal emergencies, provided the borrower furnishes the creditor a dated and signed statement requesting such waiver.

The right to rescind does not apply to a first trust or other equivalent security, including assumption of existing loans, to finance a dwelling in which the customer will reside.

Advertising

Any advertising which aids or promotes an extension of consumer credit is covered by provisions of the Act. All such advertising, whether it is by newspaper, radio, television, magazine, leaflet, billboard, or any other means, is included. Neither TIL nor Regulation Z prohibits such advertising; however, both require that if any credit terms are given, then a full disclosure must be made.

Terms used in advertising which usually would require that full disclosure be made include:

1. The amount of the downpayment, or no downpayment.

2. The amount or number of the installment payments.

3. The rate of the finance charge.

General terms such as the following would not usually require full disclosure:

1. "Excellent loan," or "Liberal terms available"

2. FHA/VA financing available

3. Low downpayments

4. Owner will finance

5. Take over existing loan

PRACTICE EXAMINATION: REAL ESTATE FINANCING

1. Which of the following statements is (are) true?

   I. A first mortgage is always larger than a second mortgage.
   II. A second mortgage cannot be foreclosed without the consent of the first mortgagee.

   (A) I only
   (B) II only
   (C) Both I and II
   (D) Neither I nor II

2. A mortgage in which there is no reduction of the principal balance until the end of the mortgage term is known as

   (A) a purchase money mortgage
   (B) an amortized mortgage
   (C) a direct-reduction mortgage
   (D) a straight mortgage

3. When a loan is assumed

   (A) the original maker is relieved of further responsibility
   (B) the purchaser becomes a co-guarantor
   (C) the purchaser must obtain a certificate of eligibility
   (D) none of the above are correct

4. Loans are usually based

   (A) on the sales price
   (B) on the appraised amount
   (C) on the appraisal amount or the sales price, whichever is less
   (D) on the amount of the down payment

5. Rates on mortgages are influenced by

   (A) interest available on corporate bonds
   (B) supply of and demand for money
   (C) neither of the above
   (D) both of the above

6. Loan discounts in FHA and VA loans are generally paid by

   (A) the lender
   (B) the purchaser
   (C) the seller
   (D) none of these

7. One point is equal to

   (A) 1 percent of the sales price
   (B) 10 percent of the down payment
   (C) 1 percent of the loan amount
   (D) none of these

8. A mortgage in which the principal amount is systematically reduced through regular monthly payments of both principal and interest is known as a (an)

   (A) junior mortgage
   (B) straight mortgage
   (C) amortized mortgage
   (D) none of the above

9. The maximum VA guarantee is

   (A) $12,500
   (B) 60 percent of the purchase price
   (C) $17,500 or 60 percent of the loan amount, whichever is lower
   (D) none of these

10. The penalty for prepaying an FHA loan is

    (A) 2 percent of the balance of the loan at time of prepayment
    (B) 1 percent of the balance of the loan at time of prepayment
    (C) 1 percent of the original loan amount
    (D) none of the above

11. Under certain conditions the FHA will

    (A) lend money on two-family houses
    (B) make a loan of $32,780
    (C) allow a second trust
    (D) none of these

12. In order to purchase property with an FHA loan, the purchaser must

    (A) be a citizen of the U.S.
    (B) usually certify he or she is going to occupy the property
    (C) both of the above
    (D) neither of the above

13. Veterans Administration loans

    (A) are limited to no more than $33,000
    (B) are insured loans
    (C) require a 10 percent down payment if the sales price is above $35,000
    (D) none of the above

14. The maximum FHA loan under the regular FHA program is

    (A) $30,000
    (B) $33,000
    (C) $35,000
    (D) none of the above

15. The major source of residential mortgage loan funds is

    (A) loan correspondents
    (B) commercial banks
    (C) savings and loan associations
    (D) insurance companies

16. If an FHA purchaser is paying more than the appraised price, the difference between the appraisal and the sales price

    (A) can be in the form of a junior mortgage
    (B) can be in the form of a straight mortgage
    (C) must come from the purchaser's assets
    (D) cannot be paid according to FHA rules

17. An agent who originates loans for others in their names would most likely be

    (A) a savings and loan official
    (B) a mortgage banker
    (C) a commercial banker
    (D) a mortgage broker

18. If you are attempting to save loan origination fees, such as points, and at the same time purchase a house as quickly as possible, your best choice of financing would usually be

    (A) an FHA loan   (C) assumption of a loan
    (B) a VA loan   (D) a conventional loan

19. Which of the following statements is (are) true?

    I. VA loans are insured loans.
    II. FHA loans are guaranteed loans.

    (A) I only   (C) Both I and II
    (B) II only   (D) Neither I nor II

20. Which of the following statements is (are) true?

    I. According to VA regulations, down payment requirements cannot exceed 10 percent of the purchase price or appraisal, whichever is lower.
    II. In order to obtain an FHA loan, the property must meet certain minimum standards.

    (A) I only   (C) Both I and II
    (B) II only   (D) Neither I nor II

Chapter 14
Following Written Instructions

Very often, Real Estate License Examinations will have problems similar to the following descriptive code problems and summary card problems to test an applicant's ability to read, comprehend, and follow written instructions. Neither the descriptive code nor the summary card problems require extensive technical knowledge. They do, however, require very careful reading and some skill in problem analysis.

DESCRIPTIVE CODE PROBLEMS

Following are explanations of the data and coding system and instructions on how to use the information in solving the problems.

In these problems, usually nine facilities of a home (living room, dining room, basement, garage, and other features such as taxes, location, or luxury features) are listed, together with a numbered code indicating a description of each feature of that facility. By using a numerical coding system it is possible to describe a home with a series of numbers. The code may later be interpreted by another person to get an exact description of that home.

Problem Explanation

DESCRIPTIVE CODE

Under "meaning of descriptive code" an explanation of the coding system is given. Note that the numbers 0, 1, and 2 are used as codes for each facility to indicate the exact features of that facility. Although the same numbers are used for each facility, they do not have the same meaning. *All* houses have a *living room, kitchen, bath,* and one or more *bedrooms.* Therefore, the number 0 in the descriptive code for each of these facilities does not necessarily mean that the house does not have that facility, but rather is a description of that facility. However, in the case of a dining room, utility room, storage room, basement, or garage, the number 0 *does* indicate that this facility is lacking in this particular problem.

Example: Bath: code 0 means "yes, this home has a bath, but only one or one and a half."
Basement: code 0 means "no, this home does not have a basement."

It should be noted from the previous example that the reader must remain alert when analyzing the data. Each facility's code must be considered independently. A zero must never be assumed to mean "none." Only in some of the codes and some of the problems is this the case. Also, a code of 1 or 2 does not always mean that that facility is present.

Before starting with a problem, one should read through all the codes and be generally familiar with the coding system.

DESCRIPTION

At the top are listed four classifications, each describing a certain type of house. The classifications are coded with the letters A, B, C, or. D. For example, in problem 1, to be classified an A type, a house must have all nine facilities with a full basement. Houses classified as B, C, and D must likewise meet certain other specified criteria.

The classification information must be correlated with the coded data in the descriptive code column. Each house can then be classified as A, B, C, or D, according to the coded description given opposite each question number.

The coded information opposite each question number describes one particular house. By correlating this information with the descriptive code column, one can

classify this house as A, B, C, or D. *Each house described will fit only one classification.*

Be careful of requests such as "*2 or more* baths." In problem 1 the bathroom code could be either 1 or 2. Other requests to look for are ones which state "*at least* $1\frac{1}{2}$ baths." In problem 1 you could not accept the code 0 under baths because the house may only have 1 bath. Either code 1 or code 2 would be acceptable.

To simplify and speed up your selection, it is usually best to eliminate the need to check each house as a possibility for each request.

To solve Problem 1, you should proceed this way.

Review the meaning of the descriptive codes under each facility to check the code that shows that that facility is missing, then mark the codes under each facility in such a way that a quick glance shows whether that facility is missing. Remember that a code of 0 does not necessarily mean that the facility is missing. Also, a code of 1 or 2 does not always mean that the facility is present. Notice the original Problem 1, then the same problem with the missing facilities marked.

Now a quick check shows that numbers 3, 6, and 9 are the only ones that have all nine facilities (no marks); therefore, any of them that have a full basement (code 2) will be an A-type house. You can quickly select numbers 3, 6, and 9 as A-type houses and mark them as such.

For type B houses, you see that you must have 7 or 8 facilities, which means you must have at least one but cannot have more than 2 marks showing missing facilities. Again, a quick check shows that numbers 1, 2, and 8 cannot be B-type houses (remember that numbers 3, 6, and 9 have already been selected as A types), so you only need to check numbers 4, 5, 7, and 10 to see if they have the code 2 under "kitchen" and "utility room;" checking shows that numbers 4, 7, and 10 fit that requirement, and so they can be marked as type B.

For the C-type houses, you need a house that has the first three facilities (the first three listed). In this problem, as in most cases, all the houses have a living room and a kitchen, so in order to determine which houses have the first three facilities you only need to check to see which houses have a dining room (code 1 or 2). With the use of the marks made to indicate missing facilities, you can readily see that all houses except numbers 2, 5, and 8 have the first three facilities. The next thing to determine is which of the others have a code of 0 in at least three other facilities (three other than the first three). This shows number 1 as the only one fitting the C category, and it can be so marked.

The rest of the houses, numbers 2, 5, and 8, can now be marked as D types.

PROBLEM 1

Each question is described by a 9-digit code. The meaning of each digit in the code is given on the left below. Your task is to recode the data for each question, choosing the appropriate letter (A, B, C, or D) as follows:

A — The house has all nine facilities with a full basement.

B — The house has 7 or 8 facilities and the code 2 in kitchen and utility room.

C — The house has the first 3 facilities and a code of 0 in at least 3 others.

D — The house does not fit any of the above.

MEANING OF DESCRIPTIVE CODE:

LIVING ROOM
  0 = without fireplace
  1 = with fireplace
  2 = with fireplace & carpets
DINING ROOM
  0 = none
  1 = small
  2 = large
KITCHEN
  0 = without eating sp.
  1 = with appliances
  2 = with eating sp. and appliances
UTILITY ROOM
  0 = none
  1 = small
  2 = large
BEDROOMS
  0 = 1 or 2
  1 = 3
  2 = 4 or more
BATHROOM
  0 = 1 or 1½
  1 = 2 or 2½
  2 = 3
STORAGE ROOM
  0 = none
  1 = small
  2 = full
BASEMENT
  0 = none
  1 = ½
  2 = full
GARAGE
  0 = none
  1 = 1 car
  2 = 2 car

ORIGINAL PROBLEM

QUESTION NUMBER	LIVING RM.	DINING RM.	KITCHEN	UTILITY RM.	BEDROOMS	BATHROOMS	STORAGE RM	BASEMENT	GARAGE	ANSWER
1	0	2	0	1	2	2	0	0	0	
2	2	0	2	0	1	2	2	0	1	
3	0	1	1	2	0	0	2	2	1	
4	2	1	2	2	1	1	1	0	0	
5	2	0	0	1	2	1	2	1	0	
6	2	2	2	1	1	1	1	2	1	
7	0	1	2	2	2	1	0	1	0	
8	2	0	0	0	0	1	0	2	0	
9	1	1	1	1	1	1	1	2	2	
10	1	1	2	2	1	1	0	1	1	
	WITH MISSING FACILITIES MARKED									
1	0	2	0	1	2	2	0̸	0̸	0̸	
2	2	0̸	2	0̸	1	2	2	0̸	1	
3	0	1	1	2	0	0	2	2	1	
4	2	1	2	2	1	1	1	0̸	0̸	
5	2	0̸	0	1	2	1	2	1	0̸	
6	2	2	2	1	1	1	1	2	1	
7	0	1	2	2	2	1	0̸	1	0̸	
8	2	0̸	0	0̸	0	1	0̸	2	0̸	
9	1	1	1	1	1	1	1	2	2	
10	1	1	2	2	1	1	0̸	1	1	

PROBLEM 2

Each question is described by a 9-digit code. The meaning of each digit in the code is given on the left below. Your task is to recode the data for each question, choosing the appropriate letter (A, B, C, or D) as follows:

A – The house has all nine facilities with a full basement and carpets in the living room.

B – The house has 7 or 8 facilities, no more or less, and has 2 or more baths and 4 bedrooms.

C – The house has the first 3 facilities and a code of 0 in at least 3 others.

D – The house does not fit any of the above.

MEANING OF DESCRIPTIVE CODE:

LIVING ROOM
    0 = without fireplace
    1 = with fireplace
    2 = with fireplace & carpets
DINING ROOM
    0 = none
    1 = small
    2 = large
KITCHEN
    0 = without eating sp.
    1 = with appliances
    2 = with eating sp. and appliances
UTILITY ROOM
    0 = none
    1 = small
    2 = large
BEDROOMS
    0 = 1 or 2
    1 = 3
    2 = 4 or more
BATHROOMS
    0 = 1 or 1½
    1 = 2
    2 = 2½ or 3
STORAGE ROOM
    0 = none
    1 = small
    2 = large
BASEMENT
    0 = none
    1 = ½
    2 = full
GARAGE
    0 = none
    1 = 1 car
    2 = 2 car

QUESTION NUMBER	LIVING RM.	DINING RM.	KITCHEN	UTILITY RM.	BEDROOMS	BATHROOMS	STORAGE RM.	BASEMENT	GARAGE	ANSWER
1	2	1	0	1	0	1	1	2	2	
2	2	1	1	0	1	0	1	2	0	
3	2	0	0	2	2	2	2	2	2	
4	2	1	1	0	1	1	1	2	1	
5	2	1	1	1	2	2	1	2	1	
6	2	2	1	1	0	2	0	0	1	
7	2	1	1	0	2	1	0	2	1	
8	2	1	0	1	0	0	2	0	1	
9	1	1	0	1	2	1	1	2	0	
10	0	1	0	1	0	1	0	0	1	

SUMMARY CARD PROBLEMS

Generally in this type of problem details regarding a parcel of real estate are listed. The information given usually includes a description of the property and important financial data regarding the existing loan or new financing available. Also listed would be information about the existing taxes (rate, assessment, and taxes). Very often only two of the items regarding taxes are given, and the applicant will have to compute the third. A calendar of events is also usually included, covering such items as when the property was listed and shown and the date any offer to purchase is made. This is generally followed by information concerning the settlement.

The applicant must be very careful in answering questions. Very often details have to be analyzed in order to choose the best answer.

PROBLEM 1

Description. A frame rambler 25' X 30' with 2 bedrooms, 1 bath, and full basement on a 200' X 200' lot. Gas hot water heater and oil hot-air heat; a drilled well and septic system.

Owner/Financial Data. Property is free and clear of loans. The owner, Henry Jackson, will take back a new trust of 75% of the purchase price at 9% interest for 30 years. Taxes for the calendar year are paid, based on a rate of $4.00 per hundred and an assessment of $4,000.

Listing/Transaction History. May 15—property listed for sale at a price to net the owner $28,200 after paying your 6% commission, under a 90-day exclusive authorization to sell.

June 5—property shown to John and Phyl Jenkins, who offer to purchase it at $1,000 less than the listed price, for all cash. They give you a $1,500 check as earnest money. Settlement to be July 1.

June 6—All terms of the offer are acceptable to Henry Jackson, who accepts the offer.

July 1—Settlement occurs.

1. Which of the following is (are) correct?

   I. Taxes on the Jackson property are $160.00 per annum.
   II. Jackson should receive a refund of part of the taxes at settlement.

(A) I only   (C) Both I and II
(B) II only   (D) Neither I nor II

2. Which of the following statements is (are) correct?

   I. The listing price is $28,200.
   II. The sales price is $29,000.

(A) I only   (C) Both I and II
(B) II only   (D) Neither I nor II

3. Which of the following statements is (are) correct?

   I. John and Phyl are husband and wife.
   II. The listing is an exclusive authorization to sell.

(A) I only   (C) Neither I nor II
(B) II only   (D) Both I and II

EXPLANATION OF PROBLEM 1

1. Correct answer is (C)—Both I and II.

Taxes = assessment times rate

Taxes = $160.00 ($4.00 X 40 hundreds)

Jackson has paid the taxes for the entire year, so he would receive a refund of those paid for the time from date of settlement to the end of the year.

2. Correct answer is (B)—II only.

Property is listed at a price which will net the owner $28,200 after paying your 6% commission.

$28,200 ÷ 94% = $30,000 listing price.

The purchaser offered $1,000 less than the listed price, or $30,000 − $1,000 = $29,000 sales price.

3. Correct answer is (B)—II only.

The summary card does not state that John and Phyl Jenkins are husband and wife; they could be brother and sister, father and daughter, brothers, or unrelated. Do not assume anything. The problem does state that the listing is an exclusive authorization to sell.

Do not let the seemingly simple format of this type of question make you overconfident. Each requires careful reading and thought.

PROBLEM 2

Description. A 3-bedroom, 5-year-old Cape Cod with vertical frame siding. It has a living room with fireplace, 2 baths, and a 2-car detached garage in the rear fenced yard. There is a gas-fired water heater and heating system, with city sewer and water connected.

Owner/Financial Data. Helen Huber, femme sole, states the loan balance of the existing loan on the date you list the property is $29,450. It was originally a 30-year VA loan at 7.5% per annum interest rate which was placed on the property when the house was constructed. The taxes of $360.00, due January 1 for this calendar year, have not been paid. The tax rate is $6.00 per hundred of the assessment.

Listing/Transaction History. *March 1*—property listed to net the owners $4,390 after paying your 6% commission under an exclusive agency.

May 15—property shown to Jim and Ann Thomas, husband and wife, who agree to pay $500 less than the listed price, assume the present loan, pay $5,000 cash, and give back a second trust for the difference. The owners accept, and settlement is set for 15 days after the offer. Settlement occurs on schedule.

1. From information given in the summary card, which of the following is (are) correct?

    I. There is a fenced rear yard.
    II. Thomas will pay Huber a tax refund.

    (A) I only   (C) Neither A nor B
    (B) II only   (D) Both A and B

2. From information given, which of the following is (are) correct?

    I. The tax assessment on the property is $3,000.
    II. The streets have curbs and gutters.

    (A) I only   (C) Neither A nor B
    (B) II only   (D) Both A and B

3. If the salesperson selling the property receives 50% of the total commission, he or she would receive

    (A) $1,080   (C) $1,015
    (B) $1,800   (D) none are within $50

4. Which of the following is (are) correct?

    I. There is more than one floor of finished living space.
    II. The range is more than likely electric.

    (A) I only   (C) Neither A nor B
    (B) II only   (D) Both A and B

5. The amount of the second trust will be

    (A) $1,550
    (B) $1,050
    (C) $1,000
    (D) none are within $100 of the correct amount

Chapter 15

Preparation of Listings, Offer to Purchase Agreements, and Settlement Statements

INFORMATION TO LICENSE APPLICANTS

Some states require all applicants for licensure to complete a Listing form and an Offer to Purchase Agreement form. Other states only require this of broker applicants. In some states the broker applicant must also complete a settlement statement.

If your state does not require completion of these forms, you may skip this chapter.

When completion of these instruments is a part of the examination, the procedure usually is as follows:

The applicants are given information about a Listing, an Offer to Purchase Agreement problem, and the proper forms on which to record the information (and, if required, the settlement information also). After completing the forms they turn in the original problems and receive a set of questions which must be answered from the information they have transferred to the forms. Some applicants may be led to believe that the manner in which the information is placed on the forms is unimportant. However, if applicants are consistent in the method they use to complete the forms, they can eventually come to tell at a glance that all the pertinent information has been properly transferred to the forms.

Before starting the listing, offer to purchase agreement, and settlement statement problems, it would be advisable to review the chapter on contracts, agency, and listings. It would also be helpful to "think through" a normal real estate transaction from the time of the initial listing of the property through the subsequent offer to purchase agreement to the final settlement. A review of Fig. 5-1 may also be helpful.

First, the seller of the property and the real estate broker enter into a listing agreement. This is a contract between the seller (the principal) and the broker (the agent) which sets forth the terms and conditions under which the seller offers to sell the property. It is a contractual agreement between seller and broker and does not bind the purchaser unless the terms of the listing are later included in the contract of sale between the purchaser and the seller.

Second, the agent locates a purchaser who either accepts the terms of the offeror (seller) or makes an offer of different terms. In some cases several offers and counteroffers are made before a final agreement and meeting of the minds occur. The contract of sale should contain all conditions of the entire agreement between the purchaser and seller, as the provisions of the listing agreement are not binding between purchaser and seller.

Third, after all conditions of the contract of sale have been met, the final transaction takes place in which the seller delivers, and the purchaser accepts, the deed transferring title to the property. This transfer is called contract settlement, or, more often, simply settlement (or closing). At this time the obligations of both seller and purchaser are fulfilled and the transaction is complete. In most states, provisions of the contract of sale have been merged in the deed, unless the contract provided for their survival.

The forms used here for these problems may not be identical to the ones used in your state. However, if you can complete these forms properly, you should not have difficulty with any variations.

The following is a detailed, step-by-step explanation of how to complete the listing forms.

LISTING AGREEMENTS

The fastest and easiest method of completing the Listing Agreement form is to transfer items from the problem to the form as they are given, then underline or mark the information on the problem sheet in such a way that when you are finished it is easy to see that all information has been transferred from the problem to the form. In order to do this rapidly and accurately, you should become familiar with the listing form. The listing form used in the uniform examination is reproduced on page 161. Heavy lines divide it into five sections, which will be discussed individually.

Do not be concerned if some blanks on the form are not filled in. Do not add anything "extra" to the information furnished in the problem.

How to Complete a Listing Agreement

Section I

Line 1.

Sales price—this will usually be stated in the problem. If not, it will be up to you to compute the gross sales price from the information given. For example, an owner wishes to net $32,900 from the sale of a house after paying your 6 percent commission. The $32,900 represents 94 percent of the gross price, so the gross price can be computed by dividing the $32,900 by 94 percent (.94), which would be $35,000.

Type home—either specifically stated or implied, such as rambler, split-level, Cape Cod, etc.

Total bedrooms—all the bedrooms in the house, regardless of their location.

Total baths—all baths in the property, regardless of location.

Line 2.

Address—street address, as given in the problem.

Jurisdiction of—city, county, and state, as given.

Section II

Line 1.

Amount of loan to be assumed—the current loan balance, or the balance as of date of settlement, if given. Unless otherwise stated, consider that the existing loan can be assumed.

As of what date—as given in the problem, or use the listing date.

Taxes and insurance included—are escrow payments to taxes and insurance included in the monthly payment? Answer yes or no.

Years to go—what is the remaining number of years on the existing loan?

Amount payable monthly—what is the total monthly payment to principal and interest, or principal, interest, taxes, and insurance, if applicable? Also, what is the interest rate on the existing loan?

Type loan—is the existing loan FHA, VA, or conventional (Conv.)?

Line 2.

Mortgage company—insert the name of the mortgagee (lender).

Second trust—if there is a current second trust on the property, record the pertinent data: amount, interest, payments, etc., as given. If the owner will take back a second trust, the pertinent information should be inserted in Section IV under "Remarks."

Line 3.

Estimated expected rent monthly—as stated in problem, or leave blank.

Type of appraisal requested—indicate whether an appraisal has been ordered, such as FHA, VA, or conventional; or if one has been received, indicate type and amount.

Line 4.

Owner's name and telephone number—as given in the problem.

Line 5.

Tenant's name and telephone number—as given in the problem.

Line 6.

Possession—the date when a purchaser can take possession of the property.

Date listed—as given, or the date you list the property.

Exclusive for—the term of your listing (60 days, 90 days, 120 days, etc.).

Date of expiration—when does the listing expire? Use a definite date, giving day, month, and year.

Line 7.

Listing broker—as given in the problem, not your sponsoring broker, unless so instructed.

Phone—as given.

Key available at—as given.

Line 8.

Listing salesman—your name.

Home phone—yours.

How to be shown—instructions for showing the property, such as "call owner" or "key in office" (KIO) so that the house can be shown even if the owner is not at home

Section III

Fifty items in this section are numbered on the listing form; most are self-explanatory. If the information is not given in the listing problem, leave it blank. The item may not be applicable to your listing.

Items 44 through 47 concern *tax information*, and the applicant will usually have to compute the taxes, assessment, or tax rate from the information given in the problem. Refer to the math chapter if you need to refresh your memory.

Section IV

Record information given regarding schools, public transportation, and shopping.

Remarks—under remarks should be entered any condition of the sale or any other pertinent information not

EXCLUSIVE AUTHORIZATION TO SELL

SEC I

SALES PRICE: _____ TYPE HOME _____ TOTAL BEDROOMS _____ TOTAL BATHS _____

ADDRESS: _____

JURISDICTION OF: _____

AMT. OF LOAN $ / TO BE ASSUMED $ _____ AS OF / WHAT DATE: _____ TAXES & INS. INCLUDED: _____ YEARS TO GO: _____ AMOUNT PAYABLE MONTHLY $ _____ @ ___ % TYPE LOAN _____

MORTGAGE COMPANY _____ 2nd TRUST $ _____

ESTIMATED EXPECTED RENT MONTHLY $ _____ TYPE OF APPRAISAL REQUESTED: _____

OWNER'S NAME _____ PHONES: (HOME) _____ (BUSINESS) _____

TENANTS NAME _____ PHONES: (HOME) _____ (BUSINESS) _____

POSSESSION _____ DATE LISTED: _____ EXCLUSIVE FOR _____ DATE OF EXPIRATION _____

SEC II

LISTING BROKER _____ PHONE _____ KEY AVAILABLE AT _____

LISTING SALESMAN _____ HOME PHONE: _____ HOW TO BE SHOWN: _____

SEC III

(1) ENTRANCE FOYER ☐ CENTER HALL ☐	(18) AGE AIR CONDITIONING ☐	(32) TYPE KITCHEN CABINETS
(2) LIVING ROOM SIZE FIREPLACE ☐	(19) ROOFING TOOL HOUSE ☐	(33) TYPE COUNTER TOPS
(3) DINING ROOM SIZE	(20) GARAGE SIZE PATIO ☐	(34) EAT-IN SIZE KITCHEN ☐
(4) BEDROOM TOTAL: DOWN UP	(21) SIDE DRIVE ☐ CIRCULAR DRIVE ☐	(35) BREAKFAST ROOM ☐
(5) BATHS TOTAL: DOWN UP	(22) PORCH ☐ SIDE ☐ REAR ☐ SCREENED ☐	(36) BUILT-IN OVEN & RANGE ☐
(6) DEN SIZE FIREPLACE ☐	(23) FENCED YARD OUTDOOR GRILL ☐	(37) SEPARATE STOVE INCLUDED ☐
(7) FAMILY ROOM SIZE FIREPLACE ☐	(24) STORM WINDOWS ☐ STORM DOORS ☐	(38) REFRIGERATOR INCLUDED ☐
(8) RECREATION ROOM SIZE FIREPLACE ☐	(25) CURBS & GUTTERS ☐ SIDEWALKS ☐	(39) DISHWASHER INCLUDED
(9) BASEMENT SIZE	(26) STORM SEWERS ☐ ALLEY ☐	(40) DISPOSAL INCLUDED ☐
NONE ☐ 1/4 ☐ 1/3 ☐ 1/2 ☐ 3/4 ☐ FULL ☐	(27) WATER SUPPLY	(41) DOUBLE SINK ☐ SINGLE SINK ☐
(10) UTILITY ROOM SIZE	(28) SEWER ☐ SEPTIC ☐	STAINLESS STEEL ☐ PORCELAIN ☐
TYPE HOT WATER SYSTEM:	(29) TYPE GAS: NATURAL ☐ BOTTLED ☐	(42) WASHER INCLUDED ☐ DRYER INCLUDED ☐
(11) TYPE HEAT	(30) WHY SELLING	(43) PANTRY ☐ EXHAUST FAN ☐
(12) EST. FUEL COST		(44) LAND ASSESSMENT $
(13) ATTIC	(31) DIRECTIONS TO PROPERTY	(45) IMPROVEMENTS $
PULL DOWN STAIRWAY ☐ REGULAR STAIRWAY ☐ TRAP DOOR ☐		(46) TOTAL ASSESSMENT $
(14) MAIDS ROOM ☐ TYPE BATH		(47) TAX RATE
LOCATION		(48) TOTAL ANNUAL TAXES $
(15) NAME OF BUILDER		(49) LOT SIZE
(16) SQUARE FOOTAGE		(50) LOT NO. BLOCK SECTION
(17) EXTERIOR OF HOUSE		

NAME OF SCHOOLS: ELEMENTARY: _____ JR. HIGH: _____

HIGH _____ PAROCHIAL: _____

SEC IV

PUBLIC TRANSPORTATION: _____

NEAREST SHOPPING AREA: _____

REMARKS: _____

Date: _____

In consideration of the services of _____ (herein called "Broker") to be rendered to the undersigned (herein called "Owner"), and of the promise of Broker to make reasonable efforts to obtain a Purchaser therefor, Owner hereby lists with Broker the real estate and all improvements thereon which are described above (all herein called "the property"), and Owner hereby grants to Broker the exclusive and irrevocable right to sell such property from 12:00 Noon on *SEC V* _____, 19_____ until 12:00 Midnight on _____, 19_____ (herein called "period of time"), for the price of _____ Dollars ($ _____) or for such other price and upon such other terms (including exchange) as Owner may subsequently authorize during the period of time.

It is understood by Owner that the above sum or any other price subsequently authorized by Owner shall include a cash fee of _____ per cent of such price or other price which shall be payable by Owner to Broker upon consummation by any Purchaser or Purchasers of a valid contract of sale of the property during the period of time and whether or not Broker was a procuring cause of any such contract of sale.

If the property is sold or exchanged by Owner, or by Broker or by any other person to any Purchaser to whom the property was shown by Broker or any representative of Broker within sixty (60) days after the expiration of the period of time mentioned above, Owner agrees to pay to Broker a cash fee which shall be the same percentage of the purchase price as the percentage mentioned above.

Broker is hereby authorized by Owner to place a "For Sale" sign on the property and to remove all signs of other brokers or salesmen during the period of time, and Owner hereby agrees to make the property available to Broker at all reasonable hours for the purpose of showing it to prospective Purchasers.

Owner agrees to convey the property to the Purchaser by warranty deed with the usual covenants of title and free and clear from all encumbrances, tenancies, liens (for taxes or otherwise), but subject to applicable restrictive covenants of record. Owner acknowledges receipt of a copy of this agreement.

WITNESS the following signature(s) and seal(s):

Date Signed: _____   _____ (SEAL)
(Owner)

Listing Broker _____

Address _____ Telephone _____   _____ (SEAL)
(Owner)

_____

Figure 15-1. Sample form for a Listing Agreement.

otherwise included. Listed below are examples of items that might be found in this section.

1. Owner will not sell VA or FHA.

2. Owner will not pay more than _____ points as a loan placement fee.

3. Property being sold subject to an existing lease, which expires on _____, 19_____.

4. Owner to move shrubs or some other item which would normally be considered real estate and included in the sale.

5. Possession to be given _____ days after settlement.

6. Owner to make some repairs, such as painting gutters or repairing back steps.

7. Owner is willing to sell only if purchaser buys the lawn mower, or some other item, under a separate bill of sale, for $_____.

8. Owner will take back a second trust for $_____ at _____% interest for _____ years.

9. Owner will sell only if some event does or does not occur, such as "owner receiving final transfer orders" or "owner purchasing another house."

Section V

This is the legal section of the listing form and is self-explanatory. Some information that has been entered on other parts of the listing is also entered here. Make sure you insert the amount of the commission rate.

Now refer to Listing Problem 1 below and Listing Form 1 on the opposite page showing how that problem has been transferred to the form.

Notice that, for purposes of simplification, much of the information normally obtained when listing a house has been omitted.

Instructions for Listing Problem 1

Study Listing Problem 1 and its suggested solution. Then study Offer to Purchase Problem 1 and its suggested solution.

When you have become familiar with the solutions, review the 10 sample questions in Practice Examination 1, which pertain to Listing Problem 1 and Offer to Purchase Problem 1.

After you have reviewed the sample questions, proceed to complete Listing and Offer to Purchase Problems 2 and 3, along with the practice examinations applicable to each.

Remember that in an actual examination situation, you will have turned in the instruction sheet and will be required to answer the questions from the listing and offer to purchase forms only. Therefore, do not refer back to the instructions.

When you have finished the practice examinations, refer to the approved solutions and answers for the practice examinations, which start on page 202. Keep in mind that the method used in the approved solutions is not the only way that these forms can be completed and still be legal; it is only one recommended solution.

When you have completed the listing and offer to purchase problems, proceed to the settlement statement section if the state examination for which you are preparing requires this.

LISTING PROBLEM 1

On June 15 of this year, you, as a salesperson for Argo Realty, obtain a 90-day exclusive right to sell agreement on property at 123 Rose Street, Farmdale, belonging to Ebner Jones and his wife, Mary. It is a frame, 2-bedroom rambler with 1 bath. The house has a full basement, 25' X 30', with an outside entrance. There is a 30-gallon gas-fired water heater and an oil-fired hot-water heating system. The measurements are: living room, 10' X 15'; dining room, 8' X 10'. There is a drilled well and a septic system. The lot is 200' X 200', and the legal description is Lot 3, Bloomfield Subdivision, Bourbon County, your state. The house is 50 years old. The composition roof was replaced last year at the same time the owners installed storm doors and windows. Mr. Jones states he does not owe anything on the house and will take back a 15-year, 7% mortgage if the purchaser makes a down payment of 25% of the purchase price, to be repaid in 180 equal monthly installments to principal and interest. The property is assessed at $4,000, and the tax rate is $4.00 per hundred. The sellers will leave the stove, refrigerator, and washing machine. They will, however, remove the tagged shrub at the front door. Place the house on the market at a price to net Mr. and Mrs. Jones $23,500 after paying your 6% commission. Possession is to be given at settlement.

EXCLUSIVE AUTHORIZATION TO SELL

SALES PRICE: _25,000_ TYPE HOME _RAMBLER_ TOTAL BEDROOMS _2_ TOTAL BATHS _1_

ADDRESS: _123 ROSE STREET, FARMDALE_ JURISDICTION OF: _BOURBON COUNTY - YOUR STATE_

AMT. OF LOAN TO BE ASSUMED $ _CLEAR_ AS OF WHAT DATE: ___ TAXES & INS. INCLUDED: ___ YEARS TO GO: ___ AMOUNT PAYABLE MONTHLY $ ___ @ ___ % LOAN TYPE ___

MORTGAGE COMPANY ___ 2nd TRUST $ ___

ESTIMATED EXPECTED RENT MONTHLY $ ___ TYPE OF APPRAISAL REQUESTED: ___

OWNER'S NAME _ELMER JONES AND HIS WIFE MARY_ PHONES: (HOME) ___ (BUSINESS) ___

TENANTS NAME ___ PHONES: (HOME) ___ (BUSINESS) ___

POSSESSION _AT SETTLEMENT_ DATE LISTED: _6-15-THIS YEAR_ EXCLUSIVE FOR _90 DAYS_ DATE OF EXPIRATION _9-15-THIS YR._

LISTING BROKER _ARGO REALTY_ PHONE ___ KEY AVAILABLE AT ___

LISTING SALESMAN _YOU_ HOME PHONE: ___ HOW TO BE SHOWN: ___

---

(1) ENTRANCE FOYER ☐   CENTER HALL ☐
(2) LIVING ROOM SIZE _10 x 15_   FIREPLACE ☐
(3) DINING ROOM SIZE _8 x 10_
(4) BEDROOM TOTAL: _2_ DOWN _2_ UP
(5) BATHS TOTAL: _1_ DOWN _1_ UP
(6) DEN SIZE ___   FIREPLACE ☐
(7) FAMILY ROOM SIZE ___   FIREPLACE ☐
(8) RECREATION ROOM SIZE ___   FIREPLACE ☐
(9) BASEMENT SIZE _25 x 30_
NONE ☐ 1/4 ☐ 1/3 ☐ 1/2 ☐ 3/4 ☐ FULL ☒
(10) UTILITY ROOM SIZE ___
TYPE HOT WATER SYSTEM: _30 GAL GAS_
(11) TYPE HEAT _OIL - HOT WATER_
(12) EST. FUEL COST ___
(13) ATTIC ☐
PULL DOWN STAIRWAY ☐   REGULAR STAIRWAY ☐   TRAP DOOR ☐
(14) MAIDS ROOM ☐   TYPE BATH ___
LOCATION ___
(15) NAME OF BUILDER ___
(16) SQUARE FOOTAGE ___
(17) EXTERIOR OF HOUSE _FRAME_

(18) AGE _50 YRS._   AIR CONDITIONING ☐
(19) ROOFING _COMP - NEW_   TOOL HOUSE ☐
(20) GARAGE SIZE ___   PATIO ☐
(21) SIDE DRIVE ☐   CIRCULAR DRIVE ☐
(22) PORCH ☐ SIDE ☐ REAR ☐   SCREENED ☐
(23) FENCED YARD ☐   OUTDOOR GRILL ☐
(24) STORM WINDOWS ☒   STORM DOORS ☒
(25) CURBS & GUTTERS ☐   SIDEWALKS ☐
(26) STORM SEWERS ☐   ALLEY ☐
(27) WATER SUPPLY _DRILLED WELL_
(28) SEWER ☐   SEPTIC ☒
(29) TYPE GAS: NATURAL ☐   BOTTLED ☐
(30) WHY SELLING ___
(31) DIRECTIONS TO PROPERTY ___

(32) TYPE KITCHEN CABINETS ___
(33) TYPE COUNTER TOPS ___
(34) EAT-IN SIZE KITCHEN ☐
(35) BREAKFAST ROOM ☐
(36) BUILT-IN OVEN & RANGE ☐
(37) SEPARATE STOVE INCLUDED ☒
(38) REFRIGERATOR INCLUDED ☒
(39) DISHWASHER INCLUDED ☐
(40) DISPOSAL INCLUDED ☐
(41) DOUBLE SINK ☐   SINGLE SINK ☐   STAINLESS STEEL ☐   PORCELAIN ☐
(42) WASHER INCLUDED ☒   DRYER INCLUDED ☐
(43) PANTRY ☐   EXHAUST FAN ☐
(44) LAND ASSESSMENT $ ___
(45) IMPROVEMENTS $ ___
(46) TOTAL ASSESSMENT $ _4,000_
(47) TAX RATE _4 00_ PER HUNDRED
(48) TOTAL ANNUAL TAXES $ ___
(49) LOT SIZE _200' x 200'_
(50) LOT NO. _3_ BLOCK ___ SECTION ___
BLOOMFIELD SUB. BOURBON CO. - YOUR STATE

NAME OF SCHOOLS: ELEMENTARY: ___ JR. HIGH: ___
HIGH ___ PAROCHIAL: ___

PUBLIC TRANSPORTATION: ___

NEAREST SHOPPING AREA: ___

REMARKS: _OWNER WILL TAKE BACK A 15 YEAR 7% MORTGAGE IF PURCHASER MAKES A DOWN PAYMENT OF 25% - OWNER TO REMOVE TAGGED SHRUB AT FRONT DOOR_

Date: _6-15- THIS YEAR_

In consideration of the services of _ARGO REALTY_ (herein called "Broker") to be rendered to the undersigned (herein called "Owner"), and of the promise of Broker to make reasonable efforts to obtain a Purchaser therefor, Owner hereby lists with Broker the real estate and all improvements thereon which are described above (all herein called "the property"), and Owner hereby grants to Broker the exclusive and irrevocable right to sell such property from 12:00 Noon on _6-15_, 19 _THIS YEAR_ until 12:00 Midnight on _9-15_, 19 _THIS YEAR_ (herein called "period of time"), for the price of _TWENTY FIVE THOUSAND AND 00/100_ Dollars ($ _25,000.00_) or for such other price and upon such other terms (including exchange) as Owner may subsequently authorize during the period of time.

It is understood by Owner that the above sum or any other price subsequently authorized by Owner shall include a cash fee of _6%_ per cent of such price or other price which shall be payable by Owner to Broker upon consummation by any Purchaser or Purchasers of a valid contract of sale of the property during the period of time and whether or not Broker was a procuring cause of any such contract of sale.

If the property is sold or exchanged by Owner, or by Broker or by any other person to any Purchaser to whom the property was shown by Broker or any representative of Broker within sixty (60) days after the expiration of the period of time mentioned above, Owner agrees to pay to Broker a cash fee which shall be the same percentage of the purchase price as the percentage mentioned above.

Broker is hereby authorized by Owner to place a "For Sale" sign on the property and to remove all signs of other brokers or salesmen during the period of time, and Owner hereby agrees to make the property available to Broker at all reasonable hours for the purpose of showing it to prospective Purchasers.

Owner agrees to convey the property to the Purchaser by warranty deed with the usual covenants of title and free and clear from all encumbrances, tenancies, liens (for taxes or otherwise), but subject to applicable restrictive covenants of record. Owner acknowledges receipt of a copy of this agreement.

WITNESS the following signature(s) and seal(s):

Date Signed: _6-15- THIS YEAR_

Listing Broker _Argo Realty By: You_

Address _As given_ Telephone ___

Elmer Jones (SEAL) (Owner)

Mary Jones (SEAL) (Owner)

Figure 15-2. Listing Form 1. Suggested solution for Listing Problem 1.

OFFER TO PURCHASE AGREEMENT (SALES CONTRACT)

The following is a detailed explanation of the Offer to Purchase Agreement, also known as the sales contract. It, too, has been broken down into sections for easy reference.

Remember that some of the information will be transferred from the listing agreement unless it has been changed by the agreement between purchaser and seller.

How to Complete an Offer to Purchase Agreement

Section I

This section establishes the date of the agreement and identifies the purchaser, seller, and broker. Fill them in as they are given in the problem, identifying them as husband and wife, brother and sister, single, or however they are listed.

Section II

You might say this section describes what is and what is not included in the sales price. It is a good idea to always complete this in the same order, such as:

Real estate included—the legal description.

Real estate excluded—is some item of real estate going to be removed, such as a shrub or a chandelier?

Chattels included—what is included in the sale, such as stoves or refrigerators.

Chattels excluded—as a matter of clarification, if items customarily included are not going to be left, then they should be so listed.

Section III

Line 1. The purchase price of the property would be inserted. Below that would be a breakdown of how that purchase price would be paid; for example:

$1,500 deposit acknowledged in paragraph 2, below

$3,500 additional cash down payment at settlement

$30,000 by conventional first deed of trust at _____ % per year for _____ years

When this section is completed, you should always add up the deposit, the additional down payment, and the trust. The total should equal the purchase price.

Section IV

Line 2. This should incorporate the amount of the earnest money deposited, with a notice as to the form of deposit, i.e., by note, check, or cash.

Line 3. Does not require any information.

Line 4. Indicates where and when settlement is to occur.

Lines 5 and 6. Require no information.

Line 7. The percentage of the broker's fee should be filled in.

"Subject to:"—this is one of the most important portions of the Offer to Purchase Agreement. In this section are to be inserted any conditions of the purchase or sale which must be fulfilled prior to settlement date. If there are any contingencies attached to the sale, they should also be inserted here, such as:

"This contract is contingent upon seller locating and purchasing another house by _____ date."

"This contract is contingent upon purchaser selling his present house by _____ date."

"This contract is contingent upon buyer securing financing, as outlined."

Also included in this section would be any agreement between buyer and seller which is not covered anywhere else in the Offer to Purchase Agreement.

Lines 8 and 9. Require no information.

Line 10. Insert the jurisdiction in which the property is located.

Section V

This section is self-explanatory.

Remember, when you complete the Offer to Purchase Agreement, do not add or subtract from the information supplied to you in the problem, even though in your particular area certain other information would generally be found in an actual contract.

OFFER TO PURCHASE AGREEMENT

This AGREEMENT made as of_____, 19_____ ,

among_____(herein called "Purchaser"),

SEC I

and_____(herein called "Seller"),

and_____(herein called "Broker"),
provides that Purchaser agrees to buy through Broker as agent for Seller, and Seller agrees to sell the following described real estate, and all improvements

thereon, located in the jurisdiction of_____

(all herein called "the property"):_____

_____

_____

SEC II

_____

_____, and more commonly known as_____

_____(street address).

    1. The purchase price of the property is_____

Dollars ($_____), and such purchase price shall be paid as follows:

_____

_____

SEC III

_____

_____

    2. Purchaser has made a deposit of_____Dollars ($_____)
with Broker, receipt of which is hereby acknowledged, and such deposit shall be held by Broker in escrow until the date of settlement and then applied
to the purchase price, or returned to Purchaser if the title to the property is not marketable.

    3. Seller agrees to convey the property to Purchaser by Warranty Deed with the usual covenants of title and free and clear from all encumbrances,
tenancies, liens (for taxes or otherwise), except as may be otherwise provided above, but subject to applicable restrictive covenants of record. Seller further
agrees to deliver possession of the property to Purchaser on the date of settlement and to pay the expense of preparing the deed of conveyance.

    4. Settlement shall be made at the offices of Broker or at_____on or before

_____, 19_____ , or as soon thereafter as title can be examined and necessary documents prepared, with allowance of
a reasonable time for Seller to correct any defects reported by the title examiner.

    5. All taxes, interest, rent, and F.H.A. or similar escrow deposits, if any, shall be prorated as of the date of settlement.

    6. All risk of loss or damage to the property by fire, windstorm, casualty, or other cause is assumed by Seller until the date of settlement.

    7. Purchaser and Seller agree that Broker was the sole procuring cause of this Contract of Purchase, and Seller agrees to pay Broker for services

rendered a cash fee of_____per cent of the purchase price. If either Purchaser or Seller defaults under such Contract, such defaulting party shall
be liable for the cash fee of Broker and any expenses incurred by the non-defaulting party in connection with this transaction.

Subject to:_____

_____

SEC IV

_____

    8. Purchaser represents that an inspection satisfactory to Purchaser has been made of the property, and Purchaser agrees to accept the property in
its present condition except as may be otherwise provided in the description of the property above.

    9. This Contract of Purchase constitutes the entire agreement among the parties and may not be modified or changed except by written instrument
executed by all of the parties, including Broker.

    10. This Contract of Purchase shall be construed, interpreted, and applied according to the law of the jurisdiction of_____and shall
be binding upon and shall inure to the benefit of the heirs, personal representatives, successors, and assigns of the parties.

All parties to this agreement acknowledge receipt of a certified copy.

WITNESS the following signatures and seals:

_____(SEAL)   _____(SEAL)
Seller   Purchaser

SEC V

_____(SEAL)   _____(SEAL)
Seller   Purchaser

_____(SEAL)
Broker

Deposit Rec'd $_____

Check   Cash

Sales Agent:

Figure 15-3. Sample form for an Offer to Purchase Agreement.

OFFER TO PURCHASE PROBLEM 1
(Refers to Listing Problem 1)

On August 1, this year, you show the Jones' property to Miss Elvira Swink, single, who agrees to buy it at the list price. She instructs you to draw up a contract offer with a 20% down payment and the seller to take back an 80% mortgage for 15 years at 7% interest, with 180 equal monthly payments consisting of principal and interest. She conditions her offer on the seller providing her with a certificate from the health authorities, certifying that the water supply is potable and that the septic system is approved. She desires settlement no later than September 1, this year. She gives you a check for $500 as an "earnest money" deposit.

OFFER TO PURCHASE AGREEMENT

This AGREEMENT made as of _AUGUST 1ST_____, 19 _THIS YEAR_,

among _ELVIRA SWINK - SINGLE_____
_____ (herein called "Purchaser"),

and _ELMER JONES AND HIS WIFE MARY_____
_____ (herein called "Seller"),

and _ARGO REALTY_____
_____ (herein called "Broker"),

provides that Purchaser agrees to buy through Broker as agent for Seller, and Seller agrees to sell the following described real estate, and all improvements thereon, located in the jurisdiction of _BOURBON COUNTY - YOUR STATE_____,

(all herein called "the property"): _____

_____ _LOT 3 BLOOMFIELD SUBD - BOURBON COUNTY - YOUR STATE_____

_____ _OWNER TO REMOVE TAGGED SHRUB AT FRONT DOOR_____

_____ _INCLUDED IN SALE IS STOVE, REFRIGERATOR AND WASHING MACHINE_____

_____ _FARMDALE - YOUR STATE_____, and more commonly known as _123 ROSE STREET_
(street address).

1. The purchase price of the property is _TWENTY FIVE THOUSAND AND_ _00/100_ ~~~
Dollars ($_25,000.00_), and such purchase price shall be paid as follows:

$500.00 DEPOSIT ACKNOWLEDGED IN PARAGRAPH 2 BELOW

$4,500.00 ADDITIONAL CASH DOWNPAYMENT AT SETTLEMENT

$20,000.00 MORTGAGE AT 7% INTEREST FOR 15 YEARS TO BE REPAID IN
180 EQUAL MONTHLY INSTALLMENTS TO PRINCIPAL AND INTEREST
TO BE TAKEN BACK BY SELLER.

2. Purchaser has made a deposit of _FIVE HUNDRED AND 00/100 (BY CHECK)_ Dollars ($_500.00_)
with Broker, receipt of which is hereby acknowledged, and such deposit shall be held by Broker in escrow until the date of settlement and then applied to the purchase price, or returned to Purchaser if the title to the property is not marketable.

3. Seller agrees to convey the property to Purchaser by Warranty Deed with the usual covenants of title and free and clear from all encumbrances, tenancies, liens (for taxes or otherwise), except as may be otherwise provided above, but subject to applicable restrictive covenants of record. Seller further agrees to deliver possession of the property to Purchaser on the date of settlement and to pay the expense of preparing the deed of conveyance.

4. Settlement shall be made at the offices of Broker or at _____ on or before _SEPTEMBER 1_____, 19 _THIS YEAR_, or as soon thereafter as title can be examined and necessary documents prepared, with allowance of a reasonable time for Seller to correct any defects reported by the title examiner.

5. All taxes, interest, rent, and F.H.A. or similar escrow deposits, if any, shall be prorated as of the date of settlement.

6. All risk of loss or damage to the property by fire, windstorm, casualty, or other cause is assumed by Seller until the date of settlement.

7. Purchaser and Seller agree that Broker was the sole procuring cause of this Contract of Purchase, and Seller agrees to pay Broker for services rendered a cash fee of _6%_ per cent of the purchase price. If either Purchaser or Seller defaults under such Contract, such defaulting party shall be liable for the cash fee of Broker and any expenses incurred by the non-defaulting party in connection with this transaction.

Subject to: _SELLER TO PROVIDE PURCHASER WITH A CERTIFICATE FROM THE_
HEALTH AUTHORITIES CERTIFYING THAT THE WATER SUPPLY IS POTABLE
AND THAT THE SEPTIC SYSTEM IS APPROVED

8. Purchaser represents that an inspection satisfactory to Purchaser has been made of the property, and Purchaser agrees to accept the property in its present condition except as may be otherwise provided in the description of the property above.

9. This Contract of Purchase constitutes the entire agreement among the parties and may not be modified or changed except by written instrument executed by all of the parties, including Broker.

10. This Contract of Purchase shall be construed, interpreted, and applied according to the law of the jurisdiction of _YOUR STATE_ and shall be binding upon and shall inure to the benefit of the heirs, personal representatives, successors, and assigns of the parties.

All parties to this agreement acknowledge receipt of a certified copy.

WITNESS the following signatures and seals:

Elmer Jones (SEAL) Seller   _Elvira Swink_ (SEAL) Purchaser

Mary Jones (SEAL) Seller   _Single_ (SEAL) Purchaser

Argo Realty: By - You (SEAL) Broker

Deposit Rec'd $ _500.00_

(Check)   Cash

Sales Agent: _Your Signature_

Figure 15-4. Offer to Purchase Form 1. Suggested solution for Offer to Purchase Problem 1.

PRACTICE EXAMINATION 1
(*Refer to Listing and Offer to Purchase Forms 1 Only*)

1. Which of the following statements regarding the property are true?

   I. The lot contains 40,000 square feet.
   II. The house contains 750 square feet.

   (A) I only
   (B) II only
   (C) Both I and II
   (D) Neither I nor II

2. The water supply comes from

   (A) a dug well
   (B) city services
   (C) a drilled well
   (D) none of these

3. The taxes on the property are

   (A) $400
   (B) $160
   (C) $240
   (D) $1,600

4. The hot-water heater is

   (A) electric, 40 gallons
   (B) oil, 30 gallons
   (C) electric, 30 gallons
   (D) gas, 30 gallons

5. The property is

   (A) brick
   (B) asbestos shingle
   (C) concrete block
   (D) frame

6. The purchase price is

   (A) $25,000
   (B) $24,910
   (C) $23,500
   (D) none of these

7. In addition to the deposit, how much additional down payment will the purchaser have to make?

   (A) $2,000
   (B) $5,000
   (C) $4,500
   (D) none of these

8. Settlement should be

   (A) August 1 this year
   (B) September 1 this year
   (C) November 1 this year
   (D) none of these

9. The terms of the loan the seller is taking back include

   (A) $9,500 with interest at 8% for 20 years
   (B) $20,000 with interest at 7% for 15 years
   (C) $21,500 with interest at 7% for 20 years
   (D) none of these

10. The agent's commission will be

    (A) 6%
    (B) 5%
    (C) $1,250
    (D) none of these

LISTING PROBLEM 2

On April 15, this year, you, as agent for Zenith Realty Company, list the home of Oliver Smith and his wife, Agnes, at 17 Petunia Place, Wysteria, your state, for 90 days. It is a $1\frac{1}{2}$-story, brick Cape Cod, 20 years old. It has a full basement, 28' X 40'; living room with fireplace, 12' X 18'; dining room, 10' X 9'; and 3 bedrooms and 2 baths, with 1 bedroom and bath on the first floor. The eat-in kitchen has a double sink and a separate stove and refrigerator, which will be included, along with a built-in dishwasher and garbage disposal. The heating system is oil hot-water baseboard, and there are storm windows and doors. There is a 1-car, attached garage with an asphalt side drive. The roof is composition shingle. The lot, described as Lot 4, Block 9, Section 1, Picadilly Subdivision, Brandy County, your state, has a 75' frontage on Petunia Place and is 120' deep. The property is assessed at $15,000, with taxes of $615. The property is served by all city utility services. The owners are moving and feel they should net $45,120 for their property after paying your 6% commission. They will take back a second trust for $4,000 at 9% interest for up to 5 years. The present 30-year first trust was placed on the property 6 years ago by the Sectional National Savings and Loan Association. As of July 1, the remaining balance will be approximately $37,500, with principal and interest payments of $293.51, including interest at 8% per annum. Taxes and insurance are paid directly by the owners. (Use form following Index.)

OFFER TO PURCHASE PROBLEM 2
(Refers to Listing Problem 2)

On July 4, this year, Mr. Joseph Chance and his wife, Nellie, were shown the Smith house. Both Mr. and Mrs. Chance like the house, but state they will not pay more than $46,000 for it and its fixtures "as is," with cash above the existing first trust. The Chances insist on settlement by July 20. They place a time limit on their offer, which will expire at 12:00 P.M., midnight, the following day if it has not been accepted. The Chances further specify that settlement is to be held in the law offices of Jones and Jackson. Mr. Chance agrees to make a $500 "earnest money" deposit in the form of a check.

You prepare a contract incorporating these terms, which the Chances sign. You present the offer that evening to the Smiths, who decide to make a counterproposal of $47,000, with cash above the existing trust.

The Chances accept the new price and ratify the changes. You then advise the Smiths that the counterproposal is accepted and bring them their copy of the final agreement. (Use form following Index.)

PRACTICE EXAMINATION 2
(Refer to Listing and Offer to Purchase Forms 2 Only)

1. The present loan payment is

   (A) $293.51 to principal, interest, taxes, and insurance
   (B) $293.51 to principal and interest
   (C) $392.25 to principal, interest, taxes, and insurance
   (D) none of these.

2. The term of your listing is

   (A) 90 days   (C) 120 days
   (B) 60 days   (D) none of these

3. The house size is

   (A) 26' X 38'   (C) 28' X 40'
   (B) 28' X 42'   (D) 1,000 square feet

4. How many bedrooms are upstairs?

   (A) 1   (C) 3
   (B) 2   (D) None

5. What is the tax rate?

   (A) $2.44 per hundred   (C) 41¢ per hundred
   (B) $6.15 per hundred   (D) $4.10 per hundred

6. What was the Chances' first offer on the house?

   (A) $47,000   (C) $46,000
   (B) $46,500   (D) None of these

7. Where will settlement be conducted?

   (A) In your broker's office
   (B) At the seller's home
   (C) At the office of Chance
   (D) At the office of Jones and Jackson

8. How much total down payment is the purchaser required to make?

   (A) $8,500   (C) $8,000
   (B) $9,500   (D) None of these

9. The property contains

   (A) a 9,000-square-foot lot
   (B) a 1-car garage
   (C) both of the above
   (D) neither A nor B

10. Which of the following statements are true?

    I. There are 2 baths—1 upstairs and 1 down.
    II. The house has both storm windows and storm doors.

    (A) I only   (C) Both I and II
    (B) II only   (D) Neither I nor II

LISTING PROBLEM 3

On June 15 this year, you, as agent for Estes, Inc., Realtors, list the home of William Bell and his wife, Liberty, at 73 Rancho Grande Boulevard, Juansville, your state. Their telephone number is 555-1021. The legal description is Lot 3, Block 9, Section 2 of El Sombrero Subdivision, Mucho County, your state. The house is a 3-bedroom rambler with vertical wood siding. There is a 12' × 18' living room with fireplace, a 10' × 12' dining room, 2 baths, and an eat-in kitchen with natural wood cabinets and Formica counter tops. The kitchen is equipped with a built-in oven and range, double stainless steel sink, dishwasher, disposal, and separate refrigerator, all of which will be included. The basement is full size, 28' × 45'. The hot water tank is gas-fired, 30 gallons; the heating system is gas, forced hot air. The washer and dryer are also included. There is a paved side drive, curbs, gutters, sidewalks, storm sewers, and city water and sanitary sewers. The lot is 90' × 110'. The current tax assessment is $3,200 to the land and $12,800 to the improvements; the tax rate is $4.30 per hundred of assessment. Taxes due January 1 in advance have been paid. The key is in your broker's office; the telephone number is 533-3333.

The present loan balance as of April 15 was $16,980 with principal and interest payments of $128.88. This is a 6%, 25-year, conventional loan placed 7 years ago when the house was new. It may be assumed without fee, but there is a $150 fee if it is prepaid.

List the house for $49,950 for 120 days, with a 6% commission. The owners state they will not pay any points as a loan placement fee. (Use form following Index.)

OFFER TO PURCHASE PROBLEM 3
(*Refers to Listing Problem 3*)

On August 1, this year, you show the Bell property to George E. Brown and his wife, Betty, who agree to purchase it at the listed price. The Browns wish to obtain their own financing, and make their offer contingent upon obtaining a commitment for an 80% loan to run for at least 25 years, at an interest rate of not more than 8% per year. The Browns agree to make application for the loan within 3 working days following acceptance of their offer by Mr. and Mrs. Bell. Mr. Brown gives you his personal check for $500 as a deposit to be held in escrow and credited against the purchase price. The Browns desire settlement on or before September 1.

The Bells agree to these terms and accept the contract. (Use form following Index.)

PRACTICE EXAMINATION 3
(Refer to Listing and Offer to Purchase Forms 3 Only)

1. The term of the listing is

   (A) 60 days   (C) 90 days
   (B) 120 days   (D) not stated

2. What are the taxes?

   (A) $550   (C) $688
   (B) $137.60   (D) None of these

3. The house contains how many square feet?

   (A) 1,260   (C) 1,176
   (B) 1,350   (D) None of these

4. The monthly payment of $128.88 includes

   (A) principal, interest, and taxes
   (B) principal, interest, taxes, and insurance
   (C) principal and interest
   (D) principal, interest, and insurance

5. The exterior of the house is

   (A) brick
   (B) vertical wood siding
   (C) frame
   (D) none of these

6. In addition to the deposit, what is the buyer's down payment at settlement?

   (A) $9,490   (C) $9,960
   (B) $9,990   (D) None are within $200

7. Based on the contract, how much will the seller pay as a loan placement fee?

   (A) $399.60   (C) $94.90
   (B) $499.50   (D) None of these

8. Which of the following statements is (are) true?

   I. The listing expires October 15 this year.
   II. The hot water tank is 30 gallons.

   (A) I only   (C) Both I and II
   (B) II only   (D) Neither I nor II

9. Which of the following statements is (are) true?

   I. The property has curbs, gutters, and sidewalks.
   II. The kitchen is equipped with an exhaust fan.

   (A) I only   (C) Both I and II
   (B) II only   (D) Neither I nor II

10. Which of the following statements is (are) true?

    I. The house is 7 years old.
    II. The property includes a garage.

    (A) I only   (C) Both I and II
    (B) II only   (D) Neither I nor II

SETTLEMENT STATEMENTS

How to Complete a Settlement Statement

After all conditions of a real estate sales contract have been met, the final transaction takes place in which title of the property is transferred from the seller to the buyer in exchange for whatever consideration is provided for in the contract. This transaction is most often simply called *settlement.* Basically, settlement is the time when the financial portion of the offer to purchase is finalized.

The accounting technique generally used in settlements is a very simple form of double entry bookkeeping. Although it is well known to businessmen, bankers, lawyers, and accountants, most people have little more than a passing acquaintance with this method.

The bookkeeping principles which apply to real estate closing statements are few. They can be more easily understood if the following points are kept in mind (refer to Settlement Statement form as needed):

1. The term *debit*, as the word itself suggests, is something that is owed. On the buyer's statement it is an item that is chargeable against (or subtracted from) the buyer's account. Similarly, a debit on the seller's statement is an item that is chargeable against (or subtracted from) the seller's account.

2. A *credit* is something that is receivable. On the buyer's statement, it is an item that is added or credited to the buyer's balance. On the seller's statement, it is an item added or credited to the seller.

3. The sum of the seller's debits must equal the sum of the seller's credits. Also, the sum of the buyer's debits must equal the buyer's credits.

4. The same line item in an identical amount may appear as a credit on one statement and as a debit on the other. This can occur when there is a direct transfer of equity from the seller to the buyer in such items as prorations of insurance, taxes, or rent.

With respect to the various line items on the buyer's statement and those on the seller's, it would appear that the party being charged for some of them would be standard practice in most jurisdictions. In actuality, these items are assigned in accordance with the specific provisions of the contract being settled. The closing statements are, in effect, a direct translation of the financial aspects of the contract. As a general rule, an item is usually charged or debited to the party benefiting by the item, and the party giving up something is generally credited by an amount equivalent to its value. As previously mentioned, however, there can be exceptions to this rule, depending on the custom in various areas.

Closing statements can be prepared in two basic ways: either as separate statements for buyer and seller, or as a single statement in which a combined presentation is made of the two accounts. Combined statements, such as the ones used here, are used in the Uniform Examination. They include a listing of all line item entries that apply to both the buyer and the seller, which in itself facilitates cross-checking for errors or omissions.

The exact sequence in which the line item entries appear on the closing statement is for the most part a matter of discretion, except that the purchase price is normally the first entry, and the last entries are generally those concerning how much cash the buyer will pay at closing, or what the net to the seller will be.

The line items in the following list are those frequently appearing in real estate closing statements. The list has been placed in the general form of a combined statement in which the various items appear as one might expect to find them in a typical statement. Keep in mind that these items are assigned to the buyer or seller on the basis of practices in some parts of the country. They may not agree with customs in your area. More items have been covered than will normally be found on a real estate examination in an effort to accustom the student to any possible variation which may be encountered. (Refer to Settlement Statement Worksheet, Fig. 15-5.)

Purchase Price of the Property

This is a principal expense of the buyer and is carried as a debit on the buyer's account. For the seller, it is a credit.

Deposit

This is the amount which the buyer put up as earnest money. It is a portion of the purchase price. Since the entire amount has already been debited to the buyer, the deposit here is a credit to the buyer.

Preparation of the Deed and Bargain of Sale

It is the seller's responsibility to provide a good and sufficient deed to the buyer. This is usually an expense of the seller.

Recording of Deed and Bargain of Sale

The recordation of the deed and bargain of sale is for the benefit and protection of the buyer (and lender); therefore, it is usually an expense, or debit, to the buyer.

Conveyance Tax

This is an *ad valorem* type of tax imposed on the transfer of real estate. It is an expense associated with the seller's transfer of title and is usually at the seller's expense.

Sales Commission

This is normally an expense, or debit, of the seller. Occasionally, an agent may be working for the buyer, who has agreed to pay the agent's fee. If such were the case, then this item would appear as an expense (or debit) to the buyer.

Pay Off Existing Deeds of Trust

If the existing trust is not to be assumed, then it must be paid off in order to clear the title. The balance of the existing trust, along with any payoff penalties imposed, would be charged, or debited, to the seller.

Release of Existing Trust

These are legal fees associated with paying off the existing trust and clearing the title of liens; therefore, they are debited to the seller.

Assumption of Existing Trust

If a loan or loans are being assumed, the amounts are treated as credits to the buyer. (They are part of the total amount of the purchase, and reduce the cash required from the buyer.) The same amount is then debited to the seller's account. (It reduces the amount of cash the seller is due.) In effect, the buyer agrees to assume the seller's debt in return for a credit against the purchase price.

Proceeds of New Trust

If the property is to be refinanced, the proceeds of the new trust are entered as a credit to the buyer's account. Although the trust itself constitutes a long-term obligation of the buyer to a third party, the *proceeds* of that trust provide the buyer with the means with which to pay a large part of the purchase price.

Purchase Money Deeds of Trust

A first or second trust, which is being taken back by the seller as part payment of the purchase price in lieu of cash, is handled in the same manner as an assumption (see Assumption of Existing Trust). It is considered as a credit to the buyer inasmuch as it provides a portion of the means which will be used to close the transaction. For the seller, it is considered as a debit since it reduces the net proceeds receivable by the seller at settlement. In effect, the seller has purchased a secured investment using part of the proceeds of sale that would otherwise be receivable as cash at settlement.

Title Examination

This is a fee paid to an attorney, abstract company, or title company for their opinion as to the condition of title. While this varies widely from one jurisdiction to another, the purchaser is usually charged for it; therefore, it is a debit to the buyer.

Title Insurance

Most lenders will require, as one of their conditions of making the loan, that they be supplied with an insurance policy protecting them against loss if the title is defective. If the buyer is obtaining a new loan, it is usually considered a cost of loan origination, and therefore is charged, or debited, to the buyer.

In some areas, this is debited to the seller, as it is considered part of the agreement of transferring a property free of liens. A title insurance policy, in effect, proves this, or provides the purchaser and lender with more protection than a General Warranty Deed. For our purposes, charge or debit the buyer.

Preparation of Deeds of Trust

These are legal fees for preparing deeds of trust to secure the loans obtained by the buyer. They are an expense incurred by the borrower as a condition of obtaining the loan, and are chargeable to the buyer, as a debit.

	BUYER'S STATEMENT		SELLER'S STATEMENT	
	DEBIT	CREDIT	DEBIT	CREDIT
PURCHASE PRICE	X			X
DEPOSIT		X		
PREPARATION OF THE DEED			X	
RECORDING OF THE DEED	X			
CONVEYANCE TAX			X	
SALES COMMISSION			X	
PAY-OFF OF EXISTING TRUST			X	
RELEASE OF EXISTING TRUST			X	
ASSUMPTION OF EXIST. TRUST		X	X	
PROCEEDS OF NEW TRUST		X		
PURCHASE MONEY TRUST		X	X	
TITLE EXAMINATION	X			
TITLE INSURANCE	X			
PREPARATION OF DEED OF TR.	X			
RECORDING OF DEED OF TR.	X			
LOAN DISCOUNT - POINTS	VARIES			
REAL PROPERTY TAXES				
BACK TAXES			X	
CURRENT TAXES - NOT DUE		X	X	
PREPAID TAXES	X			X
INSURANCE				
ASSUMPTION OF POLICY	X			X
NEW POLICY	X			
INTEREST				
ASSUMPTIONS		X	X	
NEW LOANS	X			
ESCROW ACCOUNTS				
PAY OFF EXISTING LOAN				X
ASSUMPTIONS	X			X
CREDIT REPORTING FEE	X			
SURVEY	X			
APPRAISAL FEE	VARIES			
SETTLEMENT FEE	VARIES			
SALE OF CHATTELS	X			X
BALANCE DUE FROM BUYER		X X		
BALANCE DUE SELLER			X X	
TOTALS	xxxxx	xxxxx	xxxxx	xxxxx

Figure 15-5. Sample Settlement Statement Worksheet.

Recording of Deeds of Trust

These are the charges consisting of clerk's fees, state deed taxes, and county or municipal deed taxes. Although the purpose of recordation is to protect the interests of the parties secured (the lenders), the costs are debited to the buyer as a condition of obtaining the loan.

Loan Discount or Placement Fees

Practices regarding loan discount and placement fees vary widely from one area to another, as well as varying with the type of loan involved. The distribution of these charges is usually specified in the contract. If this item is found on any examination, follow the instructions given.

Real Property Taxes

1. *Back taxes*—These are a lien on the property and must be paid prior to title transfer. They are debited to the seller.
2. *Current taxes not yet due*—The seller is debited and the buyer credited with the proportionate share of the unpaid taxes covering the period prior to settlement (from the date when taxes were last due and payable to the date of settlement).
3. *Prepaid taxes*—The seller is credited with the "unused" portion of the prepayment (taxes paid in advance), and the buyer, who will receive the benefit of the remaining "unused" portion, is debited. The proration is based on the date of settlement.

Insurance

If the buyer is assuming the seller's insurance policy, this is a debit to the buyer and a credit to the seller for the unused portion of the policy.

A buyer who is purchasing a new insurance policy will be debited for the amount of the policy. In this case, the seller usually will get a refund for the unused amount of the present policy directly from the insurance company. The seller does not receive a credit for that here.

Interest

If the current loan is being assumed, the seller owes the buyer for interest from the last date it was paid (usually the first of the month) until the date of settlement. Debit the seller and credit the buyer with this pro rata amount.

If a new loan is being placed, in order to adjust the payment date to the first of the month, the buyer is charged interest from the date of settlement to the end of the month, so debit the buyer. There is no credit to the seller.

Escrow Accounts

If the seller has monies on deposit with the lender and the existing loan is being paid off, these funds will be returned to the seller. The seller is credited.

If the loan is being assumed, the buyer, in effect, buys the escrow accounts. Debit the buyer and credit the seller.

Credit Reporting Fee

This is a charge against the buyer by the lending institution for investigating the buyer and the buyer's credit. Debit the buyer.

Survey

This is a charge against the buyer when a survey is required by the lender as a condition of making the loan. Debit the buyer.

Appraisal Fee

This is a charge against either the buyer or the seller, usually depending upon which party orders it. Often, the seller may order an appraisal in advance in order to enhance the marketing effort of the agent, in which case the appraisal is charged, or debited, against the seller. If the buyer orders an appraisal for loan purposes, then the fee is charged, or debited, to the buyer.

Settlement Fee

If not otherwise provided for in the sales contract, this is a charge, or debit, to the buyer for the services of an escrow agent in conducting settlement. In some areas, the settlement fee is one-half debited to buyer and one-half debited to seller.

Sale of Chattels

If the contract provides for the purchase of items, such as rugs, draperies, lawn mowers, etc., not included in the purchase price, these items are conveyed under a separate bill of sale and are carried on the settlement statement as a credit to the seller and a debit to the buyer.

Balance Due from Buyer to Close

This is the amount the buyer must pay at settlement. This figure is obtained by "forcing the balance," i.e., subtracting the total of all the buyer's credits from the total of all the buyer's debits. The balance due is carried as a credit to the buyer.

Balance Due Seller

This is the net amount the seller receives. It is also obtained by "forcing the balance," in this case subtracting all the seller's debits from the total of all the seller's credits. This balance is carried as a debit to the seller.

SETTLEMENT PROBLEM 1
(Refers to Listing and Offer to Purchase Problems 1)

All terms of the contract on the Jones property have been met, and settlement is scheduled for September 1, this year. Real estate taxes for the current year are due January 1, next year.

In addition to the purchase price, deposit, first mortgage, proration of taxes, and sales fee, the following will be charged:

Title examination: $\frac{1}{2}$% of the sales price, charged to the purchaser

Recording fee for mortgage: $50, charged to the purchaser

Appraisal fee: $40, charged to the seller

Oil in tank: the seller has just filled the tank. Purchaser is to pay $35 for the oil.

Other items are purposely not given and are not to be used.

	BUYER'S STATEMENT		SELLER'S STATEMENT	
	DEBIT	CREDIT	DEBIT	CREDIT
PURCHASE PRICE	25,000.00			25,000.00
DEPOSIT		500.00		
NEW 1ST MORT. PROCEEDS		20,000.00	20,000.00	
R.E. TAXES - PRORATED		106.67	106.67	
SALES FEE			1,560.00	
TITLE EXAMINATION	125.00			
RECORDING FEE - MORT.	50.00			
APPRAISAL FEE			40.00	
OIL IN TANK	35.00			35.00
BALANCE DUE FROM BUYER		4,603.33		
BALANCE DUE SELLER			3,388.33	
	25,210.00	25,210.00	25,035.00	25,035.00

Figure 15-6. Settlement Statement Worksheet 1. Suggested solution for Settlement Problem 1.

BROKER'S PRACTICE EXAMINATION 1
(Refer to Completed Settlement Statement 1 Only)

1. The tax proration is

    (A) debit seller $106.67, credit purchaser $106.67
    (B) credit seller $106.67, debit purchaser $106.67
    (C) debit seller $53.33, credit purchaser $106.67
    (D) credit seller $106.67, debit purchaser $53.33

2. The balance due from purchaser to close is

    (A) $3,388.33
    (B) $4,603.33
    (C) $4,496.66
    (D) none of the above are within $5.00

3. Referring to the debits and credits to the purchaser,

    (A) there are 4 debits and 4 credits
    (B) there are 3 debits and 4 credits
    (C) there are 4 debits and 3 credits
    (D) none of these

4. Referring to the debits and credits to the seller,

    (A) there are 1 credit and 3 debits
    (B) there are 3 debits and 3 credits
    (C) there are 2 credits and 3 debits
    (D) none of these

5. The balance due seller at settlement is

    (A) $21,888.33
    (B) $23,388.33
    (C) $23,281.66
    (D) none of the above are within $5.00

6. Total credits to seller are

    (A) $25,000
    (B) $24,065
    (C) $25,035
    (D) none of these are within $5.00

7. Total debits to the purchaser are

    (A) $25,160
    (B) $25,210
    (C) $25,125
    (D) none of these are within $5.00

8. The amount of the sales commission is

    (A) $1,450
    (B) $1,250
    (C) $1,500
    (D) none of these are within $50

9. Regarding the oil in the tank, which of the following statements is (are) true?

    I. The seller was debited and the purchaser was credited.
    II. The purchaser was debited and the seller was credited.

    (A) I only   (C) Both I and II
    (B) II only   (D) Neither I nor II

10. Who paid for recording the new mortgage?

    (A) The seller   (C) The purchaser
    (B) The broker   (D) There was no such charge

SETTLEMENT PROBLEM 2
(Refers to Listing and Offer to Purchase Problems 2)

Settlement of the Smith-Chance contract is scheduled for July 20. Taxes for the current year remain unpaid. The principal balance plus interest on the loan as of the date of settlement is $37,490. The purchaser will take over the seller's 3-year insurance policy, which was purchased July 20 of last year for $360.00. Lawyers' fees are $190 for the purchaser and $70 for the seller. Use any other information you need from the Listing or Offer to Purchase. (Use form following Index.)

BROKER'S PRACTICE EXAMINATION 2

(Refer to Completed Settlement Statement 2 Only)

1. The insurance proration is

   (A) seller credited $120.00, purchaser debited $120.00
   (B) purchaser credited $120.00, seller debited $120.00
   (C) seller debited $240.00, purchaser credited $240.00
   (D) purchaser debited $240.00, seller credited $240.00

2. The purchase price of the property is

   (A) debited to the purchaser, credited to the seller
   (B) credited to the purchaser, debited to the seller
   (C) Neither A nor B is correct
   (D) Both A and B are correct

3. Regarding debits and credits to the purchaser,

   (A) there are 3 credits and 4 debits
   (B) there are 3 debits and 4 credits
   (C) there are 3 debits and 3 credits
   (D) none of the above are correct

4. Regarding debits and credits to the seller,

   (A) there are 3 credits and 4 debits
   (B) there are 4 credits and 3 debits
   (C) there are 5 debits and 2 credits
   (D) there are 2 debits and 5 credits

5. The balance due from purchaser to close is

   (A) $9,098.34
   (B) $8,756.68
   (C) $8,256.68
   (D) none of the above are within $50.00

6. The balance due seller is

   (A) $6,518.34   (C) $6,176.68
   (B) $6,448.34   (D) $9,338.34

7. The total of the purchaser's debits is

   (A) $47,190
   (B) $47,670
   (C) $47,430
   (D) none of the above are within $50.00

8. The total of the seller's debits is

   (A) $47,240.00
   (B) $47,581.66
   (C) $46,898.34
   (D) none of the above are within $50.00

9. The tax proration is

   (A) $341.66 debited to purchaser and credited to seller
   (B) $341.66 debited to seller and credited to purchaser
   (C) $273.34 debited to seller and credited to purchaser
   (D) $273.34 debited to purchaser and credited to seller

10. The deposit was

    (A) credited to the seller, debited to the purchaser
    (B) credited to the purchaser, debited to the seller
    (C) both A and B are correct
    (D) neither A nor B is correct

SETTLEMENT PROBLEM 3
(Refers to Listing and Offer to Purchase Problems 3)

Mr. Brown has arranged financing to purchase the Bell property, and settlement is scheduled for September 1. In addition to items covered in the Listing and Offer to Purchase forms, the following charges are to be considered at settlement:

The lender is charging the purchaser 1 point to place the loan. The purchaser's legal fees will be $150.00 and the seller's $37.50, and the first trust has been reduced to $16,456.33.

Prepare the Settlement Statement, using the information you have been given. (Use form following Index.)

BROKER'S PRACTICE EXAMINATION 3
(Refer to Completed Settlement Statement 3 Only)

1. The real estate tax proration is

   (A) $458.68 debit to buyer and credit to seller
   (B) $458.68 credit to buyer and debit to seller
   (C) $229.32 debit to buyer and credit to seller
   (D) $229.32 credit to buyer and debit to seller

2. Balance due from buyer to close is

   (A) $10,768.92 (C) $10,498.24
   (B) $10,268.92 (D) $10,039.60

3. Balance due seller from the sale is

   (A) $30,688.49 (C) $30,309.17
   (B) $30,388.49 (D) $30,538.49

4. The total of the buyer's debits is

   (A) $50,499.60 (C) $50,329.32
   (B) $50,728.92 (D) $51,187.60

5. The total of the seller's debits is

   (A) $50,179.32
   (B) $50,408.64
   (C) $51,187.60
   (D) none of the above are within $100

6. Regarding the loan placement fee,

   (A) it was $499.50, debited to buyer
   (B) it was $499.50, debited to seller
   (C) it was $399.60, debited to buyer
   (D) it was $399.60, debited to seller

7. The buyer's total debits and credits are

   (A) 3 debits and 4 credits
   (B) 4 debits and 3 credits
   (C) 4 debits and 4 credits
   (D) 3 debits and 3 credits

8. The seller's total debits and credits are

   (A) 4 debits and 3 credits
   (B) 4 credits and 3 debits
   (C) 5 debits and 2 credits
   (D) 2 debits and 4 credits

9. Regarding the legal fees charged,

   (A) the buyer was credited $150, and the seller credited $37.50.
   (B) the seller was debited $37.50, and the buyer debited $150.00.
   (C) the seller was debited $37.50, and the buyer credited $150.00.
   (D) none of these are correct

10. The sales commission is

   (A) $2,497.50, debited to seller
   (B) $2,497.50, credited to seller
   (C) $2,997.00, debited to seller
   (D) $2,997.00, credited to seller

Chapter 16

Definitions of Words and Phrases

Abstract of title A condensed history of the legal title to a piece of property. It consists of a summary of the various links in the chain of title, together with a statement of all liens, judgments, taxes, or other encumbrances affecting a particular property. (It is a summary of the conveyances, such as deeds or wills, and legal proceedings affecting the subject property, giving names of the parties, descriptions of the land, and agreements, arranged to show the continuous history of ownership.)

Accelerated depreciation Method of depreciation which speeds up the write-off of property from income taxes at a rate greater than normal depreciation. Its purpose is to act as an incentive in attracting equity capital into apartment and commercial development.

Acceleration clause From the buyer's point of view, a stipulation in a mortgage or a loan contract that permits the borrower to repay either the entire indebtedness or a major portion of it without penalty. From the lender's point of view, upon default of payment due, the balance of the indebtedness becomes due and payable.

Access The right to enter and leave a property. *See also* EASEMENT; RIGHT-OF-WAY.

Accretion Addition to one's real estate by the gradual deposit of soil through the operation of natural causes. Usually the additional land is the result of water flowage. May include sand and earth. Opposite of erosion. *See also* ALLUVION; AVULSION; EROSION.

Acknowledgment The act, on the part of one who has executed a deed or other written instrument, of going before a competent court or officer and declaring it to be a voluntary act and deed. Usually a notary public attests to the veracity of the signature of each person who has signed the instrument.

Acre A measure of land equaling 160 square rods, or 4,840 square yards, or 43,560 square feet; or a tract about 208.71 feet square.

Ad valorem A tax assessment against real estate according to its valuation. *See* ASSESSMENT.

Administrator A person appointed by a court to manage and settle the estate of a deceased person who has left no will. An administrator handles the property of an intestate. Opposite of executor. *See* EXECUTOR.

Adverse possession A holding of property inconsistent with the right of the true owner. An occupant's right to acquire title to land despite the rights of the title (real) owner, if the occupant's possession has been *actual, continuous, hostile, visible,* and *distinct* for the statutory period. *See* TITLE BY ADVERSE POSSESSION.

Affidavit A statement in writing, sworn to in front of a notary public or other official possessing the authority to administer oaths.

Affirmation A solemn declaration in the nature of an oath, made by persons who have religious scruples against taking oaths; a nonreligious oath.

Affirmative action program A detailed plan to hire, employ, and/or train members of minority groups. *See* EQUAL OPPORTUNITY IN HOUSING.

Age of majority *See* MAJORITY AGE.

Agency A contract by which one person with greater or less discretionary power undertakes to represent another in certain business relations. A listing contract creates the principal-agent relationship in real estate. *See* EXCLUSIVE AGENCY; EXCLUSIVE AUTHORIZATION TO SELL LISTING.

Agent A person acting on behalf of another, called the principal. An agent derives authority from the principal, spelled out in the agency contract.

Agreement of sale A written agreement whereby the purchaser agrees to buy certain real estate and the seller agrees to sell upon terms and conditions set forth therein. (An agreement of sale is also known as a contract of, or for, sale.)

Air rights The ownership or lease of air space above a specific parcel of real property and the accompanying rights to build upon or otherwise use, control, and occupy. (The construction of an office building or a residential highrise on concrete and steel pillars straddling a railroad or highway right-of-way is an example of the use of air rights.)

Alluvion Soil deposited by accretion. *See also* ACCRETION; AVULSION.

Amenities Qualities and features of living that make an individual property and its location desirable and hence valuable. These include nature's gifts (trees, open space, streams, scenic views) as well as human creations (architectural design; well-maintained neighborhoods; proximity to schools, recreation, libraries, and other public facilities; and proximity to commerical services such as employment, shopping, theater, and professional offices).

American Institute of Real Estate Appraisers A national professional and trade association of appraisers and appraisal firms.

American Society of Appraisers A national professional and trade association of appraisers and appraisal firms.

American Society of Real Estate Counselors A national professional and trade association of developers, investors, and experienced advisers on all real estate matters.

Amortization The act of extinguishing an indebtedness such as a mortgage loan by equal and periodic payments to principal and interest. Real estate loans are commonly paid off through constant monthly payments on principal and interest which reduce the balance of the outstanding debt. While the monthly payment remains constant, an increasingly larger portion of it is applied to principal and hence a diminishing portion to interest. *See* CONSTANT.

Annuity A sum of money or its equivalent that constitutes one of a series of periodic payments. Any advantage that may be interpreted in terms of money and answers the requirements of regularity may be considered as an "annuity."

Appraisal An estimate and opinion of value of a piece of property; a conclusion resulting from an analysis of facts, chiefly about the market value of a parcel of real estate. *See also* CORRELATION.

Appreciation An increase in the value of a parcel of real estate resulting from market forces. In economic terms, when demand is stronger than supply, an appreciation in value usually occurs.

Appurtenance A right, privilege, or improvement belonging to and passing with a principal property; that which has been added to another thing, and which becomes an inherent part of the property, passing with it when it is sold, leased, or devised. *See* EASEMENT; RIGHT-OF-WAY.

Assessed valuation The value assigned to real estate by a local taxing authority for property taxation purposes.

Assessment An official valuation of property for tax purposes. (A special assessment refers to charges imposed on homeowners for certain public improvements, such as water and sewer mains or streets and gutters, specifically serving their property.)

Assets All forms of property, real and personal, that one owns. This may include both separately owned property and jointly owned property shared with others. Assets minus liabilities equals net worth, or equity.

Assignee One who receives an agreement or contract assigned.

Assignment Transfer of a title or interest by writing.

Assignor One who transfers a title or interest in real estate by assignment.

Associate broker A licensed real estate broker who chooses to work for another broker.

Assumption of mortgage The taking of title to property by a grantee who assumes the existing loan liability. Said grantee then becomes a co-guarantor for the payment of the assumed mortgage or deed of trust along with the original maker of the note, who is not released from responsibility. *See also* SUBJECT TO MORTGAGE.

Attachment of property A writ issued at the beginning or during progress of a legal action commanding the sheriff or other proper officer to attach the property, right, or effects of the defendant to satisfy the credit demands of the plaintiff.

Attestation Testimony or evidence given under oath.

Attorney-at-law A lawyer; an officer in a court of justice who is employed by a party in a cause to manage the same for them.

Attorney-in-fact One who is authorized to perform certain acts for another under a power of attorney; the power of attorney may be general or limited to a specific act or acts.

Avulsion Removal of land from one owner to another when a stream suddenly changes its channel. *See also* ACCRETION; ALLUVION.

Balloon mortgage A loan that is to be paid off in a lump sum at the end of the term. Opposite of amortized loan.

Bench marks Land description symbols affixed on metal posts, stones, or other durable matter permanently located in the ground which serve as major reference points for property identification.

Beneficiary A person designated as the recipient of funds or other property under a trust, insurance policy, or other such document. Under a deed of trust, the beneficiary is the lender.

Bilateral contract One person's promise in exchange for the other person's promise. The usual contract specifies an exchange of promises—a promise to purchase property for a cash consideration, and a promise to sell the property for the same cash consideration. *See also* UNILATERAL CONTRACT.

Bill of sale A written instrument transferring right, title, and interest in personal property to another. A bill of sale may accompany the contract of sale on real property if items of personal property have not been included within the contract of sale instrument.

Binder Deposit paid to cover a portion of or the total down payment for the purchase of real estate, as evidence of good faith on the part of the purchaser. The payment of deposit money or earnest money by the purchaser to secure the property until the sale can be completed is a binder. *See also* EARNEST MONEY.

Blanket mortgage A single mortgage which covers two or more parcels of real estate. It is commonly used in subdivision construction and home improvement work.

Blockbusting Employing fear tactics to induce panic selling of houses in a neighborhood. Such practice is illegal.

Bona fide In good faith, without fraud.

Bond Any obligation under seal. A real estate bond is a written obligation, usually issued on security of a mortgage or a trust deed. A bond, or a note, shows indebtedness and promises to repay the loan.

Breach The violation of an obligation, engagement, or duty. In case of breach of contract by one party, there are legal remedies which may be instituted by the other, nondefaulting party.

Break-even point That amount of income which just covers all expenses.

Broker One who, for compensation, acts as an agent for another.

Broker—real estate Any person, partnership, association, or corporation who, for a compensation or valuable consideration, sells or offers for sale, buys or offers to buy, or negotiates the purchase or sale or exchange of real estate, or who leases or offers to lease, or rents or offers to rent, any real estate or the improvements thereon for others, as a whole or partial vocation. *See also* ASSOCIATE BROKER.

Building code Regulations established by a local government setting forth the structural requirements for construction.

Building line A line fixed at a certain distance from the front and/or sides of a lot, beyond which no building can project. Should this line be exceeded, an encroachment may occur.

By-laws Rules and regulations governing the day-to-day operation of a condominium project, and usually appended to the Master Deed and also recorded.

CAI See COMMUNITY ASSOCIATIONS INSTITUTE.

Capitalization The process of computing current value from expected future income. Annual net income, divided by a capitalization rate which has been carefully selected based on a thorough knowledge of market conditions, gives an indication of the current value of the property.

Capitalization rate A percentage made up of the interest rate on the investment plus the recapture rate of the investment in the improvement.

Cash flow In real estate, a net income stream from gross real property receipts, after mortgage payments and other expenses are paid.

Caveat emptor Let the buyer beware. The rule means that the purchaser should carefully, and completely, specify the conditions of purchase in the contract of purchase.

Chain A unit of land measurement, 66 feet. (In a survey of real property, distances may be expressed in chains.)

Chattels Either movable or immovable items, other than real estate; in law, any property other than a freehold or fee estate in land. Chattels are divisible into chattels-real and chattels-personal. Chattels-real are annexed to real estate and are thus a part of the real property, while chattels-personal are movable and hence personalty.

Closing costs Costs for transfer of title (ownership) which are added to the price of a property; they include mortgage loan charges (points), title search and title insurance, state and local transfer taxes, and the broker's sales commission.

Closing statement *See* SETTLEMENT STATEMENT.

Cloud on the title An outstanding claim or encumbrance which, if valid, would affect or impair the owner's title; a deed of trust or judgment. The existence of a cloud on the title impairs the marketability of the property. *See also* QUIETING TITLE.

Collateral security A separate obligation attached to a contract to guarantee its performance; the transfer of property or of other contracts or valuables to ensure the performance of a principal agreement. (It is an additional security intended to guarantee contract performance. For example, additional property of the mortgagor may be encumbered to guarantee the repayment of a large loan extended to the mortgagor.)

Color of title An apparent title founded upon a written instrument such as a deed, levy of execution, or decree of court. It is that which appears to be good title, but as a matter of fact is not good title.

Commingle To mix together separate funds, as a salesperson's savings account with deposit money of a client. The practice of commingling funds is expressly forbidden, under threat of suspension or revocation of one's real estate license.

Commission This word has two meanings: (1) payment of money or other valuable consideration to a real estate broker for services performed, to satisfy the terms of the listing contract between principal (seller of real estate) and agent (real estate broker). *See also* FEE.

(2) The administrative and regulatory body charged with enforcement of the state's real estate license laws (for example, the Maryland Real Estate Commission).

Commitment A pledge or promise or firm agreement. For example, if a mortgage loan commitment has been made by a mortgagee, at some later date the mortgagee will honor the commitment and make a loan to the mortgagor on certain stipulated terms.

Community Associations Institute (CAI) A national organization of homeowner associations (for example, condominium homeowner associations). *See* HOMEOWNER ASSOCIATIONS.

Community property Property (usually obtained through joint efforts during marrige) in which husband and wife have equal, undivided half interests.

Compound interest Interest paid on both the original principal and the accrued interest which has accumulated. Sometimes popularly called "double" interest, or interest on top of interest. (Savings accounts draw compound interest.)

Condemnation This word has two meanings: (1) Taking of private property for public use by a political subdivision under the right of eminent domain. (2) Declaration that a structure is unfit for use. (Note that the two separate definitions both involve actions taken in the public interest by separate public agencies.)

Condominium (ownership) A multiunit structure made up of individually owned units with separate deeds, but with undivided, joint, and shared ownership of the common facilities (elevators, heating plant, etc.), areas (hallways, lobby, garage, etc.), and grounds. The condominium master deed in multifamily housing provides for individual owners to have separate deeds for their private living quarters. Bylaws provide policies governing the management and operation of the total structure, and a homeowners' association may provide interpretive policy along with rules and regulations. *See also* COOPERATIVE.

Condominium conversion The process of turning a rental structure into individually owned units.

Consideration Some right, interest, property, or benefit accruing to one party, or some forebearance, detriment, loss, or responsibility given, suffered, or undertaken by the other. That which induces a contract; it may be money, commodity exchange, a benefit to the promissor, or a detriment to the promisee. A promise for a promise.

Constant A combination of interest and loan amortization payments expressed as a percentage of the principal mortgage loan. The monthly or yearly payment on an amortized loan. Of the total payment to principal and interest, the amount used to pay interest declines each month, while the amount credited to principal increases. However, the combined total payment remains constant. *See* AMORTIZATION.

Construction loan *See* INTERIM FINANCING.

Contiguous Side by side, or adjacent and touching. (Property which is contiguous to other property abuts it on one of its sides.)

Contract A deliberate engagement between two competent parties based upon a legal consideration to do or to abstain from doing some act. *See also* BILATERAL CONTRACT; IMPLIED CONTRACT; LAND CONTRACT; LISTING CONTRACT; RECISSION OF CONTRACT; UNILATERAL CONTRACT.

Contract for sale *See* AGREEMENT OF SALE.

Conventional home A home built and assembled at the site of construction (or, on-site). Opposite of factory-built or mobile housing.

Convey Transfer; grant. To transfer and grant.

Conveyance The act of, or the instrument used in, transferring and granting title to real estate. (A deed is the most common instrument.)

Cooperative (ownership) Stock ownership in a multifamily structure made up of individually owned, *nondeeded* units with *shares* of ownership, together with joint and shared ownership of the common areas of the structure and grounds. Owners of units may not deed their separate units; rather, the cooperative ownership venture repurchases the shares or otherwise disposes of the units as decided by its governing body. *See also* CONDOMINIUM.

Corporeal Physical or tangible. *See* HEREDITAMENTS.

Correlation The appraisal technique of arriving at a final estimate of value by making an independent assessment using each of the three separate approaches to value—the cost approach, the sales comparison or market data approach, and the income approach—and then weighting the results. *See also* APPRAISAL.

Counsel Advice, opinion, or instruction given in directing the judgment or conduct of another; also, a lawyer engaged to give such advice, or to conduct a case in court. *See also* ATTORNEY-AT-LAW.

Covenant An agreement between two or more persons, entered into by deed, whereby one of the parties promises to perform certain acts, or that a given state does or shall, or does not or shall not, exist. (Essentially, a covenant is a promise. Covenants are clauses in the deed.)

Covert Hidden or concealed, not open, as in undiscovered or undiscoverable defects of title.

Curtesy A life estate in real estate owned by his wife which a husband is entitled to upon her death. Rights of curtesy or dower do not give an interest in the land until the spouse's death. *See also* DOWER.

Debenture A promissory note backed by the reputation and credit of a company and usually not secured by a mortgage or lien on any specific asset.

Debt An outstanding loan or obligation which must be repaid.

Debt capital The total amount of loans outstanding. The ability to raise debt capital is the ability to get loans, which is a function of the borrower's income sources and credit standing, the worth of the property or the undertaking, and the borrower's "track record." Opposite of equity capital. *See* EQUITY INTEREST.

Debt service The principal and interest payment to repay a loan.

Decedent A deceased person.

Decree A judgment of a court of equity.

Dedication To convey title in privately-held property over to public use.

Deed An instrument in writing duly executed and delivered for the purpose of conveying title to real estate.

Deed of trust *See* TRUST DEED.

Default The nonperformance of a duty. Default by one party to a contract, or the nonperformance of a condition or a term of the contract, creates certain legal remedies available to the nondefaulting party.

Defeasance clause The second clause in a mortgage contract that voids the conveyance of the property (found in the first clause); it takes effect when the debt is repaid and all other conditions are performed and satisfied by the mortgagor (debtor).

Defendant The party sued or called to answer in any legal suit. The party initiating the legal action is referred to as the plaintiff.

Deficiency judgment Court award to a creditor resulting from a foreclosure sale in which net receipts from sale are not equal to the mortgage debt.

Delinquency A loan in default; an overdue loan.

Delivery Irrevocable transfer of deed from seller to buyer (as in the transfer of title).

Demise The conveyance of an estate, chiefly by lease. (Conveyance or transfer of interest may also be made by will.)

Density The number of dwelling and commercial units per acre of land.

Deposit *See* EARNEST MONEY.

Depreciation Decrease in value, brought about by deterioration through ordinary wear and tear, action of the elements, or functional or economic obsolescence.

Developer An entrepreneur who financially and physically creates a real estate investment.

Devise A gift of real estate by will or last testament.

Disintermediation An outflow of savings from savings and loan associations and from mutual savings banks; a "reverse" flow of funds outward from financial institutions, as when depositors withdraw their savings to reinvest them wherever the return on their money will be higher.

Dispossess To deprive a person of the possession and/or use of real property. *See also* EJECTMENT; EVICTION.

Domicile The place which is a person's true, fixed, and permanent home and principal establishment, and to which whenever they are absent they have the intention of returning.

Dower A life estate in real estate owned by her husband which a wife is entitled to upon his death. It is based on common law and varies according to state laws. *See also* CURTESY.

Down payment The purchaser's equity at the time of property settlement. The sales price of real estate equals the mortgage loan plus the down payment. Sales price minus loan(s) equals down payment. *See* EARNEST MONEY.

Downzoning Public action by local government reducing the allowable density for subsequent development. After a parcel of property is downzoned, less development (i.e., fewer housing units, or fewer stories, or residential rather than commercial use) is allowed than formerly was permitted. Under the police power of government action, no recompense is paid to the private property owner.

Duress Unlawful force over someone used to compel that person to execute an instrument or otherwise perform some action against his or her will.

Earnest money A sum paid by a potential purchaser of real estate as evidence of good faith. The sum may be only a deposit or the total down payment. *See also* BINDER.

Easement A legal privilege granting a nonowner of a piece of property the use of a certain portion of the land for a specific purpose. The easement may run with the land and be transferred to another in the conveyance of title, called an easement appurtenant, or the easement may be a personal one, called an easement-in-gross, which does not run with the land.

"Easy" money A condition of the money markets in which savings institutions have ample funds available which can be used to make mortgage loans. With such a ready supply of mortgage funds, it is *easy* for the consumer to find a housing loan on favorable terms, including low down payment, maximum loan maturity, high loan-to-value ratio, and low interest rate. Opposite of "tight" money. *See* "TIGHT" MONEY.

Economic life The period over which a property will yield a return on the investment, over and above the economic or ground rent due to land. It is the life-span over which the improvement on the land can return an income to its owner.

Ejectment A form of action to regain the possession of real property, with damages payable for its unlawful retention. *See also* DISPOSSESS; EVICTION.

Emblements Crops which grow on the land and require annual planting and cultivating. Emblements normally belong to the tenant.

Eminent domain The superior right of every sovereign state to take private property for public use, upon payment of fair and just compensation to the private property owner. (Examples include private lands taken by a public authority for urban renewal, highway expansion, transit routes and stations, or flood control.) *See* CONDEMNATION (1).

Empty nester An older family whose children have grown and left home.

Encroachment Trespass; the building of a structure or any improvements partly or wholly intruding upon the property of another. (A survey determines whether or not encroachment has occurred.)

Encumbrance Any right to, or interest in, land which may reside in another person, to the diminution of value of the property.

Equal opportunity in housing A condition required by Title VIII of the Civil Rights Act of 1968, called the Federal Fair Housing Law, which stipulates that no person shall be discriminated against in the exercise of his or her housing choice because of race, color, religion, or national origin. The Civil Rights Act also forbids discrimination based on sex.

Equity This word has two meanings: (1) the interest or value which an owner has in real estate over and above the debts against it, also known as equity investment. (2) Jurisprudence, or a body of doctrines and rules developed in England and followed in the United States which serves to supplement and remedy the limitations and inflexibility of the common law.

Equity interest The total combined worth of (1) the down payment on the property, (2) the amortization of the loan(s) on the property, or principal accumulation, and (3) the appreciation of the property. (Equity capital includes the retained earnings or savings of a company. Opposite of debt capital. *See* DEBT CAPITAL.

Equity of redemption See REDEMPTION.

Equity participation A percentage of the rent receipts or other return on the investment which the lender requires in addition to the interest received from financing a real estate project.

Erosion Loss of one's real estate by the gradual wearing away of soil through the operation of natural causes. Coastal surf, stream flowage, and strong winds are influences which cause either soil addition or soil subtraction. Opposite of accretion. *See* ACCRETION.

Escheat The reversion of property to the state by reason of failure of persons legally entitled to hold or when heirs capable of inheriting are lacking.

Escrow A contract, deed, bond, or other written agreement deposited with a third person, by whom it is to be delivered to the grantee or promisee on the fulfillment of some condition. For example, a title company's instructions may require it to hold the buyer's funds and the seller's deed until the provisions of the contract of sale have been complied with and completed.

Estate The degree, quantity, nature, and extent of interest which a person has in real property. (Right in property.)

Ethics, code of Principles of behavior calling for personal integrity and professional duty, with highest standards over the broadest range of conduct. (The NATIONAL ASSOCIATION OF REALTORS abides by a Code of Ethics.)

Eviction The deprivation of the possession of lands or tenements. *See also* DISPOSSESS; EJECTMENT.

Exclusive agency The appointment of one real estate broker as the sole agent for the sale of a property for a designated period of time. The owner, however, reserves the right to sell the property personally without paying the agent a commission. *See also* LISTING CONTRACT.

Exclusive authorization to sell listing A written agreement between owner and agent giving agent the right to collect a commission if the property is sold by anyone whatsoever during the term of the agreement. Also known as exclusive right to sell contract.

Executor The person named in a last will to execute that will and testament. The term *executrix* is sometimes used when the position is held by a woman. Opposite of administrator. *See* ADMINISTRATOR.

Express contract An oral or written agreement; deliberately stipulated. *See* IMPLIED CONTRACT.

Fair housing See EQUAL OPPORTUNITY IN HOUSING.

Fannie Mae See FEDERAL NATIONAL MORTGAGE ASSOCIATION.

Farmers Home Administration (FmHA) Rural housing agency of the U.S. Department of Agriculture supplying credit and supportive services for rural development.

FED See FEDERAL RESERVE BOARD.

Federal Home Loan Mortgage Corporation (FHLMC) A secondary market operation of the Federal Home Loan Bank System that buys and sells conventional, FHA, and VA loans. (Popularly known as "Freddie Mac.")

Federal Housing Authority (FHA) The FHA, within the U.S. Department of Housing and Urban Development, insures mortgage loans made to home buyers by approved conventional lenders, with the home buyer paying the loan insurance premium.

Federal National Mortgage Association (FNMA) A government-sponsored but privately owned secondary market corporation that buys and sells mortgage loans. (Popularly known as "Fannie Mae.")

Federal Reserve Board (FED) The United States central bank, ruled by a Board of Governors. It establishes monetary policy and the cost and availability of credit and regulates commercial banks.

Fee A charge or billing by independent consultants for professional services performed. In real estate, a member of the American Society of Real Estate Counselors (with initials "C.R.E." after the name), a member of an appraisal society, and an accredited property manager are examples of realty professionals who charge fees for their professional services. *See also* COMMISSION (1).

Fee; Fee simple The largest possible estate which a person can have in real estate; an absolute fee ownership, without limitations. However, the private ownership right is subject to public rights of eminent domain, escheat, police power, and taxation.

FHA *See* FEDERAL HOUSING AUTHORITY.

FHLMC *See* FEDERAL HOME LOAN MORTGAGE CORPORATION.

Fiduciary A person to whom property is entrusted, to hold, control, or manage for another. (A real estate broker is a fiduciary for the principal.)

Filtering concept A "chain of moves" wherein one family usually moves to larger, more expensive (perhaps new) housing and vacates a used house, releasing it so it can be purchased by another upwardly mobile family. The family units filter upward, while the used housing units filter downward.

Fixture A chattel, movable or immovable, affixed or attached to a building and used in connection with it. An article that was once personalty but has become real estate by reason of its permanent attachment to the real property.

FmHA *See* FARMERS HOME ADMINISTRATION.

FNMA *See* FEDERAL NATIONAL MORTGAGE ASSOCIATION.

Foreclosure A legal remedy to collect a debt secured by a mortgage on property. (When a delinquent loan extends too long, a foreclosure may result and title may be relinquished.)

Freddie Mac *See* FEDERAL HOME LOAN MORTGAGE CORPORATION.

Freehold An interest in real estate of not less than a life estate; a life estate and a fee simple estate are freeholds.

Freeze *See* MORATORIUM.

Front-end money *See* SEED MONEY.

Front foot A standard of measurement; the front footage is the number of feet of frontage upon a street that a parcel of real estate possesses.

Fructus industriales Fruits of the soil which result from human industry.

Fructus naturales Fruits of the soil which are produced by nature.

General warranty A covenant in the deed whereby the grantor agrees to protect the title that grantee holds against the world.

G.I. loan *See* VA LOAN.

Ginnie Mae *See* GOVERNMENT NATIONAL MORTGAGE ASSOCIATION.

Government National Mortgage Association (GNMA) A secondary market corporation, under HUD supervision, that provides special assistance for the purchase of federally subsidized mortgage loans (certain FHA and VA loans), and also guarantees mortgage-backed securities. (Popularly known as "Ginnie Mae.")

Grant This word has two meanings: (1) A generic term applicable to all transfers of real property. (2) A technical term used in deeds of conveyance of lands to indicate a transfer of title.

Grantee A person to whom real estate is conveyed; the buyer of real estate. Grantee also becomes mortgagor if a loan is taken on the property in order to buy it.

Grantor A person who conveys real estate by deed; the seller of real estate. Grantor may become mortgagee if a purchase money mortgage is taken back as part payment of the purchase price.

GRM *See* GROSS RENT MULTIPLIER.

Gross lease A situation in which lessor agrees to pay all charges against the property. This includes maintenance as well as repairs; it may include utilities.

Gross Rent Multiplier (GRM) The GRM is derived by dividing the value of the property by either the annual or the monthly gross income. Once derived, the GRM provides an appraiser with a rough estimate of the value of similar properties.

Ground rent Earnings of improved property credited to earnings of the ground itself, after allowance is made for earnings of improvements.

Habendum clause The "to have and to hold" clause which defines or limits the quantity of the estate granted in the deed.

Hereditaments Usually, real estate and all that goes with it as being incidental thereto; every sort of *inheritable* property, whether real, personal, corporeal, or incorporeal. The largest classification of property. *See also* TENEMENTS.

Homeowner associations Incorporated private organizations operating under recorded land agreements, for the purpose of maintaining the common property of a group living arrangement (for example, condominium or planned unit development) and providing other services for the common enjoyment of all residents. *See*

COMMUNITY ASSOCIATIONS INSTITUTE; PLANNED UNIT DEVELOPMENT.

Homestead The place of a home or house; in certain states, a home upon which the owner has recorded a declaration of homestead, and in which the family is living; also, the land or city lot upon which the family residence, together with outbuildings, is situated.

Homestead exemption Certain state laws provide for the homestead, up to a certain value, to be exempt from forced sale to satisfy certain debts owed by the homeowner. Creditors with judgment liens may have recourse to the portion of the home's value which is in excess of the homestead exemption only by resorting to special legal proceedings.

Horizontal property acts State enabling laws which are passed by each state legislature, creating the condominium form of property ownership.

Housing and Urban Development, U.S. Department of (HUD) A Federal agency responsible for housing and certain real estate matters.

Housing code Regulations established by a local government setting forth the residence requirements for habitation.

Housing starts Term used by the U.S. Bureau of Census to denote newly constructed housing units. The term includes single-family and 1- to 4-family housing as well as multiunit housing of 5 or more units.

Housing stock The total inventory of dwelling units in the United States, including single-family houses, multifamily buildings, mobile homes, and vacation or second homes. The term covers both new construction and existing older units, and both ownership and rental units. [The 1970 Census of Housing counted 69 million homes (dwelling units), up from 58 million in 1960.]

HUD *See* HOUSING AND URBAN DEVELOPMENT, U.S. DEPARTMENT OF.

Hypothecate To give a thing as security without the necessity of giving up possession of it. A mortgage loan hypothecates the home of the mortgagor.

Implied contract An agreement that comes into being when the acts of one party are consented to by the inaction of another party. For example, if a new roof is mistakenly laid by a roofer, but with the knowledge of the recipient property owner, then consent is implied if the property owner takes no step to correct the error in progress. Silence may be construed as consent, and an implied contract is the result. *See* EXPRESS CONTRACT.

Income stream The gross or total money received from employment, interest payments and other cash receipts, and investment sources including real estate.

Incorporeal Intangible or legal rights or interests. *See* HEREDITAMENTS.

Inflation Loss of *real* purchasing power which results when the rate of price increases is larger than advances in productivity.

Infrastructure The network of public facilities located within a community (e.g., roads, schools, sewer and water systems, utilities.)

Injunction A writ or order of a court to restrain one or more parties to a suit or proceeding from doing an inequitable or unjust act in regard to the rights of some other party in the suit or proceeding. One party is enjoined or stopped from doing an unjust act to another; for example, during a lengthy court proceeding of foreclosure, removal of fixtures may be prohibited.

Institute of Real Estate Management A national professional and trade association of property managers and property management firms.

Instrument A formal written document used in real estate transactions. An instrument may be any piece in writing, such as a contract, deed, or lease.

Interest in property The degree of estate, from freehold estates (total fee ownership to partial ownerships) to nonfreehold estates (leaseholds) to easements. (See Figure 6-1).

Interest rate The cost of borrowed money; the percentage of interest which must be paid on a loan. *See also* COMPOUND INTEREST.

Interim financing The development loan that covers construction costs and other expenses which arise during the creation of the real estate investment. *See also* PERMANENT LOAN; SEED MONEY; WORKING CAPITAL.

Intestate The condition of one who dies having made no will or a will which is defective in form. Escheat occurs when an intestate leaves no heirs. *See also* TESTATE.

Investment The sum total of equity plus debt. Investment capital is equity capital plus debt capital. Thus, an investment in a parcel of real estate consists of the down payment, or one's equity, plus the mortgage loan, or debt.

Joint tenancy The holding by two or more persons of identical interests and amounts in the same asset, such as real estate, acquired simultaneously from the same source, in the same instrument, and commencing at the same time. *See also* TENANCY BY THE ENTIRETIES.

Joint venture A sharing of equity and debt obligations in a real estate investment.

Judgment The decision or sentence of the law, given by a court of justice or other competent tribunal, as the result of proceedings instituted therein for the redress of an injury. Judgments against persons state their indebtedness and become general liens against all assets of the debtor.

Judgment creditor One who has obtained a judgment against a debtor, the execution of which can be enforced.

Judgment debtor One against whom a judgment has been obtained.

Junior mortgage A mortgage second in lien or claim to a previous mortgage. (A second recorded mortgage is a junior mortgage.) The junior mortgage loan usually carries a higher interest rate because of the higher risk that it may not be repaid. The loan amount may be either greater or less than that of the first mortgage.

Jurisdiction The authority by which judicial officers take cognizance of and decide causes.

Land The word "land" or "lands" and the words "real estate" shall be construed to include land, tenements and hereditaments, and all rights thereto and interest therein, other than a chattel interest.

Land contract A contract of sale under which a down payment is made on land, followed by periodic installment payments until the consideration price is paid in full, at which time the deed is transferred. Many vacation lots are sold on the land contract basis. The seller retains title and the buyer receives possession of the land. If the buyer defaults on payment, he or she risks losing all the money paid to that date. *See* LAND SALES REGULATION.

Land sales regulators HUD's Office of Interstate Land Sales Regulation (OILSR).

Land use plan An official map and designation by a local community specifying the future uses of land, including both public facilities and private developments and improvements.

Landlord An owner of property who rents that property to another; a lessor.

Lease A type of contract, written or oral, for the possession and use of lands and tenements either for life or for a certain period of time or during the pleasure of the parties. (A lease contract enables the lessee to have possession and enjoyment of the property, upon consideration of rental payments paid to the lessor.) *See also* GROSS LEASE; NET LEASE.

Leaseback The purchase of improved property and the leasing of it back to the seller.

"Leased housing" Popular term denoting privately owned single-family housing units which are leased by local government for the benefit of large families and the elderly, and which are subsidized by HUD.

Leasehold The interest or estate which a lessee has in real estate by virtue of a lease. The leasehold is classified as personal property.

Leasehold policy A policy of title insurance taken out by a lessee to protect a lease interest in the property. Used more in commercial property leaseholds, where the value of fixtures, equipment, and modification to the rental structure can be substantial. *See* MORTGAGEE POLICY; OWNER'S POLICY.

Legal description A method of exactly identifying property, including its boundaries, dimensions, and distances, enabling its specific location and area to be ascertained precisely by later survey.

Lessee A person who leases property from another. (A renter or tenant.) *See also* TENANT.

Lessor A party who leases property to a tenant, or lessee. (Often referred to as the landlord.)

Leverage Maximum usage of borrowed funds and minimum usage of personal equity. A 95 percent loan-to-value ratio gives more leverage, or usage of borrowed funds, than a 90 percent loan. With the 95 percent loan, personal equity or down payment only amounts to 5 percent, whereas with the 90 percent loan the personal equity is 10 percent.

LHA See LOCAL HOUSING AUTHORITY.

Liability This word has two meanings: (1) A debt. (2) A responsibility; the state of one who is bound in law and justice to do something which may be enforced by action. A contract's terms impose dual responsibilities on the principals to the contract.

License In real estate, the state-granted authority to conduct the business of real estate, acting either as a salesperson or as a broker. (Such a license is an essential prerequisite and qualification to transact and carry on the business of real estate on behalf of others.)

A license may also be a personal right granted by the holder of an interest in property giving the licensee certain rights and privileges in that property.

Lien A claim recorded against a property of another as security for payment of some debt or charge. Examples include mechanic's liens, unpaid taxes, judgments of the court, and mortgages. *See also* RELEASE OF LIEN.

Life estate An estate or interest in real estate held during the term of a certain person's life. (A life estate terminates upon the death of the holder. It may be held by one or more persons, and can be contingent upon certain happenings. The remainderman succeeds to the title when the life estate terminates.) *See also* REMAINDERMAN.

Liquidity The extent to which a person is in a cash position, or possesses investments easily convertible into cash. For example, checking and savings accounts or short-term loans are held to be liquid investments, and so an investor in these is in a liquid position. Real estate or long-term loans, on the other hand, are commonly believed to be illiquid holdings, difficult to convert into cash.

Listing contract Written agreement between principal (owner of the real property) and agent (broker) employing broker to sell (or lease) owner's property. *See also* EXCLUSIVE AGENCY; EXCLUSIVE

AUTHORIZATION TO SELL LISTING; OPEN LISTING.

Litigation A contest, authorized by law, in a court of justice for the purpose of enforcing a right.

Loan discount *See* POINTS.

Loan maturity The length of the loan; the amount of time that will be required to amortize or pay back the debt. For example, the maturity of a 30-year loan is 30 years.

Loan origination fees *See* POINTS.

Loan-to-value ratio The relationship between the amount of mortgage debt that can be loaned and the market value (or sales price) of the property. For example, a 70 percent loan-to-value ratio means that on a $50,000 property a mortgage loan of $35,000 can be advanced. A higher loan-to-value ratio means greater leverage, and a smaller down payment (and thus smaller usage of one's personal equity funds.) *See* LEVERAGE.

Local Housing Authority (LHA) Body usually concerned with public housing. *See* PUBLIC HOUSING.

Magic financing A private mortgage insurance (PMI) policy that enables a home buyer to obtain a mortgage loan higher than would otherwise be obtainable from regulated lenders, and hence requires a lower down payment. "Magic" insures the mortgagee on the top portion of the loan. The name "magic" came from the initials of the Mortgage Guarantee Insurance Corp. (MGIC), one of the first private mortgage insurors. *See also* MORTGAGE INSURANCE COMPANIES OF AMERICA (MICA).

Majority age Legal age, adulthood; the age at which a person is able to enter into binding contractual relationships.

Market value The amount for which a property would sell if it were put on the open market and sold in the manner in which property is ordinarily sold in the community in which it is situated. An open market makes the assumptions that both the parties are fully informed, act intelligently, exercise due care, and have sufficient or unhurried time to carry out their transaction. *See also* APPRAISAL.

Marketable or merchantable title A title which a reasonable purchaser would be willing and ought to accept, being well informed as to the facts and their legal bearing, willing and anxious to perform the contract, and exercising that prudence which business agents ordinarily bring to bear in such transactions. (Such a title as a court would compel a purchaser to accept; it is free from any serious encumbrances or clouds.)

Master deed Basic title document used in the creation of a condominium, which divides the project into separate fee units as well as common interests.

Mechanic's lien A type of lien created by statute which exists in favor of persons who have performed work or furnished materials in the construction, improvement, or maintenance of real estate.

Metes and bounds The boundary lines of land, with their terminal points and angles. (Sometimes popularly referred to as measurements and boundaries. A metes and bounds description of property refers to its directions and distances.)

MICA *See* MORTGAGE INSURANCE COMPANIES OF AMERICA.

Mobile home A manufactured standardized home, constructed in a factory. Opposite of conventional home.

Model License Law Officially titled "Suggested Pattern: Real Estate License Law and Supplementary Rules and Regulations," a code developed by the License Law Committee of the NATIONAL ASSOCIATION OF REALTORS.

Moratorium An action by a governmental body temporarily halting public processes. For example, local county governments have adopted zoning, sewer, and condominium conversion moratoriums. HUD, at the national level, adopted a moratorium on subsidized housing programs. Commonly referred to as a "freeze" or cessation of activity.

Mortgage A conditional conveyance of property designed as security for the payment of money, the fulfillment of some contract, or the performance of some act, and to be void upon such payment, fulfillment, or performance. *See* TRUST DEED *for contrast. See also* ASSUMPTION OF MORTGAGE; BLANKET MORTGAGE; JUNIOR MORTGAGE; PURCHASE MONEY MORTGAGE.

Mortgage Bankers Association of America A national professional and trade association of mortgage bankers and mortgage brokers.

Mortgage commitment A written notice from a lending institution promising a future mortgage loan under specified terms and conditions.

Mortgage Insurance Companies of America (MICA) A national professional and trade association of private mortgage insurance companies. *See also* MAGIC FINANCING.

Mortgage loan discount *See* POINTS.

Mortgagee The recipient of a mortgage; the lender.

Mortgagee policy A policy of title insurance which protects the lender's mortgage loan. Paid for by the mortgagor. *See* LEASEHOLD POLICY; OWNER'S POLICY.

Mortgagor The maker of a mortgage; the borrower. A buyer who seeks financing to purchase property and conditionally transfers the real property as security for the payment of the debt.

Multiple listing An arrangement among real estate boards or exchange members whereby each broker brings his or her listings to the attention of the other members; if a sale results, the commission is divided between the broker bringing the listing and the broker making the sale. For the seller of the property, a multiple listing means that the chances of sale are increased because all board members are informed about the listing and the characteristics of the property.

Mutual Savings Bank A thrift institution specializing in making residential mortgage loans.

National Association of Home Builders A national professional and trade association of building and construction firms and individuals.

National Association of Real Estate Boards (NAREB) *See* NATIONAL ASSOCIATION OF REALTORS.

National Association of Real Estate License Law Officials (NARELLO) An association comprised of Real Estate Commissioners and other officials who are charged with the responsibility of enforcing the license laws.

NATIONAL ASSOCIATION OF REALTORS New name for the National Association of Real Estate Boards, which comprises numerous local boards of *REALTORS* throughout the United States.

National Savings and Loan League A national professional and trade association of individual savings and loan firms.

Necessaries Essentials for existence, including food, shelter and clothing.

Net lease A situation in which lessee (tenant) agrees to pay all charges against the property. Lessor or landlord thus "nets" or clears the rental payments received, with no outstanding charges or expenses to be paid.

Net listing A price below which the owner will not sell the property and at which the broker will not receive a commission; the broker receives any excess over and above the designated selling price as commission. Net listings are usually prohibited either by state license laws or by local real estate board policies.

Net worth *See* EQUITY.

Nonresident One not residing within the state; not from that state.

Note A legal instrument evidencing debt. *See* BOND.

Obsolescence As applied to real estate, the loss of value due to structural, economic, or social changes—becoming outmoded. Loss of value results from lessened desirability or lessened usefulness, and thus lessened ability to compete in the market place and command premium market prices.

Offer To proffer terms subject to another's acceptance. An offer is not a contract.

Offeree The recipient of an offer. In the case of a property listed for sale, the prospective purchaser to whom property is submitted is the offeree.

Offeror The maker of an offer, such as the seller who has offered property for sale.

Open-end mortgage A mortgage written to enable additional advances beyond the amount of the original loan.

Open housing *See* EQUAL OPPORTUNITY IN HOUSING.

Open listing An oral or general listing. More than one broker can work to sell the property, as can the owner. The broker who makes the sale will earn the commission. If the owner sells, no broker receives a commission.

Open-space communities *See* COMMUNITY ASSOCIATIONS INSTITUTE; HOMEOWNER ASSOCIATIONS; PLANNED UNIT DEVELOPMENT.

Option A privilege, acquired in exchange for a consideration, to carry out a transaction within a specified time upon stipulated terms. The person who holds the option may or may not exercise it during the option period. For example, the right to buy property at an agreed-upon price by some later date, in exchange for some form of consideration.

Optionee The recipient of an option; the prospective purchaser of a property under option.

Optionor The giver of an option; an owner who for a consideration gives the optionee the right to buy property on terms stipulated in the option.

Ordinances Laws and regulations by local government to protect the general public.

Overt Open or publicly disclosed, as in discoverable defects of title.

Owner's policy A policy of title insurance taken out by the mortgagor or property owner to protect his or her interest in the property. *See* LEASEHOLD POLICY; MORTGAGEE POLICY.

Ownership An estate in real property, evidenced by title (deed) to the property.

Packaged mortgages Individual mortgage loans of like denomination and character which have been pooled together by mortgage brokers and others for resale to the federally supported agencies (FNMA, GNMA, and FHLMC) in the secondary mortgage market.

Parcel A specific piece of land.

Parol Oral, as distinguished from written.

Partition The division of real estate made between tenants in common and joint tenants. For example, such tenants can petition the court for a partition decree setting forth their individual interests in a given parcel of real estate.

Pass-through securities program GNMA's mortgage-backed security program wherein principal and interest on mortgages purchased are passed through to the investor as collected on those mortgages.

Percentage lease A lease of property in which the rental is based upon the volume of sales made on the leased premises. Such a lease benefits the lessee during the slow, early start-up stages of the business, and later the lessor as the pace of business quickens and brings to both additional revenues.

Permanent loan The long-term mortgage loan or trust deed. *See also* MORTGAGE COMMITMENT.

Personal property Property of a temporary or movable nature; all articles, things, and property which are not real estate.

Personalty Collective noun covering personal property; all articles of property that are not real estate. *See also* CHATTELS.

PITI Common real estate term meaning "principal, interest, taxes, and insurance," or the monthly payment that a homeowner can be expected to make.

Plaintiff *See* DEFENDANT.

Planned unit development (P.U.D) A preferred method of conserving land by developing more efficient arrangements of housing units, as in clusters and townhouses. *See* COMMUNITY ASSOCIATIONS INSTITUTE; HOMEOWNERS ASSOCIATIONS.

Plat book A public record of various recorded plans in the municipality or county. Much urban real estate has recorded subdivision plats with numerous individual lots and block numbers, each usually signifying the property of an individual homeowner.

Plottage Joining two or more smaller parcels of land, which are under different ownerships, into one large parcel under one ownership. The creation of large office buildings downtown, as well as the assemblage of outlying land for new towns, requires plottage on a grand scale.

Points A one-time charge assessed by a lending institution when the loan is originated to increase the yield from the mortgage loan to a level competitive with the yield from other types of investments; also referred to as loan origination fees.

Police power The right of the state government to enact legislation protecting the general public's health, safety, welfare, and morals. The state constitution generally delegates this right to local government to enact zoning ordinances, master plans, building and housing codes, subdivision regulations, etc. Compensation need not be paid to an adversely affected private property owner. *See also* CONDEMNATION.

Policy of title insurance *See* TITLE INSURANCE.

Power of attorney An instrument authorizing a person to act as the agent of the person granting it. The authorized agent can perform only those specific acts expressly enumerated in the power of attorney.

Prepaid expenses Funds advanced at time of closing to provide for payment of later charges as they become due, including property taxes, insurance, and mortgage insurance premiums.

Price That amount asked for something of value. The "asking price" of a house tends to set its upper value.

Prima facie "On the face of it"; "first view." Prima facie evidence of fact is in law sufficient to establish the fact unless rebutted. It is assumed to be correct until overcome by additional evidence.

Principal This word has several meanings: (1) the comparatively more important; (2) a capital sum lent at interest; (3) one who appoints an agent to act for and in one's stead; (4) showing the degree of crime committed by a person, i.e., the person can be principal or accessory.

Private mortgage insurance (PMI) *See* MAGIC FINANCING.

Promulgate To publish; to declare.

Property The right or interest which an individual has in lands and chattels to the exclusion of all others. Any subject, or object, of value that may lawfully be acquired and held; anything that may be owned. A group of rights in relation to physical things, as the right to possess, use, and dispose of them. *See also* ATTACHMENT OF PROPERTY.

Prospectus A printed advertisement for a new enterprise, such as a rural property or subdivision. Pertinent financial and physical details are noted.

Public housing Multifamily housing structures owned by local government and subsidized by HUD. *See* LOCAL HOUSING AUTHORITY.

Public policy The law considers the conservation and promotion of the public welfare to be the first and highest duty of government and will not countenance any transaction which contravenes a sound public policy.

P.U.D. *See* Planned unit development.

Purchase money mortgage A mortgage given by a grantee to the grantor in part payment of the purchase price of real estate. Commonly used where the purchaser's small down payment requires the seller to carry back a mortgage, and where the seller does not wish to receive all the money due from the sale of the property.

Quiet enjoyment The right of an owner or a tenant to possession of the property without interference.

Quieting title The removal of a cloud from a title by proper action in a court of competent jurisdiction; a court action brought to establish title and remove a cloud from the title. *See also* CLOUD ON THE TITLE.

Quitclaim deed A deed given when the grantee already has, or claims, complete or partial title to the premises and the grantor has a possible interest that otherwise would constitute a cloud upon the title. Given without warranty of title.

Racial steering An unlawful practice which is designed to influence a minority prospect's choice of housing.

Real estate Land, tenements and hereditaments, and all rights thereto and interests therein, other than chattels-personal.

Real property Same as real estate. *See* REAL ESTATE.

Reality of consent The agreement to a contract must be real and free from fraud, duress, undue influence, misrepresentation, or mistake.

REALTOR® A trademark used to designate an active member of a real estate board affiliated with the NATIONAL ASSOCIATION OF REALTORS®.

REALTOR®-ASSOCIATE real estate salesperson who is either an employee of, or is associated with, a REALTOR® as an independent contractor.

Realty A term sometimes used collectively to mean real property or real estate; used as a synonym for real estate or real property.

Redemption The right to redeem property during the foreclosure period; the right of an owner to redeem the property after a sale for taxes. Often referred to as equity of redemption.

Regulation Q That regulation which allows the Treasury Department and various other regulatory agencies to establish interest rate differentials on savings deposits between commercial banks and thrift institutions.

Regulation Z The regulations regarding credit disclosure issued by the Board of Governors of the Federal Reserve System to implement the Truth in Lending Act. *See also* TRUTH IN LENDING ACT.

Rehabilitation The restoration of a building to improve its habitability.

Release The giving up or abandoning of a claim or right to the person against whom the claim exists or the right is to be exercised or enforced. The person who receives a release thus increases his or her interest or estate in the property.

Release of lien The discharge of certain property from the lien of a judgment, mortgage, or claim.

Remainderman Holder of a residual estate in real property. *See also* LIFE ESTATE; REVERSION.

Rent A compensation, in either money, provisions, chattels, or labor, received by the owner of real estate from the occupant thereof. Rent is usually received for the enjoyment of possession of the property. *See also* GROUND RENT.

Rent control Public regulatory action by local government limiting the amount of rent a landlord can charge.

Replacement cost Present cost of an equally desirable substitute property; cost of a property of like utility.

Reproduction cost Present cost of exact duplication of a property, to the greatest extent possible.

Rescission of contract The abrogating or annulling of a contract; the revocation or repealing of a contract by mutual consent of the parties to the contract, or for cause by either party to the contract.

Residuary estate That which remains of a testator's estate after deducting the debts, bequests, and devises.

Restriction covenant A clause in a deed limiting the use of the property conveyed for a certain period of time. May be stated in the negative, such as, this property may *not* be used for the sale of alcoholic beverages.

Retained earnings Income above and beyond that which is paid in salaries or to stockholders and which is kept within the company; a type of savings. *See also* EQUITY CAPITAL.

Reversion The residue of an estate left and remaining in the grantors, who commence in possession after the termination of some particular estate granted out by them. The return of land to the grantors and their heirs after the grant is over; also, the return of leased premises after the lease. Reversion occurs after the cessation of a life estate, for example.

Revocation The recall of a power or authority conferred, or the vacating of an instrument previously made.

Right of survivorship Right to acquire the interest of a deceased joint owner.

Right-of-way The privilege which an individual or a group of individuals has of going over another's ground, for example, installation and maintenance of transmission lines. The privilege is a right, which can be either expressed or implied, an appurtenance or a personal right not running with the property.

Riparian owners Those who own lands bounding upon a water course.

Sale-leaseback *See* LEASEBACK.

Satisfaction piece A recorded document which releases, pays in full, or satisfies the debt of the mortgagor (the mortgage).

Savings and Loan Association A thrift institution specializing in making residential mortgage loans.

Second mortgage *See* JUNIOR MORTGAGE.

Second trust *See* JUNIOR MORTGAGE; TRUST DEED.

Section 8 Leased housing program for lower-income families.

Security *See* COLLATERAL SECURITY; HYPOTHECATE.

Security deposit A tenant's payment of advance funds; both rental payments, as the first and last month's rent, and funds as collateral to restore habitability of the dwelling unit after tenant vacates, should that be necessary.

Seed money Funds needed to acquire or control the site, obtain zoning, develop preliminary plans, and complete all feasibility studies. *See* DEVELOPER; WORKING CAPITAL.

Seisin The possession of real estate with the intent to claim at least a life estate therein, by one so entitled.

Setback The distance from the curb or other established line within which no buildings may be erected. Justified under the police power authority of the government.

Settlement statement An accounting of all funds in a real estate transaction showing receipts and disbursements. *See* CLOSING COSTS.

Severalty ownership Sole ownership; owned by one person only. Ownership by husband and wife may be regarded as sole ownership, or ownership as one.

Site A specific piece of land.

Society of Real Estate Appraisers A national trade association of appraisers and appraisal firms.

Special warranty A covenant in the deed wherein the grantors limit their liability to the grantee for defective title to anyone claiming by, from, through, or under them, the grantors. Thus grantors warrant good title only during the period they owned the property.

"Stagflation" An economic condition in which there is both stagnation (no growth) and inflation (rapid and large price increases). *See* INFLATION.

Standby commitment A lender's agreement to make loan funds available at some future date, at specified terms.

Statute A law established by act of the legislative power; an act of the legislature.

Statute of frauds Legislation requiring that certain contracts concerning real estate must be in writing in order to be enforceable by the courts. These contracts include contracts of sale, deeds, leases over 1 year, mortgages, and deeds of trust.

Subdivision A tract of land divided into lots for residential construction. A subdivision is recorded in the plat book.

Subject to mortgage The taking of title to property wherein the purchaser is not responsible for payment of the mortgage. In case of foreclosure with a deficiency, the most the purchaser can lose is the equity. The original maker of the note (the seller) is still liable to the mortgagee for any deficiency. *See also* ASSUMPTION OF MORTGAGE.

Subletting A leasing by a tenant to another, who holds under the tenant. Original lessee is still obligated to lessor, under the terms of the original lease contract.

Subordinate loan *See* JUNIOR MORTGAGE.

Subordination The willingness of the holder of a lien (e.g., mortgage) to accept payment behind another creditor.

Subsidized housing Public housing and below-market interest rate mortgage loan assistance by HUD for the purpose of construction or rehabilitation of multifamily and single-unit housing.

Surety One who guarantees the performance of another; the guarantor. A large mortgage loan may require the added security of a surety.

Survey The act by which the quantity and boundaries of a piece of land are ascertained. The certified paper containing a statement of the courses, distance, and quantity of land is also called a survey. A survey establishes the legal description of property.

Tandem plan Secondary mortgage market plan whereby GNMA purchases certain original mortgages at a supported price for subsequent resale to FNMA and other investors.

Taxation The right of a unit of government (federal, state, or local) to levy funds for the provision of necessary public services. Examples of taxes include the property tax, which is levied by the local government; sales taxes, which the state may charge; and inheritance and income taxes, which the federal government requires. *See also* ASSESSMENT.

Tenancy at sufferance A tenancy arising when the tenant remains after the lease expires.

Tenancy at will A tenancy which is subject to termination at the desire of either party (lessor or lessee).

Tenancy by the entireties A holding of title by husband and wife as joint owners of property acquired during marriage. According to most states' law, upon the death of one spouse, the entire property belongs to the survivor. *See also* JOINT TENANCY.

Tenancy in common The holding of an estate in lands by several persons, with several and distinct titles but unity of possession. Each tenant in common is the owner of an undivided share of the whole mass. The estates or interests of tenants in common need not be identical or equal.

Tenant In a broad sense, one who holds or possesses lands or tenements by any kind of title, either in fee, for life, for years, or at will. In a popular sense, the tenant is a resident who has only temporary use and occupancy of lands or tenements which belong to another. The duration and other terms of occupancy are usually defined by an agreement called a lease, while the parties thereto are placed in the relationship of landlord and tenant.

Tenements A broad term including the land and its incorporeal rights of ownership, such as an intangible right to receive rents. *See also* HEREDITAMENTS.

Term of loan *See* LOAN MATURITY.

Testate The condition of one who leaves a valid will at the time of his or her death; the will stipulates who the heirs will be and how the property is to be divided. *See also* INTESTATE.

Testator Maker of a will.

"Testers" Those who test nondiscriminatory compliance with the Federal Fair Housing Law by seeking housing on behalf of minority groups. Such practice is lawful.

"Tight" money A situation in which mortgage money is virtually not available to consumers to finance housing purchases. Money available for loan purposes of any nature (including mortgage loans) becomes very scarce, and thus expensive. Hence, the consumer who is fortunate enough to find a loan pays dearly for it, with a higher down payment, shorter loan maturity, lower loan-to-value ratio, and a very high interest rate. Money becomes *tight*. Opposite of "easy" money. *See* "EASY" MONEY.

Title Evidence of a person's legal right to ownership of property (for example, by deed). In relation to real estate, title is the sum of all the facts on which ownership is founded, or by which ownership is proved. *See also* ABSTRACT OF TITLE; CLOUD ON THE TITLE; COLOR OF TITLE; QUIETING TITLE.

Title by adverse possession A holding acquired by occupancy and recognized despite the claims of the paper title owner.

Title insurance A policy of insurance which indemnifies the holder for loss sustained by reason of defects in the title. Such defects may have been in existence but undisclosed at the time the policy was issued. Defects may be either undiscovered or undiscoverable.

Torrens system A public registration of titles to property, wherein the registry shows the name(s) of the owner(s) of the property and all liens and encumbrances against it.

Tort A wrongful act; wrong; injury; violation of a legal right.

Townhouse A dwelling unit attached to another; a house having a common wall with another. Formerly referred to as rowhouse.

"Track record" Prior ability to produce; past performance.

Trust deed (deed of trust) A deed conveying land to a trustee as collateral security for the payment of a debt. Upon payment of a debt secured thereby, the deed of trust is released; upon default, the trustee has the power to sell the land and pay the debt.

Trustee A person in whom some estate, interest, or power in property of any description is vested for the benefit of another.

Trustor The maker of, or the person who takes out, a deed of trust.

Truth in Lending Act (TIL) A portion of the Consumer Credit Protection Act (Public Law 90-231) which requires that borrowers be informed of true credit costs. *See also* REGULATION Z.

Turnkey Housing initially developed by private sponsors for later sale to local housing authorities for lower-income families.

Unilateral contract One person's promise to undertake to do something without the other person's promise to perform anything. For example, a person may formally, by contract, undertake to do something for his or her spouse, son, or daughter without receiving any promise of performance in return. *See also* BILATERAL CONTRACT.

Urban renewal Authority of a public agency to acquire, demolish, and rebuild or redevelop deteriorated urban areas.

U.S. Savings and Loan League A national professional and trade association of individual savings and loan firms.

Usury Lending money at a rate of interest above the legal rate. Usurious interest is illegal interest; an illegal rate charged for interest.

VA loan The Veterans Administration guarantees the mortgage loan of a qualified veteran who establishes his or her certificate of eligibility; the actual loan is made by an approved mortgage lender.

Valid Having force, or binding force; legally sufficient and authorized by law.

Vendee A purchaser; a buyer; the person to whom a thing is rendered or sold. (Grantee.)

Vendor The seller; one who disposes of a thing for a consideration. (Grantor.)

Void That which is unenforceable; having no force or effect.

Voidable That which is capable of being adjudged void, but is not void unless action is taken to make it so, for example, contracts executed by minors.

Waiver The renunciation, abandonment, or surrender of some claim, right, or privilege. For example, lessees may waive their rights to sublet under the lease contract.

Warranty deed One that contains a covenant that the grantor will protect the title of the grantee against any claimant. *See also* GENERAL WARRANTY; SPECIAL WARRANTY.

Waste Willful destruction of any part of the land which would injure or prejudice the landlord's reversionary right. Lessee must not waste the property during the period of possession.

Will A legal declaration of a person's wishes concerning the disposition of property after death. To die testate is to leave a will, with an executor or executrix named therein to carry out its provisions.

Working capital Cash and other liquid assets available to develop a real estate investment. *See* DEVELOPER; SEED MONEY.

Wraparound loan A loan used when it is not feasible to retire the first mortgage. A junior mortgage loan incorporates the full loan amount desired, with higher loan repayment out of which must be paid the existing first mortgage loan.

Yield The rate of return (or interest) received on an investment (for example, a mortgage).

Zoning ordinance The valid use of the police power of a municipality to control and regulate the character and use of property. Subdivisions and other private developments must conform to zoning ordinances.

Master Answer Sheet to the Practice Examinations

License Laws, Regulations, and Ethical Conduct

1. (C)	5. (B)	9. (D)	13. (D)	17. (C)
2. (C)	6. (A)	10. (A)	14. (C)	18. (C)
3. (B)	7. (A)	11. (D)	15. (A)	19. (D)
4. (D)	8. (C)	12. (D)	16. (B)	20. (A)

Equal Opportunity in Housing

1. (D)	5. (A)	9. (B)	13. (D)	17. (B)
2. (A)	6. (D)	10. (C)	14. (C)	18. (D)
3. (C)	7. (B)	11. (A)	15. (C)	19. (C)
4. (B)	8. (C)	12. (A)	16. (B)	20. (A)

Contracts, Agency, and Listings

1. (B)	5. (B)	9. (D)	13. (B)	17. (C)
2. (C)	6. (B)	10. (B)	14. (D)	18. (B)
3. (C)	7. (A)	11. (C)	15. (C)	19. (B)
4. (D)	8. (C)	12. (D)	16. (B)	20. (A)

Real Property Interests

1. (D)	5. (C)	9. (A)	13. (B)	17. (A)
2. (D)	6. (D)	10. (B)	14. (C)	18. (B)
3. (D)	7. (D)	11. (B)	15. (C)	19. (B)
4. (A)	8. (C)	12. (D)	16. (C)	20. (B)

Transfer of Title to Real Property

1. (A)	5. (C)	9. (A)	13. (C)	17. (A)
2. (A)	6. (C)	10. (B)	14. (D)	18. (D)
3. (A)	7. (C)	11. (B)	15. (C)	19. (C)
4. (B)	8. (B)	12. (C)	16. (C)	20. (D)

Metes and Bounds, Lot and Block, and Monuments

1. (A)	3. (C)	5. (A)	7. (C)	9. (B)
2. (B)	4. (B)	6. (B)	8. (D)	10. (B)

Government Rectangular Survey

1. (C)	3. (B)	5. (B)	7. (B)	9. (B)
2. (B)	4. (A)	6. (C)	8. (C)	10. (C)

Title Insurance

1. (C)	5. (D)	9. (B)	13. (A)	17. (C)
2. (C)	6. (C)	10. (C)	14. (B)	18. (B)
3. (A)	7. (D)	11. (D)	15. (D)	19. (A)
4. (A)	8. (A)	12. (D)	16. (D)	20. (D)

Real Estate Appraisal

1. (A)	5. (C)	9. (B)	13. (B)	17. (C)
2. (A)	6. (D)	10. (B)	14. (D)	18. (C)
3. (B)	7. (A)	11. (A)	15. (C)	19. (D)
4. (C)	8. (C)	12. (A)	16. (C)	20. (D)

Real Estate Mathematics

1. (C)	7. (D)	13. (B)	19. (A)	25. (A)
2. (D)	8. (D)	14. (C)	20. (B)	26. (A)
3. (C)	9. (C)	15. (C)	21. (C)	27. (B)
4. (D)	10. (A)	16. (A)	22. (A)	28. (D)
5. (D)	11. (C)	17. (B)	23. (C)	29. (B)
6. (A)	12. (A)	18. (D)	24. (C)	30. (D)

Detailed suggested solutions follow.

1. $3,091 received − $800 salary = $2,291 from sales

    $2,291 = 3% of sales

    $2,291 ÷ 3% = $76,366 in real estate sales

2.

    $460 per month X 12 months = $5,520 per year gross

    $5,520 − $1,730 (expenses) = $3,790 per year net

    $3,790 ÷ .06 (rate) = $63,166 investment

3.

$6,500 sales price ÷ (100% − 4%) = $6,500 ÷ .96
                                        = $6,770 cost

4. First person invests $35,000

    Second person invests 13% of $96,000 =   12,480

    Third person invests   33,520

        Total of three investors $81,000

    $96,000 − $81,000 = $15,000 for fourth investor

    $15,000 ÷ $96,000 = .156 = 15.6%

5. *On the Lot*

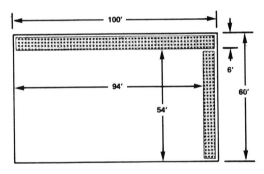

    100′ × 6′ = 600 sq ft

     54′ × 6′ = 324 sq ft

    Total   924 sq ft

    Around the Lot

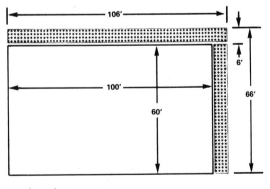

    106′ × 6′ = 636 sq ft

     60′ × 6′ = 360 sq ft

    Total   996 sq ft

    Difference

    996 sq ft − 924 sq ft = 72 sq ft

6. Frontage fencing: 155′ × $2.75 = $ 426.25 cost

    Balance of lot: 90′ + 155′ + 90′ = 335′

    335′ × $1.85 =   619.75

        Total Cost $1,046.00

7. One investor pays $\frac{3}{8}$ of cost

    3 ÷ 8 =   37.5%

    $12\frac{1}{2}$% of cost = 12.5%

    .25 of cost =   25.0%

                      75.0%

    100% − 75% = 25% = $15,000

    $15,000 ÷ .25 = $60,000 total investment

8.

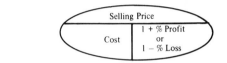

    20 offices × $375 = $7,500 per month

    $7,500 × 12 = $90,000 per year gross

    $90,000 − $15,000 = $75,000 per year net

    $75,000 ÷ $295,000 = .254 = 25.4%

9.

    $25,000 × (100% + 15% profit) = $25,000 × 1.15
                                  = $28,750 net price
                                    required

    Net Price

    Selling Price | 1 − % Commission

    $28,750 ÷ .95 = $30,263 required sales price

10.

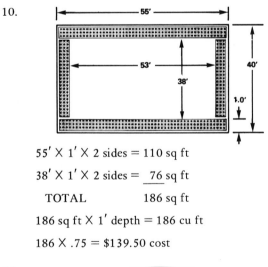

    55′ × 1′ × 2 sides = 110 sq ft

    38′ × 1′ × 2 sides = 76 sq ft

        TOTAL   186 sq ft

    186 sq ft × 1′ depth = 186 cu ft

    186 × .75 = $139.50 cost

11.

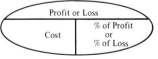

    Cost is more than sales price; therefore, there is a loss.

    $16,200 − $14,500 = $1,700 loss

    $1,700 ÷ $16,200 = .1049 = 10.49%

12. Total area of lot is
$95' \times 125' =$ 11,875 sq ft

House and patio =
$45\% \times 11,875 =$ 5,343.75 sq ft

Property sold =
$15\% \times 11,875 =$ 1,781.25 sq ft
                 7,125.00 sq ft $- 7,125$ sq ft

Property remaining =   4,750 sq ft

13. Value of lot today = $\$1,200 \times 3 = \$3,600$

Increase in value of lot = $\$3,600 - \$1,200 =$ \$2,400

Increase in value of house =   4,000

Total profit   \$6,400

14.

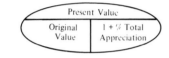

Appreciation $3\% \times 7$ years = 21% total

$\$25,000 \div (100\% + 21\%) = \$25,000 \div 1.21$
                          = \$20,661 original value

15. Commission on \$65,000 is 6%,
$\$65,000 \times .06 =$ \$3,900

Commission on \$35,000 is 5%,
$\$35,000 \times .05 =$ 1,750

Commission on \$27,500 is 5%,
$\$27,500 \times .05 =$ 1,375

Total commissions   \$7,025

16.

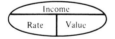

$\$266.88 \times 12$ months = \$3,202.56 per year

$\$3,202.56 \div \$45,750 = .07 = 7\%$ rate

17. Price reduction = 12% of \$43,750 = \$5,250

$\$43,750 - \$5,250 = \$38,500$ new sales price

$\$38,500 \times .06 = \$2,310$ to agent

18. Converting inches to feet (1 in = 2 ft)

$6'' \times 2 = 12$ ft

$8\frac{1}{4}'' \times 2 = 16.5$ ft

$12' \times 16.5' = 198$ sq ft

19.

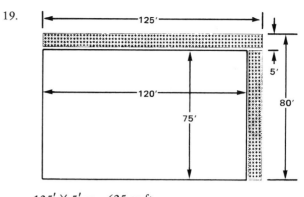

$125' \times 5' =$ 625 sq ft
$75' \times 5' =$ 375 sq ft
            1,000 sq ft

1,000 sq ft $\times .5\ (6'') = 500$ cu ft

20. 10 feet square = 100 sq ft

10 square feet =   10 sq ft

Difference   90 sq ft

21. $3,150 \div 6$ hours = 525 gallons used by 7 A/Cs in 1 hour

$525 \div 7$ A/C = 75 gallons used by 1 A/C in 1 hour

75 gallons $\times 4$ hours = 300 gallons used by 1 A/C in 4 hours

$3,600$ gallons $\div 300 = 12$ A/Cs required

22.

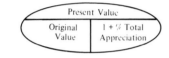

\$6,250 income $\div .12 = \$52,083$ value

23.

$\$216.50 \times 12$ months = \$2,598 annual interest

$\$2,598 \div \$35,750 = .0726 = 7.26\%$ interest

24. 4.2 showings $\times 2,400$ sales = 10,080 showings

25.

$\$70,000 \times 65\% = \$45,500$ assessed value

$\$45,500 \div 100 = 455$ hundreds

$455 \times \$3.90$ rate = \$1,774.50 annual taxes

$\$1,774.50 \div 12$ months = \$147.87 monthly taxes

26.

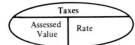

$900.79 taxes ÷ $3.82 rate = 235.81 hundreds

$235.81 × 100 = $23,581 assessment

$23.581 ÷ $67,000 value = .35 = 35% assessment ratio

27. 70′ + 90′ + 70′ + 90′ = 320′ total perimeter

320′ × $1.84 = $588.80 cost

28.

12 apts. × $150 = $1,800 per month

$1,800 × 12 months = $21,600 gross income

$21,600 − $3,560 expenses = $18,040 net income

$18,040 ÷ $112,000 = .161 = 16.1% rate of return

29.

$26,000 × (100% + 16%) = $26,000 × 1.16
   = $30,160 sales price

30.

Net Price / Selling Price / 1 − % Commission

(A) $24,000 net + $720 expenses = $24,720

   $24,720 ÷ 95% = $26,021

(B) $24,000 net + $1,100 expenses = $25,100

   $25,100 ÷ 95% = $26,421

(C) $24,000 net + $1,500 expenses = $25,500

   $25,500 ÷ 95% = $26,842

   Answer therefore is (D)

Landlord and Tenant

1. (D)	5. (C)	9. (B)	13. (C)	17. (C)
2. (B)	6. (B)	10. (A)	14. (A)	18. (B)
3. (D)	7. (A)	11. (C)	15. (B)	19. (D)
4. (D)	8. (A)	12. (D)	16. (A)	20. (A)

Real Estate Financing

1. (D)	5. (D)	9. (C)	13. (D)	17. (D)
2. (D)	6. (C)	10. (D)	14. (D)	18. (C)
3. (B)	7. (C)	11. (D)	15. (C)	19. (D)
4. (C)	8. (C)	12. (B)	16. (C)	20. (B)

Following Written Instructions

Descriptive Code Problems

Problem 1

1. (C)	3. (A)	5. (D)	7. (B)	9. (A)
2. (D)	4. (B)	6. (A)	8. (D)	10. (B)

Problem 2

1. (A)	3. (B)	5. (A)	7. (B)	9. (B)
2. (C)	4. (D)	6. (C)	8. (C)	10. (C)

Summary Card Problems

Problem 1

1. (C)	2. (B)	3. (B)

Problem 2

1. (A)	2. (A)	3. (A)	4. (C)	5. (A)

Listing and Offer to Purchase Examinations

Practice Examination 1

1. (C)	3. (B)	5. (D)	7. (C)	9. (B)
2. (C)	4. (D)	6. (A)	8. (B)	10. (A)

Practice Examination 2

1. (B)	3. (C)	5. (D)	7. (D)	9. (C)
2. (A)	4. (B)	6. (C)	8. (B)	10. (C)

Practice Examination 3

1. (B)	3. (A)	5. (B)	7. (D)	9. (A)
2. (C)	4. (C)	6. (A)	8. (C)	10. (A)

Settlement Statement Problems

Broker's Practice Examination 1

1. (A)	3. (A)	5. (D)	7. (B)	9. (B)
2. (B)	4. (D)	6. (C)	8. (C)	10. (C)

Broker's Practice Examination 2

1. (D)	3. (B)	5. (A)	7. (C)	9. (B)
2. (A)	4. (C)	6. (A)	8. (A)	10. (D)

Broker's Practice Examination 3

1. (C)	3. (D)	5. (A)	7. (B)	9. (B)
2. (B)	4. (B)	6. (C)	8. (C)	10. (C)

EXCLUSIVE AUTHORIZATION TO SELL

SALES PRICE: $48,000 TYPE HOME _Cape Cod_ TOTAL BEDROOMS 3 TOTAL BATHS 2

ADDRESS: _17 Petunia Place - Wysteria_ JURISDICTION OF: _Brandy Co. - Your State_

AMT. OF LOAN TO BE ASSUMED $ _App $37,500_ AS OF WHAT DATE: _7/1_ TAXES & INS. INCLUDED: _No_ YEARS TO GO _24_ AMOUNT PAYABLE MONTHLY $ _293.51_ @ _8_ % TYPE LOAN

MORTGAGE COMPANY _Sectional S&L_ 2nd TRUST $

ESTIMATED EXPECTED RENT MONTHLY $ TYPE OF APPRAISAL REQUESTED:

OWNER'S NAME _Oliver Smith and his wife Agnes_ PHONES: (HOME) ___ (BUSINESS) ___

TENANTS NAME ___ PHONES: (HOME) ___ (BUSINESS) ___

POSSESSION ___ DATE LISTED: _4-15-this yr._ EXCLUSIVE FOR _90 days_ DATE OF EXPIRATION _7-15-this yr._

LISTING BROKER _Zenith Realty Co._ PHONE ___ KEY AVAILABLE AT ___

LISTING SALESMAN _You_ HOME PHONE: ___ HOW TO BE SHOWN: ___

(1) ENTRANCE FOYER ☐ CENTER HALL ☐	(18) AGE _20 yrs._ AIR CONDITIONING ☐	(32) TYPE KITCHEN CABINETS
(2) LIVING ROOM SIZE _12 x 18_ FIREPLACE ☒	(19) ROOFING _Comp._ TOOL HOUSE ☐	(33) TYPE COUNTER TOPS
(3) DINING ROOM SIZE _10 x 9_	(20) GARAGE SIZE _1 car att._ PATIO ☐	(34) EAT-IN SIZE KITCHEN ☒
(4) BEDROOM TOTAL: _3_ DOWN _1_ UP _2_	(21) SIDE DRIVE ☒ _Asph._ CIRCULAR DRIVE ☐	(35) BREAKFAST ROOM ☐
(5) BATHS TOTAL: _2_ DOWN _1_ UP _1_	(22) PORCH ☐ SIDE ☐ REAR ☐ SCREENED ☐	(36) BUILT-IN OVEN & RANGE ☐
(6) DEN SIZE FIREPLACE ☐	(23) FENCED YARD OUTDOOR GRILL ☐	(37) SEPARATE STOVE INCLUDED ☒
(7) FAMILY ROOM SIZE FIREPLACE ☐	(24) STORM WINDOWS ☒ STORM DOORS ☒	(38) REFRIGERATOR INCLUDED ☒
(8) RECREATION ROOM SIZE FIREPLACE ☐	(25) CURBS & GUTTERS ☐ SIDEWALKS ☐	(39) DISHWASHER INCLUDED _Yes_
(9) BASEMENT SIZE _28 x 40_	(26) STORM SEWERS ☒ ALLEY ☐	(40) DISPOSAL INCLUDED ☒
NONE ☐ 1/4 ☐ 1/3 ☐ 1/2 ☐ 3/4 ☐ FULL ☒	(27) WATER SUPPLY _City_	(41) DOUBLE SINK ☐ SINGLE SINK ☐
(10) UTILITY ROOM SIZE	(28) SEWER ☒ SEPTIC ☐	STAINLESS STEEL ☐ PORCELAIN ☐
TYPE HOT WATER SYSTEM:	(29) TYPE GAS: NATURAL ☐ BOTTLED ☐	(42) WASHER INCLUDED ☐ DRYER INCLUDED ☐
(11) TYPE HEAT _Oil Hot Water Baseboard_	(30) WHY SELLING	(43) PANTRY ☐ EXHAUST FAN ☐
(12) EST. FUEL COST		(44) LAND ASSESSMENT $
(13) ATTIC ☐	(31) DIRECTIONS TO PROPERTY	(45) IMPROVEMENTS $
PULL DOWN STAIRWAY ☐ REGULAR STAIRWAY ☐ TRAP DOOR ☐		(46) TOTAL ASSESSMENT $ _15,000_
(14) MAIDS ROOM ☐ TYPE BATH		(47) TAX RATE
LOCATION		(48) TOTAL ANNUAL TAXES $ _615.00_
(15) NAME OF BUILDER		(49) LOT SIZE _75' x 120'_
(16) SQUARE FOOTAGE _(1,120 ☐)_		(50) LOT NO. _4_ BLOCK _9_ SECTION _1_
(17) EXTERIOR OF HOUSE _Brick_	_Picadilly Sub, Brandy Co. - Your State_	

NAME OF SCHOOLS: ELEMENTARY: ___ JR. HIGH: ___

HIGH ___ PAROCHIAL: ___

PUBLIC TRANSPORTATION: ___

NEAREST SHOPPING AREA: ___

REMARKS: _Owner will take back a second trust for $4,000 @ 9% interest for up to 5 years_

Date: _4-15- this year_

In consideration of the services of _Zenith Realty Co._ (herein called "Broker") to be rendered to the undersigned (herein called "Owner"), and of the promise of Broker to make reasonable efforts to obtain a Purchaser therefor, Owner hereby lists with Broker the real estate and all improvements thereon which are described above (all herein called "the property"), and Owner hereby grants to Broker the exclusive and irrevocable right to sell such property from 12:00 Noon on _4-15_, 19 _this year_ until 12:00 Midnight on _7-15_, 19 _this year_ (herein called "period of time"), for the price of _Forty Eight Thousand and 00/100_ Dollars ($ _48,000.00_) or for such other price and upon such other terms (including exchange) as Owner may subsequently authorize during the period of time.

It is understood by Owner that the above sum or any other price subsequently authorized by Owner shall include a cash fee of _6%_ per cent of such price or other price which shall be payable by Owner to Broker upon consummation by any Purchaser or Purchasers of a valid contract of sale of the property during the period of time and whether or not Broker was a procuring cause of any such contract of sale.

If the property is sold or exchanged by Owner, or by Broker or by any other person to any Purchaser to whom the property was shown by Broker or any representative of Broker within sixty (60) days after the expiration of the period of time mentioned above, Owner agrees to pay to Broker a cash fee which shall be the same percentage of the purchase price as the percentage mentioned above.

Broker is hereby authorized by Owner to place a "For Sale" sign on the property and to remove all signs of other brokers or salesmen during the period of time, and Owner hereby agrees to make the property available to Broker at all reasonable hours for the purpose of showing it to prospective Purchasers.

Owner agrees to convey the property to the Purchaser by warranty deed with the usual covenants of title and free and clear from all encumbrances, tenancies, liens (for taxes or otherwise), but subject to applicable restrictive covenants of record. Owner acknowledges receipt of a copy of this agreement.

WITNESS the following signature(s) and seal(s):

Date Signed: _4-15- this year_ _Oliver Smith_ (SEAL) (Owner)

Listing Broker _Zenith Realty Co By: You_ _Agnes Smith_ (SEAL) (Owner)

Address ___ Telephone ___

Suggested solution for Listing Problem 2.

OFFER TO PURCHASE AGREEMENT

This AGREEMENT made as of _JULY 4TH_____, 19 _THIS YEAR_,

among _JOSEPH CHANCE AND HIS WIFE NELLIE_____ (herein called "Purchaser"),

and _OLIVER SMITH AND HIS WIFE AGNES_____ (herein called "Seller"),

and _ZENITH REALTY CO._____ (herein called "Broker"),

provides that Purchaser agrees to buy through Broker as agent for Seller, and Seller agrees to sell the following described real estate, and all improvements thereon, located in the jurisdiction of _BRANDY COUNTY - YOUR STATE_____,

(all herein called "the property"):

LOT 4, BLOCK 9, SECTION 1, PICADILLY SUBDIVISION, BRANDY CO.-
YOUR STATE
INCLUDED IN SALE IS STOVE, DISHWASHER, REFRIGERATOR AND GARBAGE
_DISPOSER_____, and more commonly known as _17 PETUNIA PLACE_
_WYSTERIA - YOUR STATE_____ (street address).

1. The purchase price of the property is ~~FORTY SIX THOUSAND AND~~ 00/100 FORTY SEVEN THOUSAND _JC_ _NC_ Dollars ($ ~~46,000.00~~), and such purchase price shall be paid as follows: _OS_ _AS_

_JC_ _NC_ $500.00 DEPOSIT ACKNOWLEDGED IN PARAGRAPH 2 BELOW

_OS_ _AS_ $9,000 ~~$8,000.00~~ ADDITIONAL CASH AT SETTLEMENT

_JC_ _NC_ $37,500.00 BY ASSUMPTION OF THE EXISTING TRUST, PAYABLE $293.51

_OS_ _AS_   MONTHLY TO PRINCIPAL AND INTEREST AT 8% PER ANNUM

2. Purchaser has made a deposit of _FIVE HUNDRED AND_ 00/100 _(BY CHECK)_ Dollars ($ _500.00_) with Broker, receipt of which is hereby acknowledged, and such deposit shall be held by Broker in escrow until the date of settlement and then applied to the purchase price, or returned to Purchaser if the title to the property is not marketable.

3. Seller agrees to convey the property to Purchaser by Warranty Deed with the usual covenants of title and free and clear from all encumbrances, tenancies, liens (for taxes or otherwise), except as may be otherwise provided above, but subject to applicable restrictive covenants of record. Seller further agrees to deliver possession of the property to Purchaser on the date of settlement and to pay the expense of preparing the deed of conveyance.

4. Settlement shall be made at the offices of Broker or at _JONES AND JACKSON_____ on or before _JULY 20_____, 19 _THIS YEAR_, or as soon thereafter as title can be examined and necessary documents prepared, with allowance of a reasonable time for Seller to correct any defects reported by the title examiner.

5. All taxes, interest, rent, and F.H.A. or similar escrow deposits, if any, shall be prorated as of the date of settlement.

6. All risk of loss or damage to the property by fire, windstorm, casualty, or other cause is assumed by Seller until the date of settlement.

7. Purchaser and Seller agree that Broker was the sole procuring cause of this Contract of Purchase, and Seller agrees to pay Broker for services rendered a cash fee of _6%_____ per cent of the purchase price. If either Purchaser or Seller defaults under such Contract, such defaulting party shall be liable for the cash fee of Broker and any expenses incurred by the non-defaulting party in connection with this transaction.

Subject to: _THIS OFFER WILL EXPIRE AT 12:00 PM MIDNIGHT JULY 5, THIS YEAR_
IF IT HAS NOT BEEN ACCEPTED. PROPERTY BEING SOLD "AS IS".

8. Purchaser represents that an inspection satisfactory to Purchaser has been made of the property, and Purchaser agrees to accept the property in its present condition except as may be otherwise provided in the description of the property above.

9. This Contract of Purchase constitutes the entire agreement among the parties and may not be modified or changed except by written instrument executed by all of the parties, including Broker.

10. This Contract of Purchase shall be construed, interpreted, and applied according to the law of the jurisdiction of _YOUR STATE_ and shall be binding upon and shall inure to the benefit of the heirs, personal representatives, successors, and assigns of the parties.

All parties to this agreement acknowledge receipt of a certified copy.

WITNESS the following signatures and seals:

_Oliver Smith_____ (SEAL) Seller   _Joseph Chance_____ (SEAL) Purchaser

_Agnes Smith_____ (SEAL) Seller   _Nellie Chance_____ (SEAL) Purchaser

Zenith Realty Co By: You (SEAL) Broker

Deposit Rec'd $ _500.00_____

(Check)   Cash

Sales Agent: _You_____

Suggested solution for Offer to Purchase Problem 2.

EXCLUSIVE AUTHORIZATION TO SELL

SALES PRICE: **$49,950** TYPE HOME **RAMBLER** TOTAL BEDROOMS **3** TOTAL BATHS **2**

ADDRESS: **73 RANCHO GRANDE BLVD. — JUANSVILLE** JURISDICTION OF **MUCHO CO. — YOUR STATE**

AMT. OF LOAN TO BE ASSUMED $ **16,980** AS OF WHAT DATE: **4-15** TAXES & INS INCLUDED **NO** YEARS TO GO **18** AMOUNT PAYABLE MONTHLY $ **123.88** @ **6** % TYPE LOAN _____

MORTGAGE COMPANY _____ 2nd TRUST $ _____

ESTIMATED EXPECTED RENT MONTHLY $ _____ TYPE OF APPRAISAL REQUESTED: _____

OWNER'S NAME **WILLIAM BELL AND HIS WIFE LIBERTY** PHONES: (HOME) **555-1021** (BUSINESS) _____

TENANTS NAME _____ PHONES: (HOME) _____ (BUSINESS) _____

POSSESSION _____ DATE LISTED: **6-15-THIS YR** EXCLUSIVE FOR **120 DAYS** DATE OF EXPIRATION **10-15-THIS YR**

LISTING BROKER **ESTES INC. - REALTORS** PHONE **533-3333** KEY AVAILABLE AT **BROKERS OFFICE**

LISTING SALESMAN **YOU** HOME PHONE: _____ HOW TO BE SHOWN: _____

(1) ENTRANCE FOYER ☐ CENTER HALL ☐	(18) AGE **7 YEARS** AIR CONDITIONING ☐	(32) TYPE KITCHEN CABINETS **NATURAL WOOD**
(2) LIVING ROOM SIZE **12×18** FIREPLACE ☐	(19) ROOFING TOOL HOUSE ☐	(33) TYPE COUNTER TOPS **FORMICA**
(3) DINING ROOM SIZE **10×12**	(20) GARAGE SIZE PATIO ☐	(34) EAT-IN SIZE KITCHEN ☒
(4) BEDROOM TOTAL: **3** DOWN **3** UP	(21) SIDE DRIVE ☒ **PAVED** CIRCULAR DRIVE ☐	(35) BREAKFAST ROOM ☐
(5) BATHS TOTAL: **2** DOWN **2** UP	(22) PORCH ☐ SIDE ☐ REAR ☐ SCREENED ☐	(36) BUILT-IN OVEN & RANGE ☒
(6) DEN SIZE FIREPLACE ☐	(23) FENCED YARD OUTDOOR GRILL ☐	(37) SEPARATE STOVE INCLUDED ☐
(7) FAMILY ROOM SIZE FIREPLACE ☐	(24) STORM WINDOWS ☐ STORM DOORS ☐	(38) REFRIGERATOR INCLUDED ☒
(8) RECREATION ROOM SIZE FIREPLACE ☐	(25) CURBS & GUTTERS ☒ SIDEWALKS ☒	(39) DISHWASHER INCLUDED **YES**
(9) BASEMENT SIZE **28×45**	(26) STORM SEWERS ☒ ALLEY ☐	(40) DISPOSAL INCLUDED ☒
NONE ☐ 1/4 ☐ 1/3 ☐ 1/2 ☐ 3/4 ☐ FULL ☒	(27) WATER SUPPLY **CITY**	(41) DOUBLE SINK ☒ SINGLE SINK ☐
(10) UTILITY ROOM SIZE	(28) SEWER ☒ **CITY** SEPTIC ☐	STAINLESS STEEL ☒ PORCELAIN ☐
TYPE HOT WATER SYSTEM **GAS 30 GAL**	(29) TYPE GAS: NATURAL ☐ BOTTLED ☐	(42) WASHER INCLUDED ☒ DRYER INCLUDED ☒
(11) TYPE HEAT **GAS - FORCED HOT AIR**	(30) WHY SELLING	(43) PANTRY ☐ EXHAUST FAN ☐
(12) EST. FUEL COST		(44) LAND ASSESSMENT $ **3,200**
(13) ATTIC ☐	(31) DIRECTIONS TO PROPERTY	(45) IMPROVEMENTS $ **12,800**
PULL DOWN STAIRWAY ☐ REGULAR STAIRWAY ☐ TRAP DOOR ☐		(46) TOTAL ASSESSMENT $ **16,000**
(14) MAIDS ROOM ☐ TYPE BATH		(47) TAX RATE **4.30 PER HUNDRED**
LOCATION		(48) TOTAL ANNUAL TAXES $
(15) NAME OF BUILDER		(49) LOT SIZE **90'×110'**
(16) SQUARE FOOTAGE **(1260 ☐)**		(50) LOT NO. **3** BLOCK **9** SECTION **2**
(17) EXTERIOR OF HOUSE **VERTICAL WOOD SIDING**	**EL SOMBRERO SUBD. MUCHO CO. - YOUR STATE**	

NAME OF SCHOOLS: ELEMENTARY: _____ JR. HIGH: _____

HIGH _____ PAROCHIAL _____

PUBLIC TRANSPORTATION: _____

NEAREST SHOPPING AREA: _____

REMARKS: **$150.00 PENALTY FOR PREPAYING THE EXISTING LOAN - SELLERS WILL NOT PAY ANY POINTS TO PLACE A NEW LOAN. TAXES FOR THE YEAR HAVE BEEN PAID.**

Date: **6-15- THIS YEAR**

In consideration of the services of **ESTES INC., REALTORS** (herein called "Broker") to be rendered to the undersigned (herein called "Owner"), and of the promise of Broker to make reasonable efforts to obtain a Purchaser therefor, Owner hereby lists with Broker the real estate and all improvements thereon which are described above (all herein called "the property"), and Owner hereby grants to Broker the exclusive and irrevocable right to sell such property from 12:00 Noon on **6-15**, 19 **THIS YEAR** until 12:00 Midnight on **10-15**, 19 **THIS YEAR** (herein called "period of time"), for the price of **FORTY NINE THOUSAND NINE HUNDRED FIFTY AND 00/100** Dollars ($ **49,950.00**) or for such other price and upon such other terms (including exchange) as Owner may subsequently authorize during the period of time.

It is understood by Owner that the above sum or any other price subsequently authorized by Owner shall include a cash fee of **6** per cent of such price or other price which shall be payable by Owner to Broker upon consummation by any Purchaser or Purchasers of a valid contract of sale of the property during the period of time and whether or not Broker was a procuring cause of any such contract of sale.

If the property is sold or exchanged by Owner, or by Broker or by any other person to any Purchaser to whom the property was shown by Broker or any representative of Broker within sixty (60) days after the expiration of the period of time mentioned above, Owner agrees to pay to Broker a cash fee which shall be the same percentage of the purchase price as the percentage mentioned above.

Broker is hereby authorized by Owner to place a "For Sale" sign on the property and to remove all signs of other brokers or salesmen during the period of time, and Owner hereby agrees to make the property available to Broker at all reasonable hours for the purpose of showing it to prospective Purchasers.

Owner agrees to convey the property to the Purchaser by warranty deed with the usual covenants of title and free and clear from all encumbrances, tenancies, liens (for taxes or otherwise), but subject to applicable restrictive covenants of record. Owner acknowledges receipt of a copy of this agreement.

WITNESS the following signature(s) and seal(s):

Date Signed: **6-15- THIS YEAR**

Listing Broker **Estes Inc., Realtors By: You**

Address _____ Telephone _____

William Bell (SEAL) (Owner)

Liberty Bell (SEAL) (Owner)

Suggested solution for Listing Problem 3.

205

OFFER TO PURCHASE AGREEMENT

This AGREEMENT made as of ___August 1st___, 19___THIS YEAR___,

among ___George E. Brown and His Wife Betty___ (herein called "Purchaser"),

and ___William Bell and His Wife Liberty___ (herein called "Seller"),

and ___Estes Inc. Realtors___ (herein called "Broker"),

provides that Purchaser agrees to buy through Broker as agent for Seller, and Seller agrees to sell the following described real estate, and all improvements thereon, located in the jurisdiction of ___Mucho County - Your State___,

(all herein called "the property"): ___Lot 3, Block 9, Section 2, El Sombrero Subd., Mucho Co - Your State___
___Included in Sale is: Built in Range, Refrigerator, Dishwasher,___
___Disposal, Washer and Dryer___

_____, and more commonly known as ___73 Rancho Grande___
___Blvd., Ivansville - Your State___ (street address).

1. The purchase price of the property is ___Forty Nine Thousand Nine Hundred Fifty and 00/100___
Dollars ($ ___49,950___), and such purchase price shall be paid as follows:

___$500.00 Deposit Acknowledged in Paragraph 2 Below___
___$9,490.00 Additional Down Payment at Settlement___
___$39,960.00 By New 1st Deed of Trust to be Placed by Purchaser for___
___At Least 25 Years at No More Than 8% Interest Per Annum___

2. Purchaser has made a deposit of ___Five Hundred and 00/100 (By Check)___ Dollars ($ ___500.00___) with Broker, receipt of which is hereby acknowledged, and such deposit shall be held by Broker in escrow until the date of settlement and then applied to the purchase price, or returned to Purchaser if the title to the property is not marketable.

3. Seller agrees to convey the property to Purchaser by Warranty Deed with the usual covenants of title and free and clear from all encumbrances, tenancies, liens (for taxes or otherwise), except as may be otherwise provided above, but subject to applicable restrictive covenants of record. Seller further agrees to deliver possession of the property to Purchaser on the date of settlement and to pay the expense of preparing the deed of conveyance.

4. Settlement shall be made at the offices of Broker or at _____ on or before
___Sept. 1___, 19___THIS YEAR___, or as soon thereafter as title can be examined and necessary documents prepared, with allowance of a reasonable time for Seller to correct any defects reported by the title examiner.

5. All taxes, interest, rent, and F.H.A. or similar escrow deposits, if any, shall be prorated as of the date of settlement.

6. All risk of loss or damage to the property by fire, windstorm, casualty, or other cause is assumed by Seller until the date of settlement.

7. Purchaser and Seller agree that Broker was the sole procuring cause of this Contract of Purchase, and Seller agrees to pay Broker for services rendered a cash fee of ___6___ per cent of the purchase price. If either Purchaser or Seller defaults under such Contract, such defaulting party shall be liable for the cash fee of Broker and any expenses incurred by the non-defaulting party in connection with this transaction.

Subject to: ___Purchaser's Ability to Secure 1st Trust as Specified Above___
___Purchaser to Make Loan Application Within 3 Working Days Following___
___Acceptance of This Offer. Seller Will Not Pay Any Points to Place___
___The New Loan.___

8. Purchaser represents that an inspection satisfactory to Purchaser has been made of the property, and Purchaser agrees to accept the property in its present condition except as may be otherwise provided in the description of the property above.

9. This Contract of Purchase constitutes the entire agreement among the parties and may not be modified or changed except by written instrument executed by all of the parties, including Broker.

10. This Contract of Purchase shall be construed, interpreted, and applied according to the law of the jurisdiction of ___Your State___ and shall be binding upon and shall inure to the benefit of the heirs, personal representatives, successors, and assigns of the parties.

All parties to this agreement acknowledge receipt of a certified copy.

WITNESS the following signatures and seals:

___William Bell___ (SEAL) Seller   ___George E. Brown___ (SEAL) Purchaser

___Liberty Bell___ (SEAL) Seller   ___Betty Brown___ (SEAL) Purchaser

___Estes Inc Realtors___ (SEAL) Broker

Deposit Rec'd $ ___500.00___

(Check)   Cash

Sales Agent: ___You___

Suggested solution for Offer to Purchase Problem 3.

	BUYER'S STATEMENT		SELLER'S STATEMENT	
	DEBIT	CREDIT	DEBIT	CREDIT
PURCHASE PRICE	47,000.00			47,000.00
DEPOSIT		500.00		
ASSUMPTION OF TRUST		37,490.00	37,490.00	
R.E. TAXES - PRO-RATED		341.66	341.66	
ASSUMPTION INS. POLICY	240.00			240.00
LEGAL FEES - SELLER			70.00	
LEGAL FEES - BUYER	190.00			
SALES FEE			2,820.00	
BALANCE DUE FROM BUYER		9,098.34		
BALANCE DUE SELLER			6,518.34	
	47,430.00	47,430.00	47,240.00	47,240.00

Suggested solution for Settlement Problem 2.

	BUYER'S STATEMENT		SELLER'S STATEMENT	
	DEBIT	CREDIT	DEBIT	CREDIT
PURCHASE PRICE	49,950.00			49,950.00
DEPOSIT		500.00		
PAY OFF - EXISTING TRUST			16,456.33	
PAY OFF PENALTY			150.00	
PROCEEDS - NEW TRUST		39,960.00		
POINTS - PLACEMENT FEE	399.60			
LEGAL FEES	150.00		37.50	
R. E. TAXES - PRO-RATED	229.32			229.32
SALES FEE			2,997.00	
BALANCE DUE FROM BUYER		10,268.92		
BALANCE DUE SELLER			30,538.49	
	50,728.92	50,728.92	50,179.32	50,179.32

Suggested solution for Settlement Problem 3.

Practice Final Examinations

Salesperson and Broker

Before taking the sample final examination for salesperson or broker, it would be well to review once again the instructions in Chapter 2 on how to take a test, as well as the information bulletin published by the Educational Testing Service, as reprinted in Chapter 1.

Both the salesperson and broker examinations consist entirely of multiple choice questions. *You are always to select the best answer.*

The sample questions in these examinations are comprehensive and designed to be typical of, but not identical to, questions found on the Uniform Real Estate Examinations in those states which have adopted the Educational Testing Service examinations. The questions are also similar to those asked by states not using the Uniform Examination. They require careful reading and thought.

The recommended answers for these sample questions

follow each examination. These answers are based on the common and statutory law in most jurisdictions. They could be different in your area.

It is suggested that you time yourself on these examinations. They are designed to be completed in 4 hours for the salesperson and $4\frac{1}{2}$ hours for the broker examination.

The use of any reference materials is not allowed. You also may not use slide rules, calculators, or any other mechanical aids. Scratch paper is not furnished; you must use the margin or spaces on the examination. Do not make any marks on the answer sheet except those made to answer the questions.

After you have taken the practice examination for which you are preparing and have reviewed the questions you missed, you may wish to take the other examination as additional preparation. (Use forms following Index.)

PRACTICE FINAL EXAMINATION: SALESPERSON

Part A: Arithmetic

1. You are going to construct a sidewalk $5\frac{1}{2}$ ft wide and 4 in deep on a corner lot 180 ft by 80 ft. If concrete is 72 cents a cubic foot, how much would the materials for the sidewalk cost?

   (A) $343.00   (C) $350.00
   (B) $336.00   (D) $3,456

2. A trust in the amount of $16,000 was originated March 10 of this year at $8\frac{1}{2}$% per annum interest. If no payments have been made, how much would be required to pay off the trust as of September 30 of this year?

   (A) $16,869   (C) $856
   (B) $16,756   (D) None are within $50

3. The lot shown below sold for $1.65 per sq ft. What was the sale price?

   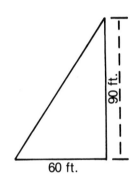

   (A) $8,910   (C) $89
   (B) $4,455   (D) $45

4. The building shown by the shaded area in the figure below cost $22.50 per square foot to construct. What was its total cost?

   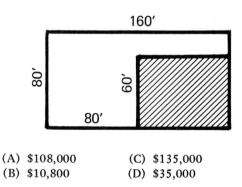

   (A) $108,000   (C) $135,000
   (B) $10,800   (D) $35,000

5. A 3-year insurance policy was purchased August 30 last year for $389. If it is canceled as of February 20 of next year, how much refund would be due?

   (A) $328   (C) $190
   (B) $198   (D) $202

6. The lot outlined below contains what portion of an acre?

   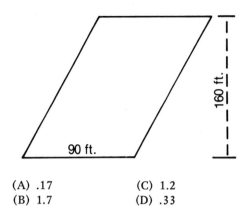

   (A) .17   (C) 1.2
   (B) 1.7   (D) .33

7. You invest $145,000 in a 10-unit apartment house; your expenses are $2,600 per annum. If you want to make a 12% return on your investment, how much monthly rent will you need to charge for each apartment?

   (A) $185   (C) $226
   (B) $200   (D) None are within $15

8. If you purchase 239,580 sq ft of land at 17¢ per square foot and divide it into $\frac{1}{2}$-acre lots and sell them for $3,500 each, how much profit would you make?

   (A) $14,207   (C) $33,475
   (B) $1,421   (D) None. There was a loss.

9. If the annual taxes on an $18,000 property assessed at 33% are $378, what is the tax rate per hundred?

   (A) $6.30   (C) $4.40
   (B) $3.30   (D) $5.20

10. A home originally valued at $33,000 12 years ago has depreciated $1\frac{1}{2}$% per annum. The lot on which the home is located was originally valued at $3,500 and has increased in value $4,500 during the 12 years. What is the total value of the property today?

    (A) $38,060   (C) $35,060
    (B) $32,560   (D) $31,500

11. The scale of a blueprint is $\frac{1}{4}'' = 1$ ft. If a room on a blueprint measures $8\frac{1}{2}'' \times 9\frac{3}{4}''$, how much area does the actual room contain?

    (A) 83 sq in
    (B) 1,326 sq ft
    (C) 504 sq ft
    (D) None are within 400 sq ft

12. Four people decided to purchase a property for $88,000. The first person had $20,500 to invest, the second $12,500, and the third $22,000. How much of the ownership was left for the fourth?

    (A) $42\frac{1}{2}$%   (C) $\frac{1}{3}$
    (B) 55%   (D) $\frac{3}{8}$

13. If 15 air conditioners use 5,760 gal of water in 8 hr, how many air conditioners will use 7,920 gal of water in 3 hr?

    (A) 45   (C) 60
    (B) 55   (D) 35

14. A property sold for $43,050, which included a profit of 23%. What was its cost?

    (A) $18,700
    (B) $35,000
    (C) $53,500
    (D) None of these are within $1,000

15. A property cost $43,250. In order to make a 13% profit, what would you have to sell it for?

    (A) $48,875   (C) $48,975
    (B) $48,800   (D) $47,750

16. You receive $500 per month salary from your broker, plus 5% commission on your real estate sales. If you were paid $2,575 this month, how much real estate did you sell?

    (A) $51,500   (C) $63,750
    (B) $41,500   (D) $31,500

17. You receive $84 per month from each of 10 apartments. If your annual expenses are $1,440 and your investment is $72,000, what rate of return are you getting on your investment?

    (A) 14%   (C) 11%
    (B) 12%   (D) None of these

18. You own a farm which has 320 acres planted in corn, $\frac{3}{16}$ of the farm planted in oats, and 18.75% in wheat, and .125 of the farm is left for the house and barn. How large is the total farm?

    (A) 320 acres   (C) 640 acres
    (B) 440 acres   (D) 750 acres

19. An owner wishes to net $18,000 from the sale of a property after paying your 6% commission, the present first trust of $23,450, and a personal note of $1,085. What would be the sales price?

    (A) $45,087   (C) $42,535
    (B) $45,250   (D) None are within $200

20. Unpaid taxes on a property are $278.40 and were due January 1. What would be the proration if the property was sold May 10?

    (A) Credit buyer $100.46, debit seller $100.46
    (B) Credit seller $177.94, debit buyer $100.46
    (C) Debit buyer $123.66, credit seller $154.76
    (D) Debit seller $123.66, credit buyer $123.66

21. The original cost of a house was $22,000. It later sold for $28,600. What was the percentage of profit?

    (A) 66%   (C) 30%
    (B) 33%   (D) 13%

22. How much would the amount of principal be reduced by the first month's payment on a $23,500 loan at 9% if the monthly payment to principal and interest is $250.00?

    (A) $176   (C) $74
    (B) $211   (D) None are within $5.00

23. If property is assessed at 45% of its value, what would the taxes be on a house valued at $37,500 if the tax rate is $4.30 per hundred?

    (A) $1,612   (C) $725
    (B) $161   (D) $894

24. You are going to pour a footing for a building. The outside measurements of the footing are 80 ft by 90 ft. The footing is to be 18 in wide and $1\frac{1}{2}$ ft deep. How many cubic yards of concrete will you need?

    (A) 30 cu yd   (C) 75 cu yd
    (B) 28 cu yd   (D) 40 cu yd

25. What interest rate are you paying on a loan of $23,500 if your monthly interest payment is $107.70?

    (A) 6%   (C) $6\frac{1}{2}$%
    (B) $5\frac{1}{2}$%   (D) None are within $\frac{1}{2}$%

26. You own a rectangular lot which is 70′ X 90′. You decide to fence it with fencing that has a post every 10 ft. How many fence posts are needed?

    (A) 34   (C) 33
    (B) 31   (D) 32

27. Which of the following sales would net the broker exactly $2,890 after paying the expenses noted, if the commission rate is 6% of the sales price?

	Sales Price	Expenses
(A)	$72,000	$1,450
(B)	$68,000	$1,200
(C)	$57,000	$530
(D)	$53,000	$300

28. An apartment building sells for $120,000. If the tax rate in the area is $4.30 per hundred, based on an assessment of 60% of value, how much are the annual taxes?

    (A) $5,160   (C) $4,244
    (B) $2,064   (D) $3,096

29. You agree to sell a property listed for $26,000 for a 5% brokerage fee. What is your loss if the seller accepts a contract for 10% less than the listed price?

    (A) $117   (C) $154
    (B) $130   (D) $174

30. If you purchase 8 lots for $6,200 each and decide to keep one lot for yourself, what would you have to sell the other lots for to make a profit of $8,500 plus your lot?

    (A) $8,300   (C) $7,260
    (B) $8,500   (D) $7,085

Part B: Comprehension of Real Estate Subject Matter

31. The *habendum* clause is found in a

    (A) will   (C) deed
    (B) deed of trust   (D) offer to purchase

32. To hypothecate means to

    (A) fabricate a story
    (B) pledge something as security without giving up possession of it
    (C) dispense medicine or drugs
    (D) render a judicial opinion

33. To convey most nearly means to

    (A) buy   (C) obligate
    (B) warrant   (D) transfer

34. Which of the following is out of place?

    (A) Offer and acceptance
    (B) Reality of consent
    (C) Seal or consideration
    (D) Words of conveyance

35. Demise refers to

    (A) a will
    (B) a conveyance of real estate
    (C) condemnation
    (D) a small cup of coffee

36. The interest which a purchaser acquires when the offer to purchase has been accepted is

    (A) an estate in fee simple
    (B) legal title
    (C) a freehold estate
    (D) equitable title

37. A contract based on a consideration which comprised a promise in exchange for another promise could be described as a

    (A) multilateral contract
    (B) bilateral contract
    (C) unilateral contract
    (D) binary contract

38. Physical deterioration results from

    (A) tax liens
    (B) deferred maintenance
    (C) overcrowded occupancy
    (D) poor basement drains

39. Which one of the following is out of place?

    (A) The grantee in a deed of trust
    (B) The grantee in a deed of release
    (C) The grantee in a deed
    (D) The vendee

40. Which of the following is out of place?

    (A) Vendee–purchaser
    (B) Grantor–seller
    (C) Mortgagor–lender
    (D) Borrower–trustor

41. One who appoints another to act for him or her and in his or her stead is a

    (A) trustee   (C) principal
    (B) agent   (D) broker

42. If the contract of sale contains no provisions to the contrary, a fire which destroys a home between the date of the contract and the date of settlement would cause

    (A) the seller to suffer the loss
    (B) the purchaser to suffer the loss
    (C) the contract to become null and void
    (D) none of the above are correct

43. The terms "utility," "scarcity," and "purchasing power" are most important in considering which of the following?

    (A) Economic obsolescence
    (B) Value
    (C) The consistent use theory
    (D) The cost approach to value

44. The right which a landlord has after termination of a valid tenancy is known as

    (A) reversionary interest
    (B) tenancy by sufferance
    (C) right to receive rent
    (D) right of reentry

45. An "as is" clause in a lease which is contrary to public policy, or perhaps detrimental to health, would probably be overturned under

    (A) the tenant's rights
    (B) an implied covenant of habitability
    (C) the rights of the landlord
    (D) none of these

46. Which of the following written instruments normally accompanies a mortgage?

    I. A note
    II. A deed

    (A) I only   (C) Both I and II
    (B) II only   (D) Neither I nor II

47. A competent title search could easily fail to discover which of the following title defects?

    I. Execution of a deed by an insane person
    II. Easements obtained by adverse possession

    (A) I only   (C) Both I and II
    (B) II only   (D) Neither I nor II

48. Which of the following is not a method of estimating depreciation in the appraisal process?

    (A) Age-life
    (B) Gross rent multiplier
    (C) Observed condition
    (D) Escalation

49. Which one of the following is not covered by a mortgagee's policy of title insurance?

    (A) Forged deeds
    (B) Mistakes in the records
    (C) Overcharges by an attorney
    (D) All are covered

50. The unities of time, interest, title, and possession are essential to

    (A) tenancy in common
    (B) joint tenancy
    (C) tenancy for years
    (D) tenancy from year to year

51. A wrongful act or the violation of a legal right is best described as a

    (A) litigation   (C) tort
    (B) violation   (D) setback

52. Which of the following are examples of severalty ownership?

    (A) Joint tenancy
    (B) Tenancy in common
    (C) Tenancy from year to year
    (D) None of these

53. The best surety that title to property is good is by means of

    (A) a title search   (C) an abstract of title
    (B) a title certificate   (D) title insurance

54. Monthly payments in the form of "direct reduction" would most likely be associated with

    (A) a straight mortgage
    (B) a blanket mortgage
    (C) a flexible-payment mortgage
    (D) none of these

55. Loan discounts, or points, are a means whereby the lender can

    I. adjust the effective yield on loans
    II. overcome the effect of inflation

    (A) I only   (C) Both I and II
    (B) II only   (D) Neither I nor II

Questions 56 to 61 test your ability to interpret correctly information about houses and to transfer specific details from one kind of document to another.

Each question is described by a 9-digit code. The meaning of each digit in the code is given above the problem. Your task is to recode the data for each question, choosing the appropriate letter (A, B, C, or D) as follows:

A – The house has all 9 facilities and 3 or more bedrooms.

B – The house has 7 or 8, not more or less facilities, and *both* bath and utility room codes are 1 or under.

C – The house has the first 3 main facilities and at least 3 bedrooms and 3 other codes below 1.

D – The house does not fit any of the categories above.

MEANING OF DESCRIPTIVE CODE:

LIVING ROOM:
- 0 = large w/fireplace
- 1 = with w/w carpeting
- 2 = with neither of above

DINING ROOM:
- 0 = separate room
- 1 = dining el
- 2 = none

REC ROOM OR DEN:
- 0 = lg. w/fireplace on main floor
- 1 = lg. w/fireplace in basement
- 2 = none

KITCHEN:
- 0 = no eating space
- 1 = w/appliances
- 2 = eating space and appliances

BEDROOMS:
- 0 = 1 or 2
- 1 = 2 or 3
- 2 = 4 or more

BATHROOMS:
- 0 = 1 - 1½
- 1 = 2 full
- 2 = 2½

BASEMENT:
- 0 = full
- 1 = half
- 2 = none

UTILITY ROOM:
- 0 = on main floor
- 1 = in basement
- 2 = none

GARAGE:
- 0 = 1 car or carport
- 1 = 2 car
- 2 = none

QUESTION NUMBER	LIVING RM.	DINING RM.	REC. RM. OR DEN	KITCHEN	BEDROOMS	BATHROOMS	BASEMENT	UTILITY RM.	GARAGE	ANSWER
56	0	0	1	0	1	2	0	1	0	
57	2	0	2	1	2	0	2	1	1	
58	0	0	0	0	2	2	0	2	0	
59	2	0	0	0	1	1	1	0	2	
60	1	1	2	1	0	0	2	2	1	
61	0	0	1	0	2	1	0	1	1	

Read the following summary card, then answer questions 62–65.

SUMMARY CARD

Description. A brick rambler 33′ × 50′ with 3 bedrooms on the main floor and 1 on the completely finished lower level. There are 3 baths, a laundry room, large recreation room with raised hearth, fireplace, gas hot-water baseboard heat, and central air conditioning; property is connected to city water and sewer facilities. The heavily wooded lot contains 68,340 sq ft of land.

Owner/Financial Data. The present owners, Jack and Jean Edwards, state the present conventional loan balance is $33,340 as of the listing date. The interest rate is 8.5%, and monthly payments are $336. Taxes for the calendar year are $1,248, based on an assessment of 40% of value and rate of $4.30 per hundred, and they have been paid by the Edwards' directly to the county.

Listing/Transaction History. October 1—property is listed under a 90-day exclusive at a price as indicated by the tax assessment rounded to the nearest multiple of $100 with a 6% commission.

October 10—Steve and Sid Stevens are shown the property and make an offer of $2,500 less than the listed price, which the owner accepts provided settlement occurs in 20 days. This is agreeable to the purchaser.

Settlement is conducted on time.

62. From information given on the summary card, which of the following statements is (are) correct?

    I. Stevens will receive a credit at settlement for real estate taxes.
    II. The assessed evaluation is less than $30,000.

(A) I only   (C) Both I and II
(B) II only   (D) Neither I nor II

63. Which of the following statements is (are) correct?

    I. The property is listed for more than $73,000.
    II. The property is served by sidewalks.

(A) I only   (C) Both I and II
(B) II only   (D) Neither I nor II

64. Which of the following can be determined by the summary card?

    I. Your listing is an exclusive authorization to sell at a 6% commission.
    II. If the cost to build the Edwards house was $25 per square foot of finished space, the cost of construction exceeded $80,000.

(A) I only   (C) Both I and II
(B) II only   (D) Neither I nor II

65. Which of the following statements is (are) correct?

    I. If the salesperson selling the property receives 30% of the total sales commission, he or she will receive more than $1,250.
    II. The monthly payment includes principal, interest, taxes, and insurance.

(A) I only   (C) Both I and II
(B) II only   (D) Neither I nor II

Questions 66 to 70 are to be answered from information contained on the plat of Melee Subdivision.

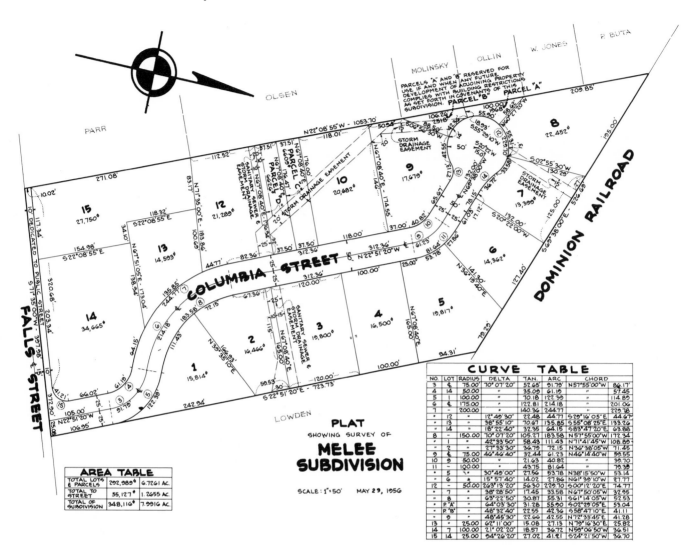

PLAT

SHOWING SURVEY OF

MELEE SUBDIVISION

SCALE: 1"=50'   MAY 29, 1956

AREA TABLE		
TOTAL LOTS & PARCELS	292,989°	6.7261 AC.
TOTAL TO STREET	55,127°	1.2655 AC.
TOTAL OF SUBDIVISION	348,116°	7.9916 AC.

CURVE TABLE

NO.	LOT	RADIUS	DELTA	TAN.	ARC	CHORD	
3	₵	75.00	70°07'20"	52.65	91.79	N57°55'00"W	86.17
4	14	50.00	"	35.09	61.19	"	57.45
5	1	100.00	"	70.18	122.39	"	114.89
6	₵	175.00	"	122.81	214.18	"	201.06
7	–	200.00	"	140.36	244.77	"	229.78
"	12	"	12°49'30"	22.48	44.77	S29°16'05"E	44.67
"	13	"	38°55'10"	70.61	135.85	S55°08'25"E	133.26
"	14	"	18°22'40"	32.35	64.15	S83°47'20"E	63.88
8	–	150.00	70°07'20"	105.27	183.58	N57°55'00"W	172.34
"	1	"	42°33'50"	58.43	111.43	N71°41'45"W	108.89
"	2	"	27°33'30"	36.79	72.15	N36°38'05"W	71.45
9	₵	75.00	46°46'40"	32.44	61.23	N46°14'40"W	59.55
10	9	50.00	"	21.63	40.82	"	39.70
11	–	100.00	"	43.75	81.64	"	79.39
"	5	"	30°49'00"	27.56	53.78	N38°15'50"W	53.14
"	6	"	15°57'40"	14.02	27.86	N61°39'10"W	27.77
12	"	50.00	263°13'20"	56.30	229.70	S00°12'20"E	74.77
"	7	"	38°28'50"	17.45	33.58	N67°50'05"W	32.95
"	8	"	63°22'50"	30.87	55.31	S61°14'05"W	52.53
"	P."A"	"	64°03'30"	31.28	55.90	S02°29'05"E	53.04
"	P."B"	"	48°32'40"	22.55	42.36	S58°47'10"E	41.11
"	9	"	48°45'30"	22.66	42.55	N72°33'45"E	41.28
13	"	25.00	62°11'00"	15.08	27.13	N79°16'30"E	25.82
14	7	100.00	21°02'20"	18.57	36.72	N59°06'50"W	36.51
15	14	25.00	94°26'20"	27.02	41.21	S24°21'50"W	36.70

66. The total frontage of Lot 2, Melee Subdivision is

    (A) 129.51 ft   (C) 67.36 ft
    (B) 139.51 ft   (D) 72.15 ft

67. Which best describes the following?

A point along the easterly boundary of Melee Subdivision, which point is S 22°51'20" E 194.31 ft from the southwesterly boundary of Dominion Railroad.

    (A) A corner common to Lot 3 and Lot 4
    (B) A corner common to Lot 4 and Lot 5
    (C) A rear corner common to Lot 3 and Lot 4 and along the line of Lowden
    (D) A rear corner common to Lot 6 and Lot 7

68. Which lot has the longest frontage on Columbia Street?

    (A) Lot 14   (C) Lot 9
    (B) Lot 1   (D) Lot 2

69. Proceeding along the line common to Lots 3 and 4 from the line of Lowden to Columbia Street would best be described as

    (A) N 67°08'40" E 165.00'
    (B) N 67°08'40" E 150.00'
    (C) S 67°08'40" W 150.00'
    (D) S 67°08'40" W 165.00'

70. Which of the following statements is (are) correct?

    I. Parcels "A" and "B" would most likely be used if Ollin and Molinsky decided to develop their land.
    II. Melee Subdivision is served by city sewers.

    (A) I only   (C) Both I and II
    (B) II only   (D) Neither I nor II

Part C: Licensing Laws, Rules, and Regulations

71. Appointments to the Real Estate Commission are usually made by

    (A) the state legislature
    (B) the governor
    (C) general elections
    (D) the state association of REALTORS

72. Regarding real estate license examinations, which of the following statements is (are) correct?

    I. An applicant must pass the examination in order to be licensed.
    II. Examinations are generally scheduled according to the needs of each individual state.

    (A) I only   (C) Both I and II
    (B) II only   (D) Neither I nor II

73. Generally, real estate licensees may accept commissions from

    (A) all parties to a real estate transaction
    (B) any person, but primarily from their licensed real estate broker
    (C) only from clients whom they successfully represent
    (D) none of the above

74. Regarding Real Estate Commissions, which of the following statements is (are) correct?

    I. Commissioners are generally paid for each day they work on Commission business.
    II. Terms for commissioners are generally staggered in such a way that only a small number leave office each year.

    (A) I only   (C) Both I and II
    (B) II only   (D) Neither I nor II

75. Which of the following actions on the part of a real estate licensee could generally result in suspension or revocation of license?

    I. Any action which constitutes improper, fraudulent, or dishonest dealings.
    II. Placing a "for sale" sign on a property without permission of the owners.

    (A) I only   (C) Both I and II
    (B) II only   (D) Neither I nor II

76. A real estate recovery fund, as legislated in a growing number of real estate license laws, primarily provides

    (A) money earmarked for the further, continuing education of real estate licensees
    (B) money earmarked for research purposes to further the advancement of the real estate industry
    (C) money earmarked for customer restitution if complaints are found to be valid
    (D) none of these

77. If a real estate licensee is convicted of a felony, which of the following statements is (are) correct?

    I. The license could be suspended or revoked.
    II. The licensee could be fined or imprisoned.

    (A) I only   (C) Both I and II
    (B) II only   (D) Neither I nor II

78. Which of the following statements is (are) correct?

    I. A nonlicensed person would not usually be successful in suing to collect a real estate commission.
    II. Resident managers of apartment houses are generally not required to have real estate licenses.

    (A) I only   (C) Both I and II
    (B) II only   (D) Neither I nor II

79. When a real estate license is on an inactive status, a licensee generally

    (A) must continue to enroll in educational courses in real estate
    (B) must continue to pay the regular license renewal fees
    (C) must continue to pay the regular license renewal fees, as well as a fee to reactivate the license
    (D) none of the above

80. A real estate commission may be earned by which of the following?

    (A) Any person bringing an offer which you accept
    (B) An attorney-in-fact
    (C) An attorney-at-law
    (D) None of the above

81. Causes for suspension or revocation of a real estate license generally include

    I. denial of equal opportunity in housing by any licensee
    II. paying a nonlicensed person a portion of a sales commission for a referral

    (A) I only   (C) Both I and II
    (B) II only   (D) Neither I nor II

82. License laws generally provide for suspension or revocation of the license of any licensee who

    I. fails to give a copy of a listing to the principal immediately upon obtaining signatures on it
    II. fails to give the purchaser a copy of an offer to purchase

    (A) I only   (C) Both I and II
    (B) II only   (D) Neither I nor II

83. Qualifications for membership on the state regulatory body which is charged with enforcement of the license laws generally include

    I. previous experience as a licensed broker or salesperson for a stipulated period
    II. membership on a Board of REALTORS

(A) I only   (C) Both I and II
(B) II only   (D) Neither I nor II

84. Failure to provide a definite termination date in an exclusive listing may result in

    I. suspension or revocation of a real estate license
    II. the listing being valid until the property is sold

(A) I only   (C) Both I and II
(B) II only   (D) Neither I nor II

85. Which of the following can act as a real estate broker or salesperson without a license?

    I. A trustee
    II. An administrator

(A) I only   (C) Both I and II
(B) II only   (D) Neither I nor II

86. Funds collected by Real Estate Commissions are generally

    I. put into the state treasury
    II. kept by the Commissions to help defray the operating expenses of the Commission

(A) I only   (C) Both I and II
(B) II only   (D) Neither I nor II

87. A licensed real estate salesperson

    I. must be under the supervision of a real estate broker
    II. may have his or her license suspended or revoked if he or she makes false promises which are likely to induce a prospect to act

(A) I only   (C) Both I and II
(B) II only   (D) Neither I nor II

88. Regarding educational requirements for licensure, which of the following statements is (are) true?

    I. Proof of meeting the requirements is usually a part of the license application.
    II. Provisions for exemption by substitution of experience are often provided.

(A) I only   (C) Both I and II
(B) II only   (D) Neither I nor II

89. Which of the following can have a real estate broker's license?

    I. A person or partnership
    II. An association or corporation

(A) I only   (C) Either I or II
(B) II only   (D) Neither I nor II

90. In order to sell property belonging to an estate, the executor must

    I. have a broker's license
    II. have a salesperson's license

(A) I only   (C) Either I or II
(B) II only   (D) Neither I nor II

91. Generally, when a person is employed by a licensed real estate broker solely to collect rents and negotiate the rental of properties which the broker manages, that person

    I. should have a real estate license
    II. could be a salaried employee of the broker without having a license

(A) I only   (C) Both I and II
(B) II only   (D) Neither I nor II

92. Membership on Real Estate Commissions is generally restricted to

    I. REALTORS from specified geographic areas
    II. those active in the political affairs of the real estate associations

(A) I only   (C) Both I and II
(B) II only   (D) Neither I nor II

93. Which of the following actions by a licensed broker or salesperson would generally be cause for suspension or revocation of license?

    I. Quoting to a prospective purchaser prices or terms other than those authorized by the principal.
    II. Failing to submit to an owner a bona fide written offer, when this offer is less than one previously rejected by the owner.

(A) I only   (C) Either I or II
(B) II only   (D) Neither I nor II

94. Which of the following most nearly defines promulgate?

(A) To announce   (C) To enforce
(B) To declare   (D) To enact

95. Which, if any, of the following actions would generally be grounds for suspension or revocation of a real estate broker's license?

    I. Advertising a property, using false information regarding favorable financing available, in an effort to sell the property.

    II. Consistently selling property for a lower commission than other brokers within a particular jurisdiction.

(A) I only   (C) Both I and II

(B) II only   (D) Neither I nor II

96. A licensed real estate broker would usually be in violation of the license laws if

    I. the broker failed to produce records regarding a real estate transaction when requested to do so by a real estate commissioner or an agent of the Commission

    II. the broker failed to provide information regarding a real estate transaction when requested to do so by the Real Estate Commission or their agents

(A) I only   (C) Both I and II

(B) II only   (D) Neither I nor II

97. The state Real Estate Commission would generally be authorized to perform which of the following?

    I. Change the license examination to control the number of new licensees, especially if there are already more than a sufficient number of real estate sales agents and brokers in an area.

    II. Promulgate operating standards of the local board of REALTORS.

(A) I only   (C) Both I and II

(B) II only   (D) Neither I nor II

98. You would be likely to have your license suspended or revoked if

    I. you encouraged a prospective purchaser to purchase because you felt a profit could be made at a later date

    II. you are managing a property and charge a commission on expenditures made for the owner

(A) I only   (C) Both I and II

(B) II only   (D) Neither I nor II

99. Regarding the license laws in effect in most states, which of the following statements is (are) correct?

    I. All advertisements listing property for sale must contain the selling price of the property.

    II. A broker can legally accept other than a cash deposit on a sales contract, provided the purchaser is made aware of the form of the deposit.

(A) I only   (C) Both I and II

(B) II only   (D) Neither I nor II

100. License laws usually contain provisions whereby certain individuals who have dealings in real estate are exempt from the requirement of obtaining a real estate license. Generally included in this group is (are)

    I. officials of regulated utilities selling their personally owned property

    II. those acting under a court order to dispose of property

(A) I only   (C) Both I and II

(B) II only   (D) Neither I nor II

ANSWER KEY

Part A: Arithmetic

1. (B)	7. (D)	13. (B)	19. (B)	25. (B)
2. (B)	8. (D)	14. (B)	20. (A)	26. (D)
3. (B)	9. (A)	15. (A)	21. (C)	27. (C)
4. (A)	10. (C)	16. (B)	22. (C)	28. (D)
5. (D)	11. (B)	17. (B)	23. (C)	29. (B)
6. (D)	12. (D)	18. (C)	24. (B)	30. (A)

Suggested detailed solutions follow.

1.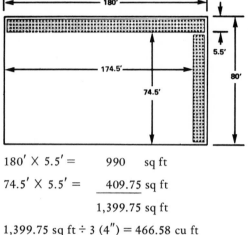

    $180' \times 5.5' = \quad\quad 990 \quad$ sq ft

    $74.5' \times 5.5' = \quad \underline{409.75}$ sq ft

    $\quad\quad\quad\quad\quad\quad 1,399.75$ sq ft

    $1,399.75$ sq ft $\div 3$ (4″) $= 466.58$ cu ft

    $466.58 \times 72¢ = \$335.94$ cost

2. $\$16,000 \times .085 = \$1,360$ per annum interest

    $\$1,360 \div 12$ months $= \$113.33$ per month interest

    March 10 to September 30 $= 6\frac{2}{3}$ months

    $\$113.33 \times 6.67 = \$755.91$ interest due

    $\$16,000 + \$755.91 = \$16,755.91$ payoff

3. Lot $60' \times 90' = 5,400$ sq ft $\div 2 = 2,700$ sq ft

    $2,700$ sq ft $\times \$1.65 = \$4,455$ sales price

4. Building $60' \times 80' = 4,800$ sq ft

    $4,800 \times \$22.50 = \$108,000$ cost

5. From August 30 last year to February 20 next year =
    1 year, 5 months, and 10 days, or 17.33 months

    36 months $- 17.33$ months $= 18.67$ months unused

    $\$389 \div 36$ months $= \$10.81$ per month

    $18.67 \times \$10.81 = \$201.82$ refund due

6. Lot $90' \times 160' = 14,400$ sq ft $\div 43,560$ sq ft (1
    acre) $= .33$

7.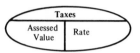

Income	
Rate	Value

    $\$145,000 \times .12 = \$17,400$ net income required

    $\$17,400 + \$2,600 = \$20,000$ gross income required

    $\$20,000 \div 10$ apartments $= \$2,000$ per apartment per
    year required

    $\$2,000 \div 12$ months $= \$166.67$ per apartment per
    month

    Answer, therefore, is (D)

8. $239,580$ sq ft $\times .17 = \$40,728.60$ cost

    $239,580$ sq ft $\div 43,560 = 5.5$ acres $\times 2$ ($\frac{1}{2}$-acre
    lots) $= 11$ lots

    11 lots $\times \$3,500 = \$38,500$ sales price

    $\$40,728.60$ cost $- \$38,500$ sales price $= \$2,228.60$
    loss

9.
Taxes	
Assessed Value	Rate

    $\$18,000$ value $\times .33 = \$5,940$ assessment

    $\$5,940 \div 100 = 59.4$ hundreds

    $\$378$ taxes $\div 59.4 = \$6.36$ per hundred rate

10.
Present Value	
Original Value	1 − % Total Depreciation

    Depreciation $1.5\% \times 12$ years $= 18\%$ total

    $\$33,000 \times .82$ (100% − 18%) $= \quad\quad \$27,060$

    Value of lot today $= \$3,500 + \$4,500 = \quad \underline{8,000}$

    Total value today $\quad\quad\quad\quad\quad \$35,060$

11. Convert in to feet (1 in $=$ 4 ft)

    $8.5'' \times 4 = 34$ ft

    $9.75'' \times 4 = 39$ ft

    34 ft $\times 39$ ft $= 1,326$ sq ft

12. $\$20,500 + \$12,500 + \$22,000 = \$55,000$ taken by
    three owners

    $\$88,000$ cost $- \$55,000 = \$33,000$ left for fourth
    owner

    $\dfrac{\$33,000}{\$88,000} = \dfrac{3}{8}$

13. $5,760$ gal $\div 15$ A/Cs $= 384$ gal used by 1 A/C in 8 hr

    $384 \div 8$ hr $= 48$ gal used by 1 A/C in 1 hr

    48 gal $\times 3$ hr $= 144$ gal used by 1 A/C in 3 hr

    $7,920 \div 144$ gal $= 55$ A/Cs required

14.

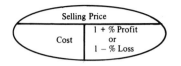

$43,050 sales price ÷ (100% + 23%) = $43,050 ÷ 1.23 = $35,000 cost

15.

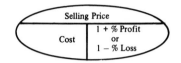

$43,250 cost × (100% + 13%) = $43,250 × 1.13 = $48,872.50 sales price

16. $2,575 − $500 salary = $2,075 from sales, which equals 5% of total

$2,075 ÷ .05 = $41,500 in real estate sales

17.

$84 per month × 10 apartments = $840 per month income

$840 × 12 months = $10,080 gross annual income

$10,080 − $1,440 = $8,640 net annual income

$8,640 ÷ $72,000 = .12 = 12% rate of return

18. $\frac{3}{16}$ = 3 ÷ 16 =   18.75% in oats

      18.75% in wheat

.125 =   12.5% in house and barn

      50%

100% − 50% = 50% left for the 320 acres in corn

320 ÷ .50 = 640 acres total

19.

$18,000 + $23,450 + $1,085 = $42,535

$42,535 = 94% of sales price

$42,535 ÷ .94 = $45,250 sales price

20. $278.40 ÷ 12 months = $23.20 per month taxes

January 1 to May 10 = $4\frac{1}{3}$ months

$23.20 × 4.33 = $100.46 credit to buyer and debit to seller

21.

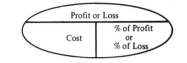

$28,600 sales price − $22,000 cost = $6,600 profit

$6,600 ÷ $22,000 = .30 = 30% profit

22. $23,500 × .09 = $2,115 per annum interest

$2,115 ÷ 12 months = $176.25 per month interest

$250 payment − $176.25 interest = $73.75 principal reduction

23.

Value $37,500 × .45 assessment ratio = $16,875 assessment

$16,875 ÷ 100 = 168.75 hundreds

168.75 × $4.30 = $725.63 taxes

24.

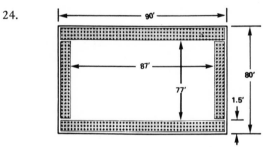

90′ × 1.5′ × 2 = 270 sq ft

77′ × 1.5′ × 2 = 231 sq ft

      501 sq ft

501 × 1.5′ depth = 751.5 cu ft

751.5 ÷ 27 = 27.83 cu yd

25.

$107.70 × 12 months = $1,292.40 per annum interest

$1,292.40 ÷ $23,500 = .055 = 5.5% interest rate

26. 70′ + 90′ + 70′ + 90′ = 320 linear feet

320′ ÷ 10′ (spacing) = 32 posts required

27. $72,000 × 6% = $4,320 − $1,450 expenses = $2,870 net to broker

$68,000 × 6% = $4,080 − $1,200 expenses = $2,880 net to broker

$57,000 × 6% = $3,420 − $530 expenses = $2,890 net to broker

28.

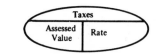

$120,000 \times .60 = \$72,000$ assessment

$72,000 \div 100 = 720$ hundreds

$720 \times \$4.30$ rate $= \$3,096$ taxes

29. $26,000 \times 10\% = \$2,600$ reduction

$2,600 \times 5\% = \$130$ loss

30.   8 lots $\times \$6,200 = \$49,600$ cost

$49,600 + \$8,500$ profit $= \$58,100$ sales price required

$58,100 \div 7$ lots $= \$8,300$ sales price per lot

Part B: Comprehension of Real Estate Subject Matter

31. (C)	39. (A)	47. (C)	55. (A)	63. (D)
32. (B)	40. (C)	48. (D)	56. (D)	64. (B)
33. (D)	41. (C)	49. (C)	57. (B)	65. (A)
34. (D)	42. (B)	50. (B)	58. (C)	66. (B)
35. (B)	43. (B)	51. (C)	59. (B)	67. (C)
36. (D)	44. (A)	52. (D)	60. (D)	68. (B)
37. (B)	45. (B)	53. (D)	61. (A)	69. (D)
38. (B)	46. (A)	54. (D)	62. (B)	70. (C)

Part C: Licensing Laws, Rules, and Regulations

71. (B)	77. (C)	83. (A)	89. (C)	95. (A)
72. (C)	78. (C)	84. (A)	90. (D)	96. (C)
73. (D)	79. (C)	85. (D)	91. (A)	97. (D)
74. (C)	80. (D)	86. (A)	92. (D)	98. (D)
75. (C)	81. (C)	87. (C)	93. (C)	99. (D)
76. (C)	82. (C)	88. (C)	94. (B)	100. (C)

PRACTICE FINAL EXAMINATION: BROKER

Part A: Instrument Preparation

In this part of the practice final examination for the broker's license, the applicant is asked to complete an Exclusive Authorization to Sell, an Offer to Purchase Agreement, and a Settlement Statement from the problems given. After the applicant has completed the forms, the problems are returned to the examiner, who gives the applicant a set of questions which must be answered from the information contained from the three completed forms. (Use forms following Index.)

Therefore, when completing this portion of the practice examination, do not refer back to the problems once the forms have been completed and you have started to answer the questions.

LISTING PROBLEM

On March 15, this year, you as agent for Sellmore Realty Company obtain a 120-day listing on property located at 3418 Anders Street, Anytown, Hope County, Your State, belonging to Edward B. Dobbs and his wife, Edna R. It is a 3-bedroom, 2-bath brick rambler on a $100' \times 90'$ lot. There is a side screened porch and a 2-car garage. It has a $12' \times 20'$ living room, a $10' \times 12'$ dining room, and a $12' \times 12'$ den with fireplace. There is table space in the kitchen, which has a built-in oven, range, and refrigerator. Also included are washer and dryer.

Taxes of $314.40 for the year, due January 1, have not been paid. The first trust balance as of April 1 is $28,500, payable in equal monthly installments to P & I of $233.80 to First National Savings and Loan Association at 7% interest. The loan is assumable with a $50.00 charge to the purchaser. If prepaid there is a penalty of 1% of the balance so prepaid.

The owners want to list the property at a price which will net them $4,000 after paying off the first trust, your 6% fee, and $3,220 they owe on a car.

The legal description is Lot 6, Section 8, Fairhope Subdivision. The owners state they will remove the living room chandelier. They also want to sell the lawnmower for $50 under a separate bill of sale.

OFFER TO PURCHASE PROBLEM
(Refers to Listing Problem)

On May 15, this year, you show the Dobbs house to Elmer A. Friend and his wife, Eleanor B., who offer to purchase it for $37,500, with the seller keeping the washer and dryer. They want to refinance the property with 10% down, a new 80% first trust for 30 years at 8% interest, and the owner taking back the balance in a second trust for 5 years at 8% interest. They agree to pay $1\frac{1}{2}$ points loan placement fee, and the sellers will have to pay 1. They give you a deposit of $1,000 by check.

They also agree to the other terms of the listing, with settlement at the office of Bean and Jones on June 15, this year.

The Dobbs agree to these terms and sign the Offer to Purchase.

SETTLEMENT PROBLEM
(Refers to Listing and Offer to Purchase Problems)

Settlement of the Dobbs to Friend contract is scheduled as per terms of the contract. In addition to items covered in the listing and contract, the following is furnished for your information.

The first trust balance has been reduced to $28,300. The purchaser is placing a new insurance policy which costs $112.00. The lenders insist that the purchaser furnish them with a mortgagee's title insurance policy in the amount of the loan, which costs $2.50 per thousand; the lenders also want interest on the first trust in advance from the date of settlement to the first of the following month. In addition, they require a tax escrow of 2 months taxes.

After you have completed the required forms, answer Questions 1 to 30.

1. The listed price of the Dobbs home is

   (A) $38,500   (C) $37,860
   (B) $38,000   (D) none are within $50.00

2. The listing will expire

   (A) January 15 next year
   (B) March 15 this year
   (C) July 15 this year
   (D) June 15 this year

3. The monthly principal and interest payments on the present loan would be closest to

   (A) $233   (C) $190
   (B) $200   (D) $180

4. The exterior of the Dobbs house is

   (A) frame   (C) stone
   (B) brick   (D) none of these

5. Regarding equipment to be left with the Dobbs house at the time of the listing, which of the following statements is (are) true?

   I. The washer and dryer are included.
   II. The range and refrigerator are not included.

   (A) I only   (C) Both I and II
   (B) II only   (D) Neither I nor II

6. What item normally considered real estate is being removed by the seller?

   (A) Washer   (C) Chandelier
   (B) Dryer   (D) Shrubs

7. From the listing information, which of the following statements is (are) true?

   I. There are 3 bedrooms, 2 downstairs and 1 upstairs.
   II. There are 2 baths, 1 on the main floor and 1 in the basement.

   (A) I only   (C) Both I and II
   (B) II only   (D) Neither I nor II

8. Regarding the existing trust, which of the following statements is (are) true?

   I. The mortgagor is a savings & loan.
   II. The interest rate is 7% per annum.

   (A) I only   (C) Both I and II
   (B) II only   (D) Neither I nor II

9. Included in the Dobbs house is

   I. a carport
   II. a garage

   (A) I only   (C) Both I and II
   (B) II only   (D) Neither I nor II

10. According to the listing, the seller is willing to

    I. give immediate possession
    II. sell the carpets separately

    (A) I only   (C) Both I and II
    (B) II only   (D) Neither I nor II

11. The total down payment in the Offer to Purchase is

    (A) $2,750   (C) $3,750
    (B) $7,500   (D) none are within $100

12. The earnest money deposit is

    (A) $1,000 by cash   (C) $1,500 by cash
    (B) $1,000 by check   (D) $1,500 by note

13. The second trust being taken back by the seller is at _____% per annum.

    (A) $8\frac{1}{2}$ (C) 8
    (B) $7\frac{1}{2}$ (D) 7

14. According to the Offer to Purchase Agreement, which of the following statements regarding the loan placement fee is correct?

    (A) The purchaser is to pay $562.50.
    (B) The seller is to pay $562.50.
    (C) The purchaser is to pay $450.
    (D) The seller is to pay $450.

15. The sales fee to the broker for services will be

    (A) $1,875   (C) $2,250
    (B) $2,280   (D) none are within $100

16. The Dobbs to Friend contract will settle

    (A) in the broker's office
    (B) at Bean and Jones
    (C) at Smith and Jones
    (D) not specified

17. The purchaser at settlement will

    (A) purchase the garden tractor for $100
    (B) purchase the garden tractor for $50
    (C) purchase the lawn mower for $100
    (D) none of the above

18. The new first trust will be for

    (A) 30 years @ $8\frac{1}{2}$%   (C) 30 years @ 8%
    (B) 25 years @ 8%   (D) 25 years @ $7\frac{1}{2}$%

19. The seller is taking back a second trust for

    (A) $2,750   (C) $4,750
    (B) $3,750   (D) none of the above

20. Settlement is scheduled for

    (A) July 15   (C) June 15
    (B) March 15   (D) none of the above

21. The total amount of the buyer's debits is

    (A) $38,284.40   (C) $38,384.40
    (B) $38,339.40   (D) none are within $20.00

22. The total number of the buyer's debits and credits are

    (A) 6 debits, 5 credits
    (B) 5 credits, 5 debits
    (C) 7 debits, 5 credits
    (D) none of the above

23. The tax proration is

    (A) $170.30 credit to seller, $170.30 debit to buyer
    (B) $170.30 credit to buyer, $170.30 debit to seller
    (C) $144.10 debit to buyer, $144.10 credit to seller
    (D) $144.10 credit to buyer, $144.10 debit to seller

24. The interest from date of settlement to the end of the month debited to buyer is

    (A) $210   (C) $218.75
    (B) $100   (D) none of these

25. The total amount of the seller's debits is

    (A) $37,550   (C) $37,257
    (B) $37,250   (D) $37,405.09

26. The total number of the seller's debits and credits are

    (A) 2 credits, 5 debits
    (B) 5 debits, 2 credits
    (C) 7 debits, 2 credits
    (D) 6 credits, 2 debits

27. The tax escrow is

    (A) $52.40, debited to buyer
    (B) $52.40, credited to seller
    (C) $52.40, debited to seller
    (D) none of the above

28. Points paid in the transaction are

    (A) $300 debit to seller, $450 debit to buyer
    (B) $450 credit to seller, $300 credit to buyer
    (C) $450 debit to seller, $300 debit to buyer
    (D) none of these are correct

29. Balance due from buyer to close is

    (A) $3,500.32   (C) $3,400.30
    (B) $3,445.30   (D) none are within $25

30. Balance of cash due seller from settlement

    (A) $2,572.90   (C) $2,522.90
    (B) $2,472.90   (D) $2,805.90

Part B: Arithmetic

31. The house shown below cost $21 per square foot to construct 8 years ago. Today it would cost $28 per square foot. What is the percentage of increase in construction costs?

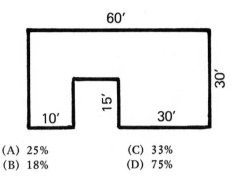

(A) 25%   (C) 33%
(B) 18%   (D) 75%

32. An investor purchased 65 acres at a price of $1,200 per acre. Taxes on the property for 5 years have averaged $600 annually. What must the selling price be to make a net profit of 12% on the total investment?

(A) $9,720   (C) $87,360
(B) $90,720   (D) none are within $2,000

33. A broker lists a property for $48,000. A prospective purchaser offers $46,000 with a new loan of $40,000, which the seller accepts. Assuming a brokerage fee of 5%, 3 points discount, and other closing costs to the seller of $700, how much will the seller net?

(A) $42,000   (C) $41,620
(B) $41,800   (D) $43,460

34. You are constructing a new house. The excavation for the basement is 24 ft by 48 ft. The basement height is 8 ft and will be about one-half above the existing grade. How many cubic yards of dirt must you remove?

(A) 341
(B) 460
(C) 171
(D) none are within 10 cu yd

35. You borrow $2,800 at 11% interest January 1 of this year. If no payments have been made, how much do you owe as of August 1?

(A) $3,104   (C) $2,980
(B) $3,056   (D) $2,954

36. What is the amount of a trust if the interest rate is 9.5% and the monthly payment to interest is $344.38?

(A) $43,500   (C) $41,325
(B) $34,400   (D) None are within $1,500

37. Annual taxes on a property were $756 and were prepaid for the calendar year. What refund would the seller be due if the property were sold May 15?

(A) $383.50   (C) $630.50
(B) $409.50   (D) $472.50

38. If you purchased a property 5 years ago for $28,000 and it has appreciated in value 6% per annum, what is its value today?

(A) $34,600   (C) $37,600
(B) $38,900   (D) $36,400

39. If you purchased a property 6 years ago for $44,000 and sold it this year for $38,000, what was the percentage of loss?

(A) 16%   (C) 15%
(B) 14%   (D) None are within 2%

40. A property sold for $35,000, which included a profit of 15%. What did the property cost?

(A) $30,435   (C) $31,450
(B) $29,750   (D) None are within $800

41. A building measures 40′ × 60′ around the exterior. The walls are 6 in thick. There are 8 interior posts 1 ft square. What is the clear floor area of the building?

(A) 2,293 sq ft   (C) 2,274 sq ft
(B) 2,156 sq ft   (D) 2,282 sq ft

42. If you purchase 196,020 sq ft of land at 18¢ per square foot, divide it into ¼-acre lots, and sell them for $1,800 each, how much profit will you make?

(A) $1,960
(B) $2,883
(C) $4,500
(D) None of these are correct

43. You list a property at a price which will net the owner $30,000 after paying $710 expenses of sale, the present first trust of $13,000, and your 6% commission. What is the listing price?

(A) $47,500   (C) $46,330
(B) $43,710   (D) $46,500

44. An office building has a net return of $43,000 per annum after paying annual expenses of $22,000. If it is paying a 12% return on the investment, what is the investment?

(A) $183,333   (C) $541,666
(B) $358,333   (D) $279,070

45. If you borrow $52,000 and have to pay $368.33 per month interest, what is the interest rate?

   (A) 8.5%   (C) 9.0%
   (B) 8.0%   (D) 7.5%

46. If you draw $2,420 this month, $530 of which is salary, and get 3% commission on your real estate sales, how much real estate did you sell?

   (A) $80,666   (C) $17,666
   (B) $63,000   (D) $66,000

47. You purchase property with an 80% loan at 9.5% per annum. If your first monthly interest payment is $395.83, what was the purchase price?

   (A) $50,000   (C) $60,000
   (B) $55,000   (D) $62,500

48. The lot shown below cost $20,000. If it sold for $2.00 per square foot, what was the percentage of profit?

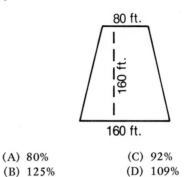

   (A) 80%   (C) 92%
   (B) 125%   (D) 109%

49. You dig a footing for a building, the outside measurements of which are 50 ft by 30 ft. If the footing is 12 in wide and 18 in deep, how many cubic yards of concrete will you need?

   (A) 23.4   (C) 8.67
   (B) 16.0   (D) 86.0

50. You receive a commission of $1,285.35 from listing and selling a property. If you are paid 25% for listing and 30% for selling, what was the selling price if the commission rate is 6%?

   (A) $17,520   (C) $21,420
   (B) $38,950   (D) $47,605

Part C: Real Estate Transactions

51. A contract of sale entered into for the performance of an act which is prohibited by law, would be

    (A) valid
    (B) void
    (C) voidable
    (D) none of the above

52. Because of a statute of frauds, an oral contract for the sale of real estate

    I. cannot be used as a basis of transfer of ownership
    II. is enforceable if one party breaches the terms of agreement

    (A) I only
    (B) II only
    (C) Both I and II
    (D) Neither I nor II

53. An owner of property has received $1,000 in exchange for his agreement to sell the property on stipulated terms to Jones, should Jones decide to purchase. The owner has entered into a (an)

    (A) offer to purchase
    (B) option
    (C) binder
    (D) none of these

54. An agency agreement can be terminated by

    I. revocation by the principal
    II. bankruptcy of the broker

    (A) I only
    (B) II only
    (C) Both I and II
    (D) Neither I nor II

55. An owner's title insurance policy terminates

    I. when the purchaser dies
    II. when the purchaser sells the property

    (A) I only
    (B) II only
    (C) Both I and II
    (D) Neither I nor II

56. In order to have a valid contract certain essentials are required to be present. They include

    I. offer and acceptance and words of conveyance
    II. reality of consent and legal capacity to contract

    (A) I only
    (B) II only
    (C) Both I and II
    (D) Neither I nor II

57. A single-family residence located in a neighborhood which has many commercial and industrial uses suffers from

    (A) overimprovement
    (B) economic obsolescence
    (C) functional obsolescence
    (D) none of the above

58. If a contract was obtained under threat of personal injury, it was

    (A) obtained by duress and would be voidable
    (B) obtained by duress and would be void
    (C) obtained by undue influence and would be voidable
    (D) none of the above

59. If an original warranty deed is defective, the grantor is obligated to execute another deed correcting the defect without additional payment under a

    (A) covenant of seisin
    (B) covenant against encumbrances
    (C) covenant of further assurance
    (D) none of the above

60. Concurrent ownership of property could be

    I. joint tenancy
    II. tenancy in common

    (A) I only
    (B) II only
    (C) Either I or II
    (D) Neither I nor II

61. With regard to a deed, which of the following statements is (are) correct?

    (A) The deed must be recorded in order to transfer title.
    (B) It is good policy to include the property address.
    (C) The grantee and his wife must execute the deed in order to ensure a valid transfer of title.
    (D) All the above are correct.

62. Assuming there are no contractual terms covering the event, if a fire destroys an improvement to property between the date of the contract of sale and the date of closing, which of the following would be correct?

    (A) The purchaser must proceed with the purchase.
    (B) The seller is not obligated to rebuild.
    (C) Neither A nor B is correct.
    (D) Both A and B are correct.

63. The provisions of the Civil Rights Act

    I. apply throughout the United States
    II. apply to all persons, whether they are real estate licensees or members of the public

    (A) I only
    (B) II only
    (C) Both I and II
    (D) Neither I nor II

64. Regarding obsolescence, which of the following statements is (are) true?

    I. Economic obsolescence is generally not curable.
    II. Functional obsolescence is generally within the property and may or may not be curable.

    (A) I only   (C) Both I and II
    (B) II only   (D) Neither I nor II

65. The difference between reproduction cost new and the present value of a property is best described as

    (A) depreciation   (C) cost approach
    (B) obsolescence   (D) physical deterioration

66. The Federal Fair Housing Laws

    I. prohibit inducing fear among property owners so that they will move when members of a minority group move into the neighborhood
    II. do not apply to members of minority groups when they are selling or renting their own property

    (A) I only   (C) Both I and II
    (B) II only   (D) Neither I nor II

67. The act of estimating value from expected future income is best described as

    (A) remaining economic life
    (B) capitalization
    (C) speculation
    (D) none of these

68. The most profitable likely use of a property, the one which will yield the greatest return to land, is best described as

    (A) the best economic life
    (B) the highest and best use
    (C) the consistent use theory
    (D) the principle of substitution

69. Regarding FHA loans, which of the following statements is (are) true?

    I. Down payments must generally be from the purchaser's assets.
    II. The seller can take back a second trust when selling and allowing an existing FHA loan to be assumed.

    (A) I only   (C) Both I and II
    (B) II only   (D) Neither I nor II

70. In the event a grantor takes back a portion of the sales price in the form of a trust, which of the following statements is (are) correct?

    I. The seller is taking back a purchase money note.
    II. In the event of a foreclosure, the seller is in a riskier position than the first trust holder.

    (A) I only   (C) Both I and II
    (B) II only   (D) Neither I nor II

71. A written instrument used to transfer right, title, and interest in personal property to another would most likely be a

    (A) chattel mortgage   (C) bill of sale
    (B) binder   (D) none of these

72. A purchaser is induced by fraud to enter into a contract to purchase real estate. The purchaser can probably have the contract declared

    (A) valid   (C) negotiable
    (B) expressed   (D) void

73. The interest or estate a tenant obtains by virtue of a lease is

    I. a leasehold estate
    II. personal property

    (A) I only   (C) Both I and II
    (B) II only   (D) Neither I nor II

74. Which of the following is out of place?

    (A) Tenancy at will
    (B) Tenancy by the entireties
    (C) Tenancy for years
    (D) Tenancy by sufferance

75. Which of the following is out of place?

    (A) Execution, delivery–contract
    (B) Contract–reality of consent
    (C) Deed–English covenants
    (D) Offer and acceptance–contract

76. An express contract can be

    I. oral
    II. written

    (A) I only   (C) Either I or II
    (B) II only   (D) Neither I nor II

77. Which of the following is found in a quitclaim deed?

    I. The terms "grant," "bargain," "sell," and "convey"
    II. A granting clause

    (A) I only   (C) Both I and II
    (B) II only   (D) Neither I nor II

78. Which of the following statements is (are) correct?

    (A) A tenancy for years is the most common leasehold interest.
    (B) A tenancy from year to year is most often created by a tenant staying on after a tenancy for years.
    (C) A tenancy for years and a tenancy from year to year are considered personal property.
    (D) All the above are correct.

79. An owner listing property restricts the sale to persons of a specific religious group. You, as the broker, should

    I. refuse to accept the listing
    II. accept the listing, but ignore the owner's request

    (A) I only   (C) Either I or II
    (B) II only   (D) Neither I nor II

80. An owner has entered into a valid contract to sell but has refused to fulfill the terms of the contract. The purchaser can

    I. initiate court action for specific performance
    II. sue for actual damages incurred because of the owner's failure to perform

    (A) I only   (C) Either I or II
    (B) II only   (D) Neither I nor II

81. An owner appoints an agent, but retains the right to sell without paying a commission. Such a listing is probably

    (A) illegal
    (B) an exclusive agency
    (C) an exclusive authorization to sell
    (D) a multiple listing

82. The extent of the interest that a person has in land is best described as a (an)

    (A) lien   (C) freehold
    (B) estate   (D) fee

83. Which of the following statements is (are) correct?

    I. A life estate can be created by law, by will, or by contract.
    II. A life estate cannot be sold.

    (A) I only   (C) Both I and II
    (B) II only   (D) Neither I nor II

84. The right to use another's land can be which of the following?

    I. An easement appurtenant
    II. An easement-in-gross

    (A) I only   (C) Either I or II
    (B) II only   (D) Neither I nor II

85. Which of the following is out of place?

    (A) Words of conveyance
    (B) Grantor
    (C) Covenants
    (D) Vendor

86. In the event a borrower fails to make mortgage payments, a mortgagee can usually recover property pledged as security sooner

    (A) under a mortgage
    (B) if a quitclaim deed has been used
    (C) if a release deed has been used
    (D) if a deed of trust has been used

87. The term "government-backed loans" would apply to which of the following?

    I. Federal Housing Administration loans
    II. A loan from a federally chartered savings and loan

    (A) I only   (C) Both I and II
    (B) II only   (D) Neither I nor II

88. The terms "mortgage insurance premium," "insured," and "no prepayment penalty" would suggest which of the following types of loan?

    (A) VA   (C) FHA
    (B) Conventional   (D) All the above

89. Possession of property which is inconsistent with and detrimental to the rights of the owner is best described as

    (A) tenancy by sufferance
    (B) adverse possession
    (C) undue influence
    (D) exclusive possession

90. Which of the following statements is (are) correct?

    I. A title insurance policy is not needed if a competent title search has been made.
    II. A certificate of title from a competent attorney affords as much protection as a title insurance policy.

    (A) I only   (C) Both I and II
    (B) II only   (D) Neither I nor II

91. The terms "loyalty," "notice," and "fiduciary responsibility" would apply to

    I. a principal in an agency agreement
    II. an appraiser

    (A) I only   (C) Both I and II
    (B) II only   (D) Neither I nor II

92. Which of the following is out of place?

    (A) Contract–agency
    (B) Administrator–will
    (C) Agent–broker
    (D) Bilateral–contract

93. The term "conveyance" is best described as

    (A) a release   (C) an instrument
    (B) transportation   (D) to take

94. Which of the following types of loans reacts most rapidly to changes in the economy?

    (A) Government-backed loans
    (B) Conventional loans
    (C) Straight loans
    (D) Amortized loans

95. In government-backed loans, which of the following statements is (are) correct?

      I. The interest rates are adjusted according to the rise and fall of the cost of living index.
     II. A second trust is never allowed when the loan is originated.

    (A) I only   (C) Both I and II
    (B) II only   (D) Neither I nor II

96. An appraisal technique that considers the relationship between the value of a property and the amount of rent that property can command in the marketplace makes use of

    (A) the income approach
    (B) a gross rent multiplier
    (C) economic life
    (D) capitalization

97. After considering the three approaches to value, the appraiser should

    (A) average the three appraisals to arrive at the estimate of value
    (B) place the greatest reliance on the cost approach
    (C) place most reliance on the one approach most relevant to the purpose of the appraisal
    (D) none of the above

98. Should the state or governing authorities desire to take private property to be used for the benefit of the public, they have the right to do so under

    (A) escheat   (C) adverse possession
    (B) condemnation   (D) none of these

99. To devise is to transfer property by

    (A) deed   (C) will
    (B) trust agreement   (D) adverse possession

100. Which of the following statements is (are) correct?

      I. Coverage under an owner's policy of title insurance declines as the loan declines.
     II. Coverage under a mortgagee policy of title insurance remains constant.

    (A) I only   (C) Both I and II
    (B) II only   (D) Neither I nor II

Part D: Licensing Laws, Rules, and Regulations

101. Procedures prior to suspension or revocation of any real estate license normally include

    I. a request for the licensee's answer to the complaint
    II. reasonable notice of the date and place for any hearing

    (A) I only   (C) Both I and II
    (B) II only   (D) Neither I nor II

102. Making false promises in an effort to persuade would

    I. be considered good sales techniques
    II. probably be cause for suspension or revocation of license

    (A) I only   (C) Both I and II
    (B) II only   (D) Neither I nor II

103. In most jurisdictions, which of the following statements is (are) correct?

    I. Violation of the license laws is a misdemeanor.
    II. A licensee who violates the license laws as well as the civil or criminal laws could have his or her real estate license suspended or revoked and then be charged under the civil or criminal laws of the state.

    (A) I only   (C) Both I and II
    (B) II only   (D) Neither I nor II

104. Real Estate Commissions are generally given the authority to

    I. enforce and administer the license laws
    II. publish rules and regulations

    (A) I only   (C) Both I and II
    (B) II only   (D) Neither I nor II

105. Regarding qualification for licensure, which of the following statements is (are) correct?

    I. The applicant must prove his or her competence to transact the business for which he or she is applying for licensure.
    II. The applicant must have citizens attest to his or her character and honesty.

    (A) I only   (C) Both I and II
    (B) II only   (D) Neither I nor II

106. A licensed real estate salesperson

    I. is employed either directly or indirectly by a real estate broker
    II. may work from his or her own place of business

    (A) I only   (C) Both I and II
    (B) II only   (D) Neither I nor II

107. Funds coming into a broker's possession which belong to others must generally be placed

    I. in an insured depository
    II. in a safety deposit box

    (A) I only   (C) Both I and II
    (B) II only   (D) Neither I nor II

108. License laws generally include provisions which prohibit

    I. using the trade name of an association or organization in advertising unless the person using it is actually a member of that association
    II. a broker from ever collecting a commission from both parties to a transaction

    (A) I only   (C) Both I and II
    (B) II only   (D) Neither I nor II

109. Real Estate Commissions are generally authorized and created by

    (A) the state association of REALTORS
    (B) the license laws
    (C) the rules and regulations of the state association
    (D) the governor

110. Real estate licenses, once issued, generally

    I. remain in effect for limited and definite terms only
    II. allow the holder to open a real estate office

    (A) I only   (C) Both I and II
    (B) II only   (D) Neither I nor II

111. Should a real estate broker have a license suspended or revoked, which of the following statements is (are) correct?

    I. The salespeople working for that broker would, in effect, be put out of business, pending transfer to another broker.
    II. The broker is usually given 60 days to complete contracts being processed, before the suspension or revocation becoming effective.

    (A) I only   (C) Both I and II
    (B) II only   (D) Neither I nor II

112. Any person should have a license who for compensation for others sells or leases or attempts to sell or lease which of the following?

    I. Leasehold interests
    II. Freehold interests

    (A) I only   (C) Both I and II
    (B) II only   (D) Neither I nor II

113. A real estate licensee can lose a license for

    I. violating the statute of limitations
    II. immoral conduct

    (A) I only
    (B) II only
    (C) Both I and II
    (D) Neither I nor II

114. Which of the following would constitute "acting" as a broker or salesperson?

    I. Selling property for a friend when authorized to do so by a power of attorney
    II. Attempting, but failing, to sell property for a friend, expecting to receive a small amount of money if successful

    (A) I only
    (B) II only
    (C) Both I and II
    (D) Neither I nor II

115. You must have a real estate license if you

    I. buy or offer to buy, lease or offer to lease, real estate
    II. negotiate the purchase or sale of real estate

    (A) I only
    (B) II only
    (C) Both I and II
    (D) Neither I nor II

116. A person authorized to perform limited or specified acts for another would best be described as

    (A) an attorney-at-law
    (B) an agent
    (C) a principal
    (D) an attorney-in-fact

117. Regarding the regulatory bodies whose duties include enforcement of the real estate license laws, which of the following statements is (are) correct?

    I. The regulatory body is generally given broadly defined powers and duties.
    II. Members of the regulatory body are usually appointed by the governor of the state.

    (A) I only
    (B) II only
    (C) Both I and II
    (D) Neither I nor II

118. Regarding license laws, which of the following statements is (are) correct?

    I. All states except two have some form of license laws.
    II. Many states have patterned their license laws after the suggested Model Real Estate License Law.

    (A) I only
    (B) II only
    (C) Both I and II
    (D) Neither I nor II

119. You and a fellow REALTOR have a dispute over which was the procuring cause of a real estate sale. Which of the following statements is (are) correct?

    (A) You should immediately send a report to the state real estate regulatory body.
    (B) You should make a report to the local real estate board.
    (C) You should file a suit in the local court.
    (D) You should take whichever of the above actions is most likely to get you the commission.

120. Which of the following statements is (are) correct?

    I. The acceptance of a commission or rebate on expenditures made for a principal is prohibited, without exception.
    II. Payment of a sales commission directly to a real estate salesperson by the seller is not usually a violation of the license laws.

    (A) I only
    (B) II only
    (C) Both 1 and II
    (D) Neither I nor II

121. Which of the following statements is (are) correct regarding a salaried employee of a builder specifically employed to sell properties the builder is constructing?

    I. The employee must be licensed.
    II. The employee cannot be paid a commission without violating the license laws.

    (A) I only
    (B) II only
    (C) Both I and II
    (D) Neither I nor II

122. Read the following statements:

    I. "Licenses shall be granted only to persons who are competent to transact the business for which they are seeking licensure and who have a reputation for honesty, truthfulness, and fair dealing."
    II. "Salesperson applicants usually must have a sponsoringbroker before they can be licensed."

    (A) Both statements are correct.
    (B) Both statements are false.
    (C) One statement is correct, one is false.
    (D) None of the above answers is correct.

123. Paying the personnel director of a corporation monies for leads would generally cause a real estate licensee to

    I. be in violation of the license laws
    II. be in violation of the criminal laws of the state

    (A) I only
    (B) II only
    (C) Both I and II
    (D) Neither I nor II

124. Licenses of real estate salespersons are generally

    I. carried by the salesperson whenever he or she is engaged in real estate activities
    II. held by the Real Estate Commission

(A) I only   (C) Both I and II
(B) II only   (D) Neither I nor II

125. Which of the following statements is (are) correct with regard to funds which a real estate broker is holding for others?

    I. The funds may be used as collateral, but may not be spent.
    II. The funds must be in an interest-bearing account.

(A) I only   (C) Both I and II
(B) II only   (D) Neither I nor II

126. Real estate license laws are applicable to

    I. any person who has a real estate license
    II. any person

(A) I only   (C) Both I and II
(B) II only   (D) Neither I nor II

127. An unlicensed secretary employed by a broker can

    I. take listings from clients over the phone, but not show property
    II. help a salesperson to negotiate leases with prospective tenants

(A) I only   (C) Both I and II
(B) II only   (D) Neither I nor II

128. Should a broker's license be suspended or revoked, what effect if any, does this have on the salespersons working for that broker?

    I. They may continue to operate pending transfer of their licenses to another broker.
    II. They may continue to operate for a reasonable time, usually 90 days.

(A) I only   (C) Both I and II
(B) II only   (D) Neither I nor II

129. Which of the following acts would generally be in violation of the real estate license laws?

    I. Owners selling their own property.
    II. A relative of an owner who sells the owner's property when acting as an attorney-in-fact.

(A) I only   (C) Both I and II
(B) II only   (D) Neither I nor II

130. The term "REALTOR" applies to which of the following?

(A) Any person who has a broker's license.
(B) Any person who has either a broker's or a salesperson's license.
(C) Both A and B
(D) Neither A nor B

ANSWER KEY

Part A: Instrument Preparation

1. (B)	7. (D)	13. (C)	19. (B)	25. (A)
2. (C)	8. (B)	14. (C)	20. (C)	26. (C)
3. (A)	9. (B)	15. (C)	21. (B)	27. (A)
4. (B)	10. (D)	16. (B)	22. (C)	28. (A)
5. (A)	11. (C)	17. (D)	23. (D)	29. (B)
6. (C)	12. (B)	18. (C)	24. (B)	30. (C)

See suggested solutions to Exclusive Authorization to Sell, Offer to Purchase, and Settlement Statement, which follow.

EXCLUSIVE AUTHORIZATION TO SELL

SALES PRICE: $38,000 TYPE HOME _Rambler_ TOTAL BEDROOMS 3 TOTAL BATHS 2

ADDRESS: _3418 Anders St., Anytown_ JURISDICTION OF: _Hope County_

AMT. OF LOAN TO BE ASSUMED $ _28,500_ AS OF WHAT DATE: _4/1_ TAXES & INS INCLUDED: _No_ YEARS TO GO: AMOUNT PAYABLE MONTHLY $ _233.40_ @ _7_ % TYPE LOAN _Conv._

MORTGAGE COMPANY _First National S&L_ 2nd TRUST $

ESTIMATED EXPECTED RENT MONTHLY $ TYPE OF APPRAISAL REQUESTED:

OWNER'S NAME _Edward B. Dobbs and his wife Edna R._ PHONES: (HOME) (BUSINESS)

TENANTS NAME PHONES: (HOME) (BUSINESS)

POSSESSION DATE LISTED: _3-15-this yr._ EXCLUSIVE FOR _120 days_ DATE OF EXPIRATION _7-15-this yr._

LISTING BROKER _Sellmore Realty Co._ PHONE KEY AVAILABLE AT

LISTING SALESMAN _You_ HOME PHONE: HOW TO BE SHOWN:

(1) ENTRANCE FOYER □ CENTER HALL □ (18) AGE AIR CONDITIONING □ (32) TYPE KITCHEN CABINETS

(2) LIVING ROOM SIZE _12 x 20_ FIREPLACE □ (19) ROOFING TOOL HOUSE □ (33) TYPE COUNTER TOPS

(3) DINING ROOM SIZE _10 x 12_ (20) GARAGE SIZE _2 car_ PATIO □ (34) EAT-IN SIZE KITCHEN □

(4) BEDROOM TOTAL: 3 DOWN 3 UP (21) SIDE DRIVE CIRCULAR DRIVE □ (35) BREAKFAST ROOM □

(5) BATHS TOTAL: 2 DOWN 2 UP (22) PORCH □ SIDE ☒ REAR □ SCREENED ☒ (36) BUILT-IN OVEN & RANGE ☒

(6) DEN SIZE _12 x 12_ FIREPLACE ☒ (23) FENCED YARD OUTDOOR GRILL □ (37) SEPARATE STOVE INCLUDED □

(7) FAMILY ROOM SIZE FIREPLACE □ (24) STORM WINDOWS □ STORM DOORS □ (38) REFRIGERATOR INCLUDED ☒

(8) RECREATION ROOM SIZE FIREPLACE □ (25) CURBS & GUTTERS □ SIDEWALKS □ (39) DISHWASHER INCLUDED □

(9) BASEMENT SIZE (26) STORM SEWERS □ ALLEY □ (40) DISPOSAL INCLUDED □

NONE □ 1/4 □ 1/3 □ 1/2 □ 3/4 □ FULL □ (27) WATER SUPPLY (41) DOUBLE SINK □ SINGLE SINK □

(10) UTILITY ROOM SIZE (28) SEWER □ SEPTIC □ STAINLESS STEEL □ PORCELAIN □

TYPE HOT WATER SYSTEM: (29) TYPE GAS: NATURAL □ BOTTLED □ (42) WASHER INCLUDED ☒ DRYER INCLUDED ☒

(11) TYPE HEAT (30) WHY SELLING (43) PANTRY □ EXHAUST FAN □

(12) EST. FUEL COST (44) LAND ASSESSMENT $

(13) ATTIC □ (31) DIRECTIONS TO PROPERTY (45) IMPROVEMENTS $

PULL DOWN STAIRWAY □ REGULAR STAIRWAY □ TRAP DOOR □ (46) TOTAL ASSESSMENT $

(14) MAIDS ROOM □ TYPE BATH (47) TAX RATE

LOCATION (48) TOTAL ANNUAL TAXES $ _314.40 unpaid_

(15) NAME OF BUILDER (49) LOT SIZE _100 x 190_

(16) SQUARE FOOTAGE (50) LOT NO. _6_ BLOCK SECTION _8_

(17) EXTERIOR OF HOUSE _Brick_ _Fairhope Sub. Hope Co. - Your State_

NAME OF SCHOOLS: ELEMENTARY: JR. HIGH:

HIGH PAROCHIAL:

PUBLIC TRANSPORTATION:

NEAREST SHOPPING AREA:

REMARKS: _Sellers to remove LR chandelier - they want to sell the lawn mower for $50 under separate bill of sale - 1% prepayment penalty on balance of loan if prepaid. $50 loan assumption fee_

Date: _3-15 - this year_

In consideration of the services of _Sellmore Realty Co._ (herein called "Broker") to be rendered to the undersigned (herein called "Owner"), and of the promise of Broker to make reasonable efforts to obtain a Purchaser therefor, Owner hereby lists with Broker the real estate and all improvements thereon which are described above (all herein called "the property"), and Owner hereby grants to Broker the exclusive and irrevocable right to sell such property from 12:00 Noon on _3-15_, 19 _this year_ until 12:00 Midnight on _7-15_, 19 _this year_ (herein called "period of time"), for the price of _Thirty Eight Thousand and 00/100_ Dollars ($ _38,000_) or for such other price and upon such other terms (including exchange) as Owner may subsequently authorize during the period of time.

It is understood by Owner that the above sum or any other price subsequently authorized by Owner shall include a cash fee of _6_ % per cent of such price or other price which shall be payable by Owner to Broker upon consummation by any Purchaser or Purchasers of a valid contract of sale of the property during the period of time and whether or not Broker was a procuring cause of any such contract of sale.

If the property is sold or exchanged by Owner, or by Broker or by any other person to any Purchaser to whom the property was shown by Broker or any representative of Broker within sixty (60) days after the expiration of the period of time mentioned above, Owner agrees to pay to Broker a cash fee which shall be the same percentage of the purchase price as the percentage mentioned above.

Broker is hereby authorized by Owner to place a "For Sale" sign on the property and to remove all signs of other brokers or salesmen during the period of time, and Owner hereby agrees to make the property available to Broker at all reasonable hours for the purpose of showing it to prospective Purchasers.

Owner agrees to convey the property to the Purchaser by warranty deed with the usual covenants of title and free and clear from all encumbrances, tenancies, liens (for taxes or otherwise), but subject to applicable restrictive covenants of record. Owner acknowledges receipt of a copy of this agreement.

WITNESS the following signature(s) and seal(s):

Date Signed: _3-15 - this year_

Listing Broker _Sellmore Realty Co By: You_

Address Telephone

Edward B. Dobbs (SEAL) (Owner)

Edna R. Dobbs (SEAL) (Owner)

Suggested solution for Exclusive Authorization to Sell.

OFFER TO PURCHASE AGREEMENT

This AGREEMENT made as of _MAY 15TH_ _____, 19 _THIS YEAR_.

among _ELMER A. FRIEND AND HIS WIFE ELEANOR B._ _____ (herein called "Purchaser"),

and _EDWARD B. DOBBS AND HIS WIFE EDNA R._ _____ (herein called "Seller"),

and _SELLMORE REALTY CO._ _____ (herein called "Broker"),

provides that Purchaser agrees to buy through Broker as agent for Seller, and Seller agrees to sell the following described real estate, and all improvements thereon, located in the jurisdiction of _HOPE COUNTY - YOUR STATE_ _____

(all herein called "the property"): _____

LOT 6, SECTION 8, FAIRHOPE SUB. - YOUR STATE

OWNER TO REMOVE LR CHANDELIER

BUILT IN OVEN AND RANGE AND REFRIGERATOR INCLUDED IN SALE

OWNER TO REMOVE WASHER AND DRYER , and more commonly known as _3418 ANDERS STREET_ _ANYTOWN - YOUR STATE_ _____ (street address).

1. The purchase price of the property is _THIRTY SEVEN THOUSAND FIVE HUNDRED AND 00/100_

Dollars ($ _37,500_), and such purchase price shall be paid as follows:

$1,000 DEPOSIT ACKNOWLEDGED IN PAR. 2 BELOW

$2,750 ADDITIONAL CASH AT SETTLEMENT

$30,000 BY NEW 1ST DEED OF TRUST FOR 30 YEARS AT 8% PER ANNUM INTEREST

$3,750 BY OWNER TAKING BACK A SECOND DEED OF TRUST FOR 5 YEARS AT 8% PER ANNUM INTEREST

2. Purchaser has made a deposit of _ONE THOUSAND AND 00/100 (BY CHECK)_ Dollars ($ _1,000.00_) with Broker, receipt of which is hereby acknowledged, and such deposit shall be held by Broker in escrow until the date of settlement and then applied to the purchase price, or returned to Purchaser if the title to the property is not marketable.

3. Seller agrees to convey the property to Purchaser by Warranty Deed with the usual covenants of title and free and clear from all encumbrances, tenancies, liens (for taxes or otherwise), except as may be otherwise provided above, but subject to applicable restrictive covenants of record. Seller further agrees to deliver possession of the property to Purchaser on the date of settlement and to pay the expense of preparing the deed of conveyance.

4. Settlement shall be made at the offices of Broker or at _BEAN AND JONES_ _____ on or before _JUNE 15_ _____, 19 _THIS YEAR_, or as soon thereafter as title can be examined and necessary documents prepared, with allowance of a reasonable time for Seller to correct any defects reported by the title examiner.

5. All taxes, interest, rent, and F.H.A. or similar escrow deposits, if any, shall be prorated as of the date of settlement.

6. All risk of loss or damage to the property by fire, windstorm, casualty, or other cause is assumed by Seller until the date of settlement.

7. Purchaser and Seller agree that Broker was the sole procuring cause of this Contract of Purchase, and Seller agrees to pay Broker for services rendered a cash fee of _6_ per cent of the purchase price. If either Purchaser or Seller defaults under such Contract, such defaulting party shall be liable for the cash fee of Broker and any expenses incurred by the non-defaulting party in connection with this transaction.

Subject to: _PURCHASER TO PURCHASE LAWN MOWER FOR $50 UNDER A SEPARATE BILL OF SALE. PURCHASER TO PAY 1½ POINTS LOAN PLACEMENT FEE AND SELLER TO PAY 1 POINT._

8. Purchaser represents that an inspection satisfactory to Purchaser has been made of the property, and Purchaser agrees to accept the property in its present condition except as may be otherwise provided in the description of the property above.

9. This Contract of Purchase constitutes the entire agreement among the parties and may not be modified or changed except by written instrument executed by all of the parties, including Broker.

10. This Contract of Purchase shall be construed, interpreted, and applied according to the law of the jurisdiction of _HOPE CO._ and shall be binding upon and shall inure to the benefit of the heirs, personal representatives, successors, and assigns of the parties.

All parties to this agreement acknowledge receipt of a certified copy.

WITNESS the following signatures and seals:

Edward B. Dobbs (SEAL) Seller   _Elmer A. Friend_ (SEAL) Purchaser

Edna R. Dobbs (SEAL) Seller   _Eleanor B. Friend_ (SEAL) Purchaser

Sellmore Realty Co. (SEAL) Broker

Deposit Rec'd $ _1,000.00_

(Check)   Cash

Sales Agent: _You_

Suggested solution for Offer to Purchase.

	BUYER'S STATEMENT		SELLER'S STATEMENT	
	DEBIT	CREDIT	DEBIT	CREDIT
PURCHASE PRICE	37,500.00			37,500.00
DEPOSIT		1,000.00		
TAXES PRO-RATED		144.10	144.10	
PAY OFF - EXISTING TRUST			28,300.00	
PREPAYMENT PENALTY			283.00	
NEW 1ST TRUST		30,000.00		
POINTS - PLACEMENT FEE	450.00		300.00	
2ND TRUST		3,750.00	3,750.00	
SALES FEE			2,250.00	
INSURANCY POLICY	112.00			
TITLE INSURANCE	75.00			
INTEREST ON NEW LOAN 15 DAYS	100.00			
TAX ESCROW - 2 MO.'S	52.40			
LAWN MOWER UNDER SEPARATE BILL OF SALE	50.00			50.00
BALANCE DUE FROM PURCHASER		3,445.30		
BALANCE DUE SELLER			2,522.90	
	38,339.40	38,339.40	37,550.00	37,550.00

Suggested solution for Settlement Statement.

Part B: Arithmetic

31. (C)	35. (C)	39. (B)	43. (D)	47. (D)
32. (B)	36. (A)	40. (A)	44. (B)	48. (C)
33. (B)	37. (D)	41. (A)	45. (A)	49. (C)
34. (C)	38. (D)	42. (D)	46. (B)	50. (B)

Suggested detailed solutions follow.

31.

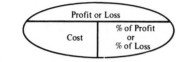

Present cost $28 − $21 original cost = $7 increase

$7 ÷ $21 = .33 = 33% increase in cost

32.

65 acres × $1,200 = $78,000 cost
Taxes: 5 years × $600 = 3,000

Total cost = $81,000

$81,000 × (100% + 12%) =
$81,000 × 1.12 = $90,720 sales price required

33. $46,000 sales price × 5% commission = $2,300
$40,000 loan × 3 points = 1,200
$700 other closing costs = 700
Total expenses $4,200

$46,000 − $4,200 expenses = $41,800 net to seller

34. Basement 24′ × 48′ × 4′ (½ below ground) = 4,608 cu ft

4,608 ÷ 27 = 170.67 cu yd

35. $2,800 × .11 = $308 per annum interest

$308 ÷ 12 months = $25.67 per month interest

January 1 to August 1 = 7 months

$25.67 × 7 months = $179.69 total interest due

$2,800 + $179.69 = $2,979.69 total owed

36.

$344.38 × 12 months = $4,132.56 per annum interest

$4,132.56 ÷ .095 = $43,500 trust amount

37. $756 taxes ÷ 12 months = $63 per month

May 15 to December 31 = 7.5 months remaining

$63 × 7.5 = $472.50 refund due seller

38.

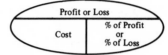

Appreciation 6% × 5 years = 30% total

$28,000 × (100% + 30%) = $28,000 × 1.30 = $36,400 value today

39.

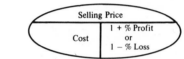

Cost $44,000 − $38,000 sales price = $6,000 loss

$6,000 ÷ $44,000 = .136 = 13.6% loss

40.

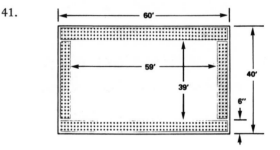

Sales price $35,000 ÷ (100% + 15%) = $35,000 ÷ 1.15 = $30,435 cost

41.

Building 60′ × 40′ = 2,400 sq ft
Walls 60′ × .5 (6″) × 2 = 60 sq ft
39′ × .5 (6″) × 2 = 39 sq ft
Posts 1′ × 1′ × 8 = 8 sq ft
Total loss 107 sq ft

107 sq ft
Clear floor area 2,293 sq ft

42. 196,020 sq ft × .18 = $35,238.60 cost

196,020 sq ft ÷ 43,560 = 4.5 acres

4.5 acres × 4 (¼-acre lots) = 18 lots

18 lots × $1,800 = $32,400 sales price

$35,283.60 − $32,400 = $2,883.60 loss

43.

$30,000 + $710 + $13,000 = $43,710 net price

$43,710 ÷ (100% − 6%) =

$43,710 ÷ .94 = $46,500 listed price

44.

$43,000 per annum net ÷ .12 = $358,333 investment

45.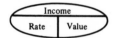

$368.33 per month × 12 months = $4,419.96 ÷
$52,000 = .085 = 8.5% interest

46. $2,420 income − $530 salary = $1,890 income from
sales at 3%

$1,890 ÷ .03 = $63,000 in real estate sales

47.
$395.83 × 12 months = $4,749.96 per annum
interest

$4,749.96 ÷ .095 = $49,999.58 loan amount

$49,999.58 loan amount = 80% of purchase price

$49,999.58 ÷ .80 = $62,499.48 purchase price

48.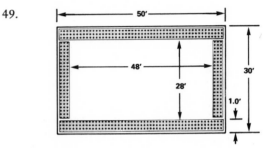

80′ + 160′ = 240′ ÷ 2 = 120′

120′ × 160′ = 19,200 sq ft

19,200 × $2 = $38,400 sales price

$38,400 − $20,000 = $18,400 profit

$18,400 ÷ 20,000 = .92 = 92% profit

49.

50′ × 1.0′ × 2 = 100 sq ft

28′ × 1.0′ × 2 = 56 sq ft

Total 156 sq ft

156 × 1.5′ = 234 cu ft

234 ÷ 27 = 8.67 cu yd

50. $1,285.35 ÷ .55 (25% + 30%) = $2,337 commission
@ 6%

$2,337 ÷ .06 = $38,950 sales price

Part C: Real Estate Transactions

51. (B)	61. (B)	71. (C)	81. (B)	91. (D)
52. (D)	62. (D)	72. (D)	82. (B)	92. (B)
53. (B)	63. (C)	73. (C)	83. (A)	93. (C)
54. (C)	64. (C)	74. (B)	84. (C)	94. (B)
55. (D)	65. (A)	75. (A)	85. (D)	95. (D)
56. (B)	66. (A)	76. (C)	86. (D)	96. (B)
57. (B)	67. (B)	77. (B)	87. (A)	97. (C)
58. (A)	68. (B)	78. (D)	88. (C)	98. (D)
59. (C)	69. (C)	79. (A)	89. (B)	99. (C)
60. (C)	70. (C)	80. (C)	90. (D)	100. (D)

Part D: Licensing Laws, Rules, and Regulations

101. (C)	107. (A)	113. (D)	119. (B)	125. (D)
102. (B)	108. (A)	114. (B)	120. (D)	126. (C)
103. (C)	109. (B)	115. (D)	121. (B)	127. (D)
104. (C)	110. (A)	116. (D)	122. (A)	128. (D)
105. (C)	111. (A)	117. (C)	123. (A)	129. (D)
106. (A)	112. (C)	118. (B)	124. (D)	130. (D)

Index

EXCLUSIVE AUTHORIZATION TO SELL

SALES PRICE: _____ TYPE HOME _____ TOTAL BEDROOMS _____ TOTAL BATHS _____

ADDRESS: _____ JURISDICTION OF: _____

AMT. OF LOAN
TO BE ASSUMED $ _____ AS OF
WHAT DATE: _____ TAXES & INS.
INCLUDED: YEARS
TO GO: _____ AMOUNT PAYABLE
MONTHLY $ _____ @ ___ TYPE
% LOAN _____

MORTGAGE COMPANY _____ 2nd TRUST $ _____

ESTIMATED
EXPECTED RENT MONTHLY $ _____ TYPE OF APPRAISAL
REQUESTED: _____

OWNER'S NAME _____ PHONES: (HOME) _____ (BUSINESS) _____

TENANTS NAME _____ PHONES: (HOME) _____ (BUSINESS) _____

POSSESSION _____ DATE LISTED: _____ EXCLUSIVE FOR _____ DATE OF EXPIRATION _____

LISTING BROKER _____ PHONE _____ KEY AVAILABLE AT _____

LISTING SALESMAN _____ HOME PHONE: _____ HOW TO BE SHOWN: _____

(1) ENTRANCE FOYER ☐ CENTER HALL ☐	(18) AGE	AIR CONDITIONING ☐	(32) TYPE KITCHEN CABINETS
(2) LIVING ROOM SIZE FIREPLACE ☐	(19) ROOFING	TOOL HOUSE ☐	(33) TYPE COUNTER TOPS
(3) DINING ROOM SIZE	(20) GARAGE SIZE	PATIO ☐	(34) EAT-IN SIZE KITCHEN ☐
(4) BEDROOM TOTAL: DOWN UP	(21) SIDE DRIVE ☐ CIRCULAR DRIVE ☐		(35) BREAKFAST ROOM ☐
(5) BATHS TOTAL: DOWN UP	(22) PORCH ☐ SIDE ☐ REAR ☐ SCREENED ☐		(36) BUILT-IN OVEN & RANGE ☐
(6) DEN SIZE FIREPLACE ☐	(23) FENCED YARD	OUTDOOR GRILL ☐	(37) SEPARATE STOVE INCLUDED ☐
(7) FAMILY ROOM SIZE FIREPLACE ☐	(24) STORM WINDOWS ☐	STORM DOORS ☐	(38) REFRIGERATOR INCLUDED ☐
(8) RECREATION ROOM SIZE FIREPLACE ☐	(25) CURBS & GUTTERS ☐	SIDEWALKS ☐	(39) DISHWASHER INCLUDED
(9) BASEMENT SIZE	(26) STORM SEWERS ☐	ALLEY ☐	(40) DISPOSAL INCLUDED ☐
NONE ☐ 1/4 ☐ 1/3 ☐ 1/2 ☐ 3/4 ☐ FULL ☐	(27) WATER SUPPLY		(41) DOUBLE SINK ☐ SINGLE SINK ☐
(10) UTILITY ROOM SIZE	(28) SEWER ☐	SEPTIC ☐	STAINLESS STEEL ☐ PORCELAIN ☐
TYPE HOT WATER SYSTEM:	(29) TYPE GAS: NATURAL ☐	BOTTLED ☐	(42) WASHER INCLUDED ☐ DRYER INCLUDED ☐
(11) TYPE HEAT	(30) WHY SELLING		(43) PANTRY ☐ EXHAUST FAN ☐
(12) EST. FUEL COST			(44) LAND ASSESSMENT $
(13) ATTIC ☐	(31) DIRECTIONS TO PROPERTY		(45) IMPROVEMENTS $
PULL DOWN STAIRWAY ☐ REGULAR STAIRWAY ☐ TRAP DOOR ☐			(46) TOTAL ASSESSMENT $
(14) MAIDS ROOM ☐ TYPE BATH			(47) TAX RATE
LOCATION			(48) TOTAL ANNUAL TAXES $
(15) NAME OF BUILDER			(49) LOT SIZE
(16) SQUARE FOOTAGE			(50) LOT NO. BLOCK SECTION
(17) EXTERIOR OF HOUSE			

NAME OF SCHOOLS: ELEMENTARY: _____ JR. HIGH: _____

HIGH _____ PAROCHIAL: _____

PUBLIC TRANSPORTATION: _____

NEAREST SHOPPING AREA: _____

REMARKS: _____

Date: _____

In consideration of the services of_____(herein called "Broker") to be rendered to the undersigned (herein called "Owner"), and of the promise of Broker to make reasonable efforts to obtain a Purchaser therefor, Owner hereby lists with Broker the real estate and all improvements thereon which are described above (all herein called "the property"), and Owner hereby grants to Broker the exclusive and irrevocable right to sell such property from 12:00 Noon on_____, 19_____until 12:00 Midnight on_____, 19_____ (herein called "period of time"), for the price of_____Dollars ($_____) or for such other price and upon such other terms (including exchange) as Owner may subsequently authorize during the period of time.

It is understood by Owner that the above sum or any other price subsequently authorized by Owner shall include a cash fee of_____ per cent of such price or other price which shall be payable by Owner to Broker upon consummation by any Purchaser or Purchasers of a valid contract of sale of the property during the period of time and whether or not Broker was a procuring cause of any such contract of sale.

If the property is sold or exchanged by Owner, or by Broker or by any other person to any Purchaser to whom the property was shown by Broker or any representative of Broker within sixty (60) days after the expiration of the period of time mentioned above, Owner agrees to pay to Broker a cash fee which shall be the same percentage of the purchase price as the percentage mentioned above.

Broker is hereby authorized by Owner to place a "For Sale" sign on the property and to remove all signs of other brokers or salesmen during the period of time, and Owner hereby agrees to make the property available to Broker at all reasonable hours for the purpose of showing it to prospective Purchasers.

Owner agrees to convey the property to the Purchaser by warranty deed with the usual covenants of title and free and clear from all encumbrances, tenancies, liens (for taxes or otherwise), but subject to applicable restrictive covenants of record. Owner acknowledges receipt of a copy of this agreement.

WITNESS the following signature(s) and seal(s):

Date Signed:_____ _____ (SEAL)
(Owner)

Listing Broker_____

Address_____ Telephone_____ _____ (SEAL)
(Owner)

_____

EXCLUSIVE AUTHORIZATION TO SELL

SALES PRICE: _____ TYPE HOME _____ TOTAL BEDROOMS _____ TOTAL BATHS _____

ADDRESS: _____ JURISDICTION OF: _____

AMT. OF LOAN $ _____ AS OF _____ TAXES & INS. YEARS AMOUNT PAYABLE TYPE
TO BE ASSUMED $ _____ WHAT DATE: _____ INCLUDED: ____ TO GO: _____ MONTHLY $ _____ @ __ % LOAN _____

MORTGAGE COMPANY _____ 2nd TRUST $ _____
ESTIMATED   TYPE OF APPRAISAL
EXPECTED RENT MONTHLY $ _____ REQUESTED: _____

OWNER'S NAME _____ PHONES: (HOME) _____ (BUSINESS) _____

TENANTS NAME _____ PHONES: (HOME) _____ (BUSINESS) _____

POSSESSION _____ DATE LISTED: _____ EXCLUSIVE FOR _____ DATE OF EXPIRATION _____

LISTING BROKER _____ PHONE _____ KEY AVAILABLE AT _____

LISTING SALESMAN _____ HOME PHONE: _____ HOW TO BE SHOWN: _____

(1) ENTRANCE FOYER ☐ CENTER HALL ☐	(18) AGE AIR CONDITIONING ☐	(32) TYPE KITCHEN CABINETS
(2) LIVING ROOM SIZE FIREPLACE ☐	(19) ROOFING TOOL HOUSE ☐	(33) TYPE COUNTER TOPS
(3) DINING ROOM SIZE	(20) GARAGE SIZE PATIO ☐	(34) EAT-IN SIZE KITCHEN ☐
(4) BEDROOM TOTAL: DOWN UP	(21) SIDE DRIVE ☐ CIRCULAR DRIVE ☐	(35) BREAKFAST ROOM ☐
(5) BATHS TOTAL: DOWN UP	(22) PORCH ☐ SIDE ☐ REAR ☐ SCREENED ☐	(36) BUILT-IN OVEN & RANGE ☐
(6) DEN SIZE FIREPLACE ☐	(23) FENCED YARD OUTDOOR GRILL ☐	(37) SEPARATE STOVE INCLUDED ☐
(7) FAMILY ROOM SIZE FIREPLACE ☐	(24) STORM WINDOWS ☐ STORM DOORS ☐	(38) REFRIGERATOR INCLUDED ☐
(8) RECREATION ROOM SIZE FIREPLACE ☐	(25) CURBS & GUTTERS ☐ SIDEWALKS ☐	(39) DISHWASHER INCLUDED
(9) BASEMENT SIZE	(26) STORM SEWERS ☐ ALLEY ☐	(40) DISPOSAL INCLUDED ☐
NONE ☐ 1/4 ☐ 1/3 ☐ 1/2 ☐ 3/4 ☐ FULL ☐	(27) WATER SUPPLY	(41) DOUBLE SINK ☐ SINGLE SINK ☐
(10) UTILITY ROOM SIZE	(28) SEWER ☐ SEPTIC ☐	STAINLESS STEEL ☐ PORCELAIN ☐
TYPE HOT WATER SYSTEM:	(29) TYPE GAS: NATURAL ☐ BOTTLED ☐	(42) WASHER INCLUDED ☐ DRYER INCLUDED ☐
(11) TYPE HEAT	(30) WHY SELLING	(43) PANTRY ☐ EXHAUST FAN ☐
(12) EST. FUEL COST		(44) LAND ASSESSMENT $
(13) ATTIC ☐	(31) DIRECTIONS TO PROPERTY	(45) IMPROVEMENTS $
PULL DOWN STAIRWAY ☐ REGULAR STAIRWAY ☐ TRAP DOOR ☐		(46) TOTAL ASSESSMENT $
(14) MAIDS ROOM ☐ TYPE BATH		(47) TAX RATE
LOCATION		(48) TOTAL ANNUAL TAXES $
(15) NAME OF BUILDER		(49) LOT SIZE
(16) SQUARE FOOTAGE		(50) LOT NO. BLOCK SECTION
(17) EXTERIOR OF HOUSE		

NAME OF SCHOOLS: ELEMENTARY: _____ JR. HIGH: _____

HIGH _____ PAROCHIAL: _____

PUBLIC TRANSPORTATION: _____

NEAREST SHOPPING AREA: _____

REMARKS: _____

Date: _____

In consideration of the services of_____(herein called "Broker") to be rendered to the undersigned (herein called "Owner"), and of the promise of Broker to make reasonable efforts to obtain a Purchaser therefor, Owner hereby lists with Broker the real estate and all improvements thereon which are described above (all herein called "the property"), and Owner hereby grants to Broker the exclusive and irrevocable right to sell such property from 12:00 Noon on_____, 19_____until 12:00 Midnight on_____, 19_____ (herein called "period of time"), for the price of_____ Dollars ($_____) or for such other price and upon such other terms (including exchange) as Owner may subsequently authorize during the period of time.

It is understood by Owner that the above sum or any other price subsequently authorized by Owner shall include a cash fee of_____ per cent of such price or other price which shall be payable by Owner to Broker upon consummation by any Purchaser or Purchasers of a valid contract of sale of the property during the period of time and whether or not Broker was a procuring cause of any such contract of sale.

If the property is sold or exchanged by Owner, or by Broker or by any other person to any Purchaser to whom the property was shown by Broker or any representative of Broker within sixty (60) days after the expiration of the period of time mentioned above, Owner agrees to pay to Broker a cash fee which shall be the same percentage of the purchase price as the percentage mentioned above.

Broker is hereby authorized by Owner to place a "For Sale" sign on the property and to remove all signs of other brokers or salesmen during the period of time, and Owner hereby agrees to make the property available to Broker at all reasonable hours for the purpose of showing it to prospective Purchasers.

Owner agrees to convey the property to the Purchaser by warranty deed with the usual covenants of title and free and clear from all encumbrances, tenancies, liens (for taxes or otherwise), but subject to applicable restrictive covenants of record. Owner acknowledges receipt of a copy of this agreement.

WITNESS the following signature(s) and seal(s):

Date Signed:_____   _____ (SEAL)
                                                                  (Owner)

Listing Broker_____

Address_____ Telephone_____   _____ (SEAL)
                                                                  (Owner)

_____

EXCLUSIVE AUTHORIZATION TO SELL

SALES PRICE: _____ TYPE HOME _____ TOTAL BEDROOMS _____ TOTAL BATHS _____

ADDRESS: _____ JURISDICTION OF: _____

AMT. OF LOAN   AS OF   TAXES & INS.   YEARS   AMOUNT PAYABLE   TYPE
TO BE ASSUMED $ _____   WHAT DATE: _____ INCLUDED: ____ TO GO: ___ MONTHLY $ _____ @ ___ % LOAN

MORTGAGE COMPANY _____ 2nd TRUST $ _____

ESTIMATED   TYPE OF APPRAISAL
EXPECTED RENT MONTHLY $ _____   REQUESTED: _____

OWNER'S NAME _____ PHONES: (HOME) _____ (BUSINESS) _____

TENANTS NAME _____ PHONES: (HOME) _____ (BUSINESS) _____

POSSESSION _____ DATE LISTED: _____ EXCLUSIVE FOR _____ DATE OF EXPIRATION _____

LISTING BROKER _____ PHONE _____ KEY AVAILABLE AT _____

LISTING SALESMAN _____ HOME PHONE: _____ HOW TO BE SHOWN: _____

(1) ENTRANCE FOYER ☐ CENTER HALL ☐	(18) AGE	AIR CONDITIONING ☐	(32) TYPE KITCHEN CABINETS
(2) LIVING ROOM SIZE FIREPLACE ☐	(19) ROOFING	TOOL HOUSE ☐	(33) TYPE COUNTER TOPS
(3) DINING ROOM SIZE	(20) GARAGE SIZE	PATIO ☐	(34) EAT-IN SIZE KITCHEN ☐
(4) BEDROOM TOTAL: DOWN UP	(21) SIDE DRIVE ☐	CIRCULAR DRIVE ☐	(35) BREAKFAST ROOM ☐
(5) BATHS TOTAL: DOWN UP	(22) PORCH ☐ SIDE ☐ REAR ☐	SCREENED ☐	(36) BUILT-IN OVEN & RANGE ☐
(6) DEN SIZE FIREPLACE ☐	(23) FENCED YARD	OUTDOOR GRILL ☐	(37) SEPARATE STOVE INCLUDED ☐
(7) FAMILY ROOM SIZE FIREPLACE ☐	(24) STORM WINDOWS ☐	STORM DOORS ☐	(38) REFRIGERATOR INCLUDED ☐
(8) RECREATION ROOM SIZE FIREPLACE ☐	(25) CURBS & GUTTERS ☐	SIDEWALKS ☐	(39) DISHWASHER INCLUDED
(9) BASEMENT SIZE	(26) STORM SEWERS ☐	ALLEY ☐	(40) DISPOSAL INCLUDED ☐
NONE ☐ 1/4 ☐ 1/3 ☐ 1/2 ☐ 3/4 ☐ FULL ☐	(27) WATER SUPPLY		(41) DOUBLE SINK ☐ SINGLE SINK ☐
(10) UTILITY ROOM SIZE	(28) SEWER ☐	SEPTIC ☐	STAINLESS STEEL ☐ PORCELAIN ☐
TYPE HOT WATER SYSTEM:	(29) TYPE GAS: NATURAL ☐	BOTTLED ☐	(42) WASHER INCLUDED ☐ DRYER INCLUDED ☐
(11) TYPE HEAT	(30) WHY SELLING		(43) PANTRY ☐ EXHAUST FAN ☐
(12) EST. FUEL COST			(44) LAND ASSESSMENT $
(13) ATTIC ☐	(31) DIRECTIONS TO PROPERTY		(45) IMPROVEMENTS $
PULL DOWN STAIRWAY ☐ REGULAR STAIRWAY ☐ TRAP DOOR ☐			(46) TOTAL ASSESSMENT $
(14) MAIDS ROOM ☐ TYPE BATH			(47) TAX RATE
LOCATION			(48) TOTAL ANNUAL TAXES $
(15) NAME OF BUILDER			(49) LOT SIZE
(16) SQUARE FOOTAGE			(50) LOT NO. BLOCK SECTION
(17) EXTERIOR OF HOUSE			

NAME OF SCHOOLS: ELEMENTARY: _____ JR. HIGH: _____

HIGH _____ PAROCHIAL: _____

PUBLIC TRANSPORTATION: _____

NEAREST SHOPPING AREA: _____

REMARKS: _____
_____
_____

Date: _____

In consideration of the services of_____(herein called "Broker") to be rendered to the undersigned (herein called "Owner"), and of the promise of Broker to make reasonable efforts to obtain a Purchaser therefor, Owner hereby lists with Broker the real estate and all improvements thereon which are described above (all herein called "the property"), and Owner hereby grants to Broker the exclusive and irrevocable right to sell such property from 12:00 Noon on_____, 19____until 12:00 Midnight on _____, 19____ (herein called "period of time"), for the price of_____ Dollars ($ _____) or for such other price and upon such other terms (including exchange) as Owner may subsequently authorize during the period of time.

It is understood by Owner that the above sum or any other price subsequently authorized by Owner shall include a cash fee of_____ per cent of such price or other price which shall be payable by Owner to Broker upon consummation by any Purchaser or Purchasers of a valid contract of sale of the property during the period of time and whether or not Broker was a procuring cause of any such contract of sale.

If the property is sold or exchanged by Owner, or by Broker or by any other person to any Purchaser to whom the property was shown by Broker or any representative of Broker within sixty (60) days after the expiration of the period of time mentioned above, Owner agrees to pay to Broker a cash fee which shall be the same percentage of the purchase price as the percentage mentioned above.

Broker is hereby authorized by Owner to place a "For Sale" sign on the property and to remove all signs of other brokers or salesmen during the period of time, and Owner hereby agrees to make the property available to Broker at all reasonable hours for the purpose of showing it to prospective Purchasers.

Owner agrees to convey the property to the Purchaser by warranty deed with the usual covenants of title and free and clear from all encumbrances, tenancies, liens (for taxes or otherwise), but subject to applicable restrictive covenants of record. Owner acknowledges receipt of a copy of this agreement.

WITNESS the following signature(s) and seal(s):

Date Signed:_____   _____ (SEAL)
                                                                          (Owner)

Listing Broker_____

Address_____ Telephone_____   _____ (SEAL)
                                                                          (Owner)

_____

EXCLUSIVE AUTHORIZATION TO SELL

SALES PRICE: _____ TYPE HOME _____ TOTAL BEDROOMS _____ TOTAL BATHS _____

ADDRESS: _____

JURISDICTION OF: _____

AMT. OF LOAN $ _____ AS OF _____ TAXES & INS. YEARS AMOUNT PAYABLE TYPE
TO BE ASSUMED $ _____ WHAT DATE: _____ INCLUDED: ___ TO GO: ___ MONTHLY $ _____ @ __ % LOAN _____

MORTGAGE COMPANY _____ 2nd TRUST $ _____

ESTIMATED TYPE OF APPRAISAL
EXPECTED RENT MONTHLY $ _____ REQUESTED: _____

OWNER'S NAME _____ PHONES: (HOME) _____ (BUSINESS) _____

TENANTS NAME _____ PHONES: (HOME) _____ (BUSINESS) _____

POSSESSION _____ DATE LISTED: _____ EXCLUSIVE FOR _____ DATE OF EXPIRATION _____

LISTING BROKER _____ PHONE _____ KEY AVAILABLE AT _____

LISTING SALESMAN _____ HOME PHONE: _____ HOW TO BE SHOWN: _____

(1) ENTRANCE FOYER ☐ CENTER HALL ☐	(18) AGE	AIR CONDITIONING ☐	(32) TYPE KITCHEN CABINETS
(2) LIVING ROOM SIZE FIREPLACE ☐	(19) ROOFING	TOOL HOUSE ☐	(33) TYPE COUNTER TOPS
(3) DINING ROOM SIZE	(20) GARAGE SIZE	PATIO ☐	(34) EAT-IN SIZE KITCHEN ☐
(4) BEDROOM TOTAL: DOWN UP	(21) SIDE DRIVE ☐	CIRCULAR DRIVE ☐	(35) BREAKFAST ROOM ☐
(5) BATHS TOTAL: DOWN UP	(22) PORCH ☐ SIDE ☐ REAR ☐	SCREENED ☐	(36) BUILT-IN OVEN & RANGE ☐
(6) DEN SIZE FIREPLACE ☐	(23) FENCED YARD	OUTDOOR GRILL ☐	(37) SEPARATE STOVE INCLUDED ☐
(7) FAMILY ROOM SIZE FIREPLACE ☐	(24) STORM WINDOWS ☐	STORM DOORS ☐	(38) REFRIGERATOR INCLUDED ☐
(8) RECREATION ROOM SIZE FIREPLACE ☐	(25) CURBS & GUTTERS ☐	SIDEWALKS ☐	(39) DISHWASHER INCLUDED ☐
(9) BASEMENT SIZE	(26) STORM SEWERS ☐	ALLEY ☐	(40) DISPOSAL INCLUDED ☐
NONE ☐ 1/4 ☐ 1/3 ☐ 1/2 ☐ 3/4 ☐ FULL ☐	(27) WATER SUPPLY		(41) DOUBLE SINK ☐ SINGLE SINK ☐
(10) UTILITY ROOM SIZE	(28) SEWER ☐	SEPTIC ☐	STAINLESS STEEL ☐ PORCELAIN ☐
TYPE HOT WATER SYSTEM:	(29) TYPE GAS: NATURAL ☐	BOTTLED ☐	(42) WASHER INCLUDED ☐ DRYER INCLUDED ☐
(11) TYPE HEAT	(30) WHY SELLING		(43) PANTRY ☐ EXHAUST FAN ☐
(12) EST. FUEL COST			(44) LAND ASSESSMENT $
(13) ATTIC ☐	(31) DIRECTIONS TO PROPERTY		(45) IMPROVEMENTS $
PULL DOWN STAIRWAY ☐ REGULAR STAIRWAY ☐ TRAP DOOR ☐			(46) TOTAL ASSESSMENT $
(14) MAIDS ROOM ☐ TYPE BATH			(47) TAX RATE
LOCATION			(48) TOTAL ANNUAL TAXES $
(15) NAME OF BUILDER			(49) LOT SIZE
(16) SQUARE FOOTAGE			(50) LOT NO. BLOCK SECTION
(17) EXTERIOR OF HOUSE			

NAME OF SCHOOLS: ELEMENTARY: _____ JR. HIGH: _____

HIGH _____ PAROCHIAL: _____

PUBLIC TRANSPORTATION: _____

NEAREST SHOPPING AREA: _____

REMARKS: _____

Date: _____

In consideration of the services of _____ (herein called "Broker") to be rendered to the undersigned (herein called "Owner"), and of the promise of Broker to make reasonable efforts to obtain a Purchaser therefor, Owner hereby lists with Broker the real estate and all improvements thereon which are described above (all herein called "the property"), and Owner hereby grants to Broker the exclusive and irrevocable right to sell such property from 12:00 Noon on _____, 19_____ until 12:00 Midnight on _____, 19_____ (herein called "period of time"), for the price of _____ Dollars ($ _____) or for such other price and upon such other terms (including exchange) as Owner may subsequently authorize during the period of time.

It is understood by Owner that the above sum or any other price subsequently authorized by Owner shall include a cash fee of _____ per cent of such price or other price which shall be payable by Owner to Broker upon consummation by any Purchaser or Purchasers of a valid contract of sale of the property during the period of time and whether or not Broker was a procuring cause of any such contract of sale.

If the property is sold or exchanged by Owner, or by Broker or by any other person to any Purchaser to whom the property was shown by Broker or any representative of Broker within sixty (60) days after the expiration of the period of time mentioned above, Owner agrees to pay to Broker a cash fee which shall be the same percentage of the purchase price as the percentage mentioned above.

Broker is hereby authorized by Owner to place a "For Sale" sign on the property and to remove all signs of other brokers or salesmen during the period of time, and Owner hereby agrees to make the property available to Broker at all reasonable hours for the purpose of showing it to prospective Purchasers.

Owner agrees to convey the property to the Purchaser by warranty deed with the usual covenants of title and free and clear from all encumbrances, tenancies, liens (for taxes or otherwise), but subject to applicable restrictive covenants of record. Owner acknowledges receipt of a copy of this agreement.

WITNESS the following signature(s) and seal(s):

Date Signed: _____ _____ (SEAL)
(Owner)

Listing Broker _____

Address _____ Telephone _____ _____ (SEAL)
(Owner)

_____

OFFER TO PURCHASE AGREEMENT

This AGREEMENT made as of_____, 19_____,

among_____ (herein called "Purchaser"),

and_____ (herein called "Seller"),

and_____ (herein called "Broker"),
provides that Purchaser agrees to buy through Broker as agent for Seller, and Seller agrees to sell the following described real estate, and all improvements
thereon, located in the jurisdiction of_____,
(all herein called "the property"):_____

_____

_____

_____

_____, and more commonly known as_____

_____(street address).

    1. The purchase price of the property is_____
Dollars ($_____), and such purchase price shall be paid as follows:

_____

_____

_____

_____

_____

    2. Purchaser has made a deposit of_____Dollars ($_____)
with Broker, receipt of which is hereby acknowledged, and such deposit shall be held by Broker in escrow until the date of settlement and then applied
to the purchase price, or returned to Purchaser if the title to the property is not marketable.

    3. Seller agrees to convey the property to Purchaser by Warranty Deed with the usual covenants of title and free and clear from all encumbrances,
tenancies, liens (for taxes or otherwise), except as may be otherwise provided above, but subject to applicable restrictive covenants of record. Seller further
agrees to deliver possession of the property to Purchaser on the date of settlement and to pay the expense of preparing the deed of conveyance.

    4. Settlement shall be made at the offices of Broker or at_____on or before
_____, 19_____, or as soon thereafter as title can be examined and necessary documents prepared, with allowance of
a reasonable time for Seller to correct any defects reported by the title examiner.

    5. All taxes, interest, rent, and F.H.A. or similar escrow deposits, if any, shall be prorated as of the date of settlement.

    6. All risk of loss or damage to the property by fire, windstorm, casualty, or other cause is assumed by Seller until the date of settlement.

    7. Purchaser and Seller agree that Broker was the sole procuring cause of this Contract of Purchase, and Seller agrees to pay Broker for services
rendered a cash fee of_____per cent of the purchase price. If either Purchaser or Seller defaults under such Contract, such defaulting party shall
be liable for the cash fee of Broker and any expenses incurred by the non-defaulting party in connection with this transaction.

Subject to:_____

_____

_____

    8. Purchaser represents that an inspection satisfactory to Purchaser has been made of the property, and Purchaser agrees to accept the property in
its present condition except as may be otherwise provided in the description of the property above.

    9. This Contract of Purchase constitutes the entire agreement among the parties and may not be modified or changed except by written instrument
executed by all of the parties, including Broker.

    10. This Contract of Purchase shall be construed, interpreted, and applied according to the law of the jurisdiction of_____and shall
be binding upon and shall inure to the benefit of the heirs, personal representatives, successors, and assigns of the parties.

All parties to this agreement acknowledge receipt of a certified copy.

WITNESS the following signatures and seals:

_____(SEAL)   _____(SEAL)
Seller   Purchaser

_____(SEAL)   _____(SEAL)
Seller   Purchaser

_____(SEAL)
Broker

Deposit Rec'd $_____

Check   Cash

Sales Agent:_____

OFFER TO PURCHASE AGREEMENT

This AGREEMENT made as of_____, 19_____,

among_____(herein called "Purchaser"),

and_____(herein called "Seller"),

and_____(herein called "Broker"),
provides that Purchaser agrees to buy through Broker as agent for Seller, and Seller agrees to sell the following described real estate, and all improvements
thereon, located in the jurisdiction of_____,
(all herein called "the property"):_____

_____

_____

_____

_____, and more commonly known as_____

_____(street address).

    1. The purchase price of the property is_____
Dollars ($_____), and such purchase price shall be paid as follows:

_____

_____

_____

_____

    2. Purchaser has made a deposit of_____ Dollars ($_____)
with Broker, receipt of which is hereby acknowledged, and such deposit shall be held by Broker in escrow until the date of settlement and then applied
to the purchase price, or returned to Purchaser if the title to the property is not marketable.

    3. Seller agrees to convey the property to Purchaser by Warranty Deed with the usual covenants of title and free and clear from all encumbrances,
tenancies, liens (for taxes or otherwise), except as may be otherwise provided above, but subject to applicable restrictive covenants of record. Seller further
agrees to deliver possession of the property to Purchaser on the date of settlement and to pay the expense of preparing the deed of conveyance.

    4. Settlement shall be made at the offices of Broker or at_____on or before
_____, 19_____, or as soon thereafter as title can be examined and necessary documents prepared, with allowance of
a reasonable time for Seller to correct any defects reported by the title examiner.

    5. All taxes, interest, rent, and F.H.A. or similar escrow deposits, if any, shall be prorated as of the date of settlement.

    6. All risk of loss or damage to the property by fire, windstorm, casualty, or other cause is assumed by Seller until the date of settlement.

    7. Purchaser and Seller agree that Broker was the sole procuring cause of this Contract of Purchase, and Seller agrees to pay Broker for services
rendered a cash fee of_____per cent of the purchase price. If either Purchaser or Seller defaults under such Contract, such defaulting party shall
be liable for the cash fee of Broker and any expenses incurred by the non-defaulting party in connection with this transaction.

Subject to:_____

_____

_____

    8. Purchaser represents that an inspection satisfactory to Purchaser has been made of the property, and Purchaser agrees to accept the property in
its present condition except as may be otherwise provided in the description of the property above.

    9. This Contract of Purchase constitutes the entire agreement among the parties and may not be modified or changed except by written instrument
executed by all of the parties, including Broker.

    10. This Contract of Purchase shall be construed, interpreted, and applied according to the law of the jurisdiction of_____and shall
be binding upon and shall inure to the benefit of the heirs, personal representatives, successors, and assigns of the parties.

All parties to this agreement acknowledge receipt of a certified copy.

WITNESS the following signatures and seals:

_____(SEAL)   _____(SEAL)
Seller   Purchaser

_____(SEAL)   _____(SEAL)
Seller   Purchaser

_____(SEAL)
Broker

Deposit Rec'd $_____

Check   Cash

Sales Agent:_____

OFFER TO PURCHASE AGREEMENT

This AGREEMENT made as of_____, 19_____,

among_____(herein called "Purchaser"),

and_____(herein called "Seller"),

and_____(herein called "Broker"),
provides that Purchaser agrees to buy through Broker as agent for Seller, and Seller agrees to sell the following described real estate, and all improvements
thereon, located in the jurisdiction of_____,
(all herein called "the property"):_____

_____

_____

_____

_____ , and more commonly known as_____

_____(street address).

    1. The purchase price of the property is_____

Dollars ($_____), and such purchase price shall be paid as follows:

_____

_____

_____

_____

_____

    2. Purchaser has made a deposit of_____ Dollars ($_____)
with Broker, receipt of which is hereby acknowledged, and such deposit shall be held by Broker in escrow until the date of settlement and then applied
to the purchase price, or returned to Purchaser if the title to the property is not marketable.

    3. Seller agrees to convey the property to Purchaser by Warranty Deed with the usual covenants of title and free and clear from all encumbrances,
tenancies, liens (for taxes or otherwise), except as may be otherwise provided above, but subject to applicable restrictive covenants of record. Seller further
agrees to deliver possession of the property to Purchaser on the date of settlement and to pay the expense of preparing the deed of conveyance.

    4. Settlement shall be made at the offices of Broker or at_____ on or before
_____, 19_____, or as soon thereafter as title can be examined and necessary documents prepared, with allowance of
a reasonable time for Seller to correct any defects reported by the title examiner.

    5. All taxes, interest, rent, and F.H.A. or similar escrow deposits, if any, shall be prorated as of the date of settlement.

    6. All risk of loss or damage to the property by fire, windstorm, casualty, or other cause is assumed by Seller until the date of settlement.

    7. Purchaser and Seller agree that Broker was the sole procuring cause of this Contract of Purchase, and Seller agrees to pay Broker for services
rendered a cash fee of_____per cent of the purchase price. If either Purchaser or Seller defaults under such Contract, such defaulting party shall
be liable for the cash fee of Broker and any expenses incurred by the non-defaulting party in connection with this transaction.

Subject to:_____

_____

_____

    8. Purchaser represents that an inspection satisfactory to Purchaser has been made of the property, and Purchaser agrees to accept the property in
its present condition except as may be otherwise provided in the description of the property above.

    9. This Contract of Purchase constitutes the entire agreement among the parties and may not be modified or changed except by written instrument
executed by all of the parties, including Broker.

    10. This Contract of Purchase shall be construed, interpreted, and applied according to the law of the jurisdiction of_____ and shall
be binding upon and shall inure to the benefit of the heirs, personal representatives, successors, and assigns of the parties.

All parties to this agreement acknowledge receipt of a certified copy.

WITNESS the following signatures and seals:

_____(SEAL)   _____(SEAL)
Seller   Purchaser

_____(SEAL)   _____(SEAL)
Seller   Purchaser

_____(SEAL)
Broker

Deposit Rec'd $_____

Check   Cash

Sales Agent:_____

OFFER TO PURCHASE AGREEMENT

This AGREEMENT made as of_____, 19_____ ,

among_____ (herein called "Purchaser"),

and_____ (herein called "Seller"),

and_____ (herein called "Broker"),

provides that Purchaser agrees to buy through Broker as agent for Seller, and Seller agrees to sell the following described real estate, and all improvements

thereon, located in the jurisdiction of_____ ,

(all herein called "the property"):_____

_____

_____

_____

_____ , and more commonly known as_____

_____ (street address).

    1. The purchase price of the property is_____

Dollars ($_____), and such purchase price shall be paid as follows:

_____

_____

_____

_____

_____

    2. Purchaser has made a deposit of_____ Dollars ($_____)
with Broker, receipt of which is hereby acknowledged, and such deposit shall be held by Broker in escrow until the date of settlement and then applied
to the purchase price, or returned to Purchaser if the title to the property is not marketable.

    3. Seller agrees to convey the property to Purchaser by Warranty Deed with the usual covenants of title and free and clear from all encumbrances,
tenancies, liens (for taxes or otherwise), except as may be otherwise provided above, but subject to applicable restrictive covenants of record. Seller further
agrees to deliver possession of the property to Purchaser on the date of settlement and to pay the expense of preparing the deed of conveyance.

    4. Settlement shall be made at the offices of Broker or at_____on or before
_____ , 19_____ , or as soon thereafter as title can be examined and necessary documents prepared, with allowance of
a reasonable time for Seller to correct any defects reported by the title examiner.

    5. All taxes, interest, rent, and F.H.A. or similar escrow deposits, if any, shall be prorated as of the date of settlement.

    6. All risk of loss or damage to the property by fire, windstorm, casualty, or other cause is assumed by Seller until the date of settlement.

    7. Purchaser and Seller agree that Broker was the sole procuring cause of this Contract of Purchase, and Seller agrees to pay Broker for services
rendered a cash fee of_____per cent of the purchase price. If either Purchaser or Seller defaults under such Contract, such defaulting party shall
be liable for the cash fee of Broker and any expenses incurred by the non-defaulting party in connection with this transaction.

Subject to:_____

_____

_____

    8. Purchaser represents that an inspection satisfactory to Purchaser has been made of the property, and Purchaser agrees to accept the property in
its present condition except as may be otherwise provided in the description of the property above.

    9. This Contract of Purchase constitutes the entire agreement among the parties and may not be modified or changed except by written instrument
executed by all of the parties, including Broker.

    10. This Contract of Purchase shall be construed, interpreted, and applied according to the law of the jurisdiction of_____and shall
be binding upon and shall inure to the benefit of the heirs, personal representatives, successors, and assigns of the parties.

All parties to this agreement acknowledge receipt of a certified copy.

WITNESS the following signatures and seals:

_____(SEAL)   _____(SEAL)
Seller   Purchaser

_____(SEAL)   _____(SEAL)
Seller   Purchaser

_____(SEAL)
Broker

Deposit Rec'd $_____

Check   Cash

Sales Agent:

SETTLEMENT STATEMENT WORKSHEET

Complete the Settlement Statement Worksheet on the basis of information furnished in the Listing, Offer to Purchase Agreement, and Settlement Problems only. Do not add other items. Use the 30-day method of computation.

	BUYER'S STATEMENT		SELLER'S STATEMENT	
	DEBIT	CREDIT	DEBIT	CREDIT

SETTLEMENT STATEMENT WORKSHEET

Complete the Settlement Statement Worksheet on the basis of information furnished in the Listing, Offer to Purchase Agreement, and Settlement Problems only. Do not add other items. Use the 30-day method of computation.

	BUYER'S STATEMENT		SELLER'S STATEMENT	
	DEBIT	CREDIT	DEBIT	CREDIT

SETTLEMENT STATEMENT WORKSHEET

Complete the Settlement Statement Worksheet on the basis of information furnished in the Listing, Offer to Purchase Agreement, and Settlement Problems only. Do not add other items. Use the 30-day method of computation.

	BUYER'S STATEMENT		SELLER'S STATEMENT	
	DEBIT	CREDIT	DEBIT	CREDIT

SETTLEMENT STATEMENT WORKSHEET

Complete the Settlement Statement Worksheet on the basis of information furnished in the Listing, Offer to Purchase Agreement, and Settlement Problems only. Do not add other items. Use the 30-day method of computation.

	BUYER'S STATEMENT		SELLER'S STATEMENT	
	DEBIT	CREDIT	DEBIT	CREDIT

NAME _____

ADDRESS _____

CITY _____ STATE _____ ZIP _____

DIRECTIONS: Read each question and its numbered answers. When you have decided which answer is correct, completely blacken the corresponding space on this sheet. If you change your mind, erase your first mark completely. Always select the best answer.

1 A B C D ( ) ( ) ( ) ( )	23 A B C D ( ) ( ) ( ) ( )	45 A B C D ( ) ( ) ( ) ( )	67 A B C D ( ) ( ) ( ) ( )
2 A B C D ( ) ( ) ( ) ( )	24 A B C D ( ) ( ) ( ) ( )	46 A B C D ( ) ( ) ( ) ( )	68 A B C D ( ) ( ) ( ) ( )
3 A B C D ( ) ( ) ( ) ( )	25 A B C D ( ) ( ) ( ) ( )	47 A B C D ( ) ( ) ( ) ( )	69 A B C D ( ) ( ) ( ) ( )
4 A B C D ( ) ( ) ( ) ( )	26 A B C D ( ) ( ) ( ) ( )	48 A B C D ( ) ( ) ( ) ( )	70 A B C D ( ) ( ) ( ) ( )
5 A B C D ( ) ( ) ( ) ( )	27 A B C D ( ) ( ) ( ) ( )	49 A B D D ( ) ( ) ( ) ( )	71 A B C D ( ) ( ) ( ) ( )
6 A B C D ( ) ( ) ( ) ( )	28 A B C D ( ) ( ) ( ) ( )	50 A B C D ( ) ( ) ( ) ( )	72 A B C D ( ) ( ) ( ) ( )
7 A B C D ( ) ( ) ( ) ( )	29 A B C D ( ) ( ) ( ) ( )	51 A B C D ( ) ( ) ( ) ( )	73 A B C D ( ) ( ) ( ) ( )
8 A B C D ( ) ( ) ( ) ( )	30 A B C D ( ) ( ) ( ) ( )	52 A B C D ( ) ( ) ( ) ( )	74 A B C D ( ) ( ) ( ) ( )
9 A B C D ( ) ( ) ( ) ( )	31 A B C D ( ) ( ) ( ) ( )	53 A B C D ( ) ( ) ( ) ( )	75 A B C D ( ) ( ) ( ) ( )
10 A B C D ( ) ( ) ( ) ( )	32 A B C D ( ) ( ) ( ) ( )	54 A B C D ( ) ( ) ( ) ( )	76 A B C D ( ) ( ) ( ) ( )
11 A B C D ( ) ( ) ( ) ( )	33 A B C D ( ) ( ) ( ) ( )	55 A B C D ( ) ( ) ( ) ( )	77 A B C D ( ) ( ) ( ) ( )
12 A B C D ( ) ( ) ( ) ( )	34 A B C D ( ) ( ) ( ) ( )	56 A B C D ( ) ( ) ( ) ( )	78 A B C D ( ) ( ) ( ) ( )
13 A B C D ( ) ( ) ( ) ( )	35 A B C D ( ) ( ) ( ) ( )	57 A B C D ( ) ( ) ( ) ( )	79 A B C D ( ) ( ) ( ) ( )
14 A B C D ( ) ( ) ( ) ( )	36 A B C D ( ) ( ) ( ) ( )	58 A B C D ( ) ( ) ( ) ( )	80 A B C D ( ) ( ) ( ) ( )
15 A B C D ( ) ( ) ( ) ( )	37 A B C D ( ) ( ) ( ) ( )	59 A A C D ( ) ( ) ( ) ( )	81 A B C D ( ) ( ) ( ) ( )
16 A B C D ( ) ( ) ( ) ( )	38 A B C D ( ) ( ) ( ) ( )	60 A B D D ( ) ( ) ( ) ( )	82 A B C D ( ) ( ) ( ) ( )
17 A B C D ( ) ( ) ( ) ( )	39 A B C D ( ) ( ) ( ) ( )	61 A B C D ( ) ( ) ( ) ( )	83 A B C D ( ) ( ) ( ) ( )
18 A B C D ( ) ( ) ( ) ( )	40 A B C D ( ) ( ) ( ) ( )	62 A B C D ( ) ( ) ( ) ( )	84 A B C D ( ) ( ) ( ) ( )
19 A B C D ( ) ( ) ( ) ( )	41 A B C D ( ) ( ) ( ) ( )	63 A B C D ( ) ( ) ( ) ( )	85 A B C D ( ) ( ) ( ) ( )
20 A B C D ( ) ( ) ( ) ( )	42 A B C D ( ) ( ) ( ) ( )	64 A B C D ( ) ( ) ( ) ( )	86 A B C D ( ) ( ) ( ) ( )
21 A B C D ( ) ( ) ( ) ( )	43 A B C D ( ) ( ) ( ) ( )	65 A B C D ( ) ( ) ( ) ( )	87 A B C D ( ) ( ) ( ) ( )
22 A B C D ( ) ( ) ( ) ( )	44 A B C D ( ) ( ) ( ) ( )	66 A B C D ( ) ( ) ( ) ( )	88 A B C D ( ) ( ) ( ) ( )

89 A B C D ( ) ( ) ( ) ( )	111 A B C D ( ) ( ) ( ) ( )
90 A B C D ( ) ( ) ( ) ( )	112 A B C D ( ) ( ) ( ) ( )
91 A B C D ( ) ( ) ( ) ( )	113 A B C D ( ) ( ) ( ) ( )
92 A B C D ( ) ( ) ( ) ( )	114 A B C D ( ) ( ) ( ) ( )
93 A B C D ( ) ( ) ( ) ( )	115 A B C D ( ) ( ) ( ) ( )
94 A B C D ( ) ( ) ( ) ( )	116 A B C D ( ) ( ) ( ) ( )
95 A B C D ( ) ( ) ( ) ( )	117 A B C D ( ) ( ) ( ) ( )
96 A B C D ( ) ( ) ( ) ( )	118 A B C D ( ) ( ) ( ) ( )
97 A B C D ( ) ( ) ( ) ( )	119 A B C D ( ) ( ) ( ) ( )
98 A B C D ( ) ( ) ( ) ( )	120 A B C D ( ) ( ) ( ) ( )
99 A B C D ( ) ( ) ( ) ( )	121 A B C D ( ) ( ) ( ) ( )
100 A B C D ( ) ( ) ( ) ( )	122 A B C D ( ) ( ) ( ) ( )
101 A B C D ( ) ( ) ( ) ( )	123 A B C D ( ) ( ) ( ) ( )
102 A B C D ( ) ( ) ( ) ( )	124 A B C D ( ) ( ) ( ) ( )
103 A B C D ( ) ( ) ( ) ( )	125 A B C D ( ) ( ) ( ) ( )
104 A B C D ( ) ( ) ( ) ( )	126 A B C D ( ) ( ) ( ) ( )
105 A B C D ( ) ( ) ( ) ( )	127 A B C D ( ) ( ) ( ) ( )
106 A B C D ( ) ( ) ( ) ( )	128 A B C D ( ) ( ) ( ) ( )
107 A B C D ( ) ( ) ( ) ( )	129 A B C D ( ) ( ) ( ) ( )
108 A B C D ( ) ( ) ( ) ( )	130 A B C D ( ) ( ) ( ) ( )
109 A B C D ( ) ( ) ( ) ( )	131 A B C D ( ) ( ) ( ) ( )
110 A B C D ( ) ( ) ( ) ( )	132 A B C D ( ) ( ) ( ) ( )

NAME _____

ADDRESS _____

CITY _____ STATE _____ ZIP _____

DIRECTIONS: Read each question and its numbered answers. When you have decided which answer is correct, completely blacken the corresponding space on this sheet. If you change your mind, erase your first mark completely. Always select the best answer.

	A B C D		A B C D			A B C D		A B C D			A B C D		A B C D
1	( )( )( )( )	23	( )( )( )( )		45	( )( )( )( )	67	( )( )( )( )		89	( )( )( )( )	111	( )( )( )( )
2	( )( )( )( )	24	( )( )( )( )		46	( )( )( )( )	68	( )( )( )( )		90	( )( )( )( )	112	( )( )( )( )
3	( )( )( )( )	25	( )( )( )( )		47	( )( )( )( )	69	( )( )( )( )		91	( )( )( )( )	113	( )( )( )( )
4	( )( )( )( )	26	( )( )( )( )		48	( )( )( )( )	70	( )( )( )( )		92	( )( )( )( )	114	( )( )( )( )
5	( )( )( )( )	27	( )( )( )( )		49	( )( )( )( )	71	( )( )( )( )		93	( )( )( )( )	115	( )( )( )( )
6	( )( )( )( )	28	( )( )( )( )		50	( )( )( )( )	72	( )( )( )( )		94	( )( )( )( )	116	( )( )( )( )
7	( )( )( )( )	29	( )( )( )( )		51	( )( )( )( )	73	( )( )( )( )		95	( )( )( )( )	117	( )( )( )( )
8	( )( )( )( )	30	( )( )( )( )		52	( )( )( )( )	74	( )( )( )( )		96	( )( )( )( )	118	( )( )( )( )
9	( )( )( )( )	31	( )( )( )( )		53	( )( )( )( )	75	( )( )( )( )		97	( )( )( )( )	119	( )( )( )( )
10	( )( )( )( )	32	( )( )( )( )		54	( )( )( )( )	76	( )( )( )( )		98	( )( )( )( )	120	( )( )( )( )
11	( )( )( )( )	33	( )( )( )( )		55	( )( )( )( )	77	( )( )( )( )		99	( )( )( )( )	121	( )( )( )( )
12	( )( )( )( )	34	( )( )( )( )		56	( )( )( )( )	78	( )( )( )( )		100	( )( )( )( )	122	( )( )( )( )
13	( )( )( )( )	35	( )( )( )( )		57	( )( )( )( )	79	( )( )( )( )		101	( )( )( )( )	123	( )( )( )( )
14	( )( )( )( )	36	( )( )( )( )		58	( )( )( )( )	80	( )( )( )( )		102	( )( )( )( )	124	( )( )( )( )
15	( )( )( )( )	37	( )( )( )( )		59	( )( )( )( )	81	( )( )( )( )		103	( )( )( )( )	125	( )( )( )( )
16	( )( )( )( )	38	( )( )( )( )		60	( )( )( )( )	82	( )( )( )( )		104	( )( )( )( )	126	( )( )( )( )
17	( )( )( )( )	39	( )( )( )( )		61	( )( )( )( )	83	( )( )( )( )		105	( )( )( )( )	127	( )( )( )( )
18	( )( )( )( )	40	( )( )( )( )		62	( )( )( )( )	84	( )( )( )( )		106	( )( )( )( )	128	( )( )( )( )
19	( )( )( )( )	41	( )( )( )( )		63	( )( )( )( )	85	( )( )( )( )		107	( )( )( )( )	129	( )( )( )( )
20	( )( )( )( )	42	( )( )( )( )		64	( )( )( )( )	86	( )( )( )( )		108	( )( )( )( )	130	( )( )( )( )
21	( )( )( )( )	43	( )( )( )( )		65	( )( )( )( )	87	( )( )( )( )		109	( )( )( )( )	131	( )( )( )( )
22	( )( )( )( )	44	( )( )( )( )		66	( )( )( )( )	88	( )( )( )( )		110	( )( )( )( )	132	( )( )( )( )

NAME _____

ADDRESS _____

CITY _____ STATE _____ ZIP _____

DIRECTIONS: Read each question and its numbered answers. When you have decided which answer is correct, completely blacken the corresponding space on this sheet. If you change your mind, erase your first mark completely. Always select the best answer.

	A B C D		A B C D		A B C D		A B C D		A B C D		A B C D
1	( )( )( )( )	23	( )( )( )( )	45	( )( )( )( )	67	( )( )( )( )	89	( )( )( )( )	111	( )( )( )( )
2	( )( )( )( )	24	( )( )( )( )	46	( )( )( )( )	68	( )( )( )( )	90	( )( )( )( )	112	( )( )( )( )
3	( )( )( )( )	25	( )( )( )( )	47	( )( )( )( )	69	( )( )( )( )	91	( )( )( )( )	113	( )( )( )( )
4	( )( )( )( )	26	( )( )( )( )	48	( )( )( )( )	70	( )( )( )( )	92	( )( )( )( )	114	( )( )( )( )
5	( )( )( )( )	27	( )( )( )( )	49	( )( )( )( )	71	( )( )( )( )	93	( )( )( )( )	115	( )( )( )( )
6	( )( )( )( )	28	( )( )( )( )	50	( )( )( )( )	72	( )( )( )( )	94	( )( )( )( )	116	( )( )( )( )
7	( )( )( )( )	29	( )( )( )( )	51	( )( )( )( )	73	( )( )( )( )	95	( )( )( )( )	117	( )( )( )( )
8	( )( )( )( )	30	( )( )( )( )	52	( )( )( )( )	74	( )( )( )( )	96	( )( )( )( )	118	( )( )( )( )
9	( )( )( )( )	31	( )( )( )( )	53	( )( )( )( )	75	( )( )( )( )	97	( )( )( )( )	119	( )( )( )( )
10	( )( )( )( )	32	( )( )( )( )	54	( )( )( )( )	76	( )( )( )( )	98	( )( )( )( )	120	( )( )( )( )
11	( )( )( )( )	33	( )( )( )( )	55	( )( )( )( )	77	( )( )( )( )	99	( )( )( )( )	121	( )( )( )( )
12	( )( )( )( )	34	( )( )( )( )	56	( )( )( )( )	78	( )( )( )( )	100	( )( )( )( )	122	( )( )( )( )
13	( )( )( )( )	35	( )( )( )( )	57	( )( )( )( )	79	( )( )( )( )	101	( )( )( )( )	123	( )( )( )( )
14	( )( )( )( )	36	( )( )( )( )	58	( )( )( )( )	80	( )( )( )( )	102	( )( )( )( )	124	( )( )( )( )
15	( )( )( )( )	37	( )( )( )( )	59	( )( )( )( )	81	( )( )( )( )	103	( )( )( )( )	125	( )( )( )( )
16	( )( )( )( )	38	( )( )( )( )	60	( )( )( )( )	82	( )( )( )( )	104	( )( )( )( )	126	( )( )( )( )
17	( )( )( )( )	39	( )( )( )( )	61	( )( )( )( )	83	( )( )( )( )	105	( )( )( )( )	127	( )( )( )( )
18	( )( )( )( )	40	( )( )( )( )	62	( )( )( )( )	84	( )( )( )( )	106	( )( )( )( )	128	( )( )( )( )
19	( )( )( )( )	41	( )( )( )( )	63	( )( )( )( )	85	( )( )( )( )	107	( )( )( )( )	129	( )( )( )( )
20	( )( )( )( )	42	( )( )( )( )	64	( )( )( )( )	86	( )( )( )( )	108	( )( )( )( )	130	( )( )( )( )
21	( )( )( )( )	43	( )( )( )( )	65	( )( )( )( )	87	( )( )( )( )	109	( )( )( )( )	131	( )( )( )( )
22	( )( )( )( )	44	( )( )( )( )	66	( )( )( )( )	88	( )( )( )( )	110	( )( )( )( )	132	( )( )( )( )

NAME _____

ADDRESS _____

CITY _____ STATE _____ ZIP _____

DIRECTIONS: Read each question and its numbered answers. When you have decided which answer is correct, completely blacken the corresponding space on this sheet. If you change your mind, erase your first mark completely. Always select the best answer.

1 A ( ) B ( ) C ( ) D ( )	23 A ( ) B ( ) C ( ) D ( )	45 A ( ) B ( ) C ( ) D ( )	67 A ( ) B ( ) C ( ) D ( )
2	24	46	68
3	25	47	69
4	26	48	70
5	27	49	71
6	28	50	72
7	29	51	73
8	30	52	74
9	31	53	75
10	32	54	76
11	33	55	77
12	34	56	78
13	35	57	79
14	36	58	80
15	37	59	81
16	38	60	82
17	39	61	83
18	40	62	84
19	41	63	85
20	42	64	86
21	43	65	87
22	44	66	88

89 A ( ) B ( ) C ( ) D ( )	111 A ( ) B ( ) C ( ) D ( )
90	112
91	113
92	114
93	115
94	116
95	117
96	118
97	119
98	120
99	121
100	122
101	123
102	124
103	125
104	126
105	127
106	128
107	129
108	130
109	131
110	132